MASTER THE™
CIVIL SERVICE
EXAMS

6TH EDITION

PETERSON'S®

About Peterson's

Peterson's® has been your trusted educational publisher for over 50 years. It's a milestone we're quite proud of, as we continue to offer the most accurate, dependable, high-quality educational content in the field, providing you with everything you need to succeed. No matter where you are on your academic or professional path, you can rely on Peterson's for its books, online information, expert test-prep tools, the most up-to-date education exploration data, and the highest quality career success resources—everything you need to achieve your education goals. For our complete line of products, visit **www.petersons.com**.

For more information about Peterson's range of educational products, contact Peterson's, 8740 Lucent Blvd., Suite 400, Highlands Ranch, CO 80129, or find us online at **www.petersons.com**.

© 2019 Peterson's

Previous editions © 2001, 2003, 2005, 2009, 2013

ISBN-13: 978-0-7689-4313-9

Printed in the United States of America

10 9 8 7 6 5 4 3 2   21 20 19

Sixth Edition

Petersonspublishingcom/publishing updates

Check out our website at **www.petersonspublishing.com/publishingupdates** to see if there is any new information regarding the test and any revisions or corrections to the content of this book. We've made sure the information in this book is accurate and up-to-date; however, the test format or content may have changed since the time of publication.

Contents

Contents

PART IV: CLERICAL ABILITY

PART V: ARITHMETIC ABILITY

PART VI: FOUR PRACTICE TESTS

PART VII: APPENDIXES

Before You Begin

Master the™ Civil Service Exams gives you a structured, step-by-step tutorial program that can help you master all the basics. It covers all the key points and gives you the practice you need to score high on your civil service exam.

WHO SHOULD USE THIS BOOK?

Master the™ Civil Service Exams is written for civil service candidates who want to prepare for their exam in the smartest way possible, but whose study time is limited. This book is for you if you can answer *yes* to the following statements:

- You know that you'll get the most out of a structured, step-by-step tutorial program that takes the guesswork out of test preparation.

- You want to prepare on your own time and at your own pace, but you don't have time for a preparation program that takes weeks to complete.

- You want a guide that covers all the key points you need to know, but doesn't waste time on topics you don't absolutely have to know for the exam.

- You want to avoid taking risks with this all-important exam by relying on "beat the system" guides that are long on promises but short on substance.

HOW THIS BOOK IS ORGANIZED

- **Part I** gives you a quick overview of important facts you need to know about the civil service job market and whether you must take an entry-level exam to qualify. You'll learn where to get job information; how to apply for federal, state, and municipal positions; and what to expect on a civil service exam. You'll also get some general test-taking tips that will help you score higher on test day.

- **Part II** offers a Diagnostic Test to help you identify your areas of strength and those areas where you will need to spend more time in your review sessions.

- **Part III** focuses on the concepts and strategies you'll need to know for the verbal sections of most civil service exams. You'll cover grammar and usage, spelling, synonyms, sentence completions, verbal analogies, reading comprehension, and effective expression as they are assessed on civil service exams. At the end of each chapter, you'll apply what you learned to civil service-type practice exercises.

- **Part IV** teaches you the ins and outs of alphabetizing and filing, clerical speed and accuracy, and typing and stenography. You'll also learn the fundamentals of judgment, observation, and memory. Here, too, you'll find skill-building practice exercises.

- **Part V** focuses on the arithmetic covered on most civil service exams. You'll review fractions and decimals, percentages, ratio and proportion, graphs and tables, and arithmetic reasoning in preparation for your test. You'll learn strategies for solving each question type, and you'll sharpen your skills by working through practice exercises.

- **Part VI** contains four full-length practice tests that are as close as you can get to the real thing. Take them under timed conditions, and you'll experience just how it feels to take an actual civil service exam. Two of the practice tests give you a great opportunity to gauge your progress and focus your study in key areas, including English grammar and usage; spelling; synonyms; sentence completions; verbal analogies; reading comprehension; judgment, communication, and memory. Two additional practice tests will help you prepare for the Municipal Office Aide and Senior Office Typist exams. As you finish each exam, check your answers against the answer key and read the explanation for each question you missed. Actually, it's a good idea to read all of the answer explanations.

- The **Appendixes** provide additional information that we hope will be helpful as you begin your search for a civil service job. In Appendix A, you'll find a listing of occupations available in the federal government—professional occupations and trade, craft, or labor occupations. Appendix B offers a sample of jobs typically available in state and municipal governments. If you are a veteran looking for a civil service job, you'll find essential information in Appendix C. Appendix D provides helpful details on government hiring of individuals with disabilities.

Once you have read and worked through this intensive, focused preparation program, you'll be more than ready to score high on your civil service exam, and you will be a more attractive applicant for the position you're seeking.

SPECIAL STUDY FEATURES

Master the™ *Civil Service Exams* is designed to be as user-friendly as it is complete. To this end, it includes several features to make your preparation more efficient.

Overview

Each chapter begins with a bulleted overview listing the topics covered in the chapter. This will allow you to quickly target the areas in which you are most interested.

Bonus Information

As you work your way through the book, check the margins to find bonus information and advice. You'll find the following kinds of information:

Note

Notes highlight need-to-know information about the civil service exams, whether it's details about applying for a position, how scores are tallied, or the structure of a question type.

Tip

Tips provide valuable strategies and insider information to help you score your best on the civil service exams.

YOU'RE WELL ON YOUR WAY TO SUCCESS

You've made the decision to work for the federal government or for your state or local government and have taken a very important step in that process. *Master the™ Civil Service Exams* will help you score high and prepare you for everything you'll need to know on the day of your exam and beyond. Good luck!

GIVE US YOUR FEEDBACK

Peterson's publishes a full line of books—test prep, career preparation, education exploration, and financial aid. Peterson's publications can be found in high school guidance offices, college libraries and career centers, and your local bookstore and library. Peterson's books are also available as eBooks.

We welcome any comments or suggestions you may have about this publication. Your feedback will help us make educational dreams possible for you—and others like you.

PART I
START WITH THE BASICS

Civil Service Jobs

Chapter 1

OVERVIEW

- **Federal Employment**
- **State and Local Government Employment**
- **Obtaining Job Information**
- **How to Apply**
- **Submitting a Civil Service Job Resume**
- **Summing It Up**

FEDERAL EMPLOYMENT

The federal government is the nation's largest employer. It employs approximately 2.7 million civilian workers in the United States and thousands more (both U.S. citizens and non-citizens) in locations overseas. Government occupations other than military service represent nearly every kind of job in private employment, as well as some jobs unique to the federal government, including regulatory inspectors, foreign service officers, and Internal Revenue Service (IRS) agents. Civilian jobs are available in each of the three branches of government: the legislative branch, which includes Congress, the General Accountability Office, the Government Printing Office, and the Library of Congress; the judicial branch, which includes the Supreme Court and the federal court system; and the executive branch, which includes the 15 executive departments, such as the Departments of State, Justice, Agriculture, Housing and Urban Development, and Defense. The executive branch also includes a diverse range of independent agencies, such as the EPA, the CIA, the Federal Trade Commission, FEMA, the Peace Corps, and lesser-known agencies like the Institute of Museum Services and the Railroad Retirement Board. The great majority of federal civilian employees work for the executive branch.

Categories of Federal Jobs

Nearly every occupation in the private sector is also represented in the federal civil service. If you are seeking a career in government service, you will probably be able to put to use the skills you've already acquired. Here's a quick look at the major categories of federal positions:

- **Specialized.** These positions require knowledge in a specialized field, usually acquired through college-level or postgraduate education. Among those filling these positions are engineers, accountants, attorneys, biologists, physicists, and chemists.

- **Administrative and managerial.** Employees in these positions are responsible for overseeing contracts with the private sector and purchasing goods and services for the government. Positions include contract specialists, budget analysts, purchasing officers, claims examiners, product control specialists, administrative assistants, personnel officers, and IRS officers.

- **Investigative and law enforcement.** Several government agencies employ police officers and investigators in positions ranging from guarding property and patrolling borders to being involved in highly technical intelligence operations. These agencies include the Department of Justice, the State Department, the Treasury Department, the U.S. Postal Service, the Federal Bureau of Investigation (FBI), and the Department of Homeland Security.

- **Technical.** These positions typically employ workers involved in support work in non-routine professional or administrative fields, such as digital technology and IT.

- **Clerical.** An umbrella category for a wide range of job types, clerical work includes not only administrative assistant roles but also court reporter, information clerk, mail clerk, and much more.

- **Labor and mechanical.** Most people do not realize that the U.S. government is one of the largest employers of mechanical and manual workers and laborers in the country. Positions include mobile equipment operators, mechanics, machine tool and metal workers, maintenance and repair workers, and food preparation and service workers.

- **Unskilled.** Thousands of positions in federal government service are open to people with few skills or with only a small amount of training. These include housekeeping aides, janitors, laundry workers, and mess attendants.

Pathways for Students and Recent Graduates to Federal Careers

The Pathways Program was established under President Barack Obama to attract students and recent graduates to jobs in the federal government. It offers three types of opportunities:

- **Internship Program:** Intended to help people explore their career options at federal agencies while they're still in school, this program offers full- and part-time paid internships to students currently enrolled in high school, trade school, college, or graduate school, or at another type of qualifying institution. More information about the program as well as details about specific internships can be found at **usajobs.gov**.

- **Recent Graduates Program:** Designed to provide a foot in the door to a federal career, this program is open to people who have earned an associate's, bachelor's, master's, professional, doctorate, vocational, or technical degree or certificate within the past two years. Veterans may have up to six years to apply. The program offers yearlong "developmental experiences," including mentorship and formal training, to help prepare successful participants for a career in the federal government. Find out more at **usajobs.gov**.

- **Presidential Management Fellows (PMF) Program:** Created to develop future leaders in the federal government, this program offers entry-level opportunities for people who have earned an advanced degree within the past two years or are on their way to earning one by August 31 of the year after the program's annual open call for applications.

Applicants who successfully undergo the rigorous evaluation process to become a finalist become eligible for a two-year paid appointment, formal training, and senior-level mentorship. Some fellows use their PMF experience as a stepping stone to high-level careers in the private sector or academia. Visit **pmf.gov** and **usajobs.gov** for recent announcements about the program.

Depending on your career plans and current circumstances, if you're a student, you might also be eligible for the Department of State Student Internship program (**careers.state.gov**), which offers internships in Washington, D.C. and abroad; the Virtual Student Federal Service program (**vsfs.state.gov**), which offers "work from home"-style internships; and a range of seasonal employment options, which are detailed in the next section.

Summer Jobs and Volunteering for the Federal Government

Limited summer or seasonal employment is available throughout the federal government. Most jobs are in metropolitan areas, although jobs may also be available at national parks, historic sites, or similar locations that attract a high volume of seasonal visitors. Applications are typically accepted from December through April 15, and the jobs tend to run from mid-May through September 30. You can find information on summer jobs at **usajobs.gov**.

Unpaid volunteer assignments are another avenue for gaining work experience in the federal government. The departments that typically have accepted the largest number of student volunteers have been the Departments of Defense, Commerce, Health and Human Services, Interior, Justice, State, Treasury, and Veterans Affairs. These volunteer assignments offer training opportunities that are separate from the paid Pathways internship program to high school and college students.

The volunteer opportunities should be related to a student's academic program so that the student can explore career options while developing personal and professional skills. Assignments typically last for three to four months and are performed during the school year and/or during summer or school vacations.

A good resource for volunteering is the webpage **usa.gov/volunteer**, which features a long list of government volunteer programs, including those open to non-students. You can also directly call or email the human resources department of the specific agency in which you would like to volunteer and describe your skills and volunteer goals. This is an especially good tactic if you are a non-student, since government volunteer opportunities will be more limited.

Job Arrangements

Flex-time, telecommuting, job sharing, and nontraditional configurations of the workday and work week, such as four 10-hour days per week, are options for some positions in the federal government. Arrangements such as these must be worked out at the time of hiring.

Part-time positions from 16 to 32 hours per week are also available throughout the federal government. Visit **usajobs.gov** for information on open part-time positions by region and/or agency.

Qualifications and Requirements

Most jobs in the federal government fall under either the General Schedule (GS) or the Federal Wage System (FWS). GS encompasses most white-collar jobs, while FWS jobs are blue collar—defined by the government as "craft, trade, and labor positions." Within each system, jobs are classified by occupational series (here, "series" means a group of similar jobs), grade or pay level, and pay plan.

Each position is graded on a scale of 1 to 15 based on the level of skills, knowledge, and responsibilities needed to perform the job competently. As you consider which federal positions you're qualified for, take into consideration the pay grades of each position and compare your education level, experience, and skills to see if they match up.

Especially for GS jobs, education is an important factor that determines which pay grade you may be right for as a new hire. Most GS-1 jobs are open to those without a high school diploma, while GS-2 jobs are available to people who have a high school diploma but don't have related work experience. High school graduates with special skills may begin at grade GS-3. Graduates of two-year colleges and technical schools typically begin at GS-4, while professional and administrative employees with bachelor's degrees can enter at grades GS-5 or GS-7, depending on experience and academic record. Applicants who have a master's degree or PhD (or have equivalent experience) may enter at the GS-9 or GS-11 level.

Of course, as you gain experience and new skills in your first federal position, you become eligible for promotion to higher-level, more specialized jobs. You may also seek to switch from a GS job to an FWS job or vice versa.

For most positions, you must have either six months or one year of experience at a comparable level to that of the next lower grade level to qualify for experience for any grade higher than the entry level. For some positions at GS-11 and lower, you must have obtained experience at two levels below that of the job. Each job announcement provides specific information about the level of experience needed to qualify for the position.

The following educational and experience requirements are typical for various categories of civil service positions:

- **Specialized.** Require highly specialized knowledge. Typically, you must have a bachelor's degree or higher in a specific field.
- **Administrative and managerial.** Usually do not require specialized knowledge. A bachelor's degree and/or responsible job experience, however, is required. In general, you must begin at the trainee level and learn the duties of the job after being hired.
- **Investigative and law enforcement.** Requirements vary greatly depending on the job. In general, these positions require a bachelor's degree, specialized training, good physical condition, and/or previous relevant experience.
- **Technical and clerical.** Entry-level positions in these fields usually require a high school diploma or equivalent, although junior college or technical school training may enable you to enter a field at a higher level. No additional experience or training may be necessary.

- **Labor and mechanical.** These positions, particularly those requiring a skilled trade, often require relevant experience. Apprenticeships for those with no previous training, however, may be available for some positions.
- **Unskilled.** Many positions require little or no prior training or experience. These positions include that of janitor, maintenance worker, and messenger.

Age

In addition to education, experience, and skill requirements, you must meet general age and physical requirements for joining the civil service. The government sets no maximum age limit for federal employment. The usual minimum age is 18, but high school graduates as young as 16 may apply for many jobs. If you are younger than 18 and you are out of school but are not a high school graduate, you may be hired only if you have successfully completed a formal vocational training program or school authorities have signed a form approving your preference for work instead of additional schooling. The agency that wants to hire you will provide the form. Also, if you are at least 16 and are in high school, you may work during school vacations or during the year on a formal student employment program.

Physical Requirements

You must be physically able to perform the duties of the position that you are interested in pursuing, and you must be emotionally and mentally stable. This does not mean that a physical disability will disqualify you, as long as you can perform the work efficiently and without posing a hazard to yourself or others. Of course, there are some positions—such as border patrol agent, firefighter, and criminal investigator—that can be filled only by applicants who are in top-notch physical condition. Whenever this is the case, the physical requirements are described in detail in the job announcement. The federal government is the world's largest employer of the physically disabled and has a strong program aimed at employing those who are disabled. If you have a physical disability, contact the Selective Placement Coordinator at the agency in which you're interested for special placement assistance. State the nature of your disability on your application, so that special testing arrangements can be made to accommodate your needs.

Working Conditions and Benefits

More than one-half of federal civilian employees are paid according to the General Schedule (GS), a pay scale for those in professional, administrative, technical, and clerical jobs and for workers such as guards and messengers. Salaries under the GS are set to correspond to pay levels in similar occupations in the private sector. GS pay rates are uniform throughout most of the country, although they are adjusted upward in areas with very high cost-of-living indexes, such as New York City, Los Angeles, and San Francisco. In areas with low cost-of-living indexes, GS pay may exceed that of private-sector workers in similar jobs.

On the following pages, you'll find basic GS pay charts for annual and hourly pay by job grade, but also visit the Office of Personnel Management's website (**opm.gov**) for a list of GS pay charts by locality, many of which differ significantly from these general standards.

TIP

Some positions, particularly those in law enforcement and firefighting, have specific age limits, generally between 34 and 37 years of age, because of the nature of the work. Be sure to check job announcements carefully before applying.

If you are hired for a trade, craft, or labor job, you will probably be paid according to the Federal Wage System (FWS), a pay-setting system that was established to ensure uniform, fair pay for blue-collar federal workers within a local wage area. According to the Office of Personnel Management, which consults with labor unions and federal agencies to administer the system, as an FWS worker, "your pay will be the same as the pay of other Federal jobs like yours in your wage area, and your pay will be in line with pay for private sector jobs like yours in your wage area."

To see current wage schedules for FWS jobs, visit **https://www.opm.gov/policy-data-oversight/ pay-leave/pay-systems/federal-wage-system/** and click the "Wage Schedule" tab, or contact the Department of Defense (DoD) at 571-372-1614. (The DoD is the lead agency carrying out FWS wage surveys and issuing wage schedules, so it's become an information hub for all FWS workers, not just those at the DoD.)

Advancement to a higher pay grade generally depends on one's level of ability and work performance, as well as on the availability of jobs at higher-grade levels. Most agencies fill vacancies by promoting their own employees whenever possible. Promotions are based on increases in responsibility and the demonstration of increased experience and skill.

It's not always necessary to move to a new job to advance in pay grade. Sometimes an employee's work assignments change a great deal in the ordinary course of business—in other words, the job "grows," or expands, in responsibility. When that happens, a position classifier determines whether the position should be reclassified to a higher grade because of increased difficulty or responsibility.

Most employees receive within-grade pay increases at one-, two-, or three-year intervals if their work is acceptable or better. However, in poor economic times, the government—federal, state, and local—may declare a pay freeze, ending pay increases for a period of time. (Some managers and supervisors receive increases based on job performance rather than on time in a specific grade.) Within-grade increases may also be awarded to recognize high-quality service.

Federal jobs offer many benefits in addition to pay, including health and life insurance, retirement benefits, and holidays.

SALARY TABLE 2018-GS
INCORPORATING THE 1.4% GENERAL SCHEDULE INCREASE
EFFECTIVE JANUARY 2018

Annual Rates by Grade and Step

Grade	Step 1	Step 2	Step 3	Step 4	Step 5	Step 6	Step 7	Step 8	Step 9	Step 10	WITHIN GRADE AMOUNTS
1	$ 18,785	$ 19,414	$ 20,039	$ 20,660	$ 21,285	$ 21,650	$ 22,267	$ 22,891	$ 22,915	$ 23,502	VARIES
2	21,121	21,624	22,323	22,915	23,175	23,857	24,539	25,221	25,903	26,585	VARIES
3	23,045	23,813	24,581	25,349	26,117	26,885	27,653	28,421	29,189	29,957	768
4	25,871	26,733	27,595	28,457	29,319	30,181	31,043	31,905	32,767	33,629	862
5	28,945	29,910	30,875	31,840	32,805	33,770	34,735	35,700	36,665	37,630	965
6	32,264	33,339	34,414	35,489	36,564	37,639	38,714	39,789	40,864	41,939	1,075
7	35,854	37,049	38,244	39,439	40,634	41,829	43,024	44,219	45,414	46,609	1,195
8	39,707	41,031	42,355	43,679	45,003	46,327	47,651	48,975	50,299	51,623	1,324
9	43,857	45,319	46,781	48,243	49,705	51,167	52,629	54,091	55,553	57,015	1,462
10	48,297	49,907	51,517	53,127	54,737	56,347	57,957	59,567	61,177	62,787	1,610
11	53,062	54,831	56,600	58,369	60,138	61,907	63,676	65,445	67,214	68,983	1,769
12	63,600	65,720	67,840	69,960	72,080	74,200	76,320	78,440	80,560	82,680	2,120
13	75,628	78,149	80,670	83,191	85,712	88,233	90,754	93,275	95,796	98,317	2,521
14	89,370	92,349	95,328	98,307	101,286	104,265	107,244	110,223	113,202	116,181	2,979
15	105,123	108,627	112,131	115,635	119,139	122,643	126,147	129,651	133,155	136,659	3,504

Source: The U.S. Office of Personnel Management (OPM).

SALARY TABLE 2018-GS
INCORPORATING THE 1.4% GENERAL SCHEDULE INCREASE
EFFECTIVE JANUARY 2018

Hourly Basic (B) Rates by Grade and Step
Hourly Title 5 Overtime (O) Rates for FLSA-Exempt Employees by Grade and Step

Grade	B/O	Step 1	Step 2	Step 3	Step 4	Step 5	Step 6	Step 7	Step 8	Step 9	Step 10
1	B	$ 9.00	$ 9.30	$ 9.60	$ 9.90	$ 10.20	$ 10.37	$ 10.67	$ 10.97	$ 10.98	$ 11.26
	O	13.50	13.95	14.40	14.85	15.30	15.56	16.01	16.46	16.47	16.89
2	B	10.12	10.36	10.70	10.98	11.10	11.43	11.76	12.08	12.41	12.74
	O	15.18	15.54	16.05	16.47	16.65	17.15	17.64	18.12	18.62	19.11
3	B	11.04	11.41	11.78	12.15	12.51	12.88	13.25	13.62	13.99	14.35
	O	16.56	17.12	17.67	18.23	18.77	19.32	19.88	20.43	20.99	21.53
4	B	12.40	12.81	13.22	13.64	14.05	14.46	14.87	15.29	15.70	16.11
	O	18.60	19.22	19.83	20.46	21.08	21.69	22.31	22.94	23.55	24.17
5	B	13.87	14.33	14.79	15.26	15.72	16.18	16.64	17.11	17.57	18.03
	O	20.81	21.50	22.19	22.89	23.58	24.27	24.96	25.67	26.36	27.05
6	B	15.46	15.97	16.49	17.00	17.52	18.03	18.55	19.07	19.58	20.10
	O	23.19	23.96	24.74	25.50	26.28	27.05	27.83	28.61	29.37	30.15
7	B	17.18	17.75	18.32	18.90	19.47	20.04	20.62	21.19	21.76	22.33
	O	25.77	26.63	27.48	28.35	29.21	30.06	30.93	31.79	32.64	33.50
8	B	19.03	19.66	20.29	20.93	21.56	22.20	22.83	23.47	24.10	24.74
	O	28.55	29.49	30.44	31.40	32.34	33.30	34.25	34.71	34.71	34.71
9	B	21.01	21.71	22.42	23.12	23.82	24.52	25.22	25.92	26.62	27.32
	O	31.52	32.57	33.63	34.68	34.71	34.71	34.71	34.71	34.71	34.71
10	B	23.14	23.91	24.68	25.46	26.23	27.00	27.77	28.54	29.31	30.08
	O	34.71	34.71	34.71	34.71	34.71	34.71	34.71	34.71	34.71	34.71
11	B	25.43	26.27	27.12	27.97	28.82	29.66	30.51	31.36	32.21	33.05
	O	34.71	34.71	34.71	34.71	34.71	34.71	34.71	34.71	34.71	34.71
12	B	30.47	31.49	32.51	33.52	34.54	35.55	36.57	37.59	38.60	39.62
	O	34.71	34.71	34.71	34.71	34.71	35.55	36.57	37.59	38.60	39.62
13	B	36.24	37.45	38.65	39.86	41.07	42.28	43.49	44.69	45.90	47.11
	O	36.24	37.45	38.65	39.86	41.07	42.28	43.49	44.69	45.90	47.11
14	B	42.82	44.25	45.68	47.10	48.53	49.96	51.39	52.81	54.24	55.67
	O	42.82	44.25	45.68	47.10	48.53	49.96	51.39	52.81	54.24	55.67
15	B	50.37	52.05	53.73	55.41	57.09	58.77	60.44	62.12	63.80	65.48
	O	50.37	52.05	53.73	55.41	57.09	58.77	60.44	62.12	63.80	65.48

Source: The U.S Office of Personnel Management (OPM).

Work Hours

The usual government work week is 40 hours. Most government employees work eight hours per day, Monday through Friday. In some cases, the nature of the work may call for a different work week, and as in many other businesses, employees sometimes have to work overtime. If you are required to work overtime, you will either be paid for the extra time or given time off as compensation.

Training

Training for increased responsibility in a government position is often provided on the job, and employees are encouraged to continue their own training and education. You may participate in individual career development programs and receive job-related training in your own agency, in other agencies, or outside the government (in industrial plants and universities, for example). In addition, the government sponsors formal training courses and may pay for outside training that is directly related to improving job performance.

Benefits

Federal employees are regularly rated on their job performance. While each agency may develop its own terms or rating system, performance is typically evaluated according to the following scale: Level 5, Outstanding; Level 4, Exceeds Fully Successful; Level 3, Fully Successful; Level 2, Minimally Satisfactory; and Level 1, Unsatisfactory. Employees with "outstanding" ratings receive extra credit toward retention in case of layoffs. An employee whose rating is "unsatisfactory" may be dismissed or assigned to another position.

INCENTIVE AWARDS

Government agencies encourage employees to suggest better, simpler, or more economical ways to perform their work. A suggestion or invention that results in savings or improved service may result in a cash award for you, or you may be rewarded for outstanding job performance or other acts deserving recognition.

VACATION AND SICK LEAVE

New full-time federal employees earn four hours of vacation time (termed "annual leave") per pay period, which adds up to 13 days of annual leave per year. That amount increases after three years of employment, and after 15 years, employees are eligible to accrue 26 vacation days annually. Sick leave for new and tenured workers is 13 days per year. There are numerous other types of leave, including court leave, bereavement leave, sick leave for adoption, and administrative leave, so depending on your life or work circumstances, you may have more flexibility beyond standard sick and vacation days. Part-time workers also earn paid time off, but on a different accrual schedule.

INJURY COMPENSATION

The government provides generous compensation benefits, including medical care, for employees who suffer injuries in the performance of their official duties. Death benefits are provided to survivors should such injuries result in death.

GROUP LIFE INSURANCE

As a federal employee, you receive low-cost basic term life insurance and also accidental death and dismemberment insurance. The government pays part of the premium, and the employee pays the rest. Employees may also upgrade to an optional policy with better benefits.

Health Care

The government sponsors a voluntary health insurance program for federal employees. The program offers a variety of plans to meet individual needs, including basic coverage and major medical protection against costly illnesses. The government contributes part of the premium and the employee pays the balance through payroll deductions.

Retirement Program

Under the Federal Employees Retirement System (FERS), federal employees are covered under a combined Social Security and supplemental retirement program of Basic Benefits and a Thrift Savings Plan. The Social Security system is the same one to which most U.S. workers contribute. Federal employees also contribute to a Basic Benefits Plan, which is an annuity. The Thrift Savings Plan is similar to a 401(k) plan that workers may contribute to on their own or through their employer. The federal government matches employee contributions up to a certain percentage, set by law. The earnings grow tax-free.

Paid Holidays

Government workers are entitled to the following 10 regular paid holidays each year:

- New Year's Day (January 1)
- Martin Luther King, Jr.'s Birthday (third Monday in January)
- Presidents' Day (third Monday in February)
- Memorial Day (last Monday in May)
- Independence Day (July 4)
- Labor Day (first Monday in September)
- Columbus Day (second Monday in October)
- Veterans Day (November 11)
- Thanksgiving Day (fourth Thursday in November)
- Christmas Day (December 25)

STATE AND LOCAL GOVERNMENT EMPLOYMENT

State and local governments provide a large and expanding source of job opportunities in a variety of fields. More than 19 million people work for state and local agencies throughout the United States; about three-fourths of these employees work in local government, such as county, municipality, town, and school district governments.

As with federal employment, nearly every kind of job available in the private sector is also available in state and local employment. However, some positions are unique to state and local government, including the following:

- **Public education.** Educational services comprise the majority of jobs in state and local government—10.9 million. School systems, colleges, and universities employ not only teachers, but also administrative personnel, librarians, guidance counselors, nurses, dieticians, clerks, and maintenance workers.

- **Health services.** More than 1.5 million people are employed in health and hospital work, including physicians, nurses, medical laboratory technicians, and hospital attendants.

- **Highway work.** More than 500,000 people work in highway construction and maintenance. Positions include civil engineers, surveyors, equipment operators, truck drivers, concrete finishers, carpenters, and construction workers.

- **Governmental control and finance.** These positions account for about 1.3 million employees, including those in the justice system, tax enforcement, and general administration. Specific positions include city managers, property assessors, and budget analysts, as well as clerks and database managers.

- **Law enforcement and firefighting.** More than 1.7 million people work in law enforcement. This includes not only police officers and detectives, but also administrative, clerical, and custodial workers. Local governments employ 383,000 non-volunteer firefighters, many of whom work part-time.

You can find other state and local government work in these fields:

- Corrections
- Housing and urban renewal
- Libraries
- Local utilities
- Natural resources
- Parks and recreation
- Public transportation
- Public welfare
- Sanitation
- Sewage disposal

These types of positions require people with diverse experiences, such as economists, electrical engineers, electricians, pipe fitters, clerks, foresters, and bus drivers. State and local government job requirements, salary scales, and benefits vary from state to state and from one municipality to another, but in general they're comparable to those of federal government employment. As with federal jobs, applicants must meet certain educational and/or experience requirements, show evidence of having the required skills, and pass a job-related written test.

OBTAINING JOB INFORMATION

When government agencies need to fill positions, they publish job announcements or examination announcements. Such an announcement lists nearly all you need to know about the job, including work requirements, salary, duties, and location. It also tells you when and where to file for the exam, which application forms you must complete, and where you can find the forms.

Most job announcements also provide a deadline for filing your application. No application submitted past the deadline date is considered. If the top of the first page of the announcement says "No Closing Date," this means that no deadline has been set and that applications are accepted until all open positions are filled.

Study the job announcement carefully. It will answer many of your questions and help you decide whether you want the position and are qualified for it. The specific duties of the position are outlined in detail, usually under the heading "Description of Work." Before you apply, make sure that your experience and ability match the range of duties listed, and that you meet all the educational, experience, and special requirements.

The job announcement also describes the type of test, if any, you will need to take to be considered for the position—so pay close attention to this section of the announcement. It tells you what areas are covered in the written test and lists the specific subjects on which questions will be asked. Sometimes an announcement will also provide sample questions or describe the method of rating the exam. This is invaluable information when you're preparing to take the exam. In some cases, you will not be required to take an exam; instead, you'll be considered based on your education, experience, and achievements. You may need to answer questions about yourself, however. They may be in the form of what is known as a KSA essay for knowledge, skills, and abilities, or they may be a series of assessment questions that ask about your experience, skills, and abilities. Both measure how well you fit the requirements of the job you're applying for.

Learning About Federal Jobs

Federal government job openings across most parts of the federal government and in all areas of the country are listed at **usajobs.gov**. The USAJOBS website is operated by the Office of Personnel Management (OPM) and lists thousands of vacancies for federal positions. As many as 20,000 job openings may be posted on the site at any one time. However, some agencies post jobs only on their own websites. If you're looking for a job at a specific agency, do a search of their employment sections and employment information pages.

USAJOBS is the portal for applying for most federal jobs. You can register and create an account where you can develop multiple versions of your resume to suit different job descriptions, set up job search agents, and upload and save documents such as transcripts. Once you have an account, you can begin your search for job openings that fit your career goals. You can fill out all the forms

TIP

The official employment website of the U.S. federal government is *usajobs.gov*.

TIP

The Office of Personnel Management's website (*opm.gov*) also offers valuable information for job seekers, including links to information on veterans' preference points, government diversity and inclusion policies, training and development programs, and similar information on policies and programs for federal government employees.

and answer all the questions required to apply for a job, as well as submit them and your supporting documents online for most jobs. However, some agencies will accept applications by mail or fax. You need to read the job announcement carefully to see what each agency will accept.

Applying online or by mail or fax may seem very impersonal, but if you have questions, job announcements generally contain the name and contact information for the hiring representative in the agency posting the job. If you do not have a computer, you can find information about federal jobs at your state's American Job Centers or by using the computers at your local public library. Local newspapers may also list available federal jobs in their classified job sections either in print or online. College and university placement offices and professional contacts can also be good sources of information.

Learning About State and Municipal Jobs

State and municipal governments make job opportunities known in various ways. Check the following resources for job announcements:

- **American Job Centers.** Funded by the Department of Labor's Employment and Training Administration, more than 2,500 AJCs are located throughout the country. Find the one nearest you at **careeronestop.org**.

- **CareerOneStop.** Billed as "the flagship career, training, and job search website for the U.S. Department of Labor," **careeronestop.org** is an invaluable website for those seeking jobs in the government as well as the private sector.

- **State Civil Service Commission** (located in your state's capital city).

- **Civil Service Commission.** Some cities—particularly large ones—have Civil Service Commissions, which sometimes go by another name such as the Department of Personnel. They would normally be listed online as a "city department."

- **City and statewide publications** devoted to civil service employees. These publications, such as the *Chief-Leader* (for New York City), often list many job openings. Local newspapers may also run a regular section on regional civil service news.

- **School boards and boards of education.** These groups employ the greatest proportions of state and local personnel. Ask directly for information about job openings. In addition to teachers and teachers' aides, school districts employ media center directors, maintenance people, and bus drivers.

- **City and state municipal buildings.** These offices usually post job openings available in your municipality. You can also check to see whether your local township has a website where job opportunities are posted.

- **Local libraries.** Check bulletin boards and other areas of public posting at your local library to see whether government jobs are listed.

- **Local college or university placement offices.** These departments can provide a wealth of information on civil service jobs.

Some resume-
writing tips include
the following:
Don't be vague;
be descriptive, but
succinct. Don't be
fancy; use plain
English.

HOW TO APPLY

The job announcement specifies which application form you should use and where to get it. Civil service application forms differ little from state to state or from one locality to another. The questions, which have been formulated through years of experimentation, are simple and direct and designed to elicit as much relevant information as possible. Many applications are now submitted online.

Applying for a Federal Job

The process for applying for a federal job is straightforward, but it will take some time. The first step is to visit **usajobs.gov** and create an account. In an effort to streamline government services, USAJOBS users are now required to create a **login.gov** account to access information stored on the USAJOBS website. Follow the onscreen steps to create your account. You will need to do this only once. When you are finished, the website will link back to USAJOBS.

Before you can apply for job openings, you will need to create a USAJOBS profile. You will be directed to enter basic information about yourself such as your full name, address, and phone number. You will also be directed to enter your citizenship, selective service information, and any federal, military, and professional experience. It is important that you complete the work experience section, as you will have the option to make your profile searchable so that agencies can find you based on your experience. You can add up to 50 separate work experience entries.

USAJOBS also requires you to complete the hiring paths section of your profile. The federal government offers the following unique hiring paths to help hire individuals that are best suited to the advertised positions:

- U.S. Citizens (including nationals or those that owe allegiance to the United States)
- Federal employees
- Veterans
- Military spouses
- National Guard & Reserves
- Students
- Recent graduates
- Senior executives
- Individuals with disabilities
- Family of overseas employees
- Native Americans
- Peace Corps & AmeriCorps VISTA
- Land & base management

These hiring paths help the government know which jobs you may or may not be eligible for. You can apply to any job, but you may not be eligible for the particular job if you do not fall into one of the required hiring paths.

You have the option at this point to provide demographic information to aid in recruitment efforts, as well as your educational history, languages that you are fluent in, organizations you are a part of, and references. This information is optional, and you can return to complete these sections at any time.

Setting up your USAJOBS profile is key to your application process. Moving forward, you will be able to do the following:

- Search, save, and archive job postings
- Customize and save your favorite job searches
- Build or upload up to five different resumes
- Apply to job openings
- Upload cover letters, transcripts, and other job-specific forms
- Monitor active job applications and archive closed applications

Once you have set up your USAJOBS profile, go back to the home page to begin your job search. You can search by keyword, job title, agency, skills, location, or control number (if you have one). Click Search and your web browser will display a listing of jobs that you can scroll through. As an example, a search for any federal jobs in Philadelphia, Pennsylvania, may produce 141 results across a variety of departments and agencies and pay. These search results can be further narrowed by using filters to search by location, hiring path, pay, work schedule, appointment type, security clearance, etc.

Once you find a job that you're interested in, click on the job title and the full job posting will appear. The posting describes the following:

- Salary range
- Open period (the length of the posting)
- Series and grade (in the civil service system)
- Position information (basic information such as full-time or part-time)
- Promotion potential
- Duty locations (cities where this type of job is open if the job announcement is not for a specific position at a specific location)
- Who may apply (note that almost all jobs are open only to U.S. citizens)
- Job summary: Description of the job
- Key requirements
- Duties
- Qualifications required
- How you will be evaluated
- Benefits
- Other information
- Instructions on how to apply
- Required documents
- Agency contact information
- What to expect next

Carefully review the qualifications listed in the Requirements section, as well as the process of how applicants will be evaluated. These two sections will detail what your application must include.

Among the items you will need to provide is your resume. Your resume should include detailed information to support your qualifications for the specific job. Keep in mind that one general resume won't necessarily highlight the experience, skills, and abilities required for the job; it is for this reason that USAJOBS allows you to create or upload up to five different resumes.

In general, most government jobs require some form of self-assessment as a part of the application. You will be able to preview the assessment or occupational questions, which are specific to the job for which you are applying, in the Evaluation section before beginning any applications. This step saves you from applying for jobs that don't really match your experience, skills, and abilities.

The Required Documents section will list any additional forms or information that need to be included in your application. Depending on the requirements listed in the job announcement, you may need to include a cover letter, transcripts, and additional government forms.

Sample Assessment Questionnaire

The following is a sample assessment questionnaire for a job as a clerical employee. As you can see, the questions are meant to measure a prospective employee's experience, skill, and abilities.

Eligibilities

1. Do you claim Veterans' Preference?

   A. No, I do not claim Veterans' Preference

   B. 0-point Sole Survivorship Preference (SSP)

   C. 5-point preference based on active duty in the U.S. Armed Forces (TP)

   D. 10-point preference for non-compensable disability or Purple Heart (XP)

   E. 10-point preference based on a compensable service-connected disability of at least 10% but less than 30% (CP)

   F. 10-point preference based on widow/widower or parent of a deceased veteran, or spouse or parent of a disabled veteran (XP)

   G. 10-point preference based on a compensable service-connected disability of 30% or more (CPS)

2. Are you a current or former federal employee displaced from the agency hiring for this position? If yes, confirm:

   - you are located in the same local commuting area of the vacancy; AND,

   - you are applying to a position that is at or below the grade level of the position from which you were or will be separated; AND,

   - you are applying to a position that does not have greater promotion potential than the position from which you were or will be separated; AND,

   - your last performance rating of record is at least fully successful or the equivalent.

To verify your eligibility, you must submit supporting documentation such as a Reduction in Force (RIF) separation notice or a Proposed Removal/Separation notice to include your latest performance rating (if the notice does not have this information included, you must submit a copy of your most recent performance appraisal) and a copy of your latest Notification of Personnel Action, Standard Form 50.

A. Yes

B. No

3. Are you a current or former federal employee displaced from a position in a Federal agency other than the agency hiring for this position? If yes, confirm:

- you are located in the same local commuting area of the vacancy; AND,

- you are applying to a position that is at or below the grade level of the position from which you were or will be separated; AND,

- you are applying to a position that does not have greater promotion potential than the position from which you were or will be separated; AND,

- your last performance rating of record is at least fully successful or the equivalent.

To verify your eligibility, you must submit supporting documentation such as a Reduction in Force (RIF) separation notice to include your latest performance rating (if the notice does not have this information included, you must submit a copy of your most recent performance appraisal) and a copy of your latest Notification of Personnel Action, Standard Form 50.

A. Yes

B. No

Preferences

1. Select the lowest grade you are willing to accept for this position.

    A. 6

    B. 7

2. Would you accept a term appointment?

    A. Yes

    B. No

Assessment 1

WARNING STATEMENT: Do not overstate or understate your level of experience and demonstrated capability. You should be aware that your ratings are subject to evaluation and verification based on the resume, and other relevant documents you submit, as well as through verification of references as appropriate. Deliberate attempts to falsify information may be grounds for disqualifying you or for dismissing you from the position following acceptance. The following questions will be used to determine your minimum qualifications for this position.

1. Carefully read the following descriptions of experience and education. Select the one that best describes your qualifications for the GS-06 Program Support Assistant. Make sure your resume supports the response that you select. Mark only one response.

   A. I have at least one year (52 weeks) of specialized experience in a pay or work status equivalent in difficulty and complexity to the GS-05 level in the Federal service. This experience must demonstrate all of the following: *Performing at least three (3) administrative functions for an organization or office, such as preparing or reviewing correspondence and/or reports for correct grammar and format; receiving and distributing mail; preparing time and attendance records; maintaining databases; monitoring progress on action items; and responding to requests for information; and *Establishing and maintaining records/files including protecting personally identifiable information; and *Utilizing computer programs, such as Microsoft Office Word, Excel, Outlook, PowerPoint, Access, Visio and Internet Explorer/Chrome to prepare correspondence, reports, spreadsheets, and other documents and conducting internet research.

   B. My education and/or experience are not reflected in any of the above statements.

2. Carefully read the following descriptions of experience and education. Select the one that best describes your qualifications for the GS-07 Program Support Assistant. Make sure your resume supports the response that you select. Mark only one response.

   A. I have at least one year (52 weeks) of specialized experience in a pay or work status equivalent in difficulty and complexity to the GS-06 level in the Federal service. This experience must demonstrate all of the following: *Performing at least four (4) administrative functions for an organization, such as reviewing correspondence and/or reports for correct grammar and format; receiving and distributing mail; preparing time and attendance records and resolving errors; maintaining databases; monitoring progress on action items; responding to requests for information; and *Establishing and maintaining records/files including protecting personally identifiable information; and *Utilizing computer programs, such as Microsoft Office Word, Excel, Outlook, PowerPoint, Access, Visio and Internet Explorer/Chrome to prepare correspondence, reports, spreadsheets, and other documents and conduct internet research.

   B. My education and/or experience are not reflected in any of the above statements.

3. To receive proper credit, please indicate the month and year as well as the average hours worked per week for each employer. Average work hours must be stated on resume to quantify each period of work experience or that experience will not be credited toward meeting the specialized experience requirement.

   Did you include month and year as well as average hours worked per week in your resume/application for each position stated? Please answer below:

   A. Yes
   B. No

For each task in the following Competencies, choose the statement from the list below that best describes your experience and/or training. Please select only one letter for each item.

4. Maintain and arrange a calendar of meetings, conferences, events, etc. for an organization using an automated system.

    A. I have no education, training, or experience in performing this task.

    B. I have had education or training in performing the task but have not yet performed it on the job.

    C. I have performed this task on the job. My work on this task was monitored closely by a supervisory or senior employee to ensure compliance with proper procedures.

    D. I have performed this task as a regular part of a job. I have performed it independently and normally without review by a supervisor or senior employee.

    E. I am considered an expert in performing this task. I am normally the person who is consulted by other workers to assist them in doing this task because of my expertise or I have supervised performance of this task.

5. Answer questions and respond to requests as appropriate and inform supervisor or other staff of issues requiring further follow up.

    A. I have no education, training, or experience in performing this task.

    B. I have had education or training in performing the task but have not yet performed it on the job.

    C. I have performed this task on the job. My work on this task was monitored closely by a supervisory or senior employee to ensure compliance with proper procedures.

    D. I have performed this task as a regular part of a job. I have performed it independently and normally without review by a supervisor or senior employee.

    E. I am considered an expert in performing this task. I am normally the person who is consulted by other workers to assist them in doing this task because of my expertise or I have supervised performance of this task.

6. Answer and transfer telephone calls to appropriate staff members using a multi-line telephone system.

    A. I have no education, training, or experience in performing this task.

    B. I have had education or training in performing the task but have not yet performed it on the job.

    C. I have performed this task on the job. My work on this task was monitored closely by a supervisory or senior employee to ensure compliance with proper procedures.

    D. I have performed this task as a regular part of a job. I have performed it independently and normally without review by a supervisor or senior employee.

    E. I am considered an expert in performing this task. I am normally the person who is consulted by other workers to assist them in doing this task because of my expertise or I have supervised performance of this task.

7. Use an email system to receive and respond to inquiries.

   A. I have no education, training, or experience in performing this task.

   B. I have had education or training in performing the task but have not yet performed it on the job.

   C. I have performed this task on the job. My work on this task was monitored closely by a supervisory or senior employee to ensure compliance with proper procedures.

   D. I have performed this task as a regular part of a job. I have performed it independently and normally without review by a supervisor or senior employee.

   E. I am considered an expert in performing this task. I am normally the person who is consulted by other workers to assist them in doing this task because of my expertise or I have supervised performance of this task.

8. To support the responses you provided to questions 4–7, please indicate the position(s) in your resume in which you communicated with others effectively orally in person or used a multi-line telephone system and other automated systems to maintain, provide, or obtain information. (Provide position title, company, and dates only.)

9. Use office application software such as Microsoft Access, Word, Excel, PowerPoint, Outlook, Visio, and Internet Explorer or comparable to generate documents, data reports, spreadsheets, conduct internet research, etc.

   A. I have no education, training, or experience in performing this task.

   B. I have had education or training in performing the task but have not yet performed it on the job.

   C. I have performed this task on the job. My work on this task was monitored closely by a supervisory or senior employee to ensure compliance with proper procedures.

   D. I have performed this task as a regular part of a job. I have performed it independently and normally without review by a supervisor or senior employee.

   E. I am considered an expert in performing this task. I am normally the person who is consulted by other workers to assist them in doing this task because of my expertise, or I have supervised performance of this task.

10. Prepare spreadsheets to compile and organize a variety of data and information.

   A. I have no education, training, or experience in performing this task.

   B. I have had education or training in performing the task but have not yet performed it on the job.

   C. I have performed this task on the job. My work on this task was monitored closely by a supervisory or senior employee to ensure compliance with proper procedures.

   D. I have performed this task as a regular part of a job. I have performed it independently and normally without review by a supervisor or senior employee.

   E. I am considered an expert in performing this task. I am normally the person who is consulted by other workers to assist them in doing this task because of my expertise or I have supervised performance of this task.

11. Use Oracle-based programs to complete assignments.

    A. I have no education, training, or experience in performing this task.

    B. I have had education or training in performing the task but have not yet performed it on the job.

    C. I have performed this task on the job. My work on this task was monitored closely by a supervisory or senior employee to ensure compliance with proper procedures.

    D. I have performed this task as a regular part of a job. I have performed it independently and normally without review by a supervisor or senior employee.

    E. I am considered an expert in performing this task. I am normally the person who is consulted by other workers to assist them in doing this task because of my expertise or I have supervised performance of this task.

12. Enter data into a variety of computer systems accurately and efficiently.

    A. I have no education, training, or experience in performing this task.

    B. I have had education or training in performing the task but have not yet performed it on the job.

    C. I have performed this task on the job. My work on this task was monitored closely by a supervisory or senior employee to ensure compliance with proper procedures.

    D. I have performed this task as a regular part of a job. I have performed it independently and normally without review by a supervisor or senior employee.

    E. I am considered an expert in performing this task. I am normally the person who is consulted by other workers to assist them in doing this task because of my expertise or I have supervised performance of this task.

13. To support the responses you provided to questions 9–12, please indicate the position(s) in your resume in which you used a computer system and software applications to prepare reports, spreadsheets, emails, and other documents. (Provide position title, company, and dates only.)

14. Comply with the requirements of a records management system and protect privacy information.

    A. I have no education, training, or experience in performing this task.

    B. I have had education or training in performing the task but have not yet performed it on the job.

    C. I have performed this task on the job. My work on this task was monitored closely by a supervisory or senior employee to ensure compliance with proper procedures.

    D. I have performed this task as a regular part of a job. I have performed it independently and normally without review by a supervisor or senior employee.

    E. I am considered an expert in performing this task. I am normally the person who is consulted by other workers to assist them in doing this task because of my expertise or I have supervised performance of this task.

15. Receive and distribute mail.

   A. I have no education, training, or experience in performing this task.

   B. I have had education or training in performing the task but have not yet performed it on the job.

   C. I have performed this task on the job. My work on this task was monitored closely by a supervisory or senior employee to ensure compliance with proper procedures.

   D. I have performed this task as a regular part of a job. I have performed it independently and normally without review by a supervisor or senior employee.

   E. I am considered an expert in performing this task. I am normally the person who is consulted by other workers to assist them in doing this task because of my expertise or I have supervised performance of this task.

16. Review internal correspondence for correct format, technical soundness, style, and typographical accuracy.

   A. I have no education, training, or experience in performing this task.

   B. I have had education or training in performing the task but have not yet performed it on the job.

   C. I have performed this task on the job. My work on this task was monitored closely by a supervisory or senior employee to ensure compliance with proper procedures.

   D. I have performed this task as a regular part of a job. I have performed it independently and normally without review by a supervisor or senior employee.

   E. I am considered an expert in performing this task. I am normally the person who is consulted by other workers to assist them in doing this task because of my expertise or I have supervised performance of this task.

17. Ensure all correspondence is in conformance with procedural notices and requirements prior to signature.

   A. I have no education, training, or experience in performing this task.

   B. I have had education or training in performing the task but have not yet performed it on the job.

   C. I have performed this task on the job. My work on this task was monitored closely by a supervisory or senior employee to ensure compliance with proper procedures.

   D. I have performed this task as a regular part of a job. I have performed it independently and normally without review by a supervisor or senior employee.

   E. I am considered an expert in performing this task. I am normally the person who is consulted by other workers to assist them in doing this task because of my expertise or I have supervised performance of this task.

18. Prepare work products which are thorough, accurate, and attentive to detail.

   A. I have no education, training, or experience in performing this task.

   B. I have had education or training in performing the task but have not yet performed it on the job.

C. I have performed this task on the job. My work on this task was monitored closely by a supervisory or senior employee to ensure compliance with proper procedures.

D. I have performed this task as a regular part of a job. I have performed it independently and normally without review by a supervisor or senior employee.

E. I am considered an expert in performing this task. I am normally the person who is consulted by other workers to assist them in doing this task because of my expertise or I have supervised performance of this task.

19. To support the responses you provided to questions 14–18, please indicate the position(s) in your resume in which you performed a variety of clerical functions, such as records management, receiving and distributing mail, and ensuring correspondence is accurate, compliant, and complete (Provide position title, company and dates only).

20. Advise staff on time and attendance policies and reporting procedures.

A. I have no education, training, or experience in performing this task.

B. I have had education or training in performing the task but have not yet performed it on the job.

C. I have performed this task on the job. My work on this task was monitored closely by a supervisory or senior employee to ensure compliance with proper procedures.

D. I have performed this task as a regular part of a job. I have performed it independently and normally without review by a supervisor or senior employee.

E. I am considered an expert in performing this task. I am normally the person who is consulted by other workers to assist them in doing this task because of my expertise or I have supervised performance of this task.

21. Track and report employees' use of overtime.

A. I have no education, training, or experience in performing this task.

B. I have had education or training in performing the task but have not yet performed it on the job.

C. I have performed this task on the job. My work on this task was monitored closely by a supervisory or senior employee to ensure compliance with proper procedures.

D. I have performed this task as a regular part of a job. I have performed it independently and normally without review by a supervisor or senior employee.

E. I am considered an expert in performing this task. I am normally the person who is consulted by other workers to assist them in doing this task because of my expertise or I have supervised performance of this task.

22. Maintain time and attendance records.

A. I have no education, training, or experience in performing this task.

B. I have had education or training in performing the task but have not yet performed it on the job.

C. I have performed this task on the job. My work on this task was monitored closely by a supervisory or senior employee to ensure compliance with proper procedures.

   D. I have performed this task as a regular part of a job. I have performed it independently and normally without review by a supervisor or senior employee.

   E. I am considered an expert in performing this task. I am normally the person who is consulted by other workers to assist them in doing this task because of my expertise or I have supervised performance of this task.

23. Maintain physical and electronic files that may contain sensitive or confidential information.

   A. I have no education, training, or experience in performing this task.

   B. I have had education or training in performing the task but have not yet performed it on the job.

   C. I have performed this task on the job. My work on this task was monitored closely by a supervisory or senior employee to ensure compliance with proper procedures.

   D. I have performed this task as a regular part of a job. I have performed it independently and normally without review by a supervisor or senior employee.

   E. I am considered an expert in performing this task. I am normally the person who is consulted by other workers to assist them in doing this task because of my expertise or I have supervised performance of this task.

24. Secure confidential files where and when necessary.

   A. I have no education, training, or experience in performing this task.

   B. I have had education or training in performing the task but have not yet performed it on the job.

   C. I have performed this task on the job. My work on this task was monitored closely by a supervisory or senior employee to ensure compliance with proper procedures.

   D. I have performed this task as a regular part of a job. I have performed it independently and normally without review by a supervisor or senior employee.

   E. I am considered an expert in performing this task. I am normally the person who is consulted by other workers to assist them in doing this task because of my expertise or I have supervised performance of this task.

25. Archive records using proper office procedures.

   A. I have no education, training, or experience in performing this task.

   B. I have had education or training in performing the task but have not yet performed it on the job.

   C. I have performed this task on the job. My work on this task was monitored closely by a supervisory or senior employee to ensure compliance with proper procedures.

   D. I have performed this task as a regular part of a job. I have performed it independently and normally without review by a supervisor or senior employee.

   E. I am considered an expert in performing this task. I am normally the person who is consulted by other workers to assist them in doing this task because of my expertise or I have supervised performance of this task.

26. Track employee assignments including deployments, travel, supplies and/or equipment.

   A. I have no education, training, or experience in performing this task.

   B. I have had education or training in performing the task but have not yet performed it on the job.

   C. I have performed this task on the job. My work on this task was monitored closely by a supervisory or senior employee to ensure compliance with proper procedures.

   D. I have performed this task as a regular part of a job. I have performed it independently and normally without review by a supervisor or senior employee.

   E. I am considered an expert in performing this task. I am normally the person who is consulted by other workers to assist them in doing this task because of my expertise or I have supervised performance of this task.

27. To support the responses you provided to questions 20–26, please indicate the position(s) in your resume in which you managed and organized information such as maintaining physical and electronic files with confidential information, monitor policies and procedures, reviewed for compliance and responded to internal and external correspondence. (Provide position title, company, and dates only.)

As previously explained, your ratings in this Occupational Questionnaire are subject to evaluation and verification based on the documents and references you submit. Deliberate attempts to falsify information may be grounds for disqualifying you or for dismissing you from the position/agency during the probation period. Please take this opportunity to review your responses to ensure their accuracy. By agreeing to the statement below, you are confirming that you: 1) Understand this warning; 2) Have reviewed your responses to this questionnaire for accuracy; and 3) Verify that your responses accurately describe your current level of experience and capability.

28. Failure to agree to the statement below will disqualify you from further consideration for the position.

   A. Yes, I verify that all of my responses to this questionnaire are true and accurate. I accept that if my supporting documentation and/or later steps in the selection process do not support one or more of my responses to the questionnaire that my application may be rated lower and/or I may be removed from further consideration.

   B. No, I do not accept this agreement and/or I no longer wish to be considered for this position.

> **NOTE**
> You will be asked on your application whether someone may contact your present employer. If you say no, it will not affect your employment opportunities—but try to provide some form of evaluation or letter of recommendation to compensate.

NOTE: It is the applicant's responsibility to verify that information entered, uploaded, or faxed (i.e., resume, veterans' preference documentation, assessment questions and answers, and SF 50s) is accurate and received by the agency.
Source: https://apply.usastaffing.gov/ViewQuestionnaire/10218835

Federal, state, and municipal agencies looking for employees frequently contact professional societies, veterans' organizations, unions, and trade associations. Check with any organization to which you belong.

Using the Online Application Process

The OPM recommends that you download the job posting so that you can easily refer to it as you complete your application. The application process itself has five steps:

1. Create or upload a resume on **usajobs.gov**.

2. Apply online.

3. Answer the online questions and submit your online application.

4. Review and confirm your submission, which you will then be able to track through USAJOBS.

5. Submit required documents online or via mail or fax.

SUBMITTING A CIVIL SERVICE JOB RESUME

Taking an exam is now much less common than submitting a resume, an assessment or occupational questionnaire, and an application form for state and municipal government jobs as well as for federal positions. However, about 20 percent of civil service positions still involve exams. These include clerical and technology jobs that often require tests of speed, accuracy, and judgment. The remaining positions are filled based on competitive evaluation of applicants' experience, skills, abilities, and education. The following pages offer examples of three cover letters and resumes tailored to three hypothetical civil service positions at the state level.

Figure 1.2

James Johnson
123 Main Street
Dallas, Texas 53132
Phone: 555.222.1212
jjohnson@email.com

August 20, 2018

Human Resources Office
New York State Banking Department
One State Street
New York, NY 10004-1417
Re: Bank Examiner Trainee I (Exam 20-598); OC-APP-3 #20598 (4/07)

To Whom It May Concern:

I am responding to your position listing for Bank Examiner Trainee I, dated August 12, 2018. The application, my resume, and three (3) letters of reference are attached. For the past year, I have provided consulting and management training services, but I am now eager to continue with a career in banking. I would be honored to make a strong contribution to your team's efforts in this position.

After having carefully reviewed the requirements of this position, I am confident that my skills, abilities, and experience effectively match your requirements for this position. I have nearly 10 years' experience in banking and the financial industry, both in the private sector and in the government arena.

Throughout my career in banking, I have derived great satisfaction from serving clients well. I enjoy working with dynamic teams. I also enjoy working with the public, demonstrating banking services. I believe I would contribute to your professional environment because I find the banking industry to be both challenging and rewarding.

May I arrange an interview to further discuss my qualifications? I am available to meet with you at a mutually convenient time.

Thank you for your consideration of my application.

Sincerely,

James Johnson

Encl.

123 Main St., Dallas, TX 53132   Phone: 555.222.1212 Email: jjohnson@email.com

James Johnson

Objective	To work in banking as a loan officer or a bank examiner

Experience

2017–Present	Progressive Bank	Dallas, TX

Consultant and Trainer
- Conduct on-site regulatory compliance reviews and in-house training programs for bank employees, including both deposit and lending-related statutes
- Responsibilities include defining standards for project preparation, business blueprint, realization, and testing phases.

2015–2017	Progressive Bank	Dallas, TX

Bank Teller
- Served customers from diverse backgrounds in the Dallas metropolitan area
- Worked with bank officers to ensure efficient delivery of services
- Suggested new methods to increase retention of customers

2013–2014	Friendly Bank of Dallas	Dallas, TX

Bank Teller Assistant
- Helped assess the level of customer service and methods to increase delivery of great customer service
- Supervised interns in developing customer satisfaction surveys

2012–2013	Duffy Vineyards	Dallas, TX

Junior Sales Associate
- Worked with team to market local vineyard products

2011–2012	Lit Ware, Inc.	Dallas, TX

Sales Representative
- Worked in direct sales of plastic containers for home use
- Received company's highest sales award in 2012
- Helped develop training course in sales

Education	2007-2011	South Ridge State University	Dallas, TX

- Course of study. Finance and accounting; B.S. degree attained

Interests	Running, golf, tennis, computers

References	Available upon request

Figure 1.3

Jane A. Smith
4 New Street
Chicago, Illinois 60601
Phone: 555.234.5678
janesmith@email.com

August 20, 2018

H.S. Smith
Room 541
Bureau of Personnel Management
2300 S. Dirksen Parkway
Springfield, IL 62744

Re: Developmental Aide Trainee; OC-APP #4 10-010 / 10-011 (2-07L)

To Whom It May Concern:

I am responding to your listing for the Developmental Aide Trainee position, dated August 20, 2018. The application, my resume, and three letters of reference are attached. After having carefully reviewed the requirements of this position, I am confident that my skills, abilities, and experience match your requirements for this position.

For the past year, I have served as a Developmental Aide with Kinder Kids. Prior to that, I worked as a Developmental Aide with the Institute for Childhood Development in Chicago and as an assistant at a local daycare center. All of my previous positions have provided the opportunity to deepen my understanding of child development and teaching strategies.

I would be grateful for an opportunity to work for the State of Illinois as a Developmental Aide Trainee. Such an experience would be valuable to me as I pursue a career that utilizes my skills in a learning environment. I can assure you that I will devote my strong work ethic to serving your agency in this capacity.

May I arrange an interview to further discuss my qualifications? I am available for an interview at a mutually convenient time. Please feel free to contact me at the telephone number above.

Thank you for your time and consideration.

Sincerely,

Jane A. Smith

Encl.

4 New Street, Chicago, IL 60601   P: 555.234.5678 E: janesmith@email.com

Jane A. Smith

Objective

To contribute to the understanding of early childhood development through study and application of innovative methods in education and testing

Experience

2017–Present   Kinder Kids   Chicago, IL
Developmental Aide

- Emphasized learning for children 4 to 6 years of age
- Worked with children to help them understand the role of preschool in preparing them for elementary school
- Suggested new methods to increase retention of new reading skills

2015–2017   The Institute for Childhood Development Chicago, IL
Developmental Aide

- Helped assess the level of preparedness of children 6 to 8 years old for foreign language education
- Supervised interns in early childhood development

2013–2015   Bright Eyes Daycare, Inc.   Chicago, IL
Teacher Assistant

- Worked as assistant in the two-year-old class
- Helped youngsters during all activities, including meals
- Helped plan weekly activities with head teacher

Education

2009–2013   Chicago State University   Chicago, IL

- Course of study: Early Childhood Development

Interests

Running, nutrition, reading

References

Available upon request

Figure 1.4

Maria E. Jones
123 Street Avenue
Apt. 2B
Sacramento, California 94203
mej@email.com
Phone: 555.333.4444

August 20, 2018

Personnel Office
Attn: Mrs. Sylvia Smith
P.O. Box 9992
Sacramento, CA 94203

Re: Food Service Worker I; OMRDD, DOH, OC-APP #4 20-484

To Whom It May Concern:

I am responding to your position listing for Food Service Worker I, dated August 20, 2018. The application and my resume are attached. I am happy to provide letters of references upon request. After having carefully reviewed the requirements of this position, I am confident that my skills, abilities, and experience qualify me to serve as a Food Service Worker I for your organization.

For the past year, I have worked as a Food Service Technician in the cafeteria at a local hospital in Walnut Creek. I have an undergraduate degree in psychology, and I am very interested in the way that nutrition affects a person's physical well being. I would appreciate the chance to increase my knowledge and skills through hands-on experience working for the State of California. I am a dedicated, reliable employee, and I bring enthusiasm to a team environment.

May I arrange an interview to further discuss my qualifications? I am available for an interview at a mutually convenient time. Please feel free to contact me at the telephone number above.

Thank you for your consideration of my application. I look forward to hearing from you.

Sincerely,

Maria E. Jones

123 Street Avenue, Apt. 2B
Sacramento, California 94203

P: 555.333.4444 E: mej@email.com

Maria E. Jones

Objective	To work as a physical therapist in a progressive hospital

Experience

| 2017–Present | Arbor Hospital | Walnut Creek, CA |

Food Service Technician

- Emphasized efficient, safe delivery of food to patients
- Learned to keep food and food delivery costs to a minimum without sacrificing quality
- Suggested new food products that increased efficiency and nutrition

| 2015–2017 | Broadmoor Physical Therapy Institute | Capitola, CA |

Food Service Technician

- Served staff and clients during breakfast and lunch
- Supervised interns learning food service trade

| 2014–2015 | New Meadow Vineyard | Sacramento, CA |

Junior Sales Associate

- Worked with team to market local vineyard products
- Created brochures featuring product nutritional information

| 2013–2014 | ABC Nursing Home | Sacramento, CA |

Activities Assistant

- Assisted patients in all daily activities
- Responsible for compiling weekly reports for state
- Developed new reading program for patients

Education

| 2009–2013 | Prescott College | Prescott, AZ |

- Course of study: Psychology

Interests

Nutrition, gardening, running, reading

References

Available upon request

Tips for Completing Your Job Application

Give every job application serious attention. Submitting a complete application is the first important step toward getting the position you want. Consider the following tips:

- **Make a first draft.** This is especially important when you're writing your employment history and recording other types of experience. Rewrite the draft as many times as you need to until you've produced a comprehensive, well-written account. Review your background and make a list of specific on-the-job duties, outside activities, knowledge, and experiences that may enhance your qualifications for the position.

- **Provide a complete employment history.** Do not summarize; explain fully but succinctly. Be specific about which tasks you performed at each job you've had. If you're filling out a paper application, use all the lines allotted to each job description, and if you need more space, use plain white paper to continue.

- **Provide a complete educational history.** Include the names of all the schools you've attended going as far back as high school. Include school locations, the dates you attended, the subjects you studied, the total number of classroom or credit hours you earned, the diplomas or degrees you received, and any other pertinent data. Include the cities or towns, the dates you attended, your major if you have an associate or a bachelor's degree, the diplomas or degrees you received, and any other pertinent data. Also list military training, leadership orientation, career specialty training, and the like.

- **List honors and awards.** Many people are modest about awards. This is not the time to be modest. Honors and awards do not have to be earthshakingly important to be included. For example, cite scholarships and elections to any honor society and other groups if you are a recent graduate. Cite awards and honors related to your career and also any community awards if they are relevant. Recent awards are usually the most important, but if you've received only a few awards, list those that are relevant to your work, even if you received them some years ago.

- **List special qualifications, experiences, and skills.** Be honest in evaluating your abilities. Even if they do not seem directly related to the position, be sure to mention any familiarity with a foreign language, software programs, typing skills, licenses and certificates you have earned, experience with equipment or machines, membership in professional and nonprofit organizations, material you have written, examples of public speaking events, and relevant hobbies. For example, cite scholarships and elections to an honor society if you're a recent graduate. Cite awards and honors related to your career and also community awards if they are relevant. Recent awards are usually the most important, and the USAJOBS tips for resume-building says to list only awards and honors received in the last five years.

- **List available professional references.** Ask people who know you and who know your work to provide a reference. Make sure that they can be easily reached and include their phone numbers or other contact information.

- **Put the job announcement number on all application materials.** The number appears on the front of the job announcement. Also list your name, birthdate, and the position

TIP

Experience you acquired more than 15 years ago may be summarized in one block if it is not applicable to the type of position for which you are applying.

for which you're applying on all materials, in case parts of your application become separated.

- **Never embellish or falsify information.** Your application will be examined closely and facts will be checked. If you were ever fired, say so. It is better to state this openly than to have an examiner find out from a former employer.

- **Do not put employment history or other material into one long paragraph.** Aim for a clear, well-organized presentation. This is especially important if you use more space than what is provided on the application. Break up long descriptions into short sentences and paragraphs, and use headings. Also, use action verbs and avoid abbreviating or using the passive voice.

- **Consider your options carefully.** Most of the questions on the application form are straightforward. Be sure, however, to put some extra thought into answering the following:

  - *Locations where you're willing to work.* Sometimes vacancies are available in several locations. Would you accept employment in any location, or do you want to work in a specific place? Either way, list all the places where you're willing to work.

  - *Lowest grade or pay you will accept.* You will not be considered for a job that pays less than the amount you provide. Although the position salary is clearly stated in the announcement, it's possible that an earlier opening in the same occupation carries less responsibility and, thus pays a lower entrance-level salary.

  - *Temporary or part-time employment.* Temporary positions arise frequently, and part-time positions occasionally open up as well. Willingness to accept a temporary assignment or part-time position may be good ways of getting a foot in the door. Either could lead to a full-time job.

TIP

Include a college transcript only if the job announcement requests one.

SUMMING IT UP

- Major categories of federal positions include professional, administrative, investigative and law enforcement, technical, clerical, labor and mechanical, and unskilled. Each of these categories (except unskilled) requires certain educational and experience requirements.

- Some federal positions may be attained through special government programs, in which applicants do not require experience to qualify but may have to take a test to indicate aptitude for the position. These programs include part-time and summer employment, student work-study programs and student temporary employment, and the PMF program (Presidential Management Fellows Program).

- Generally, a high school diploma or previous job experience qualifies you for an entry-level job. With experience, federal employees are eligible for promotion to higher-level, more specialized jobs. You may also begin employment with the federal government at a higher grade level if you already have specialized experience or additional education.

- If you are a U.S. Armed Forces veteran, you may be eligible for Veterans' Preference points, which enable you to increase your exam score by either 5 or 10 points. If you're eligible, be sure to indicate that fact on your application or resume.

- Employment with the federal government comes with a number of benefits, including job training, generous vacation and sick time allowances, life and health insurance, and retirement benefits.

- As with federal employment, nearly every kind of job available in the private sector is also available in state and local employment. Fields that are unique to state and local government include public education, highway work, governmental control and finance, and law enforcement and firefighting.

- State and local government job requirements, salary scales, and benefits are generally comparable to those of federal government employment. As with federal jobs, applicants must meet educational and/or experience requirements and show evidence of having the required skills, and they may have to pass a job-related written test.

- Government agencies fill positions through job announcements or exam announcements. Study the announcements carefully, and be sure that you meet all the educational, experience, and special requirements before applying for a position.

- The official employment website of the U.S. federal government is **usajobs.gov**. The Office of Personnel Management's website (**opm.gov**) also provides information for job seekers, including job announcements, and detailed information about benefits and pay.

- For information on state and local government jobs, contact your American Jobs Center, **careeronestop.org**, the State Civil Service Commission, the nearest big city's Civil Service Commission, city and statewide civil service publications, school boards and boards of education, and city and state municipal offices. You might also check your local library or nearby college and university placement offices.

Exam Essentials

OVERVIEW

- **What to Expect on the Federal Civil Service Exam**
- **What to Expect on State and Municipal Exams**
- **Biographical and Achievement Inventory**
- **Preparing for a Civil Service Exam**
- **How the Exam Is Administered**
- **Exam Ratings**
- **Test-taking Strategies**
- **Summing It Up**

WHAT TO EXPECT ON THE FEDERAL CIVIL SERVICE EXAM

Congress passed the Civil Service Act to ensure that federal employees are hired based on individual merit and fitness. The Civil Service Act provides for competitive exams and the selection of new employees from among the most qualified applicants. Any U.S. citizen may take civil service exams. For most jobs, the agency seeking new employees rates exams to determine which applicants are eligible for the jobs to be filled. Some federal jobs are exempt from civil service requirements. Most of these positions, however, are covered by separate merit systems of other agencies, such as the State Department, the Federal Bureau of Investigation, the Nuclear Regulatory Commission, or the Tennessee Valley Authority.

There are two main types of civil service exams: competitive and noncompetitive. All applicants who take a competitive exam for a position compete with each other. The better your score, the better your chance of being appointed. Each applicant who takes a noncompetitive exam is tested solely to determine qualifications for a given position. You need only pass to become eligible for the job.

The purpose of civil service exams is to identify candidates who have the aptitude and ability to learn the job easily and to do it well. The subjects tested on the exam are closely related to the duties of the position. The written tests for federal occupations measure verbal, clerical, arithmetic, and any other skills needed for the job. On many clerical exams, for example, the exam consists of two tests: one measuring verbal ability, and another measuring clerical ability. Test requirements vary depending on the agency and the type of position.

Chapter 2

NOTE
For administrative civil service careers, testing is no longer mandatory.

Check the job announcement to confirm the test battery that you will have to take. If the announcement indicates that a written test will be given, you will receive a notice in the mail telling you when and where to report for the test.

Pay special attention to the section of the job announcement describing the kind of exam given for the open position. It explains what areas are covered in the written test and lists the specific subjects on which questions will be asked. Sometimes the hiring agency will provide sample questions to give applicants an idea of what to expect on the exam.

Testing Verbal Ability

Most civil service exams include a section to test verbal ability. The verbal portion of the exam tests you in the following areas:

- Spelling, meaning, and relationship of words
- Recognition of sentences that are grammatically correct
- Reading, understanding, and using written material

These areas relate to a variety of job tasks, such as proofreading and correcting typed copy, using instruction manuals, organizing new files of related materials, and carrying out written instructions.

Testing Clerical Ability

The clerical portion of the exam is a test of speed and accuracy on different clerical tasks. Because speed is being measured, this portion of the exam is more closely timed than other portions. Also, because accuracy is being measured, there is often a penalty for incorrect answers, unlike other portions of the exam. You may be tested on any or all of the following areas: alphabetic filing, name and number checking, and typing. Some clerical tests also include a stenography or coding portion.

Testing Mathematical Ability

Not all exams include a math section—it depends on the job you are applying for. Many clerical and cashiering jobs and positions in the manual trades do require some level of arithmetic ability. You may be tested on any of the following:

- Fractions, decimals, and percentages
- Graphs and tables
- Ratio and proportion
- Reasoning problems, including work, distance, taxation, and payroll problems

Other Exam Topics

Depending on the job that you are applying for, you may be tested on other topics. These include general aptitude questions for qualities necessary for the job, and questions testing specific abilities not covered in the clerical portion of the exam. For example, general aptitude questions may measure judgment and communication skills, which are necessary for many jobs. Other subjects are more specific: observation and memory for police officers, firefighters, corrections officers, court officers, and similar positions; and mechanical ability for firefighters, custodians, and mechanical workers in many trades.

WHAT TO EXPECT ON STATE AND MUNICIPAL EXAMS

Following the lead of the federal government, every state has instituted some form of merit-based hiring procedure. In matters of internal hiring, each state has complete autonomy. No higher authority tells a state which positions must be filled by examination or which exam to use. In the interests of efficiency and fairness in hiring, nearly all states fill positions through civil service exams.

Many states offer their testing services to counties and municipalities as well. Thus, if you qualify on a state-administered exam, you may have your name and ranking listed on any number of eligibility rosters in counties or towns in which you are willing to work. In other states, state testing is only for state positions, and counties and municipalities have their own independent systems.

As testing arrangements vary from state to state, so do procedures and the tests themselves. Because of the differences in state exams, it is not possible to give you the precise information you need for the exam in your state. But many state and municipal exams follow the lead of the federal civil service exam style, measuring verbal, clerical, arithmetic, and mechanical abilities, as well as other skills, depending on the job.

BIOGRAPHICAL AND ACHIEVEMENT INVENTORY

Many federal and state civil service exams conclude with a self-descriptive inventory. This inventory is set up to look like a multiple-choice test and is timed like a test, but it is not a test at all. There are no right or wrong answers. Rather, the examiners are looking for a pattern of achievements, interests, and personality traits that they can compare to the profile of currently active, successful people in the same occupation.

Aside from high school and college-related questions, you are asked about your likes and dislikes and about the impression that you make on others. There are questions about how you rank yourself in relation to other people, about what your friends think of you, and about the opinions of supervisors or teachers. Do not try to second-guess the testers to give the "right" answer on the biographical and achievement inventory. Internal checks for consistency and honesty are built into the questions. Your best bet is to answer quickly and candidly. Dwelling on the questions is not likely to help.

You cannot really study for this inventory. The only possible preparation is searching old school records to refresh your memory about subjects you studied and your attendance, grades, and extracurricular activities. If you cannot find your records, just answer to the best of your ability.

PREPARING FOR A CIVIL SERVICE EXAM

Obviously, some education is necessary to answer questions in reading, spelling, grammar, English usage, and math. But for the most part, these general subjects demand less schooling than the subjects that would be used in testing candidates for skilled, technical, or specialized jobs. Government agencies favor these general test subjects because they probe a candidate's native intelligence and

NOTE

Exam subjects and formats vary the most among law enforcement and corrections exams. By contrast, clerical exams are more limited to the nature of clerical work itself and are more universal.

aptitude for learning how to do a job and succeed in it. The agency does not want to handicap candidates who have been deprived of a full education.

Ability questions, such as those testing clerical and mechanical ability, are designed to assess the effects of a specific course of training. These tests assume that applicants have had a specific course of instruction, job apprenticeship, or other relatively uniform experience.

Because aptitude and ability tests overlap, you will clearly benefit from studying the subject matter and learning how to achieve the highest scores on general questions. Experience has shown that it is possible to improve your score and, thus, to better demonstrate your aptitude for the job. With the great variety in exams, especially among state and municipal exams, the best preparation is thorough grounding in basic skills and practice with many kinds of exam questions.

The test questions and review materials in this book are based on the requirements of a variety of job announcements, as well as on questions that have appeared on actual tests. It will be well worth your time to try your hand at all the practice questions and sample exams, even if you do not think some of the subjects or types of questions will appear on your exam. This way, you can prepare yourself for whatever type of question you may encounter. In a field of competent applicants, familiarity with different question styles and strategies can give you the competitive edge, a higher score, and an offer of employment.

Any test-taking practice will help in preparation for the exam. In addition, knowing what to expect and familiarity with techniques of effective test-taking should give you the confidence you need to do your best. The following list will help you prepare for a civil service exam, or any exam for that matter:

- **Prepare for the exam.** Do not make the test harder than it has to be by not preparing yourself. You are taking a very important step by reading this book and taking the practice tests. Doing so will help you become familiar with the test and the kinds of questions that you will have to answer. Make a study schedule and stick to it. Regular, daily study is important.

- **Answer all the practice questions.** Read the sample questions and directions for taking the test carefully. When you take the practice tests, time yourself as if you were taking a real civil service exam. If you answer a question correctly, do not be satisfied with merely the correct answer. Do some research on the other choices to see why they were incorrect. You will broaden your background and be more adequately prepared for the actual exam.

- **Don't look at the correct answers before answering the practice questions on your own.** Looking ahead can fool you into thinking that you understand a question when you really do not. Try answering the question on your own first, and then compare your answer with the one given. In a practice test, you are your own grader; you do not gain anything by pretending to understand something that you really do not. Study answer explanations whenever they are supplied because they may give you extra insights—even into the questions that you answered correctly.

- **Review what you have learned.** Once you have studied something thoroughly, review it the next day so that the information will be firmly fixed in your mind.

- **Tailor your study to the subject matter.** Do not study everything in the same manner. Give special attention to your areas of weakness and to areas that are more likely to be covered on your exam.

- **Study where you won't be interrupted or distracted.** You will concentrate better if you work away from distractions such as your phone and social media, chitchat from family, TV, and so on. Choose a comfortable, well-lit study spot that's as far as possible from the distractions of daily life. That might mean going to the public library.

- **Stay physically fit.** You cannot retain information well when you are uncomfortable, have a headache, or are tense. Try to get some exercise. You don't have to go to the gym or do an intense workout. Exercise can be as simple as going for a short walk, or getting off the bus or subway a stop or two early to walk the rest of the way to your destination. A short break for some physical exercise can help to clear your mind and improve your focus.

- **Don't try to learn too much in one study period.** If your mind starts to wander, take a short break and then return to your work.

HOW THE EXAM IS ADMINISTERED

In general, civil service exams are made up of multiple-choice questions. Most multiple-choice tests consist of a question booklet and a separate answer sheet. The question booklet begins with general instructions for taking the test, including the rules and regulations governing your exam, the number of questions, how the exam is timed, and signals used when time is up. Specific directions for different types of questions are explained in the section of the question booklet before each new type of question. Many federal agencies, states, and localities now use computer-based tests. Typically, candidates can take a tutorial to ensure they understand the functions of the software and how to use the computer for the specific test. An examiner will be in the room during the test should a problem arise. The time is shown on the screen, and the program will time out automatically. Directions are explained directly for each type of question on the screen. In the test room, the examiner will hand out forms for you to fill out or will direct you to screens to complete, and will give you the instructions that you must follow in taking the exam. The examiner will tell you how to fill in the grids on the forms and will explain time limits and timing signals. If you do not understand any of the instructions, ask questions. Do not score less than your best because the examiner did not explain something fully or you didn't understand.

Follow the examiner's instructions exactly. Fill in the grids on the forms carefully and accurately. Do not begin until you are told to begin, and stop as soon as the examiner tells you to stop. Do not turn pages until you are told to do so or go back to parts that you have already completed. If you are taking the test on a computer, you will be able to go back only within the section you are working in. Any infraction of the rules is considered cheating; your test paper will not be scored, and you will not be eligible for appointment.

Multiple-choice questions have four or five answer choices lettered **A** through **D** or **E**. Each question has one best answer. You must read the question carefully, think, choose the best answer, and blacken the matching lettered circle on the separate answer sheet, or click on the correct answer. If you take the time to clearly and neatly mark your answers, there will be no room for scoring errors. This will ensure accuracy and objectivity.

TIP

On the day of your exam, be sure to bring your ID, a pen, and any forms you received when you registered for the test. If you're taking a paper-based exam, also bring along three No. 2 pencils and an eraser.

ALERT

Make sure you complete all required forms before you arrive at the test site. Have all forms ready to turn in.

EXAM RATINGS

Applicants who meet the minimum experience and education requirements and skill levels for the job are given numerical ratings based on their written test scores. If you pass the exam, you will receive an eligible rating—that is, your name will be placed on a list for appointment, with the highest test scores at the top of the list. Eligible applicants who are not selected for the position are restored to the list for consideration for other openings. If you fail the exam, you can usually take it again as long as applications are being accepted. If you pass but want to improve your score, you can usually retake the test after a year has passed, if the announcement is open at that time.

Once you achieve a rating on a standardized exam, such as a clerical exam, you do not have to take the test again to apply for similar jobs. You also do not have to reestablish that you meet the minimum experience and education requirements or have the required skills. Your rating will expire after a certain period, as indicated on the rating form. Be sure to notify the agency that gave you a rating of address, name, or availability changes. When writing, give your full name, your Social Security number, the title of the job announcement, and the rating you received.

How the Exam Is Scored

The method of rating on all civil service exams is on a scale of 100, with 70 as the usual passing mark. Written tests are most frequently rated by machine. In some written exams, and for rating experience and training, two examiners work independently. In case of a protest about the rating, a third examiner is assigned to rate the exam again. Thus, the chances of error, arbitrary grading, or bias are almost completely eliminated.

On most exams, you get one point for each correct answer. You do not receive credit for an incorrect answer or for an unanswered question. Most important, you do not lose any credit for an incorrect answer. An incorrect answer is simply not a right answer. You do not receive any credit, but the incorrect answer itself does not work against you.

A few exams or portions of exams do not follow this scoring rule, especially clerical exams that measure accuracy under time pressure. A part of the federal clerical exam penalizes incorrect answers, for instance. In some cases, the number of incorrect answers is subtracted from the number of correct answers. More often, a portion of the incorrect answers—usually one-fourth—is subtracted from the number of correct answers.

Not many exams consist of exactly 100 questions. Some contain only 80, others 140 or more. All final scores are reported on the basis of 100. What this means is that while you get one point for each correct answer, that answer may not be adding exactly one point to your score. The examiners create a confidential formula that converts raw scores (the number you got right) to the final, scaled rating, which determines your ranking on the eligibility list. When an announcement specifies "70 percent required," it refers to the score that is reported after the conversion (and before the addition of veterans' preference points).

Rating Nontested Positions

If you applied for a job that did not require a written test, your rating is based on the experience and training you described in your application and on any required supporting evidence. When all this information has been gathered, you will be rated, and the agency will tell you how your qualifications look to the examiners. That's all there is to it, until you are called to the job.

Veterans' Preference Points

If you are a veteran of the U.S. Armed Forces, you may be eligible for veterans' preference points, a points boost that can give you an edge in the civil service hiring process. Veterans' preference points enable you to increase your exam score by either 5 or 10 points, depending on your eligibility. The veterans' preference may also allow you to submit certain job applications after the closing date for the exam.

To receive veterans' preference, you must have served in active duty and been released with an honorable or general discharge. Military retirees with a rank of major, lieutenant commander, or higher are not eligible for veterans' preference unless they are disabled veterans. (This restriction does not apply to some Reservists.) Note that the rules for veterans' preference can be complicated, so make sure to investigate your options, even if it seems at first that you don't qualify. You may.

See Appendix C for more detailed qualification rules for both 5- and 10-point credits.

TEST-TAKING STRATEGIES

When taking the exam, you can employ a number of strategies designed to boost your overall score by helping you to complete the test in an accurate and timely manner. For example:

- **Read every word of the instructions.** Aside from actually knowing the answer, careful reading is what most influences choosing the correct answer. Misreading directions causes the greatest problems and can result in a significant negative impact to your overall score. For example, if the directions ask you to choose the word that means the opposite of the underlined word, and you choose the word that means the same as the underlined word, you will mark incorrect answers for a whole series of questions. If you have time, reread the instructions after you work on the first few questions to make sure you understand and are answering the questions as directed. Whenever you are allowed to, ask the examiner to clarify anything you do not understand.

- **Read every word of every question.** Careful reading must extend beyond the reading of directions to the reading of each individual question. Qualifying words like *most, least, only, best, probably, definitely, not, all, every,* and *except* make a big difference in determining the correct answer to a specific question. Because reading is key to success with multiple-choice questions, your preparation should include a lot of attention to reading and reading-based questions. Once you have mastered the techniques of dealing with reading-based questions, you will be well-equipped to tackle all aspects of the civil service exam.

- **Make notes on scratch paper or the question booklet.** Usually, you are allowed to write in the question booklet. If this is the case, use the pages to calculate the answers to math questions, cross out eliminated answer choices, or underline key words. If you guess on a question, try placing a question mark next to the question in the booklet so that you can easily go back and review. If you are not permitted to write in the question booklet, you

TIP

If you're eligible to claim veterans' preference, make sure to indicate that on your application or resume.

TIP

For more information about veterans' preference points and your eligibility, contact the Veterans Employment Coordinator of the agency where you are seeking employment.

will be issued scratch paper. Whether you are using the booklet or scratch paper, do not forget to mark the final answer on the answer sheet. Only the answer sheet is scored; all other notes are disregarded.

- **Mark answers neatly and carefully.** The separate answer sheet is the only record of answers that is scored. Blacken your answer space firmly and completely. A correct answer response looks like this:

●

The following are incorrectly marked responses:

◐, ⊗, ☑, ∅

The scoring machine might not notice these marks. If the scoring machine does not register your answer, you will not get any credit for it. If you are taking the test on a computer, be sure you click the answer circle, and, if necessary, click "submit."

- **Manage your time.** Before you begin, take a moment to plan your progress through the test. Although you are not usually expected to finish all the questions, you should at least get an idea of how much time you need to spend on each question in order to answer them all. For example, if there are 60 questions to answer and you have 30 minutes, you will have about 30 seconds to spend on each question.

- **Check your answers.** If you finish a section or a part before the allotted time is up, use the remaining time to check that each question is answered in the right space and that you marked only one answer for each question. Return to the difficult questions and rethink them. However, keep in mind that second guessing yourself about your answers is not usually a good idea. Your first answer is often the right answer. If you cannot finish the current section or part before the allotted time expires, do not worry. If you are accurate, you can do well even without finishing. It is even possible to earn a rating of 100 without entirely finishing an exam part if you are very accurate. At any rate, do not let your performance on any one part affect your performance on any other part.

- **Guess when wrong answers do not count against you.** In most portions of the exam, incorrect answers do not take points off your score, so a guess cannot hurt you. The best guess is an educated guess. If you are not sure of the correct answer, try to eliminate the obviously incorrect answers. If you can narrow the field and guess from among fewer choices, you will raise the odds of guessing correctly.

- **Don't guess when wrong answers do count against you.** On some tests, a correct answer gives you one point, a skipped space gives you nothing at all but costs you nothing, and an incorrect answer costs you one-fourth of a point. Do not randomly guess—you could hurt your score. (Be sure to keep careful track of skipped questions so you do not mark the wrong lines on your answer sheet.) Although you should not make random guesses, an educated guess can still help you on this type of test. Do not rush to fill answer spaces randomly at the end. Instead, work as quickly as possible while concentrating on accuracy until time is called. Then, stop and leave the remaining answers blank.

TIP

Before testing begins, ask which scoring method will be used on your particular exam. You can then guide your guessing procedure accordingly.

- **Don't mark more than one answer for each question.** If more than one circle for any question is blackened, even if one of the answers is correct, the scoring machine will give no credit for that question. When you change an answer, be careful to fully and cleanly erase the first answer. You do not want the machine to misread your choice. Never cross out an answer in favor of a new choice. You must erase, or the machine will read both old and new answers and give you no credit.

- **Be careful in marking answers.** If you mark an answer in the wrong place, it will be scored as incorrect. If you notice that you have slipped out of line, you must erase all answers from the point of the error and redo all those questions. Most civil service exams allow sufficient time to finish, but you do not have the time to waste erasing and re-answering large blocks of questions. Therefore, do not skip any questions or jump around looking for easy questions to answer first. Do not omit a question even if you have no idea of the correct answer. If you are forced to guess so as to answer every question in order, then do so. If you answer every question in order, there should be no chance to slip. (The exception to this rule, of course, is when incorrect answers count against you.)

- **Don't spend too much time on any one question.** If you get stuck, do not take the puzzler as a personal challenge. Either guess and mark the question in the question booklet, or skip it entirely, marking the question as a skip and taking care to skip the answer space on the answer sheet. If you still have time when you reach the end of the exam section, you can return and give marked questions another try.

TIP

Check often to be sure that the question number matches the answer space and that you have not skipped a space by mistake.

SUMMING IT UP

- Any U.S. citizen may take civil service exams. In most cases, the agency seeking new employees rates these exams to determine which applicants are eligible for open positions.

- Civil service exams may be competitive or noncompetitive. With competitive exams, all applicants for a position compete with one another, so the higher your score, the better your chance of being hired. With noncompetitive exams, each applicant is tested to determine their qualifications for a given position and you do not compete with other applicants.

- Most federal civil service exams include a section that assesses your verbal ability. This type of section includes questions about spelling, meaning, and relationship of words; recognition of grammatically correct sentences; and reading, understanding, and using written material.

- Clerical sections of federal civil service exams test your speed and accuracy in performing various clerical tasks, including alphabetical filing, name and number checking, and typing. Some clerical exams also include a stenography or coding section.

- Some federal civil service exams include a math section. You may be tested on fractions, decimals, and percentages; graphs and tables; ratio and proportion; and reasoning problems of various sorts, including work, distance, taxation, and payroll.

- In addition to verbal ability, clerical ability, and arithmetic, some federal civil service exam questions may measure your judgment and communication skills; observation and memory skills; or mechanical ability.

- Each state has a merit-based hiring procedure and has complete autonomy over internal hiring for state civil service positions. Nearly all state governments fill positions through civil service exams, and as with the federal government, most include sections measuring verbal, clerical, arithmetic, and mechanical abilities.

- A self-descriptive inventory may also be a part of your civil service exam. This is a timed, multiple-choice test, but there are no correct or incorrect answers and you cannot study for these questions. Examiners are looking for a pattern of achievements, interests, and personality traits that they can compare to those of current employees in similar or related positions. Don't second-guess the questions; answering all questions quickly and honestly is the best way to proceed.

- The most useful way to prepare for taking a civil service exam is to be sure you've polished up your basic skills, and to practice with many types of exam questions. Review the test tips in this chapter and take the Practice Tests for experience with the kinds of test questions you're likely to see on your civil service exam.

- Applicants meeting minimum experience and education requirements and skill levels for a job are rated numerically based on their written test scores. If you've passed your civil service exam, you'll receive an eligibility rating and your name will be placed on a list for appointment. If you are not selected for the position, your name is restored to the list for consideration for other positions.

- All civil service exams are scored on a scale of 100, with 70 being the usual passing score (even if the test does not contain 100 questions). Written tests are almost always machine-scored; on most exams, you receive one point for each correct answer and no credit for an incorrect or unanswered question. Exceptions to this type of scoring include clerical exams that measure accuracy under time constraints. For positions that do not require taking a written test, your rating is based on the experience and training you described in your application and on any required supporting information.

- If you're a U.S. Armed Forces veteran, remember to indicate that fact on your application or resume. You may be eligible for veterans' preference points that increase your exam score by either 5 or 10 points, depending on your eligibility level.

- Follow the test-taking strategies outlined in this chapter to help you complete your test accurately and quickly, boosting your overall civil service exam score.

PART II

DIAGNOSING YOUR STRENGTHS AND WEAKNESSES

PRACTICE TEST 1   Diagnostic Test

ANSWER SHEET PRACTICE TEST 1: DIAGNOSTIC TEST

Verbal Ability

1. Ⓐ Ⓑ Ⓒ Ⓓ   14. Ⓐ Ⓑ Ⓒ Ⓓ   27. Ⓐ Ⓑ Ⓒ Ⓓ   40. Ⓐ Ⓑ Ⓒ Ⓓ
2. Ⓐ Ⓑ Ⓒ Ⓓ   15. Ⓐ Ⓑ Ⓒ Ⓓ   28. Ⓐ Ⓑ Ⓒ Ⓓ   41. Ⓐ Ⓑ Ⓒ Ⓓ
3. Ⓐ Ⓑ Ⓒ Ⓓ   16. Ⓐ Ⓑ Ⓒ Ⓓ   29. Ⓐ Ⓑ Ⓒ Ⓓ   42. Ⓐ Ⓑ Ⓒ Ⓓ
4. Ⓐ Ⓑ Ⓒ Ⓓ   17. Ⓐ Ⓑ Ⓒ Ⓓ   30. Ⓐ Ⓑ Ⓒ Ⓓ   43. Ⓐ Ⓑ Ⓒ Ⓓ
5. Ⓐ Ⓑ Ⓒ Ⓓ   18. Ⓐ Ⓑ Ⓒ Ⓓ   31. Ⓐ Ⓑ Ⓒ Ⓓ   44. Ⓐ Ⓑ Ⓒ Ⓓ
6. Ⓐ Ⓑ Ⓒ Ⓓ   19. Ⓐ Ⓑ Ⓒ Ⓓ   32. Ⓐ Ⓑ Ⓒ Ⓓ   45. Ⓐ Ⓑ Ⓒ Ⓓ
7. Ⓐ Ⓑ Ⓒ Ⓓ   20. Ⓐ Ⓑ Ⓒ Ⓓ   33. Ⓐ Ⓑ Ⓒ Ⓓ   46. Ⓐ Ⓑ Ⓒ Ⓓ
8. Ⓐ Ⓑ Ⓒ Ⓓ   21. Ⓐ Ⓑ Ⓒ Ⓓ   34. Ⓐ Ⓑ Ⓒ Ⓓ   47. Ⓐ Ⓑ Ⓒ Ⓓ
9. Ⓐ Ⓑ Ⓒ Ⓓ   22. Ⓐ Ⓑ Ⓒ Ⓓ   35. Ⓐ Ⓑ Ⓒ Ⓓ   48. Ⓐ Ⓑ Ⓒ Ⓓ
10. Ⓐ Ⓑ Ⓒ Ⓓ   23. Ⓐ Ⓑ Ⓒ Ⓓ   36. Ⓐ Ⓑ Ⓒ Ⓓ   49. Ⓐ Ⓑ Ⓒ Ⓓ
11. Ⓐ Ⓑ Ⓒ Ⓓ   24. Ⓐ Ⓑ Ⓒ Ⓓ   37. Ⓐ Ⓑ Ⓒ Ⓓ   50. Ⓐ Ⓑ Ⓒ Ⓓ
12. Ⓐ Ⓑ Ⓒ Ⓓ   25. Ⓐ Ⓑ Ⓒ Ⓓ   38. Ⓐ Ⓑ Ⓒ Ⓓ
13. Ⓐ Ⓑ Ⓒ Ⓓ   26. Ⓐ Ⓑ Ⓒ Ⓓ   39. Ⓐ Ⓑ Ⓒ Ⓓ

Arithmetic Ability

1. Ⓐ Ⓑ Ⓒ Ⓓ   8. Ⓐ Ⓑ Ⓒ Ⓓ   15. Ⓐ Ⓑ Ⓒ Ⓓ   22. Ⓐ Ⓑ Ⓒ Ⓓ Ⓔ
2. Ⓐ Ⓑ Ⓒ Ⓓ   9. Ⓐ Ⓑ Ⓒ Ⓓ   16. Ⓐ Ⓑ Ⓒ Ⓓ   23. Ⓐ Ⓑ Ⓒ Ⓓ Ⓔ
3. Ⓐ Ⓑ Ⓒ Ⓓ   10. Ⓐ Ⓑ Ⓒ Ⓓ   17. Ⓐ Ⓑ Ⓒ Ⓓ   24. Ⓐ Ⓑ Ⓒ Ⓓ Ⓔ
4. Ⓐ Ⓑ Ⓒ Ⓓ   11. Ⓐ Ⓑ Ⓒ Ⓓ   18. Ⓐ Ⓑ Ⓒ Ⓓ   25. Ⓐ Ⓑ Ⓒ Ⓓ Ⓔ
5. Ⓐ Ⓑ Ⓒ Ⓓ   12. Ⓐ Ⓑ Ⓒ Ⓓ   19. Ⓐ Ⓑ Ⓒ Ⓓ Ⓔ
6. Ⓐ Ⓑ Ⓒ Ⓓ   13. Ⓐ Ⓑ Ⓒ Ⓓ   20. Ⓐ Ⓑ Ⓒ Ⓓ Ⓔ
7. Ⓐ Ⓑ Ⓒ Ⓓ   14. Ⓐ Ⓑ Ⓒ Ⓓ   21. Ⓐ Ⓑ Ⓒ Ⓓ Ⓔ

answer sheet

Clerical Ability

1. Ⓐ Ⓑ Ⓒ Ⓓ Ⓔ   8. Ⓐ Ⓑ Ⓒ Ⓓ   15. Ⓐ Ⓑ Ⓒ Ⓓ   22. Ⓐ Ⓑ Ⓒ Ⓓ

2. Ⓐ Ⓑ Ⓒ Ⓓ Ⓔ   9. Ⓐ Ⓑ Ⓒ Ⓓ   16. Ⓐ Ⓑ Ⓒ Ⓓ   23. Ⓐ Ⓑ Ⓒ Ⓓ

3. Ⓐ Ⓑ Ⓒ Ⓓ Ⓔ   10. Ⓐ Ⓑ Ⓒ Ⓓ   17. Ⓐ Ⓑ Ⓒ Ⓓ   24. Ⓐ Ⓑ Ⓒ Ⓓ

4. Ⓐ Ⓑ Ⓒ Ⓓ Ⓔ   11. Ⓐ Ⓑ Ⓒ Ⓓ   18. Ⓐ Ⓑ Ⓒ Ⓓ   25. Ⓐ Ⓑ Ⓒ Ⓓ

5. Ⓐ Ⓑ Ⓒ Ⓓ Ⓔ   12. Ⓐ Ⓑ Ⓒ Ⓓ   19. Ⓐ Ⓑ Ⓒ Ⓓ

6. Ⓐ Ⓑ Ⓒ Ⓓ Ⓔ   13. Ⓐ Ⓑ Ⓒ Ⓓ   20. Ⓐ Ⓑ Ⓒ Ⓓ

7. Ⓐ Ⓑ Ⓒ Ⓓ Ⓔ   14. Ⓐ Ⓑ Ⓒ Ⓓ   21. Ⓐ Ⓑ Ⓒ Ⓓ

Practice Test 1: Diagnostic Test

CIVIL SERVICE EXAMS AND YOU

The civil service exam you will take is different from most standardized tests. Usually, tests have an exact number of questions per category, and every person taking the exam will see the same exact questions on test day. However, each civil service exam is tailored to the job you seek and the organization administering it. In fact, even if you and a friend take a civil service exam in the same state, you will likely face different tests!

That said, civil service exams all feature the same general categories, which we cover extensively in this book and its practice tests. The following diagnostic test is a great example of the elements found on most civil service exams—after taking it, you will be familiar with different question types that have commonly been found on past exams across the country. Use your results to discover your areas of strength and where you need more work. Good luck!

NOTE: While most civil service tests are not divided into timed sections, this diagnostic test has been divided with suggested timing to help you pace yourself as you answer the questions.

VERBAL ABILITY
50 Questions • 45 Minutes

Directions: In questions 1–4, the two capitalized words have a certain relationship to each other. Select the letter of the pair of words that are related in the same way as the two capitalized words.

---

1. SUGAR : CAKE ::

   A. NACHOS : TACOS
   B. ARTICLE : NEWSPAPER
   C. HOUSE : APARTMENT
   D. PIZZA : CRUST

2. LION : ROAR ::

   A. TIGER : HUNGRY
   B. DOLPHIN : SLIPPERY
   C. ZOO : ANIMALS
   D. FROG : CROAK

3. TOSS : FRISBEE ::

    A. NAIL : HAMMER

    B. LIGHT : MATCH

    C. BEVERAGE : SODA

    D. FAST : HORSE

4. ANGRY : FURIOUS ::

    A. SAD : ELATED

    B. PAIN : CRY

    C. HAPPY : JOYOUS

    D. MOAN : NOISE

Directions: In questions 5–9, choose the sentence that is most suitable for a formal letter or report with respect to grammar and usage.

NOTE

The directions are stated as if you are taking the exam in a paper-and-pencil format. If you will be taking the exam on computer, each section will have directions specific to answering questions on a computer.

5. **A.** Clerks perform a vareity of administrative and clerical duties necessary to operating state and local government.

    B. Clerical people do a lot of jobs in administrative and clerical fields to run state and local governments.

    C. Jobs at the clerk level is vital to running state and local governments effectively.

    D. Clerks perform a number of administrative and clerical duties that are necessary if state and local governments are to run smoothly.

6. **A.** Clerk-typists perform keyboarding and clerical duties, they may write short letters and memos, sort mail, filing forms, and check materials.

    B. Clerk-typists perform keyboarding and clerical duties that may include writing short letters and memos, sorting mail, filing forms, and checking materials.

    C. Clerk-typists perform keyboarding and clerical duties that may include writing short letters, memos, sorting mail, filing forms, and checking materials.

    D. Clerk-typists perform keyboarding, clerical duties, writing short letters, memos, sort mail file forms, and check materials.

7. **A.** An applicant typically must meet age and medical requirements, have a high school diploma or have served in the military, and have a personality suited to police work.

    B. Applicants typically must meet age and medical requirements and have a high school diploma or have served in the military they also need a personality suited to police work.

    C. Typically, applicants for police work has to meet age and medical requirements and a high school diploma or military service and a good personality to be a police officer.

    D. Applicants have to meet certain requirements: age and health, have a high school diploma or military service, and a personality suited to police work.

8. **A.** Him and me were looking into computer-related jobs in state government, but we needed more experience with certain types of software.

    B. Computer-related jobs appeal to him and I, but we need more experience.

    C. They were interested in computer-related jobs, but they believe they need more experience in certain software programs.

    D. State government jobs in computers pay good and interest he and I.

9. **A.** Social workers in the area of planning and policy propose ways to bring about needed change in institutions.

   B. Planing and policy initatives are important specilties in some social work positions.

   C. A social worker may have responsibil-ities in areas in which they have little training, such as developing policy.

   D. Social work is an interesting field people which are interested in helping others go into this field.

Directions: In questions 10 and 11, identify the sentence that contains an error in grammar, spelling, or punctuation.

---

10. **A.** The museum had a huge amount of art I needed several days to see it all.

    B. Everyone enjoyed the pizza party, but it was getting late and was time to go home.

    C. You can't drive a car without fuel—it needs gasoline to run properly.

    D. Have you ever taken an unexpected trip to a foreign country?

11. **A.** Don't bother showing up at the concert venue without purchasing a ticket first.

    B. The clockmaker, who is always a diligent professional, worked on his latest clock through the night.

    C. Some people feel as if there are never enough hours in the day to get every-thing done.

    D. When preparing fish, it's important to wash clean and cook it properly.

Directions: In questions 12–15, choose the correct spelling of the word. If no suggested spelling is correct, choose **D.** None of the above.

---

12. **A.** relible
    B. relyable
    C. reliable
    D. None of the above

13. **A.** restaurant
    B. restorent
    C. restorant
    D. None of the above

14. **A.** receivership
    B. recievership
    C. recievurship
    D. None of the above

15. **A.** simultaineously
    B. simultainiously
    C. similtaineously
    D. None of the above

Directions: For questions 16–18, choose the word that is spelled incorrectly.

16. **A.** acheeve
    B. judgment
    C. bask
    D. financial

17. **A.** relevant
    B. sucess
    C. cement
    D. vanquish

18. **A.** mysterious
    B. absent
    C. tomorrow
    D. imediate

Directions: Read the following passage. Then for questions 19–25, choose the best answer to each question about the passage.

A compelling question has arisen amidst the tidal wave of technological innovation and resulting consumer products that continue to flood the market and infiltrate our lives: Are we losing our ability to focus deeply on a single
Line task? The widespread proliferation and use of mobile devices has become so
5   ubiquitous and inexorably intertwined into modern American culture and behavior that there's simply no way to reverse the trend. The focus should lie on examining what the potential long-term effects of nearly constant use of these ever-present devices, and whether or not we can leverage the benefits of mobile computing without falling victim to its possible drawbacks.
10   Many studies have been investigating whether the constant shifting of focus that occurs while flipping through several TV channels, toggling back and forth through multiple apps, and juggling our perception back and forth between the outside world and our phones is, in effect, "reprogramming" our brains. Some argue that our ability to focus deeply on a single task is eroding,
15   and might continue to diminish.
Others argue that our brains are just getting accustomed to processing information in a new way. With multiple streams of constant data flowing across our consciousness at any given time, our brains are adjusting to multitasking more efficiently, and processing more information (albeit with less
20   depth of focus on any one item). Regardless of one's opinion regarding the relative merits or drawbacks of this new way of focusing, it's hard to argue against the notion that we all need to get used to being able to handle processing information this way—or risk getting left behind.

19. Which of the following **best** captures the main idea of the passage?

   A. As technology becomes more mobile and sophisticated, it also becomes more expensive.

   B. Our brains are not as complex and moral as the electronic devices we have surrounded ourselves with.

   C. The evolution of technology is changing how our brains focus on tasks, and whether it is a good or bad thing is up for debate.

   D. We should stop using smartphones immediately, because they are dangerous to our long-term health.

20. According to the author, the main potential negative effect of this new way of processing information is

   A. more money spent on purchasing the latest technology.

   B. an inability to focus deeply on a single task.

   C. greater difficulty showing up for our jobs each day.

   D. more time spent on performing each task.

21. According to the author, a potential benefit of this new way of processing information is

   A. a better understanding of the world.

   B. deeper connections with our friends.

   C. more time to spend with those we care about.

   D. an improved ability to multitask.

22. Based on how it's used in line 5, the word *ubiquitous* most nearly means:

   A. scarce

   B. commonplace

   C. expensive

   D. small

23. Which of the following is NOT an item mentioned as possibly contributing to how our ability to focus is changing?

   A. Speaking too quickly to our friends and family

   B. Flipping through several TV channels

   C. Toggling back and forth through multiple apps

   D. Going back and forth between the outside world and our smartphones

24. The author most likely feels that as a result of changing technology, this change in how our brains process information is

   A. reversible.

   B. inevitable.

   C. regrettable.

   D. inviting.

25. Which of the following **best** captures the author's opinion on the topic of how our brains' focus is changing within the passage?

   A. supportive

   B. nervous

   C. neutral

   D. furious

Directions: For questions 26–35, choose the word closest in meaning to the word given.

26. *Circumvent* most nearly means:

    A. accept

    B. cross

    C. ingest

    D. bypass

27. *Distinguish* most nearly means:

    A. differentiate

    B. delicious

    C. mingle

    D. mistake

28. *Confound* most nearly means:

    A. assure

    B. confuse

    C. circle

    D. lift

29. *Obtain* most nearly means:

    A. acquire

    B. leave

    C. avoid

    D. count

30. *Penalize* most nearly means:

    A. reward

    B. shrink

    C. punish

    D. release

31. *Substantial* most nearly means:

    A. small

    B. thick

    C. remote

    D. significant

32. *Endorse* most nearly means:

    A. frustrate

    B. carry

    C. support

    D. thwart

33. *Mentor* most nearly means:

    A. advisor

    B. leader

    C. authority

    D. supervisor

34. *Tribute* most nearly means:

    A. evidence

    B. applause

    C. honor

    D. criticism

35. *Renown* most nearly means:

    A. difference

    B. honorable

    C. fortunate

    D. fame

Directions: For questions 36–42, select the word or phrase that will best complete the meaning of the sentence as a whole and mark its corresponding letter on the answer sheet.

---

36. The debate team was unable to effectively _____ its side of the argument and couldn't convince the audience to support its point of view.

    A. forget
    B. articulate
    C. spend
    D. lament

37. The English teacher found Susan's poor excuse for not completing the assignment _____ and gave her a failing grade for the assignment.

    A. preposterous
    B. overt
    C. believable
    D. commonplace

38. The climb up the tall mountain was a(n) _____ challenge, and the group of climbers decided to carefully prepare to avoid catastrophe.

    A. humorous
    B. informative
    C. flavorful
    D. formidable

39. The cabin was a(n) _____ structure in the middle of a deep-wooded area, and no signs of life could be seen for miles around.

    A. encouraging
    B. lively
    C. remote
    D. comforting

40. The wristwatch contained numerous _____ parts and required a magnifying lens and careful hand to repair properly.

    A. useless
    B. colorful
    C. expensive
    D. intricate

41. We never saw our _____ neighbor much, and we weren't sure if she ever left her house.

    A. reclusive
    B. sociable
    C. boisterous
    D. helpful

42. The soccer player was known for his _____ behavior; he was always getting thrown out of games or fined for behaving inappropriately.

    A. supportive
    B. belligerent
    C. docile
    D. popular

Directions: Portions of the following passage are underlined and numbered. For questions 43–50, if you feel that an underlined portion is correct and stated as well as possible, mark choice **A**, **NO CHANGE**. If you feel that there is an error in the underlined portion or that one of the alternatives would be more effective, choose the correct answer.

Many economists and news pundits have been <u>focus</u> on the issue of automation
43

in various industries, and whether or not its inarguable proliferation will ulti-

mately prove to be good for both the economy <u>or</u> workforce. Some argue that
44

it <u>represents; a</u> positive and inevitable <u>evolution—as</u> industrialized societies
45   46

become more automated, many of the repetitive mechanized <u>labor task</u> that
47

traditionally required human involvement will be handled by machines and arti-

ficial intelligence <u>faster better and more efficiently</u> than ever before. <u>She further</u>
48   49

claim that this will ultimately benefit companies and industries (and their

employees), and will free people up to seek more fulfilling and challenging, and

less rote professional pursuits. Others claim that countless workers whose eco-

nomic livelihoods were inexorably <u>based, on</u> tasks that are being automated will
50

ultimately find themselves displaced and facing economic hardship, adversely

impacting large sectors of the economy as a result.

43. A. NO CHANGE
   B. focused
   C. focusing
   D. focuses

44. A. NO CHANGE
   B. if
   C. and
   D. then

45. A. NO CHANGE
   B. represents, a
   C. represents. A
   D. represents a

46. A. NO CHANGE
   B. evolution as
   C. evolution. As
   D. , evolution as

47. A. NO CHANGE
   B. labors task
   C. labor tasks
   D. labor's tasks

48. A. NO CHANGE
   B. faster better, and more efficiently
   C. faster; better and; more efficiently
   D. faster, better, and more efficiently

49. A. NO CHANGE
   B. They
   C. He
   D. We

50. A. NO CHANGE
   B. based. On
   C. based; on
   D. based on

END OF VERBAL ABILITY SECTION

---

diagnostic test

ARITHMETIC ABILITY
25 Questions • 30 Minutes

> **Directions:** For questions 1–10, perform the computation as indicated and choose the correct answer.

1. Compute: $6\frac{7}{12} - 2\frac{5}{6}$

    SHOW YOUR WORK HERE

    A. $3\frac{3}{4}$

    B. $4\frac{1}{6}$

    C. $4\frac{1}{3}$

    D. $4\frac{3}{4}$

2. Sam spends $\frac{5}{8}$ of his free time on the weekend doing household chores and errands. If he has 12 hours of free time, how many hours does he spend on chores and errands?

    A. 4.5 hours

    B. 6 hours

    C. 7.5 hours

    D. 9 hours

3. The total weight of four identical packages is $18\frac{2}{3}$ pounds. What is the weight of one of the packages?

    A. 3 pounds

    B. $4\frac{1}{3}$ pounds

    C. $4\frac{1}{2}$ pounds

    D. $4\frac{2}{3}$ pounds

4. Compute: $4.0804 \div 0.04$

    A. 0.010201

    B. 1.0201

    C. 10.201

    D. 102.01

5. A customer buys four books of stamps that cost $4.90 each, three mailing boxes that cost $4.25 each, and a package of labels that cost $3.45. What is the total bill before sales tax?

   A. $12.60
   B. $24.70
   C. $25.80
   D. $35.80

6. A scale is known to have an error of ± 0.028 ounces in what it registers as the weight of packages. If the weight of a small package registers 9.09 ounces, which of the following CANNOT be its true weight?

   A. 9.058 ounces
   B. 9.064 ounces
   C. 9.100 ounces
   D. 9.109 ounces

7. What is 120% of $2\frac{3}{4}$?

   A. $3\frac{19}{20}$
   B. $3\frac{1}{3}$
   C. $3\frac{3}{10}$
   D. $3\frac{3}{20}$

8. What percentage of 0.02 is 0.001?

   A. 0.05%
   B. 5%
   C. 20%
   D. 200%

9. A group of friends goes to dinner. The bill comes to $115.38. They give the waiter $140 and tell him to keep the change. What percentage of the bill did they leave as a tip?

   A. 18.93%
   B. 20.50%
   C. 21.34%
   D. 24.62%

SHOW YOUR WORK HERE

10. The ratio of kittens to puppies up for adoption at an animal shelter is 2 to 3. If there are 60 animals total up for adoption, how many are puppies?

    A. 20

    B. 24

    C. 30

    D. 36

SHOW YOUR WORK HERE

Directions: For questions 11 and 12, refer to the following graph.

The following line graph shows the population of Blue Hill Township between 1985 and 2015.

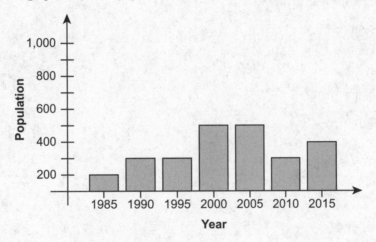

11. What is the approximate percentage increase in population from 1995 to 2000?

    A. 5%

    B. 40%

    C. 67%

    D. 200%

SHOW YOUR WORK HERE

12. If the population were to increase at the same rate as it did from 1985 to 1990, what would Blue Hill Township's population be in 2020?

    A. 450

    B. 500

    C. 600

    D. 800

Directions: For questions 13 and 14, refer to the following graph.

Wendy's monthly budget is illustrated in the following circle graph:

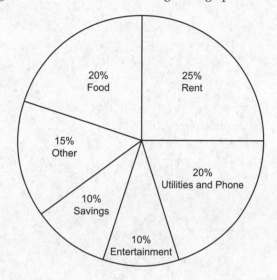

13. If Wendy's monthly income is $2,750, how much of it is spent on rent and food combined?

    SHOW YOUR WORK HERE

    A. $550.00
    B. $687.50
    C. $1,237.50
    D. $1,512.50

14. If Wendy wants to save at least $350 per month, by approximately what percentage should she increase the percentage devoted to the Savings category?

    A. 2.8%
    B. 10%
    C. 12.8%
    D. 75%

15. Assume that your duties include purchasing office equipment. You must buy nine new copiers. The subtotal comes to $1,799.91. How much is the total price when a 6% sales tax is added?

   A. $1,907.90

   B. $1,990.95

   C. $2,107.99

   D. $2,229.90

16. If a keypunch operator can complete 318 cards in one hour, how many keypunch operators are needed to complete 4,770 cards?

   A. 11

   B. 15

   C. 21

   D. 26

17. Assume your job duties include counting and recording school fees for a middle school. At the beginning of the school year, students presented you with cash and 60 checks. The checks were divided as follows: 18 checks for $75 each, 31 checks for $140, 10 checks for $130, and one check for $200 as a donation toward fees for any child who couldn't afford to pay. In addition, you received two $50 bills, two $20 bills, seven $10 bills, and three $5 bills. How much did you collect in school fees?

   A. $6,395

   B. $7,415

   C. $7,650

   D. $8,555

SHOW YOUR WORK HERE

18. During a one-week period, the Milford Police Force wrote the following number of tickets involving vehicles:

SHOW YOUR WORK HERE

Type of Ticket			
	Parking	Moving	Expired Registration
M	5	0	0
T	14	0	0
W	16	3	0
Th	31	1	1
F	42	4	0

What percentage of the total number of tickets written were moving violations?

A. 6.8%

B. 10%

C. 12.4%

D. 14.6%

19. Add: 39 + 14

A. 42

B. 49

C. 51

D. 53

E. None of the above

20. Subtract: 107 – 88

A. 9

B. 11

C. 19

D. 29

E. None of the above

21. Multiply: 24 × 32

A. 678

B. 766

C. 768

D. 867

E. None of the above

22. Divide: 546 ÷ 14   **SHOW YOUR WORK HERE**

   A. 34
   B. 39
   C. 42
   D. 46
   E. None of the above

23. Multiply: 12.46 × 0.52

   A. 5.0032
   B. 5.092
   C. 6.48
   D. 6.68
   E. None of the above

24. Add: $\dfrac{7}{14} + \dfrac{5}{42}$

   A. $\dfrac{7+5}{56}$

   B. $\dfrac{3}{10}$

   C. 78

   D. $\dfrac{35}{56}$

   E. None of the above

25. Divide: $\dfrac{4}{7} \div \dfrac{11}{7}$

   A. $\dfrac{4}{11}$

   B. 44

   C. $\dfrac{7}{4}$

   D. $\dfrac{44}{49}$

   E. None of the above

   END OF ARITHMETIC ABILTY SECTION

CLERICAL ABILITY
25 Questions • 30 Minutes

Directions: In questions 1–3, there are three names, addresses, or codes that are very much alike. Compare the three and on your answer sheet, choose:

A if ALL THREE names, addresses, or codes are exactly ALIKE.
B if only the FIRST and SECOND names, addresses, or codes are exactly ALIKE.
C if only the FIRST and THIRD names, addresses, or codes are exactly ALIKE.
D if only the SECOND and THIRD names, addresses, or codes are exactly ALIKE.
E if ALL THREE names, addresses, or codes are DIFFERENT.

---

1. Bridget Herron   Brigette Herron   Brigetta Heron

2. 6937621   6937261   6937261

3. 1401 Azalea Court   4011 Azalea Court   1401 Azalea Court

Directions: In questions 4–7, you are given a name followed by four other names in alphabetical order. Find the correct space for the given name so that the alphabetical order remains correct.

---

4. Tanaka, Hari

  A. -
     Tanaka, Harold
  B. -
     Tanaka, Howard
  C. -
     Tanna, George
  D. -
     Tanner, Michael
  E. -

5. Wong, Vivienne

  A. -
     Wang, V. W.
  B. -
     Wang, Vivian
  C. -
     Wonder, R.V. William
  D. -
     Wong, Vernon
  E. -

6. d'Orsey, Eugene

  A. -
     D'Anton, Raymond
  B. -
     D'Orcy, F. W.
  C. -
     D'Orsay, Leonard
  D. -
     D'Orsi, Edw.
  E. -

7. Blaskett, Thomas A.

  A. -
     Blankenship, Victor
  B. -
     Blankenstein, T.Victor
  C. -
     Blochner, H.A.
  D. -
     Block, Marian
  E. -

Directions: Questions 8–11 consist of a CAPITALIZED word that is to be filed correctly among the alphabetized words listed. Choose the word that should come after the capitalized word.

8. DAISIES

   A. daggers

   B. dairies

   C. dams

   D. dandelions

9. PADS

   A. pacifists

   B. packages

   C. pacts

   D. paddles

10. THEATERS

   A. thefts

   B. themes

   C. theorems

   D. therapies

11. AIRPORTS

   A. aircrafts

   B. aisles

   C. alarms

   D. albums

Directions: For questions 12–14, consider each group of names as a unit. Determine where the name printed in boldface would appear if the names in the group were correctly alphabetized. If the name in boldface should appear first, mark **A** on your answer sheet; if second, mark **B**; if third, mark **C**; and if fourth, mark **D**.

12.   David Jacobs

       David Jacobson

       David L. Jacobs

       Dave Z. Jacobson

13.   **Julie Stanton and Associates**

       Jamirez Stationary Supplies

       Junebug Home Décor, Inc.

       Jules and Company

14.   Allan Rich

       Alan Riche

       Allen K. Richards

       Al Richard

Directions: Questions 15–17 each consist of four names. For each question, select the one of the four names that should be third if the four names were arranged in alphabetical order in accordance with the rules for alphabetical filing.

15. **A.** Sixth Street Catering
    B. Mrs. Annie Quon
    C. Ms. Danielle Donato
    D. 63rd Gumdrop Company

16. **A.** 77 Lucas Drive Associated
    B. Mr. Lorenzo Semple, Jr.
    C. Salma A. Luceno
    D. Seven Sisters Pizza

17. **A.** Dr. Billie O'Brien
    B. 1 Blue Jay Way Industries
    C. Mr. Billy Brown
    D. One Way Trucking Co.

Directions: Questions 18 and 19 each give the name and identification number of an employee. You are to choose the one answer that has exactly the same identification number and name as those given in the question.

18. 876756   Meagen Entwistle

    A. 876756   Meagen Entwistle
    B. 876756   Megen Entwistle
    C. 876756   Meagan Entwistle
    D. 876756   Meagen Entwisle

19. 667553   Karen Astley-Hynde

    A. 667553   Karen Astly-Hynde
    B. 667533   Karen Astley-Hynde
    C. 667553   Karen Astley-Hynd
    D. 667553   Karen Astley-Hynde

Directions: Questions 20 and 21 each consist of three sets of names and name codes. In each question, the two names and name codes on the same line are supposed to be exactly the same. Look carefully at each set of names and codes, and choose your answer as follows:

Choose **A** if there are mistakes in all THREE sets.
Choose **B** if there are mistakes in TWO of the sets.
Choose **C** if there are mistakes in only ONE set.
Choose **D** if there are NO MISTAKES in any of the sets.

20. Louisville Shipping   S 45321   Louisville Shipping   45321 S
    Applause Theatre Co.   J 64553   Applause Theater Co.   J 64553
    W-XTC Television   A 42313   W XTC Television   A 42313

21. Ms. Claire D. Clouzot   D-53647   Ms. Claire D. Clouzot   D-53647
    Dr. Nan Berg   98767   Dr. Nan Berg   F 98767
    Mrs. Alice Brakhage   I 7658   Mrs. Alice Brakhage   1 7658

Directions: For questions 22 and 23, choose the best solution to the situation presented.

22. You are asked to lead a team on a project. One of the other people named to the team is someone you don't like, and the feeling is mutual. The best action for you to take is to

   A. tell your supervisor that you and the other employee don't get along and ask for the person to be removed from the team.

   B. ignore the person and any contributions the person makes at meetings.

   C. meet with the person before the first meeting and discuss how you two can work together on the project.

   D. meet with the person before the first meeting and tell him/her to leave the team voluntarily or you will tell your supervisor why you don't want him/her on the team.

23. Assume that your job is to check employee expense accounts before submitting them to the department head for approval. You have noticed over time that one employee appears to be overcharging for meals while on business trips. Some receipts appear to be altered. The best action for you to take would be to

   A. report the employee to your department head.

   B. ask the employee about the apparent overages and give her a chance to change them.

   C. report the employee to the auditing department.

   D. confront the employee yourself about the apparent overages.

Directions: Study the image shown for five minutes. Then answer questions 24 and 25 without referring back to the image.

https://www.pexels.com/photo/people-brasil-guys-avpaulista-109919/

24. What was the temperature at the time of this picture?

    A. 16°C

    B. 16°F

    C. 45°C

    D. 45°F

25. What is the man who is wearing glasses and crossing the street holding in his hand?

    A. A backpack

    B. A dog leash

    C. A phone

    D. A water bottle

END OF CLERICAL ABILITY SECTION

---

diagnostic test

ANSWER KEYS AND EXPLANATIONS

Verbal Ability

1. B	11. D	21. D	31. D	41. A
2. D	12. C	22. B	32. C	42. B
3. B	13. A	23. A	33. A	43. B
4. C	14. A	24. B	34. C	44. C
5. D	15. D	25. C	35. D	45. D
6. B	16. A	26. D	36. B	46. A
7. A	17. B	27. A	37. A	47. C
8. C	18. D	28. B	38. D	48. D
9. A	19. C	29. A	39. C	49. B
10. A	20. B	30. C	40. D	50. D

1. **The correct answer is B.** *Sugar* is a component of a *cake*, and an *article* is a component of a *newspaper*.

2. **The correct answer is D.** A sound a *lion* makes is a *roar*, and the sound a *frog* makes is a *croak*.

3. **The correct answer is B.** A *toss* is an action associated with a *frisbee*, and a *light* is an action associated with a *match*.

4. **The correct answer is C.** Being *angry* is a less extreme but related emotion to being *furious*, and being *happy* is a less extreme but related emotion to being *joyous*.

5. **The correct answer is D.** Choice A is incorrect because *variety* is misspelled. Choice B uses the colloquial expression "a lot of," which should not be used in formal communication, that is, job situations. Choice C is incorrect because *jobs* is plural, so its predicate should be plural. Don't be confused by any phrase that comes between the subject and verb.

6. **The correct answer is B.** Choice A is incorrect because it is a run-on sentence. Two stand-alone thoughts (independent clauses) are joined by a comma. You need either a period at the end of the first

thought, a conjunction such as *and* or *that*, or a semicolon. Also, the series of duties is not parallel; *filing* should be *file*. Choice C is incorrect because *memos* is part of the thought "writing short letters and memos." Choice D is incorrect due to numerous errors, specifically the *and* between *keyboarding* and *clerical duties* is missing; the comma between *sort mail* and *file forms* is missing; and the series of duties is not parallel.

7. **The correct answer is A.** Choice B is incorrect because it's a run-on sentence. A punctuation mark or conjunction is needed between *military* and *they*. In choice C, a phrase between the subject and verb results in the use of the correct form of the verb; *has* should be *have*. Also, a "good personality" is not the same as a "personality suited to police work." Choice D has several problems. The colon could work here if the elements were parallel. You need either to add verbs to "age and health" and "a personality suited to police work," or remove *have* from "have a high diploma or military service."

8. **The correct answer is C.** Choice A is incorrect because *him* and *me* are the objective forms of the personal pronouns, and the

subject forms are needed in the sentence; the pronouns are the subject of the sentence. Choice B is incorrect because although *him* is correct, *I* is not. The pronoun *me* is needed as the object of the preposition *to*. Choice D is incorrect because the adjective *good* should be the adverb *well*, because it modifies the verb *pay*. Also, *he* and *I* should be the objective forms *him* and *me*. They are the object of the verb *interest*.

9. **The correct answer is A.** *Planning, initiatives,* and *specialties* are misspelled, so eliminate choice B. Choice C is incorrect because *they* should be *he* (or *he or she*) to agree with its antecedent "a social worker." Choice D is incorrect because it is a run-on sentence. There should be a punctuation mark or conjunction between *field* and *people*. Also, *which* should be *who*.

10. **The correct answer is A.** This is a run-on sentence. The two independent clauses, *The museum had a huge amount of art* and *I needed several days to see it all* should be separated into two sentences or joined with a comma and an article. Correct: *The museum had a huge amount of art, and I needed several days to see it all.*

11. **The correct answer is D.** The steps to preparing fish are a list of items that each should be separated by commas. Correct: *When preparing fish, it's important to wash, clean, and cook it properly.*

12. **The correct answer is C.** The correct spelling is *reliable*.

13. **The correct answer is A.** The correct spelling is *restaurant*.

14. **The correct answer is A.** The correct spelling is *receivership*.

15. **The correct answer is D.** The correct spelling is *simultaneously*.

16. **The correct answer is A.** The correct spelling is *achieve*.

17. **The correct answer is B.** The correct spelling is *success*.

18. **The correct answer is D.** The correct spelling is *immediate*.

19. **The correct answer is C.** The passage focuses how on the evolution of technology is changing how our brains focus on tasks and looks at both sides of the debate about whether this is a good or bad thing.

20. **The correct answer is B.** Based on the information provided in the passage, the main potential negative effect of this new way of processing information is an inability to focus deeply on a single task. The other answer choices aren't explicitly mentioned in the passage as potential negative effects.

21. **The correct answer is D.** According to the passage, the author feels that a potential benefit of this new way of processing information is an improved ability to multitask. The other answer choices aren't explicitly mentioned in the passage as potential benefits.

22. **The correct answer is B.** The sentence that the word *ubiquitous* appears in is discussing how intertwined smartphones have become in our culture—a reference to how "commonplace" they currently are.

23. **The correct answer is A.** There's no mention in the passage of speaking too quickly to our friends and family as contributing to how our ability to focus is changing. The other choices are referenced in the passage.

24. The correct answer is B. The author of the passage states that "regardless of one's opinion regarding the relative merits or drawbacks of this new way of focusing, it's hard to argue against the notion that we all need to get used to being able to handle processing information this way," which suggests that she or he feels as if this change is *inevitable*.

25. The correct answer is C. The author presents both sides of the issue, and although she or he feels as if the change is inevitable, doesn't really weigh in on whether or not she or he feels as if it's a good or bad thing. Therefore, we can say that the author adopts a neutral position on the topic.

26. The correct answer is D. *Circumvent* means "to bypass."

27. The correct answer is A. *Distinguish* means "to differentiate."

28. The correct answer is B. *Confound* means "to confuse."

29. The correct answer is A. *Obtain* means "to acquire."

30. The correct answer is C. *Penalize* means "to punish."

31. The correct answer is D. *Substantial* means "significant."

32. The correct answer is C. *Endorse* means "to support."

33. The correct answer is A. A mentor helps and advises someone with less experience who is typically younger. A supervisor may be a mentor, but not necessarily.

34. The correct answer is C. A tribute is an honor, which may include applause, but that's not the meaning of tribute.

35. The correct answer is D. *Renown* means "fame."

36. The correct answer is B. In order for a debate team to win, they must communicate, or *articulate*, their point of view effectively.

37. The correct answer is A. A poor excuse that results in a failing grade is clearly not effective or believable; hence, it is *preposterous*.

38. The correct answer is D. A challenge that could result in catastrophe is a *formidable* one.

39. The correct answer is C. A cabin that has no other signs of life for miles around is distant and *remote*.

40. The correct answer is D. Parts of a small wristwatch that are hard to see with the naked eye and require a careful hand are *intricate*.

41. The correct answer is A. Someone who is seldom seen and may never leave the house can potentially be described as *reclusive*.

42. The correct answer is B. *Belligerent* behavior is a type of aggressive behavior that will get you thrown out of games or fined.

43. The correct answer is B. The correct tense of the verb *to focus*, given the context of the sentence, is *focused*.

44. The correct answer is C. Because the sentence references both the economy as well as the workforce, they should be joined by the article *and*.

45. The correct answer is D. As written, the semicolon is grammatically incorrect and creates an awkward pause in the sentence. No internal sentence punctuation is needed here.

46. **The correct answer is A.** This sentence is correct as written. An em dash helps create a long pause within a sentence.

47. **The correct answer is C.** The word *labor* should be in singular form and the multiple *tasks* being referred to should be in plural form.

48. **The correct answer is D.** Items in a list should be separated by a comma. In this case, commas should be placed after faster and better.

49. **The correct answer is B.** This sentence is still referencing the "many economists and news pundits" that were mentioned in the original sentence. Therefore, the plural pronoun *they* should be used.

50. **The correct answer is D.** As written, the comma is grammatically unnecessary and creates an awkward pause in the sentence. No internal sentence punctuation is needed here.

answers diagnostic test

Arithmetic Ability

1. A	6. A	11. C	16. B	21. C
2. C	7. C	12. C	17. B	22. B
3. D	8. B	13. C	18. A	23. C
4. D	9. C	14. A	19. D	24. E
5. D	10. D	15. A	20. C	25. A

1. **The correct answer is A.** Find a common denominator and subtract as follows:

$$6\frac{7}{12} - 2\frac{5}{6} = 6\frac{7}{12} - 2\frac{10}{12} =$$

$$5\frac{19}{12} - 2\frac{10}{12} = 3\frac{9}{12} = 3\frac{3}{4}$$

Choice B is incorrect because you did not convert $\frac{5}{6}$ correctly to an equivalent fraction whose denominator is 12. Choice C is incorrect because you cannot subtract fractions by subtracting the numerators and denominators. Choice D is incorrect because you did not borrow correctly.

2. **The correct answer is C.** Multiply $\frac{5}{8}$ times 12 to get $\frac{15}{2}$, which equals 7.5 hours. Choice A is incorrect because this is the time spent on tasks other than chores and errands. Choice B is incorrect because this is half of the time, not $\frac{5}{8}$. Choice D is incorrect because this is 75% of the time.

3. **The correct answer is D.** Divide $18\frac{2}{3}$ by 4 to get $\frac{56}{3} \div 4 = \frac{56}{3} \cdot \frac{1}{4} = \frac{14}{3} = 4\frac{2}{3}$ pounds.

Choice A is incorrect because $18\frac{2}{3}$ is a mixed number, not a product of 18 and $\frac{2}{3}$. Choice B is incorrect because you divided incorrectly. Choice C is incorrect because you ignored the fractional part of the mixed number.

4. **The correct answer is D.** $4.0804 \div 0.04 = 408.04 \div 4 = 102.01$. The other choices are the result of not moving the decimal point correctly.

5. **The correct answer is D.** The total cost is $4(\$4.90) + 3(\$4.25) + \$3.45 = \$35.80$. Choice A is incorrect because you did not multiply the cost of each item by the number of that item being purchased. Choices B and C are incorrect because when adding, you did not carry correctly.

6. **The correct answer is A.** The range is $9.09 - 0.028 = 9.062$ to $9.09 + 0.028 = 9.118$. Any value between these two numbers is a possible weight for the package. The only one not in this range is 9.058 ounces.

7. **The correct answer is C.** $2\frac{3}{4} = 2.75$ and $120\% = 1.2$. So 120% of $2\frac{3}{4}$ is $(2.75)(1.2) = 3.3$, which is equivalent to $3\frac{3}{10}$. Choice A is incorrect because you should multiply 1.2 and 2.75, not add them. Choice B is incorrect because you converted 3.3 to a fraction incorrectly. Choice D is incorrect because you only computed 120% of 2 and added it to the fractional part.

8. **The correct answer is B.** Divide 0.001 by 0.02 to get 0.05, which is 5%. Choice A is incorrect because you need to move the decimal point two places to the right when converting a decimal to a percent. Choice C is incorrect because you divided in the wrong order. Choice D is incorrect because you divided in the wrong order and the decimal point is in the wrong location.

9. **The correct answer is C.** The tip percentage is $\frac{140 - 115.83}{115.83} = 0.2134 \approx 21.34\%$.

Choice A is incorrect because you must divide the change by the amount of the bill, not the amount you tendered. Choice B is incorrect because of an arithmetic error. Choice D is incorrect because this is the change; you must now divide this by the bill amount to get the percentage.

10. **The correct answer is D.** Use the ratio to see that the number of puppies is $\frac{3}{5}$ of 60, which is $\frac{3}{5} \cdot 60 = 36$. Choice A is incorrect because you used the ratio incorrectly. Choice B is incorrect because this is the number of kittens. Choice C is incorrect because you used the ratio incorrectly.

11. **The correct answer is C.** The percentage increase is

$$\frac{500 - 300}{300} \times 100\% \approx 67\%.$$

Choice A is incorrect because 5 is the difference in the years during which the population is computed, not the actual change in population. Choice B is incorrect because you divided the difference in populations by 500 instead of 300. Choice D is incorrect because 200 is the difference in the populations, not the percentage increase.

12. **The correct answer is C.** The percentage increase from 1985 to 1990 is

$$\frac{300 - 200}{200} \times 100\% = 50\%.$$

So applying a 50% increase to 400 yields a population of 600 in 2020. Choice A is incorrect because 50% does not mean 50. Choice B is incorrect because you added the actual increase in population to the population in 2015 rather than applying the percent increase to it. Choice D is incorrect because this is a 100% increase.

13. **The correct answer is C.** 45% of $2,750 = $2,750(0.45) = $1,237.50. Choice A is incorrect because this is just the amount spent on food. Choice B is incorrect because this is just the amount spent on rent. Choice D is incorrect because this is the amount spent on everything except food and rent.

14. **The correct answer is A.** The percentage of the budget that $350 represents is $\frac{350}{2,750} \times 100\% \approx 12.73\%$. So the current allocation to savings, 10%, would need to be increased by approximately 2.8%. Choice B is incorrect because this is the current percentage of the budget devoted to savings. Choice C is incorrect because this is the total percentage of the budget that would need to be allocated to savings, not the additional percentage that must be added to the current amount. Choice D is incorrect because 75 is the number of dollars more that would need to be added to savings to bring the amount up to $350.

15. **The correct answer is A.** You don't need to know how many copiers were bought to figure out the sales tax because you already know the subtotal before the sales tax is calculated and the amount of the sales tax:

$1,799.91 × 1.06 = $1,907.9046

Rounded to the nearest tenth = $1,907.90

This is the short way to figure out the answer. You could also multiply the total price of the 9 copiers ($1,799.91) by the percentage of sales tax (0.06), and add that to the total price, but it's one step more.

16. **The correct answer is B.** You know the total and the amount completed in one hour by one person. To find how many more workers are needed: 4,770 ÷ 318 = 15.

17. **The correct answer is B.** To find the total, first multiply the number of checks by the amount on each check, determine the amount of cash, and then add it all together: $(18 \times 75) + (31 \times 140) + (10 \times 130) + 200 + (2 \times 50) + (2 \times 20) + (7 \times 10) + (3 \times 5) = 1{,}350 + 4{,}340 + 1{,}300 + 200 + 100 + 40 + 70 + 15 = \$7{,}415$.

18. **The correct answer is A.** Add the total number of tickets written and divide by the number of moving violation tickets: $5 + 14 + 16 + 31 + 42 + 3 + 1 + 4 + 1 = 117$; $8 \div 117 \times 100 = 6.8\%$

19. **The correct answer is D.** 53

20. **The correct answer is C.** 19

21. **The correct answer is C.** 768

22. **The correct answer is B.** 39

23. **The correct answer is C.** 6.48

24. **The correct answer is E.** None of the above.

25. **The correct answer is A.** $\frac{4}{11}$

Clerical Ability

1. E	**6.** D	**11.** B	**16.** D	**21.** C
2. D	**7.** C	**12.** C	**17.** B	**22.** C
3. C	**8.** C	**13.** D	**18.** A	**23.** A
4. A	**9.** D	**14.** D	**19.** D	**24.** A
5. E	**10.** A	**15.** D	**20.** A	**25.** D

1. **The correct answer is E.** All three names are different.

2. **The correct answer is D.** The second and third numbers are alike.

3. **The correct answer is C.** The first and third numbers are alike.

4. **The correct answer is A.** *Tanaka, Hari;* Tanaka, Harold; Tanaka, Howard; Tanna; George; Tanner, Michael.

5. **The correct answer is E.** Wang, V. W.; Wang, Vivian; Wonder, R. V. William; Wong, Vernon; *Wong, Vivian.*

6. **The correct answer is D.** D'Anton, Raymond; D'Orcy, F. W.; D'Orsay, Leonard; *d'Orsey, Eugene;* D'Orsi, Edw.

7. **The correct answer is C.** Blankenship, Victor; Blankenstein, T. Victor; *Blaskett, Thomas A.;* Blochner, H.A.; Block, Marian.

8. **The correct answer is C.** In alphabetical order, *daisies* comes after *dairies* and before *dams*.

9. **The correct answer is D.** In alphabetical order, *pads* comes after *pacts* and before *paddles*.

10. **The correct answer is A.** In alphabetical order, *theaters* comes before *thefts*.

11. **The correct answer is B.** In alphabetical order, *airports* comes after *aircrafts* and before *aisles*.

12. **The correct answer is C.** Names are alphabetized with importance placed on the last name first, the first name or initial second, and the middle name or initial last. Since *Jacobson* would be alphabetized after *Jacobs* but *Dave* would be alphabetized before *David*, correct alphabetical order is David Jacobs, David L. Jacobs, **Dave Z. Jacobson**, David Jacobson.

13. **The correct answer is D.** The names of organizations, institutions, and buildings are filed according to the order in which each word in the name appears, except where these names include the full names of individuals. In such cases, the last name of the person is filed first. Therefore, the correct order is: Jamirez Stationary Supplies, Jules and Company, Junebug Home Décor, Inc., **Julie Stanton and Associates**.

14. **The correct answer is D.** Names are alphabetized with importance placed on the last name first, the first name or initial second, and the middle name or initial last. Since *Alan Riche* would be alphabetized after *Allen K. Richards*, correct alphabetical order is: Allan Rich, Al Richard, Allen K. Richards, **Alan Riche**.

15. **The correct answer is D.** Business names that begin with numerals should be alphabetized as if the numerals are spelled out. Titles such as *Mrs.* and *Ms.* are disregarded when alphabetizing names. Therefore, correct alphabetical order is: Ms. Danielle Donato; Sixth Street Catering; 63rd Gumdrop Company; Mrs. Annie Quon. Choice D is the correct answer because 63rd Gumdrop Company is third in the order.

16. **The correct answer is D.** Business names that begin with numerals should be alphabetized as if the numerals are spelled out. Names are alphabetized with importance placed on the last name first, the first name or initial second, and the middle name or initial last. Therefore, correct alphabetical order is: Salma A. Luceno; Lorenzo Semple, Jr.; Seven Sisters Pizza; 77 Lucas Drive Associated. Choice D is the correct answer because Seven Sisters Pizza is third in the order.

17. **The correct answer is B.** Business names that begin with numerals should be alphabetized as if the numerals are spelled out. Titles such as *Dr.* and *Mr.* are disregarded when alphabetizing names. Therefore, correct alphabetical order is: Mr. Billy Brown; Dr. Billie O'Brien; 1 Blue Jay Way Industries; One Way Trucking Co. Choice B is the correct answer because 1 Blue Jay Way Industries is third in the order.

18. **The correct answer is A.** The identification numbers are the same in all answer choices, but there are slight spelling mistakes in all names except the one in choice A. In choices B and C, the first name is misspelled. In choice D, the last name is misspelled.

19. **The correct answer is D.** Only choice D is correctly written. In choice A, the name *Astley* is missing an *e*. In choice B, the identification number is written incorrectly. In choice C, the *e* is missing from *Hynde*.

20. **The correct answer is A.** There are mistakes in all sets. In the first set, the *S* appears at the beginning of the code in the first column but at the end in the second column. In the second set, *Theater* is spelled differently in each column. In the third set, a hyphen is missing from the company name in the second column.

21. **The correct answer is C.** There is a mistake in the third set only. In the first column, the code begins with the letter *I*. In the second column, the code begins with the number *1*.

22. **The correct answer is C.** The best idea is to meet with the person before the first meeting and discuss how you can work together on the project. Threatening a team member or trying to coerce the person (choice D) is never a good idea. It's better to be straightforward with the person. Speaking with your supervisor (choice A) is the last resort if the person obstructs the team's work or undermines the team leader's authority. Ignoring the person and any contributions he or she makes at meetings (choice B) is never a good idea.

23. **The correct answer is A.** The correct action to take is to report the employee to your department head. You don't want to get involved in expense account cheating, so you don't want to select choices B or D. Reporting the employee to the auditing department (choice C) goes over your supervisor's head, which is not a good idea.

24. **The correct answer is A.** The digital picture on the screen on the left side of the picture reads 16°C.

25. **The correct answer is D.** The man who is wearing glasses and crossing the street is holding a water bottle.

SELF-EVALUATION

Since you will receive only a comprehensive exam score, your performance on any single question type is not as crucial as it would be on other standardized tests you may have taken. To earn a high score, however, you must do well on all parts of the civil service exam you take. Using the following self-evaluation grid, determine the question types from which content areas you missed to gauge your strengths and weaknesses on the skills assessed on the Diagnostic Test. It doesn't matter if your particular exam does not have a question type given here; chances are that the content/skill area—math, accuracy, grammar, reasoning, comprehension—will be on your exam. Concentrate your efforts on improving the areas that your score shows gave you the most difficulty. The following grid indicates which chapters you should review as you study this book.

Content Area	Question Numbers	Review Chapters
Verbal Ability		
Analogies	4–7	8
Grammar and Usage	8–14	4
Effective Expression	43–50	9
Reading Comprehension	22–28	10
Sentence Completion	36–42	7
Spelling	15–21	5
Synonyms	1–3; 29–35	6
Arithmetic Ability		
Basic Arithmetic	4, 5, 19–23	15, 16, 18
Fractions and Decimals	1–3; 6, 24, 25	15
Graphs and Tables	11–14	17
Percents, Ratios, and Proportions	7–10; 18	16
Reasoning	15–17	18
Clerical Ability		
Alphabetizing and Filing	4–18	12
Clerical Accuracy	1–3; 19–22	13
Judgment, Communication, and Memory	23–25	11

PART III
VERBAL ABILITY

English Grammar and Usage

OVERVIEW

- **The Parts of Speech**
- **Rules of Sentence Structure**
- **Rules of Agreement**
- **Avoiding Common Errors**
- **Other Rules You Must Know**
- **Exercise**
- **Answer Key and Explanations**
- **Summing It Up**

THE PARTS OF SPEECH

A strong grasp of the basic rules of English grammar is essential for scoring well on this part of the exam. All of the following rules should be a review for you. Study these rules until you are sure that you understand them, so that recognizing errors in the questions on the exam will come naturally to you.

The basic parts of speech are as follows:

- **Nouns** identify people, places, things, or ideas: *teacher, city, desk, democracy.*
- **Pronouns** substitute for nouns: *he, she, they, ours, those.*
- **Adjectives** describe nouns: *warm, quick, tall, blue.*
- **Verbs** express actions or states of being: *yell, interpret, feel, are.*
- **Adverbs** modify verbs, adjectives, or other adverbs: *slowly, well, busily.*
- **Conjunctions** join words, sentences, and phrases: *and, but, or.*
- **Prepositions** show position in time or space: *in, during, after, behind.*

It's also important to understand what phrases are. A phrase is any group of related words that has no subject or predicate and that is used as a single part of speech. Phrases may be built around prepositions, articles, gerunds, or infinitives, but they cannot stand by themselves as sentences.

Chapter 4

Nouns and Pronouns

The antecedent of a pronoun is the noun to which a pronoun refers. A pronoun must agree with its antecedent in gender, person, and number. The pronoun generally refers to the nearest noun. Make certain that the grammatical antecedent is indeed the intended antecedent. Consider this sentence:

Since the mouth of the cave was masked by underbrush, it provided an excellent hiding place.

This sentence is incorrect because *it* refers grammatically to *underbrush*, not the intended antecedent *cave*. You may find that the most effective way to clear up an ambiguity is to revise the sentence so that the pronoun is not used:

Masked by underbrush, the mouth of the cave provided an excellent hiding place.

Both pronouns and nouns have three cases:

1. **Subjective:** The subject, noun/pronoun of address, or predicate noun/pronoun. Examples of subjective pronouns include *I, he, she, we,* and *they.*

2. **Objective:** The direct object, indirect object, or object of a preposition. Examples of objective pronouns include *me, him, her, us,* and *them.*

3. **Possessive:** The form that shows possession. Examples of possessive pronouns include *mine, his, hers, ours,* and *theirs.*

The following are several rules relating to noun and pronoun case that you should know:

- The subject of a verb is in the subjective case even if the verb is understood and not expressed.
  Example: They are as old as *we.* (Check your answer by silently finishing off the sentence: *as we are.*)

- Nouns or pronouns connected by a form of the verb "to be" are always in the nominative case.
  Example: It is *I.* (Not *me.*)

- *Who* and *whoever* are in the nominative case; *whom* and *whomever* are in the objective case.
  Examples: The trapeze artist *who* ran away with the clown broke the lion tamer's heart. (*Who* is the subject of the verb *ran.*) Invite *whomever* you wish to accompany you. (*Whomever* is the object of the verb *invite.*)

- The object of a preposition or transitive verb takes a pronoun in the objective case.
  Example: It would be impossible for *me* to do that job alone. (*Me* is the object of the preposition *for.*)

- A noun or pronoun modifying a gerund should be in the possessive case.
  Example: Is there any criticism of *Arthur's* going? (*Going* is the gerund.)

Verbs

You can't have a sentence without a verb. Verbs indicate action, or condition (state) of being.

- A verb that expresses action, such as *drive, make, take, bring,* or *eat*, is an **action verb**.

- There are also **helping verbs** and **linking verbs**.

TIP

Be careful using the different forms of the personal pronouns. "Jack and *me* are going" is incorrect because *me* is the objective form of the first-person pronoun, and you need a subject. "They invited Jack and *I* to go" is also incorrect. You need the objective form here.

- ○ Helping verbs combine with the main verb to form a verb phrase, such as *is going* or *has worked*. The main helping verbs are *do, does, did; have, has, had; will, would, could, should; can, may;* and *must*.

- ○ Linking verbs connect the subject with a word that describes or identifies it, for example, *Charlene is* a good *worker*. The main linking verb is the verb *to be* and its forms: *am, are, is, was, were, been*.

- ○ Other linking verbs are *appear, become, continue, feel, grow, look, remain, seen, smell, sound, taste,* and *turn*.

Verbs have four principal parts:

1. Present (*bake*)
2. Present participle (*baking*)
3. Past (*baked*)
4. Past participle (*baked*)

The *–ing* and *–ed* endings you see here are the usual way of forming present and past participles, but some verbs have irregular past and past participles, for example, *slept/slept, ate/eaten, knew/known, sat/sat*.

Verbs may be in the **active** or **passive** voice.

- When a verb is in the active voice, the subject is the doer of the action.
  Example: *Sheena opened* the door.

- When the verb is in the passive voice, the subject is not the doer.
  Example: The *door was opened* by Sheena.

Passive voice uses a form of the main verb and a form of the verb *to be*.

When you are writing, it is always better to use active voice than passive voice.

Tense indicates when something occurs or when it is done. Verbs have six tenses:

1. **Present:** It is happening now (*eat, drive, make*).
2. **Past:** It happened before (*ate, drove, made*).
3. **Future:** It is going to happen (*will eat, will drive, will make*).
4. **Present perfect:** It began in the past and continues into the present (*has eaten, have driven, have made*).
5. **Past perfect:** It happened in the past before another action happened (*had eaten, had driven, had made*).
6. **Future perfect:** It will take place in the future before another action happens (*will have eaten, will have driven, will have made*).

Verbs may be singular or plural, depending on the subject. Regardless of the voice or tense, the verb must agree in person and number with the subject. If the subject is in the third person, singular number (*he, she,* or *it*), the form of the linking or helping verb must be *is, has,* or *does*.

Adjectives and Adverbs

It is often unclear whether you should use an adjective or an adverb. Remember that adjectives modify nouns and pronouns, and adverbs modify verbs, adjectives, and other adverbs. Sometimes, context must determine which is used. Consider this sentence: "The old man looked angry." In this case, you must use an adjective because you are describing a noun, *the old man*. Consider this sentence: "The old man looked *angrily* out the window." Now, you must use an adverb because you are describing a verb, *looked*.

Adjectives answer the questions, "Which one?" "What kind?" and "How many?" Adverbs answer the questions, "Why?" "How?" "Where?" "When?" and "To what degree?"

Place adverbs, clauses, and phrases near the words they modify to prevent confusion. For example, "The man was willing to sell only one horse" is clearer than "The man was *only* willing to sell one horse," because the adverb *only* modifies the adjective *one*, rather than the verb *was willing*.

Whenever you use a modifier, it must modify something. For example, the sentence "While away on vacation, the pipes burst" is incorrect. The pipes were not on vacation, so the phrase does not modify anything. A better way to say it is "While we were on vacation, the pipes burst."

Conjunctions and Prepositions

Conjunctions connect words, phrases, and clauses. There are three general types of conjunctions:

- **Coordinate:** Placed between the words and ideas it connects. Examples of coordinate conjunctions include *and* and *but*.
- **Subordinate:** Connects a dependent idea in a sentence with the main thought. Subordinate conjunctions are used to indicate concession (*although, even if, though*), to show cause (*now that, because, as, since*), to describe a condition (*provided that, if only, except that, unless*), to indicate purpose (*in order to, so that*), or to fix a time (*as long as, ever since, until, after, when, now*).
- **Correlative:** Used in pairs and usually placed next to the words they connect. Examples of correlative conjunction pairs are: *neither/nor, either/or,* and *not only/but also*.

Prepositions are connecting words that show a noun or pronoun's relationship to other words in the sentence. They're almost always combined with other words in constructions known as *prepositional phrases*.

A prepositional phrase acts as an adjective or adverb to locate something in time and space, to modify a noun, or to describe where or under what conditions something occurred. Examples of common prepositions include *about, above, across, after, against, along, among, around, at, before, behind, below, beneath, beside, between, by, down, during, except, for, from, in, in front of, inside, instead of, into, near, off, on, on top of, onto, out of, outside, over, past, through, to, toward, under, until, up, upon, with, within,* and *without*.

In day-to-day speech, people often use prepositions where they aren't needed. Review the following examples and make sure that you understand where to eliminate or replace extraneous prepositions.

- He met ~~up with~~ the new president yesterday.
- The boy fell off ~~of~~ the bicycle.

- She threw the ball out ~~of~~ the window.
- My parents wouldn't let the dog inside ~~of~~ the house. (Or use *in* in place of *inside of*.)
- Where did Harry go ~~to~~?
- Park your car ~~in back of~~ the office building. (Use *behind* instead.)
- Where is your house ~~at~~?

RULES OF SENTENCE STRUCTURE

You should know the following basic rules of good sentence structure:

- **Every sentence must contain a verb.** A group of words without a verb is a sentence fragment, not a sentence.

- **Every sentence must have a subject.** The subject may be a noun, pronoun, phrase, or clause functioning as a noun. In commands, however, the subject is usually not expressed but is understood to be *you*.

- **A subordinate clause must never stand alone.** It is not a complete sentence, despite the fact that it has a subject and a verb. Subordinate clauses may act as adverbs, adjectives, or nouns. A subordinate adverbial clause is usually introduced by a subordinating conjunction, such as *when, while, because, as soon as, if, after, although, as before, since, than, though, until*, and *unless*. Subordinate adjective and noun clauses may be introduced by the pronouns *who, which*, and *that*.

RULES OF AGREEMENT

The following guidelines illustrate the sometimes tricky rules of subject-verb agreement and verb tense that you should know:

- A verb should agree in number with the subject of the sentence.
  Example: Poor study *habits are* the leading cause of unsatisfactory achievement in school.

- A verb should not be made to agree with a noun that is part of a phrase following the subject.
  Example: *Mount Snow*, one of my favorite ski areas, *is* in Vermont.

- A subject consisting of two or more nouns joined by a coordinating conjunction takes a plural verb.
  Example: Paul *and* Sue *were* the last to arrive.

- When the conjunctions *or, either/or*, and *neither/nor* are used, the number of the verb agrees with the last subject.
  Example: Either the cat or the *mice take* charge in the barn.

- The number of the verb is not affected when words introduced by *with, together with, no less than, as well as*, etc., modify the subject.
  Example: The *captain*, together with the rest of the team, *was delighted* by the victory celebration.

- In sentences beginning with *there is* and *there are*, the verb agrees with the noun that follows it.
  Example: There *is not* an unbroken *bone* in her body.

- Statements equally true in the past and the present are usually expressed in the present tense.
  Example: He said that Venus *is* a planet. (Although he made the statement in the past, the fact remains that Venus is a planet.)

- When expressing a condition contrary to fact or a wish, use the subjunctive form *were*.
  Example: I wish I *were* a movie star.

AVOIDING COMMON ERRORS

The following are common but subtle errors. Train yourself to concentrate on each sentence so that you can recognize errors.

- Comparisons must be logical and complete.
  Incorrect: Wilmington is larger than *any city* in Delaware.
  Correct: Wilmington is larger than any *other* city in Delaware. (Wilmington cannot be larger than itself.)

- Comparisons and other groups must be parallel.
  Incorrect: She spends all her time *eating*, *asleep*, and *on her studies*.
  Correct: She spends all her time *eating*, *sleeping*, and *studying*. (All three list items are in present participle form.)

- Avoid needless shifts in point-of-view—a change within the sentence from one verb tense to another, from one subject to another, or from one person or number to another.
  Incorrect: Mary especially *likes* math, but history *is also enjoyed* by her. (The subject shifts from Mary to history, and the voice shifts from active to passive.)
  Correct: Mary especially *likes* math, but she also *enjoys* history.

- Avoid the *is when* and *is where* constructions.
  Incorrect: A limerick *is when* a short poem has a catchy rhyme.
  Correct: *A limerick is a short poem with a catchy rhyme.*

OTHER RULES YOU MUST KNOW

The following list of rules is far from comprehensive. In fact, it is purposely kept brief so that you can learn every rule and every hint. You will find these rules invaluable for all your writing.

Capitalization Rules

- Capitalize the first word of a sentence.
- Capitalize all proper names.
- Capitalize days of the week, months of the year, and holidays.
- Do not capitalize the seasons.

- Capitalize the first and all other important words in a title including the forms of the verb *to be*.

  Example: *The Art of Promotion* or *The Winner Is a Major Shock to Fans*.

- Capitalize common nouns only when they are used as part of proper names.

  Example: Yesterday I visited *Uncle Charles*, my favorite *uncle*.

- Capitalize the points of the compass only when referring to a specific place or area.

  Example: Many retired persons spend the winter in the *South*.

- Do not capitalize the points of the compass when referring to a direction.

  Example: Many birds fly *south* in the winter.

- Capitalize languages and specific place names used as modifiers, but do not capitalize any other school subjects.

  Example: Next year I will study *French*, biology, and *English* literature.

- Capitalize the first word of a direct quotation.

  Example: Alexander Pope wrote, "*A* little learning is a dangerous thing."

- Do not capitalize the first word within quotation marks if it does not begin a complete sentence, as when a direct quotation is broken.

  Example: "I tore my stocking," she told us, "*because* the drawer was left open."

Punctuation Rules

Using the Apostrophe

Use an apostrophe in the following situations:

- To indicate possession. When indicating possession, the apostrophe means "belonging to everything to the left of the apostrophe." Use this rule to test for correct placement. For example, *childrens'* or "belonging to the childrens" is obviously incorrect, while *children's* or "belonging to the children" is correct. This placement rule applies at all times, even with compound nouns and with entities made up of two or more names. For example, *father-in-law's* means "belonging to a father-in-law," and *Brown and Sons'* delivery truck refers to a delivery truck "belonging to Brown and Sons."

- In a contraction in place of the omitted letter or letters.

  Examples: *haven't, we're, class of '85, '90s*.

- To form plurals of numbers, letters, and phrases referred to as words.

  Example: The young child pronounced his *r*'s as *w*'s.

Using the Colon

Use a colon in the following situations:

- After a salutation in a business letter.

  Example: Dear Board Member:

- To separate hours from minutes.

  Example: The eclipse occurred at 10:36 a.m.

- Use of the colon is optional in the following cases:
    - To introduce a list, especially after expressions like as *follows* or *the following*.
    - To introduce a long quotation.
    - To introduce a question, such as, "My question is this: Are you willing to punch a time clock?"

Using the Comma

Use a comma in the following situations:

- After the salutation of a personal letter.
  Example: *Dear Mary,*
- After the complimentary close of a letter.
  Example: *Cordially yours,*
- To set off a noun in direct address.
  Example: When you finish your homework, *Jeff,* take out the garbage.
- To set off an appositive—a phrase that follows a noun or pronoun and means the same thing.
  Example: Mr. Burke, *our lawyer,* gave us some good advice.
- To set off parenthetical expressions—words or phrases that interrupt the flow of the sentence—such as *however, though, for instance,* and *by the way*. Test for placement of commas in a parenthetical expression by reading aloud. If you pause before and after the expression, set it off with commas.
  Example: We could not, however, get him to agree.
- Between two or more adjectives that equally modify a noun.
  Example: The jolly, fat, ruddy man laughed.
- To separate words, phrases, or clauses in a series.
  Example: Place coats, umbrellas, and boots in the closet.
- To separate a direct quotation from the speaker.
  Example: She said, "I must leave work on time today."
- After an introductory phrase of five or more words.
  Example: Because the prisoner had a history of attempted jailbreaks, he was guarded heavily.
- After a short introductory phrase whenever the comma would aid clarity.
  Example: To Dan, Phil was a friend as well as brother.
- Before a coordinating conjunction, unless the two clauses are very short.
  Example: The boy wanted to borrow a book from the library, but the librarian would not allow him to take it until he had paid his fines.

TIP

If you can add the word *and* between the adjectives without changing the sense of the sentence, use commas.

- To set off a nonrestrictive adjective phrase or clause—one that can be omitted without changing the meaning of the sentence.
  Example: Our new sailboat, which has bright orange sails, is very seaworthy.

- A restrictive phrase or clause is vital to the meaning of a sentence and cannot be omitted. Do not set it off with commas.
  Example: A sailboat that has no sails is useless.

- If the sentence might be subject to different interpretations without a comma.
  Examples: My brother Bill is getting married. (This implies that I have more than one brother.) My brother, Bill, is getting married. (In this case, *Bill* is an appositive and presumably the only brother.)

- If a pause would make the sentence clearer and easier to read.
  Incorrect: After all crime must be punished.
  Correct: After all, crime must be punished.

Using Dashes

There are two types of dashes, en dashes and em dashes. En dashes are typically used to join numbers in a range (e.g., pages 101–115) or to join words that describe a range (e.g., January–March 2018).

Em dashes are longer in appearance and are used in the following situations:

- For emphasis or to set off an explanatory group of words. Em dashes, like parentheses, must be used in pairs unless the set-off expression ends a sentence.
  Example: The tools of his trade—probe, mirror, cotton swabs—were neatly arranged on the dentist's tray.

- To break up a thought.
  Example: There are five—remember I said five—good reasons to refuse their demands.

Using the Hyphen

Use a hyphen in the following situations:

- To divide a word at the end of a line. Always divide words between syllables.

- When spelling out numbers from twenty-one to ninety-nine.

- To join two words serving together as a single adjective before a noun.
  Example: We left the highway and proceeded on a *well-paved* road.

- When using the prefixes *ex-*, *self-*, and *all-*, and the suffix *-elect*.
  Examples: *ex-Senator, self-appointed, all-state, Governor-elect*

- To avoid ambiguity.
  Example: After the custodian *recovered* use of his right arm, he *re-covered* the office chairs.

- To avoid an awkward union of letters.
  Examples: *self-independent, shell-like*

> **NOTE**
> The pause rule is not infallible, but it is your best resort when all other rules governing use of the comma fail you.

TIP

If you are uncertain about how to use the semicolon to connect independent clauses, write two sentences instead.

Using the Semicolon

Use a semicolon in the following situations:

- To separate a series of phrases or clauses, each of which contains commas.
  Example: The old gentleman's heirs were *Margaret Whitlock, his half-sister; William Frame, companion to his late cousin, Robert Bone; and his favorite charity, the Salvation Army.*

- To avoid confusion with numbers.
  Example: Add the following: *$1.25; $7.50; and $12.89.*

- To separate two independent clauses with a semicolon. When there are two main clauses in a sentence, it is acceptable to separate the clauses with a semicolon, a conjunction, or to write as two sentences. A semicolon never precedes a coordinating conjunction. The same two clauses may be written in any one of three ways:

  ○ Autumn had *come and* the trees were almost bare.

  ○ Autumn had *come; the* trees were almost bare.

  ○ Autumn had *come. The* trees were almost bare.

Using the Period, Question Mark, and Exclamation Point

- Use a period at the end of a sentence that makes a statement, gives a command, or makes a "polite request" in the form of a question that does not require an answer.

- Use a period after an abbreviation and after the initial in a person's name.
  Example: Gen. Robert E. Lee.

- Use a question mark after a request for information.

- Use an exclamation point to express strong feeling or emotion, or to imply urgency.
  Example: Congratulations! You broke the record.

NOTE

A question must end with a question mark, even if the question does not end the entire sentence. Example: "Daddy, are we there yet?" the child asked.

Using Quotation Marks

Use quotation marks in the following situations:

- To enclose all directly quoted material. Words not quoted must remain outside the quotation marks.
  Example: "If it's hot on Sunday," she said, "we'll go to the beach."

  ○ Do not enclose an indirect quote in quotation marks.
    Example: She said that we might go to the beach on Sunday.

- To set off words used in an unusual way.
  Example: A surfer who "hangs ten" is performing a maneuver on a surfboard, not staging a mass execution.

- To enclose the title of a short story, essay, short poem, song, or article.
  Example: Robert Louis Stevenson wrote a plaintive poem called "Bed in Summer."
    It's important to note that titles of books and plays are not enclosed in quotation marks. They are printed in italics.
    Example: The song "Tradition" is from *Fiddler on the Roof.*
    In handwritten or typed manuscript, underscore titles of books and plays.
    Example: The song "Tradition" is from <u>Fiddler on the Roof.</u>

TIP

Do not use a period after postal service state name abbreviations like AZ or MI.

Remember these rules for placing quotation marks correctly:

- Periods and commas always go inside quotation marks.
  Example: She described what she heard as an "ear-splitting, thunderous boom."

- Question marks and exclamation points go inside quotation marks if they are part of the quotation. If the whole sentence containing the quotation is a question or exclamation, the punctuation goes outside the quotation marks.
  Example: What did you really mean when you said, "I do"?

- Colons and semicolons always go outside the quotation marks.
  Example: He said, "War is destructive"; she added, "Peace is constructive."

- When a multiple-paragraph passage is quoted, each paragraph of the quotation must begin with quotation marks, but ending quotation marks are used only at the end of the last quoted paragraph.

- Direct quotations are bound by all the rules of sentence structure. Beware of run-on sentences in divided quotations.
  Incorrect: "Your total is wrong," he said, "add the column again."
  Correct: "Your total is wrong," he said. "Add the column again."
  In the correct example, the two independent clauses form two separate sentences.

EXERCISE

> **Directions:** In each of the following items, there are four sentences. Choose the grammatically incorrect sentence. When you are finished, check your answers in the section immediately following the questions.

1. **A.** Everyone at camp must have his medical certificate on file before participating in competitive sports.
   B. A crate of oranges were sent from Florida for all the children in cabin six.
   C. John and Danny's room looks as if they were prepared for inspection.
   D. Three miles is too far for a young child to walk.

2. **A.** Being tired, I stretched out on a grassy knoll.
   B. While we were rowing on the lake, a sudden squall almost capsized the boat.
   C. Entering the room, a strange mark on the floor attracted my attention.
   D. Mounting the curb, the empty car crossed the sidewalk and came to rest against a building.

3. **A.** Not one in a thousand readers take the matter seriously.
   B. He was able partially to accomplish his purpose.
   C. You are not as tall as he.
   D. The people began to realize how much she had done.

4. **A.** In the case of members who are absent, a special letter will be sent.
   B. The visitors were all ready to see it.
   C. I like Burns's poem "To a Mountain Daisy."
   D. John said that he was sure he seen it.

5. **A.** Neither the critics nor the author were right about the reaction of the public.
   B. The senator depended upon whoever was willing to assist him.
   C. I don't recall any time when Edgar has broken his word.
   D. Every one of the campers but John and me is going on the hike.

6. **A.** B. Nelson & Co. has a sale on sport shirts today.
   B. Venetian blinds—called that although they probably did not originate in Venice—are no longer used as extensively as they were at one time.
   C. He determined to be guided by the opinion of whoever spoke first.
   D. There was often disagreement as to whom was the better Shakespearean actor, Evans or Gielgud.

7. **A.** Never before have I seen anyone who has the skill John has when he repairs engines.
   B. If anyone can be wholly just in his decisions, it is he.
   C. Because of his friendliness, the new neighbor was immediately accepted by the community.
   D. Imagine our embarrassment when us girls saw Miss Maltinge sitting with her beau in the front row.

8. **A.** The general regarded whomever the colonel honored with disdain.

   B. All who reads this book will think themselves knights errant on missions of heroism.

   C. The reason why the new leader was so unsuccessful was that he had fewer responsibilities.

   D. All the new mechanical devices we have today have made our daily living a great deal simpler, it is said.

9. **A.** I can but do my best.

   B. I cannot help comparing him with his predecessor.

   C. I wish that I was in Florida now.

   D. I like this kind of grapes better than any other.

10. **A.** Neither Tom nor John was present for the rehearsal.

    B. The happiness or misery of men's lives depends on their early training.

    C. Honor as well as profit are to be gained by these studies.

    D. The egg business is only incidental to the regular business of the general store.

11. **A.** The Board of Directors has prepared a manual for their own use.

    B. The company has announced its new policy of advertising.

    C. The jury was out about thirty minutes when it returned a verdict.

    D. The flock of geese creates a health hazard for visitors with allergies.

12. **A.** Two thirds of the building are finished.

    B. Where are Mr. Keene and Mr. Herbert?

    C. Neither the salespeople nor the manager want to work overtime.

    D. The committee was agreed.

13. **A.** The coming of peace effected a change in her way of life.

    B. Spain is as weak as, if not more weaker than, it was in 1900.

    C. In regard to that, I am not certain what my attitude will be.

    D. That unfortunate family faces the problem of adjusting itself to a new way of life.

14. **A.** I wondered why it was that the mayor objected to the governor's reference to the new tax law.

    B. I have never read *Les Miserables*, but I plan to read it this summer.

    C. After much talk and haranguing, the workers received an increase in wages.

    D. Charles Dole, who is a member of the committee, was asked to confer with commissioner Wilson.

15. **A.** Most employees, and he is no exception do not like to work overtime.

    B. The doctor had carelessly left all the instruments on the operating table.

    C. Despite all the power he has, I should still hate to be in his shoes.

    D. I feel bad because I gave such a poor performance in the play tonight.

16. **A.** Of London and Paris, the former is the wealthier.

    B. Of the two cities visited, White Plains is the cleanest.

    C. Chicago is larger than any other city in Illinois.

    D. The United States is the wealthiest nation, and, of all others, China is the most populous.

exercise

17. **A.** It was superior in every way to the book previously used.

    B. His testimony today is different from that of yesterday.

    C. The letter will be sent to the United States senate this week.

    D. The flowers smelled so sweet that the whole house was perfumed.

18. **A.** When either or both habits become fixed, the student improves.

    B. When the supervisor entered the room, he noticed that the book was laying on the desk.

    C. Neither his words nor his actions were justifiable.

    D. A calm almost always comes before a storm.

19. **A.** Who did they say won?

    B. Send in the candidate, Ann.

    C. The question of who should be leader arose.

    D. All the clerks including those who have been appointed recently are required to work on the new assignment.

20. **A.** Mrs. Black the supervisor of the unit has many important duties.

    B. This is the woman whom I saw.

    C. She could solve even this problem.

    D. She divided the money among the three of us.

21. **A.** He felt deep despair (and who has not?) at the evidence of man's inhumanity to people.

    B. You will be glad, I am sure, to give the book to whoever among your young friends has displayed an interest in animals.

    C. When independence day falls on a Sunday, it is officially celebrated on Monday.

    D. Being a stranger in town myself, I know how you feel.

22. **A.** The task of filing these cards is to be divided equally between you and he.

    B. A series of authentic records of Native American people is being published.

    C. The Smokies is the home of the descendants of this brave tribe.

    D. Five dollars is really not too much to pay for a book of this type.

23. **A.** The game over, the spectators rushed out on the field and tore down the goalposts.

    B. The situation was aggravated by disputes over the captaincy of the team.

    C. Yesterday they lay their uniforms aside with the usual end-of-the season regret.

    D. It is sometimes thought that politics is not for the high-minded.

24. **A.** Consider that the person which is always idle can never be happy.

    B. Because a man understands a woman does not mean they are necessarily compatible.

    C. He said that accuracy and speed are both essential.

    D. "Is it possible that the better of the two coats is less expensive?" asked Raoul.

25. **A.** Everyone entered promptly but her.

    B. Each of the messengers were busily occupied.

    C. At which exit did you leave him?

    D. The work was not done well.

ANSWER KEY AND EXPLANATIONS

1. B	6. D	11. A	16. B	21. C
2. C	7. D	12. C	17. C	22. A
3. A	8. B	13. B	18. B	23. C
4. D	9. C	14. D	19. D	24. A
5. A	10. C	15. A	20. A	25. B

1. **The correct answer is B.** The subject of the sentence is *crate*, which takes a singular verb: A crate of oranges *was* sent from Florida for all the children in cabin six.

2. **The correct answer is C.** The sentence reads as if the strange mark entered the room. A better way to write it would be: *When I entered the room, a strange mark on the floor attracted my attention.*

3. **The correct answer is A.** The subject of the sentence is *one*, which takes a singular verb: Not one in a thousand readers *takes* the matter seriously.

4. **The correct answer is D.** The verb is missing its helping verb *had*. You can't use a participle form alone as a verb. The sentence should read as follows: John said that he was sure he *had seen* it.

5. **The correct answer is A.** When two nouns (or pronouns) are joined by the correlative conjunction *neither/nor*, the verb agrees with the last subject: *Neither* the critics *nor* the author *was* right about the reaction of the public.

6. **The correct answer is D.** *Who* is the subject of the verb following it, *was*: There was often disagreement as to *who* was the better Shakespearean actor, Evans or Gielgud.

7. **The correct answer is D.** As the subject of the verb *saw*, the correct word is *we*, not *us*: Imagine our embarrassment when *we* girls saw Miss Maltinge sitting with her beau in the front row.

8. **The correct answer is B.** The sentence has a subject-verb agreement error. The indefinite pronoun *All* is plural and should take a plural verb: All who *read* this book will think themselves knights errant on missions of heroism.

9. **The correct answer is C.** Use the subjunctive, *were*, when stating a wish: I wish that I *were* in Florida now.

10. **The correct answer is C.** The phrase *as well as profit* does not add to the number of the subject, so the verb should be singular: Honor as well as profit *is* to be gained by these studies.

11. **The correct answer is A.** The sentence switches number in the middle (*Board of Directors* is singular). The sentence should read as follows: The Board of Directors has prepared a manual for *its* own use.

12. **The correct answer is C.** Because *neither/nor* is a correlative conjunction, the verb must agree with the nearest noun: Neither the salespeople nor the manager *wants* to work overtime.

13. **The correct answer is B.** You don't need both the comparative ending –*er* and the word *more* to create the comparative form. The sentence should read as follows: Spain is as weak as, *if not weaker than*, it was in 1900.

14. **The correct answer is D.** Commissioner Wilson is a specific commissioner, so the *C* must be capitalized: Charles Dole, who is a member of the committee, was asked to confer with *Commissioner* Wilson.

15. **The correct answer is A.** Parenthetical expressions must always be enclosed in commas or other punctuation. The sentence

should read as follows: Most employees, *and he is no exception*, do not like to work overtime.

16. **The correct answer is B.** The comparative *-er* is used when only two items are being compared; *-est* requires three or more items. The sentence should read as follows: Of the two cities visited, White Plains is *the cleaner*.

17. **The correct answer is C.** The specific noun *senate* must be capitalized: The letter will be sent to the United States *Senate* this week.

18. **The correct answer is B.** The verb *to lay* should be used only when it can be replaced with *to put*; at all other times, use a form of the verb *to lie*: When the supervisor entered the room, he noticed that the book *was lying* on the desk.

19. **The correct answer is D.** Omitting the clause in this sentence does not change the meaning of the remaining words, so it is nonrestrictive and should be set off by commas: All the clerks, *including those who have been appointed recently*, are required to work on the new assignment.

20. **The correct answer is A.** Appositives should be set off by commas. The sentence should read as follows: Mrs. Black, *the supervisor of the unit*, has many important duties.

21. **The correct answer is C.** Holidays are always capitalized. The sentence should read as follows: When *Independence Day* falls on a Sunday, it is officially celebrated on Monday.

22. **The correct answer is A.** Pronouns that are objects of prepositions should be in the objective case. The sentence should read as follows: The task of filing these cards is to be divided equally between you and *him*.

23. **The correct answer is C.** Because the sentence occurred in the past (yesterday), the verb should be in the past tense: Yesterday they *laid* their uniforms aside with the usual end-of-the-season regret.

24. **The correct answer is A.** Use *who* when referring to people and *which* when referring to objects. The sentence should read as follows: Consider that the person *who* is always idle can never be happy.

25. **The correct answer is B.** *Each* is singular. The sentence should read as follows: Each of the messengers *was* busily occupied.

SUMMING IT UP

- A strong grasp of basic English grammar is essential for scoring well on the civil service exams. Study the rules until you're sure you understand them so that you can easily recognize errors in the questions that appear on your exam.

- The basic parts of speech are nouns, pronouns, adjectives, verbs, adverbs, conjunctions, and prepositions. A phrase is any group of related words that has no subject or predicate and is used as a single part of speech.

- Pronouns and nouns have three cases: subjective, objective, and possessive. Make sure you know the rules relating to these cases by studying the section in this chapter devoted to nouns and pronouns.

- Verbs indicate action or condition of being. Verbs may also serve as helping or linking verbs. Verbs have six tenses and may be in the active or passive voice. Regardless of the voice or tense, verbs must agree in person and number with their subjects.

- Differentiating adjectives from adverbs is sometimes difficult. Remember that adjectives modify nouns and adverbs modify verbs, adjectives, and other adverbs. Adjectives answer the questions "Which one?" "What kind?" and "How many?" Adverbs answer the questions "Why?" "How?" "When?" and "To what degree?"

- To do well on the civil service exam, review the basic rules of sentence structure, subject-verb agreement, and verb tense.

- It pays to be sure you know the rules of capitalization and punctuation. You will see questions relating to these rules on your civil service exam.

Spelling

OVERVIEW

- **Essential Spelling Rules**
- **Strategies for Answering Common Spelling Questions**
- **Exercise 1**
- **Exercise 2**
- **Exercise 3**
- **Answer Keys and Explanations**
- **Summing It Up**

Chapter 5

ESSENTIAL SPELLING RULES

The rules outlined in this section will see you through almost any spelling question that you may face. Study these rules and their most common exceptions. Memorize as many as you can.

1. *i* before *e* except after *c* or when sounding like *ay* as in *neighbor* or *weigh*.

   Exceptions: *neither, leisure, foreign, seize, weird, height*

2. If a word ends in *y* preceded by a vowel, keep the *y* when adding a suffix.

   Examples: *day, days; attorney, attorneys*

3. If a word ends in *y* preceded by a consonant, change the *y* to *i* before adding a suffix.

   Examples: *try, tried; lady, ladies*

4. If a word ends in *y* preceded by a consonant, avoid a double *i* by retaining the *y* before the suffixes *-ing* and *-ish*.

   Examples: *fly, flying; baby, babyish.*

5. A silent *e* at the end of a word is usually dropped before a suffix beginning with a vowel.

   Examples: *dine + ing = dining; locate + ion = location; use + able = usable; offense + ive = offensive*

   Exceptions: *mileage, dyeing, acreage, canoeing*

6. Words ending in *ce* and *ge* retain *e* before the suffixes *-able* and *-ous* in order to retain the soft sounds of *e* and *g*.

   Examples: *peace + able = peaceable; courage + ous = courageous*

107

7. A silent *e* is usually kept before a suffix beginning with a consonant.

   Examples: *care + less = careless; late + ly = lately; one + ness = oneness; game + ster = gamester.*

   Exceptions: *truly, wholly, duly. awful, argument, ninth*

8. A one-syllable word that ends in a *single* consonant preceded by a *single* vowel doubles the final consonant before a suffix beginning with a vowel or *y.*

   Examples: *hit, hitting; drop, dropped; big, biggest; mud, muddy.*

   Exceptions: *Help* becomes *helping* because *help* ends in two consonants, and *need* becomes *needing* because the final consonant is preceded by two vowels.

9. A word with more than one syllable (that accents the last syllable and ends in a single consonant preceded by a single vowel) doubles the final consonant when adding a suffix beginning with a vowel.

   Examples: *begin, beginner; admit, admitted*

   Exceptions: *Enter* becomes *entered* because the accent is not on the last syllable.

10. A word ending in *-er* or *-ur* doubles the *r* in the past tense if the word is accented on the *last* syllable.

    Examples: *occur, occurred; prefer, preferred; transfer, transferred*

11. A word ending in *-er* does not double the *r* in the past tense if the accent does not fall on the last syllable.

    Examples: *answer, answered; offer, offered; differ, differed*

12. When *-full* is added to the end of a noun to form an adjective, the final *l* is dropped.

    Examples: *cheerful, cupful, hopeful*

13. All words beginning with *over* are one word.

    Examples: *overcast, overcharge, overhear*

14. All words with the prefix *self-* are hyphenated.

    Examples: *self-control, self-defense, self-evident*

15. *Percent* is never hyphenated.

16. The letter *q* is always followed by *u.*

    Examples: *quiz, bouquet, acquire*

17. *Welcome* is one word with one *l.*

18. *All right* is always two words; there is no such word as *alright. Already* means prior to some specified time; *all ready* means completely ready.

    Example: By the time I was *all ready* to go to the play, the bus had already left.

19. *Altogether* means entirely; *all together* means in sum or collectively.

    Example: There are *altogether* too many people to seat in this room when we are *all together.*

20. *Their* is the possessive of *they*; *they're* is the contraction for "they are"; and *there* is "that place."

   Example: *They're* going to put *their* books over *there*.

21. *Your* is the possessive of *you*; *you're* is the contraction for "you are."

   Example: *You're* certainly planning to leave *your* muddy boots outside.

22. *Whose* is the possessive of *who*; *who's* is the contraction for "who is."

   Example: Do you know *who's* ringing the doorbell or *whose* car is in the street?

23. *Its* is the possessive of *it*; *it's* is the contraction for "it is."

   Example: *It's* I who put *its* stamp on the letter.

Develop a personal program for improving your spelling. Think of your own private "devils"—the words that you must look up every time. Everyone has such words. Make a list of these words, correctly spelled. Keep adding to the list right up to exam day, including those words that you miss on the practice exercises. Each day that you have extra study time, type through the list three times. By typing your troublesome words correctly, your hands and fingers will get used to the "feel" of the correct spelling, and your eye will become accustomed to seeing the words correctly spelled. Frequent repetition will embed the correct spellings in your mind.

STRATEGIES FOR ANSWERING COMMON SPELLING QUESTIONS

The following exercises illustrate the three most common types of spelling questions found on civil service exams. By studying these examples, you can easily tackle the spelling questions on the actual exam.

One common variety of spelling question looks like this:

Directions: In each group of four words, one word is misspelled. Find the misspelled word and mark its letter on your answer sheet.

---

1. **A.** business
   B. manufacturer
   C. possibly
   D. recieved

In this case, you would mark **D** on your answer sheet because *recieved* is spelled incorrectly. Refer back to rule 1 in the previous section if you are unsure why choice D is incorrect.

A second common spelling question looks like this:

Directions: In each group of three words, one word may be misspelled. If you find one word that is spelled incorrectly, mark its letter on your answer sheet. If all the words are spelled correctly, mark **D**.

---

1. **A.** foreign
   B. acreage
   C. occurred
   D. none of these

In this case, all three words are spelled correctly, so the answer is **D**. If you thought one of these words was spelled incorrectly, refer back to spelling rule 1, the exceptions to rule 4, and rule 10 in the previous section.

Or you might run into spelling questions involving a sentence like this:

Directions: Choose the word that is spelled correctly and mark it on your answer sheet.

---

1. She hoped that the refurbished computer would be _____.
   A. useable
   B. usable
   C. usabel

For this question, you would mark **B**. If you are unsure why *usable* is correct, refer back to rule 4.

Try another question:

2. The population of Chuggington increased by 75 _____ in 2017.
   A. percent
   B. per-cent
   C. persent

For this question, you should mark **A** as your answer because *percent* is never hyphenated (see rule 16) and does not include an *s*.

The following spelling exercises will give you practice spotting words that are spelled incorrectly. The three most common types of spelling questions are included—one in each set of practice exercises. You will find the correct answer in the Answer Keys and Explanations section following the practice exercises. Sometimes it helps to answer spelling questions by looking away from the given choices and writing the word on the margin of your question booklet or on your scratch paper. Then, check to see if the spelling you believe is correct is given as one of the choices.

EXERCISE 1

> **Directions:** In each group of four words, one is misspelled. Mark the letter of the misspelled word.

1. **A.** hyphen
    B. index
    C. office
    D. diferent

2. **A.** corporation
    B. handel
    C. foreign
    D. material

3. **A.** adress
    B. exactly
    C. research
    D. vertical

4. **A.** occupation
    B. accross
    C. authority
    D. invoice

5. **A.** guardian
    B. certified
    C. voucher
    D. mispelled

6. **A.** trustee
    B. multipal
    C. promissory
    D. valuable

7. **A.** traveler
    B. pamphlet
    C. agencys
    D. permit

8. **A.** automatic
    B. proportion
    C. announcement
    D. municiple

9. **A.** recruitment
    B. mentioned
    C. optional
    D. commision

10. **A.** responsibility
    B. disabled
    C. vetran
    D. misleading

11. **A.** competetive
    B. review
    C. erroneous
    D. license

12. **A.** familiarity
    B. accredited
    C. payment
    D. distributer

13. **A.** localities
    B. servise
    C. central
    D. occupation

14. **A.** offerred
    B. jogging
    C. threaten
    D. advertise

15. **A.** vending
    B. tomorrow
    C. strangly
    D. barometer

16. **A.** anounce
    B. local
    C. grasshopper
    D. farmer

17. **A.** historical
    B. dustey
    C. kindly
    D. anniversary

18. **A.** current
    B. comunity
    C. cement
    D. calves

19. **A.** changeing
    B. explained
    C. diameter
    D. consent

20. **A.** sword
    B. selfassured
    C. signed
    D. taste

EXERCISE 2

Directions: In each question, identify the word spelled incorrectly and mark the corresponding blank on your answer sheet. If all the words are spelled correctly, mark **D**.

1. A. gratful
   B. census
   C. analysis
   D. none of these

2. A. installment
   B. retreive
   C. concede
   D. none of these

3. A. dismissal
   B. conscientious
   C. indelible
   D. none of these

4. A. percieve
   B. anticipate
   C. acquire
   D. none of these

5. A. facility
   B. reimburse
   C. assortment
   D. none of these

6. A. plentifull
   B. advantageous
   C. similar
   D. none of these

7. A. guarantee
   B. repel
   C. ommission
   D. none of these

8. A. maintenance
   B. liable
   C. announcement
   D. none of these

9. A. exaggerate
   B. seize
   C. condenm
   D. none of these

10. A. pospone
    B. altogether
    C. grievance
    D. none of these

11. A. argument
    B. reciept
    C. complain
    D. none of these

12. A. sufficient
    B. declaim
    C. visible
    D. none of these

13. A. expirience
    B. dissatisfy
    C. alternate
    D. none of these

14. A. occurred
    B. noticable
    C. appendix
    D. none of these

15. A. anxious
    B. warranty
    C. calender
    D. none of these

16. A. fundamental
    B. dissapear
    C. accidentally
    D. none of these

17. A. guidance
    B. across
    C. carreer
    D. none of these

18. A. pamphlet
    B. always
    C. commit
    D. none of these

19. A. excessive
    B. permited
    C. appointment
    D. none of these

20. A. personnel
    B. resource
    C. colledge
    D. none of these

EXERCISE 3

Directions: Choose the word that is spelled correctly and mark it on your answer sheet.

1. The student's assignment was completed _____.
   A. satisfactorily
   B. satisfactorally
   C. satisfactoriality

2. Caitlin was hired for her accurate _____ skills.
   A. bookeeping
   B. bookkeeping
   C. bookkeepping

3. Stephen waited anxiously for the university's _____ of his application.
   A. acknoledgment
   B. acknowlegement
   C. acknowledgment

4. Please listen to the following announcements for _____ information.
   A. pertenant
   B. pertainent
   C. pertinent

5. The retired explorer kept photo albums of all her _____.
   A. journeys
   B. journies
   C. journys

6. Mike kept _____ he would win the prize.
   A. hopeing
   B. hoping
   C. hopping

7. The team was _____ to winning the tournament.
   A. committed
   B. commited
   C. comitted

8. Corey bought a drill with _____ heads.
   A. exchangable
   B. exchangeable
   C. exchangeabel

9. Councilman Barton _____ with his political rival's stand on the junk food tax.
   A. concerred
   B. concured
   C. concurred

10. Sarah works as the _____ for the sales and marketing departments.
    A. liaison
    B. leision
    C. liassion

ANSWER KEYS AND EXPLANATIONS

Exercise 1

1. D	**5.** D	**9.** D	**13.** B	**17.** B
2. B	**6.** B	**10.** C	**14.** A	**18.** B
3. A	**7.** C	**11.** A	**15.** C	**19.** A
4. B	**8.** D	**12.** D	**16.** A	**20.** B

1. **The correct answer is D.** The correct spelling is *different*.

2. **The correct answer is B.** The correct spelling is *handle*.

3. **The correct answer is A.** The correct spelling is *address*.

4. **The correct answer is B.** The correct spelling is *across*.

5. **The correct answer is D.** The correct spelling is *misspelled*.

6. **The correct answer is B.** The correct spelling is *multiple*.

7. **The correct answer is C.** The correct spelling is *agencies*.

8. **The correct answer is D.** The correct spelling is *municipal*.

9. **The correct answer is D.** The correct spelling is *commission*.

10. **The correct answer is C.** The correct spelling is *veteran*.

11. **The correct answer is A.** The correct spelling is *competitive*.

12. **The correct answer is D.** The correct spelling is *distributor*.

13. **The correct answer is B.** The correct spelling is *service*.

14. **The correct answer is A.** The correct spelling is *offered*.

15. **The correct answer is C.** The correct spelling is *strangely*.

16. **The correct answer is A.** The correct spelling is *announce*.

17. **The correct answer is B.** The correct spelling is *dusty*.

18. **The correct answer is B.** The correct spelling is *community*.

19. **The correct answer is A.** The correct spelling is *changing*.

20. **The correct answer is B.** The correct spelling is *self–assured*.

Exercise 2

1. A	5. D	9. C	13. A	17. C
2. B	6. A	10. A	14. B	18. D
3. D	7. C	11. B	15. C	19. B
4. A	8. D	12. D	16. B	20. C

1. **The correct answer is A.** The correct spelling is *grateful*.

2. **The correct answer is B.** The correct spelling is *retrieve*.

3. **The correct answer is D.** All the words listed are spelled correctly.

4. **The correct answer is A.** The correct spelling is *perceive*.

5. **The correct answer is D.** All the words listed are spelled correctly.

6. **The correct answer is A.** The correct spelling is *plentiful*.

7. **The correct answer is C.** The correct spelling is *omission*.

8. **The correct answer is D.** All the words listed are spelled correctly.

9. **The correct answer is C.** The correct spelling is *condemn*.

10. **The correct answer is A.** The correct spelling is *postpone*.

11. **The correct answer is B.** The correct spelling is *receipt*.

12. **The correct answer is D.** All the words listed are spelled correctly.

13. **The correct answer is A.** The correct spelling is *experience*.

14. **The correct answer is B.** The correct spelling is *noticeable*.

15. **The correct answer is C.** The correct spelling is *calendar*.

16. **The correct answer is B.** The correct spelling is *disappear*.

17. **The correct answer is C.** The correct spelling is *career*.

18. **The correct answer is D.** All the words listed are spelled correctly.

19. **The correct answer is B.** The correct spelling is *permitted*.

20. **The correct answer is C.** The correct spelling is *college*.

Exercise 3

| 1. A | 3. C | 5. A | 7. A | 9. C |
| 2. B | 4. C | 6. B | 8. B | 10. A |

1. **The correct answer is A.** The correct spelling is *satisfactorily*.

2. **The correct answer is B.** The correct spelling is *bookkeeping*.

3. **The correct answer is C.** The correct spelling is *acknowledgment*. This word is an example of an exception to rule 7.

4. **The correct answer is C.** The correct spelling is *pertinent*.

5. **The correct answer is A.** The correct spelling is *journeys*. Refer to rule 2.

6. **The correct answer is B.** The correct spelling is *hoping*. The root word is *hope*, (rule 5), not *hop* (rule 8).

7. **The correct answer is A.** The correct spelling is *committed*. Refer to rule 9.

8. **The correct answer is B.** The correct spelling is *exchangeable*. Refer to rule 6.

9. **The correct answer is C.** The correct spelling is *concurred*. Refer to rule 10.

10. **The correct answer is A.** The correct spelling is *liaison*.

SUMMING IT UP

- A thorough knowledge of basic English spelling rules is essential for scoring well on the civil service exams. Study these rules and their most common exceptions and try to memorize as many as possible, so that you can easily recognize errors in the questions that appear on your exam.

- You will see three common types of spelling questions on your civil service exam. Be sure to read the directions very carefully so that you know what you are being asked:

  - One question type asks you to find the misspelled word among the answer choices.

  - A second type asks you to determine whether any of the answer choices are misspelled (they may not be).

  - The third question type will ask you to choose the correctly spelled word in the context of a sentence.

Synonyms

OVERVIEW

- **What are Synonyms?**
- **Strategies for Answering Synonym Questions**
- **Exercise 1**
- **Exercise 2**
- **Answer Keys and Explanations**
- **Summing It Up**

WHAT ARE SYNONYMS?

Two words are *synonyms* if they have the same or similar meanings. In a synonym question, you must pick the word or phrase closest in meaning to the given word. Remember that you are looking for the best match among the choices given, not necessarily a perfect match. You may also encounter another type of vocabulary question—*antonym* questions. Antonyms are two words that have opposite meanings. In an antonym question, you must choose the word or phrase that most nearly means the opposite of the given word. The strategies for tackling antonym questions are similar to those for answering synonym questions, keeping in mind that you are looking for an answer that means the opposite, rather than the closest match.

Synonym questions are more commonly found on civil service exams, however, which is why this chapter focuses on them. When dealing with vocabulary questions, you must read the directions carefully to determine whether you should choose the opposite of the given word—its antonym—or its closest match—its synonym. Not paying close attention to the directions could result in answering an entire section of the exam incorrectly.

When you are faced with a synonym question, follow these three steps to answer it:

1. Read the question carefully.
2. If you know right away that some of the answer choices are wrong, eliminate them.
3. From the remaining answer choices, select the one that most closely means the same as the given word, even if it is a word that you yourself do not normally use. The correct answer may not be a perfect synonym, but of the choices offered, it is the best fit.

Here is an example of a typical synonym question:

FACSIMILE most nearly means:

A. summary

B. exact copy

C. list

D. artist's sketch

The correct answer is B. This is a straightforward vocabulary question. The given word is rather difficult, but the choices are not tricky. A *facsimile* is a copy that looks exactly like the original—a photocopy, for instance. The word contains the root *simile*, meaning "like." *List* (choice C) has no connection with *facsimile*. The words *summary* and *artist's sketch* (choices A and D) are in a sense copies of something else, but not exact copies.

Here is another example:

FRAUDULENT most nearly means:

A. suspicious

B. deceptive

C. unfair

D. despicable

The correct answer is B. The word *fraudulent* means "characterized by deceit or trickery, especially deliberate misrepresentation." Therefore, *deceptive* is the best synonym. *Suspicious* (choice A), meaning "sensing that something is wrong without definite proof," could describe a person's reaction to a fraudulent situation. *Unfair* and *despicable* (choices C and D) could both be used to describe a fraudulent act. The basic meanings of these three words, however, are completely different from the meaning of *fraudulent*.

Some tests phrase synonym questions as a sentence. You must then make sure that your answer makes sense in the given sentence and does not change the sentence's meaning. The following is an example of this kind of synonym question:

Choose the word closest in meaning to the underlined word in the sentence.

We had to <u>terminate</u> the meeting because a fire broke out in the hall.

A. continue

B. postpone

C. end

D. extinguish

The correct answer is C. Even if you do not know what *terminate* means, you can eliminate choice A because it does not make much sense to say, "We had to continue the meeting because a fire broke out in the hall." *Postpone* (choice B) means "to put off until another time." It makes sense in the given sentence, but it also changes the meaning of the sentence. *Extinguish* (choice D) is similar in meaning to *terminate* but not as close as *end*. One can extinguish, or "put an end to," a fire but not a meeting.

STRATEGIES FOR ANSWERING SYNONYM QUESTIONS

Answering synonym questions depends largely upon your knowledge of vocabulary. You can apply the following strategies to arrive at the correct answer, if you do not recognize it immediately:

- If you have a general idea about what the word means but are having trouble choosing an answer, try using the word in a short sentence. Then substitute each of the answer choices in the same sentence to see which one seems to fit the sentence best without changing its meaning.

- Try to break the given word into parts to see if the suffix (ending) or the prefix (beginning) gives a clue about its meaning. For example, if you are asked to find the synonym for *previous*, you may remember that the prefix *pre-* usually means "before." You could use that as a clue to help you choose the correct answer.

You must watch out for traps of logic, though. Study the following example:

PERTINENT most nearly means:

- **A.** relevant
- **B.** prudent
- **C.** true
- **D.** respectful

The correct answer is A. *Pertinent* means "having some bearing on or relevance to." In the sentence "Her testimony was pertinent to the investigation," you could put *relevant* in the place of *pertinent* without changing the meaning. *Prudent* (choice B) means "careful" or "wise," and although it sounds somewhat like *pertinent*, its meaning is different. Choice C may seem possible because something that is *pertinent* should also be *true*. But watch out—not everything that is true is pertinent.

Respectful (choice D) is misleading. Its opposite, *disrespectful*, is a synonym for the word *impertinent*. You might logically guess, then, that *respectful* is a synonym for *pertinent*. The best way to avoid a trap like this is to remember how you have seen or heard the word used. You never see *pertinent* used to mean *respectful*.

EXERCISE 1

> **Directions:** Select the correct synonym or antonym in the following items.

1. RETAIN most nearly means:
   - A. pay out
   - B. play
   - C. keep
   - D. inquire

2. ENDORSE most nearly means:
   - A. sign up for
   - B. announce support for
   - C. lobby for
   - D. renounce

3. INTRACTABLE most nearly means:
   - A. confused
   - B. misleading
   - C. instinctive
   - D. unruly

4. CORRESPONDENCE most nearly means:
   - A. letters
   - B. files
   - C. testimony
   - D. response

5. Choose the word most opposite in meaning to OBLITERATE.
   - A. praise
   - B. erase
   - C. construct
   - D. reprove

6. LEGITIMATE most nearly means:
   - A. democratic
   - B. legal
   - C. genealogical
   - D. underworld

7. Choose the word most opposite in meaning to DEDUCT.
   - A. conceal
   - B. withstand
   - C. increase
   - D. terminate

8. MUTILATE most nearly means:
   - A. paint
   - B. damage
   - C. alter
   - D. rebel

9. EGRESS most nearly means:
   - A. extreme
   - B. extra supply
   - C. exit
   - D. high price

10. HORIZONTAL most nearly means:
    - A. marginal
    - B. in a circle
    - C. left and right
    - D. up and down

11. CONTROVERSY most nearly means:
    - A. publicity
    - B. debate
    - C. revolution
    - D. revocation

12. PREEMPT most nearly means:
    - A. adorn
    - B. empty
    - C. preview
    - D. appropriate

13. CATEGORY most nearly means:
    A. class
    B. adherence
    C. simplicity
    D. cataract

14. Choose the word closest in meaning to the underlined word in the sentence.

    The crowd's apathy affected the team's performance.
    A. sorrow
    B. indifference
    C. aptness
    D. sickness

15. TENTATIVE most nearly means:
    A. persistent
    B. permanent
    C. thoughtful
    D. provisional

16. PER CAPITA most nearly means:
    A. for an entire population
    B. by income
    C. for each person
    D. for every adult

17. Choose the word closest in meaning to the underlined word in the sentence.

    Structural failure resulted from deficient materials.
    A. sufficient
    B. outstanding
    C. inadequate
    D. bizarre

18. INSPECT most nearly means:
    A. disregard
    B. look at
    C. annoy
    D. criticize

19. Choose the word opposite in meaning to the underlined word in the sentence.

    Participation is optional but recommended.
    A. mandatory
    B. infrequent
    C. choosy
    D. for sale

20. IMPLIED most nearly means:
    A. acknowledged
    B. stated
    C. predicted
    D. hinted

exercises

EXERCISE 2

Directions: Select the correct synonym or antonym in the following items.

1. PRESUMABLY most nearly means:
   A. positively
   B. helplessly
   C. recklessly
   D. supposedly

2. TEXTILE most nearly means:
   A. linen
   B. cloth
   C. page
   D. garment

3. FISCAL most nearly means:
   A. critical
   B. basic
   C. personal
   D. financial

4. STRINGENT most nearly means:
   A. demanding
   B. loud
   C. flexible
   D. clear

5. PROCEED most nearly means:
   A. go forward
   B. parade
   C. refrain
   D. come before

6. BROCHURE most nearly means:
   A. ornament
   B. flowery statement
   C. breakage
   D. pamphlet

7. PERMEABLE most nearly means:
   A. penetrable
   B. durable
   C. unending
   D. allowable

8. LIMIT most nearly means:
   A. budget
   B. sky
   C. point
   D. boundary

9. Choose the word closest in meaning to the underlined word in the sentence.

   She was admired for her scrupulous attention to detail.
   A. conscientious
   B. unprincipled
   C. intricate
   D. neurotic

10. STALEMATE most nearly means:
    A. pillar
    B. deadlock
    C. maneuver
    D. work slowdown

11. Choose the word closest in meaning to the underlined word in the sentence.

    The defendant was declared competent for trial.
    A. inept
    B. informed
    C. capable
    D. caring

12. SOMATIC most nearly means:
    A. painful
    B. drowsy
    C. indefinite
    D. physical

13. OBSTACLE most nearly means:
    A. imprisonment
    B. hindrance
    C. retaining wall
    D. leap

14. REDUNDANT most nearly means:
    A. concise
    B. reappearing
    C. superfluous
    D. lying down

15. SUPPLANT most nearly means:
    A. prune
    B. conquer
    C. uproot
    D. replace

16. Choose the word closest in meaning to the underlined word in the sentence.

    The clerk's <u>haphazard</u> filing system was impossible to decipher.
    A. devious
    B. without order
    C. aberrant
    D. risky

17. COMMENSURATE most nearly means:
    A. identical
    B. of the same age
    C. proportionate
    D. measurable

18. Choose the word opposite in meaning to the underlined word in the sentence.

    The executives explored ways to <u>accelerate</u> the company's financial growth.
    A. drive fast
    B. reroute
    C. speed up
    D. hinder

19. PURCHASED most nearly means:
    A. charged
    B. bought
    C. ordered
    D. supplied

20. ZENITH most nearly means:
    A. depths
    B. astronomical system
    C. peak
    D. solar system

exercises

ANSWER KEYS AND EXPLANATIONS

Exercise 1

1. C	5. C	9. C	13. A	17. C
2. B	6. B	10. C	14. B	18. B
3. D	7. C	11. B	15. D	19. A
4. A	8. B	12. D	16. C	20. D

1. **The correct answer is C.** *Retain* means "to continue to possess, control, or utilize." *Keep* is the word closest in meaning.

2. **The correct answer is B.** *Endorse* means "to advocate or promote the cause of." The phrase "announce support for" is closest in meaning.

3. **The correct answer is D.** *Intractable* describes one who is resistant to authority or control by another. *Unruly* is closest in meaning.

4. **The correct answer is A.** One definition of *correspondence* is communication carried through the postal system. *Letters* is closest in meaning.

5. **The correct answer is C.** *Obliterate* means "to destroy entirely; annihilate." The word most nearly opposite is *construct*.

6. **The correct answer is B.** *Legitimate* means "permitted by law." *Legal* is the word closest in meaning.

7. **The correct answer is C.** *Deduct* means "to take away or subtract." The word most nearly opposite is *increase*.

8. **The correct answer is B.** *Mutilate* means "to cause permanent or severe or injury." *Damage* is the word closest in meaning.

9. **The correct answer is C.** An egress a is means of getting out; *exit* is the word closest in meaning.

10. **The correct answer is C.** If something is horizontal, it is positioned parallel to the horizon, so it can also best be described in terms of "left and right."

11. **The correct answer is B.** A controversy is an (often contentious) expression of different opinions. The word closest in meaning is *debate*.

12. **The correct answer is D.** *Preempt* is to take or use without the right or authority to do so. *Appropriate* (the verb, not the adjective) is the word closest in meaning.

13. **The correct answer is A.** A category is a division within a system of classification. *Class* is the word closest in meaning.

14. **The correct answer is B.** *Apathy* is a lack of concern or interest. *Indifference* is the word closest in meaning.

15. **The correct answer is D.** *Tentative* relates to something that is not developed or completely worked out. Something that is tentative can be provisional, as its result may be contingent upon another factor. *Provisional* is the word closest in meaning.

16. **The correct answer is C.** *Per capita* means "equally to each individual"; the phrase *for each person* is the word closest in meaning.

17. **The correct answer is C.** *Deficient* means "lacking in quality or in a necessary element." *Inadequate* is the word closest in meaning.

18. **The correct answer is B.** *Inspect* means "to view closely or inspect." *Look at* is the word closest in meaning.

19. **The correct answer is A.** *Optional* means "not mandatory."

20. **The correct answer is D.** *Implied* means "to have expressed indirectly." *Hinted* is the word closest in meaning.

answers exercises

Exercise 2

1. D	**5.** A	**9.** A	**13.** B	**17.** C
2. B	**6.** D	**10.** B	**14.** C	**18.** D
3. D	**7.** A	**11.** C	**15.** D	**19.** B
4. A	**8.** D	**12.** D	**16.** B	**20.** C

1. **The correct answer is D.** *Presumably* means "likely, or that which can be reasonably assumed." *Supposedly* is the word closest in meaning.

2. **The correct answer is B.** *Textile* refers to fabric or the fibers that are woven to make fabric. Linen is a type of textile, and textiles are used to make a garment. A page may be part of a text. *Cloth* is the word closest in meaning here.

3. **The correct answer is D.** *Fiscal* refers to financial matters. *Financial* is the word closest in meaning.

4. **The correct answer is A.** One definition of *stringent* is "characterized by strictness or severity, especially in terms of rules or standards." *Demanding* is the word closest in meaning.

5. **The correct answer is A.** *Proceed* means "to move along or advance." *Go forward* is the phrase closet in meaning.

6. **The correct answer is D.** A brochure is a booklet or pamphlet.

7. **The correct answer is A.** *Permeable* means "capable of being penetrated," so *penetrable* is the word closest in meaning.

8. **The correct answer is D.** A limit is something that confines, restricts, or restrains. *Boundary* is the word closest in meaning.

9. **The correct answer is A.** *Scrupulous* refers to acting with integrity toward what is considered proper or correct. *Conscientious* is the word closest in meaning.

10. **The correct answer is B.** A stalemate is a situation in which there is no winner; a draw. *Deadlock* is the word closest in meaning.

11. **The correct answer is C.** *Competent* means "fit, qualified, or having adequate ability." *Capable* is the word closest in meaning.

12. **The correct answer is D.** *Somatic* relates to something that affects the body. *Physical* is the word closest in meaning.

13. **The correct answer is B.** An obstacle impedes progress. *Hindrance* is the word closest in meaning.

14. **The correct answer is C.** *Redundant* means "in excess of what is needed." *Superfluous* is the word closest in meaning.

15. **The correct answer is D.** *Supplant* means "to take the place of." *Replace* is the word closest in meaning.

16. **The correct answer is B.** *Haphazard* means "disorderly; without plan or direction." The phrase closest in meaning is "without order."

17. **The correct answer is C.** *Commensurate* means corresponding in amount, degree, or extent. *Proportionate* is the word closest in meaning.

18. **The correct answer is D.** In this context, *accelerate* means to speed up progress or development; the word most nearly opposite is *hinder*.

19. **The correct answer is B.** *Purchased* means "bought."

20. **The correct answer is C.** *Zenith* refers to the highest point, either in astronomical terms, or as it relates to accomplishments. *Peak* is the word closest in meaning.

SUMMING IT UP

- The civil service exam will present questions about synonyms, which are two words that have the same or similar meanings. In these questions, you must choose the answer choice that most closely matches the given word. Remember that you are looking for the best match, not necessarily a perfect match.

- You may also encounter antonym questions on your exam: words with opposite or nearly opposite meanings. The strategy for tackling antonym questions is much like that of answering synonym questions—but keep in mind that you are looking for the opposite in meaning rather than the closest match, so read the directions very carefully.

- Take the following steps to successfully choose the correct answers to synonym questions:

    1. Read the question carefully.

    2. Eliminate any answer choices that you know for certain are incorrect.

    3. Select the remaining answer choice that most nearly means the same as the given word.

Sentence Completions

OVERVIEW

- **What Are Sentence Completions?**
- **Strategies for Answering Sentence Completion Questions**
- **Exercise**
- **Answer Key and Explanations**
- **Summing It Up**

WHAT ARE SENTENCE COMPLETIONS?

In a sentence completion question, you are given a sentence or long passage in which a portion has been omitted, indicated by a blank. A number of words or phrases are suggested to fill that blank. You must select the word or phrase that will best complete the meaning of the passage as a whole. Although more than one answer may make sense, the best choice will be the one that is most exact, appropriate, or likely, considering the information given in the sentence or passage.

STRATEGIES FOR ANSWERING SENTENCE COMPLETION QUESTIONS

Follow these four steps to answer a sentence completion question:

1. Read the question carefully and review all of the answer choices.
2. Eliminate any answer choices that are obviously incorrect.
3. Of the remaining choices, select the one that best completes the meaning of the sentence or passage given.
4. Double-check your answer by reading the sentence or passage again.

The following example shows you how to follow these steps in answering a sentence completion question:

Trespassing on private property is _____ by law.

- **A.** proscribed
- **B.** warranted
- **C.** prescribed
- **D.** eliminated

First, eliminate any choices that are obviously wrong. *Warranted* (choice B) may remind you of a warrant for arrest, which might be the result of trespassing; *warranted*, however, means "justified," which would make the given sentence obviously untrue. *Prescribed* (choice C) means "recommended"; like *warranted*, it makes no sense in the given sentence.

Now, select the best answer from the remaining choices and insert it into the blank to be sure that it makes sense in the given sentence. *Eliminated* (choice D) is a likely choice, but it doesn't fit the sentence; the law may be intended to eliminate trespassing, but it can never be completely successful in doing so. This leaves *proscribed* (choice A), which means "forbidden, especially by law," as the best answer choice. **The correct answer is A.**

Let's apply the four steps to another example.

Despite the harsh tone of her comments, she did not mean to _____ any criticism of you personally.

A. infer

B. aim

C. comply

D. imply

You can eliminate *comply* (choice C), which means "to obey," because it makes no sense in the context. *Aim* (choice B) is more likely, but it doesn't work in the sentence as given. You might say, "She did not mean to aim any criticism *at* you," but you would not normally say, "She did not mean to aim any criticism *of* you."

Be careful of *infer* (choice A); this word is often confused with *imply*. *Infer* means "conclude from reasoning or implication." A speaker implies, whereas a listener infers.

In this example, the word *imply*, meaning "to suggest indirectly," is the best fit. To double-check your answer, read the sentence again. "Despite the harsh tone of her comments, she did not mean to *imply* any criticism of you personally." **The correct answer is D.**

Sentence completion questions often contain words that act as clues to help you determine the missing word:

- **Contrast words** tell you that the missing word should contrast with another idea stated in the sentence: *although, despite, though, but, however, rather than, not, yet, instead of.*

- **Support words** tell you that the missing word is supported by another part of the sentence: *and, for, furthermore, also, because, so.*

- **Summary words** tell you that the missing word summarizes an idea already stated in the sentence: *as a result, finally, in conclusion, on the whole.*

- **Cause-and-effect words** tell you that the missing word is an effect of a cause stated in the sentence, or vice versa: *consequently, so that, thus, since, if, therefore, accordingly.*

TIP

Watch out for words that look alike but have different meanings, such as *proscribed* and *prescribed* in the first example. Read each answer choice carefully so that you will not fall for this trap.

Let's examine the following question:

The department's _____ does not allow for unlimited copying by all the instructors in the program. Each instructor can be reimbursed for copying expenses only up to ten dollars.

A. paperwork

B. staff

C. organization

D. budget

The correct answer is D. The concern here is with money. A budget puts limits on spending. *Paperwork* (choice A) and *staff* (choice B) are not appropriate to the meaning of the passage. *Organization* (choice C) is barely possible, but only because it is so vague. *Budget* both makes sense and is much more specific.

Let's tackle one more example question:

If the company offered a settlement commensurate with the damages sustained, the couple would _____ their right to a hearing.

A. cancel

B. ensue

C. waive

D. assert

The correct answer is C. *Waive* means "forego" or "give up." One *waives* something to which one is entitled, such as a right. *Cancel* (choice A) is similar in meaning but is not used in this way. One can cancel a hearing, but not a right. *Ensue* (choice B) may mislead you by its similarity to *sue*. The sentence does imply that the couple is suing or planning to sue the company for damages of some sort. However, *ensue* simply means "to follow as a result" and it makes no sense in this context. *Assert* (choice D) means the opposite of *waive*. One can *assert* a right, but the meaning of the first part of the sentence makes this choice unlikely.

TIP

If you are having trouble finding the correct answer, look for clues in the overall subject of the sentence. In the third example, the sentence is primarily about money, so you can assume that the answer is a word that relates to money—*budget*.

EXERCISE

Directions: Each of the following sentences or passages contains a blank. Select the word or phrase that will best complete the meaning of the sentence or passage as a whole.

1. He was the chief _____ of his uncle's will. After taxes, he was left with an inheritance worth close to $20,000.
   A. exemption
   B. pensioner
   C. beneficiary
   D. contestant

2. In view of the extenuating circumstances and the defendant's youth, the judge recommended _____.
   A. conviction
   B. a defense
   C. a mistrial
   D. leniency

3. The basic concept of civil service is that where a public job exists, all those who possess the _____ shall have an opportunity to compete for it.
   A. potential
   B. contacts
   C. qualifications
   D. credits

4. They would prefer to hire someone fluent in Spanish since the neighborhood in which the clinic is located is _____ Hispanic.
   A. imponderably
   B. sparsely
   C. consistently
   D. predominantly

5. The lover of democracy has an _____ toward totalitarianism.
   A. antipathy
   B. attitude
   C. empathy
   D. idolatry

6. The candidate's _____ was carefully planned; she traveled to six cities and spoke at nine rallies.
   A. pogrom
   B. itinerary
   C. adjournment
   D. apparition

7. _____ recommendations are generally more constructive than vague complaints or blanket praise.
   A. Justified
   B. Nebulous
   C. Sweeping
   D. Specific

8. In the face of an uncooperative Congress, the Chief Executive may find himself _____ to accomplish the political program to which he is committed.
   A. impotent
   B. equipped
   C. neutral
   D. contingent

9. The authorities declared an _____ on incoming freight because of the trucking strike.

   A. impression
   B. immolation
   C. embargo
   D. opprobrium

10. The information we have available on that question is _____. The form, scope, and reliability of the documents vary tremendously, so it is difficult to determine its validity.

    A. essential
    B. lacking
    C. questionable
    D. minimal

11. The _____ on the letter indicated that it had been mailed in Minnesota three weeks previously.

    A. address
    B. stamp
    C. postmark
    D. envelope

12. The television ads _____ an unprecedented public response. Sales skyrocketed and within a few months the brand name had become a household word.

    A. boosted
    B. promised
    C. elicited
    D. favored

13. The chairman submitted a _____ for the new equipment, but it will not be delivered for two weeks.

    A. requisition
    B. reason
    C. proposal
    D. plea

14. With all his courtroom experience, the attorney was able to pry very little information out of the _____ witness.

    A. cooperative
    B. recalcitrant
    C. reactionary
    D. testifying

15. Although for years substantial resources had been devoted to alleviating the problem, a satisfactory solution remained _____.

    A. costly
    B. probable
    C. elusive
    D. esoteric

16. The local police department will not accept for _____ a report of a person missing from his residence if such residence is located outside of the city.

    A. foreclosure
    B. convenience
    C. investigation
    D. control

17. The consumer group is optimistic about the _____ of the new regulations on the industry's safety standards.

    A. incision
    B. effect
    C. affectation
    D. input

18. The mayor sent a letter _____ our invitation and commending us on our work; she regrets that she will be unable to attend the opening ceremonies due to a prior commitment.

    A. rebuffing
    B. reconsidering
    C. returning
    D. acknowledging

exercise

19. His wealth of practical experience and his psychological acuity more than _____ his lack of formal academic training.
    A. concede to
    B. comprise
    C. compensate for
    D. educate for

20. Suffering from hay fever, he was _____ to spend his time indoors.
    A. coerced
    B. forced
    C. strengthened
    D. pushed

21. The treaty cannot go into _____ until it has been ratified by the Senate.
    A. distribution
    B. limit
    C. effect
    D. check

22. You will have to speak to the head of the agency; I am not _____ to give out that information.
    A. willing
    B. authorized
    C. programmed
    D. happy

23. When new individuals have proved their capability and reliability, they ought to achieve journeyman status in the company _____.
    A. intrinsically
    B. permanently
    C. automatically
    D. decisively

24. The object may be _____, but the plan as presented is far from practicable.
    A. compensatory
    B. laudable
    C. precarious
    D. subversive

25. You must _____ a copy of your latest federal income tax return before your loan application can be considered.
    A. surrender
    B. replicate
    C. supplement
    D. submit

ANSWER KEY AND EXPLANATIONS

1. C	6. B	11. C	16. C	21. C
2. D	7. D	12. C	17. B	22. B
3. C	8. A	13. A	18. D	23. C
4. D	9. C	14. B	19. C	24. B
5. A	10. C	15. C	20. B	25. D

1. **The correct answer is C.** Because the subject received a benefit from his uncle's will, *beneficiary* fits the sentence best.

2. **The correct answer is D.** The words *extenuating circumstances* and *youth* should tip you off that the judge will be merciful, or recommend leniency.

3. **The correct answer is C.** As you learned earlier in this book, you must have the *qualifications* for the job.

4. **The correct answer is D.** The cause-and-effect clue *since* tells you that the second part of the sentence is the cause of the first part. If the neighborhood is mostly or *predominantly* Hispanic, then clinic workers would preferably need to be fluent in Spanish.

5. **The correct answer is A.** Totalitarianism is the opposite of democracy, so someone who loves democracy would naturally feel *antipathy*, or a strong feeling of "distaste," toward totalitarianism.

6. **The correct answer is B.** The words *planned* and *traveled* suggest that the best answer is *itinerary*, which means "a planned route on a journey."

7. **The correct answer is D.** The word *than* contrasts the last part of the sentence with the first part; therefore, you should choose an answer that means the opposite of vague—*specific.*

8. **The correct answer is A.** In this case, *impotent* means "powerless"; if Congress is uncooperative, the President is probably powerless.

9. **The correct answer is C.** The words *because of* are a cause-and-effect clue. If truckers are on strike, then there is no one to bring in the freight, so there must be an embargo, or prohibition, of it.

10. **The correct answer is C.** If it is difficult to determine the validity of the documents, then the word *questionable* is the best answer.

11. **The correct answer is C.** A *postmark* indicates when and where a letter was mailed.

12. **The correct answer is C.** *Elicited* means "brought out" or "provoked"; the ads brought out an unprecedented response, as indicated by the following sentence.

13. **The correct answer is A.** In a business context, the correct term is *requisition*, meaning "a formal request for."

14. **The correct answer is B.** Since the witness gave very little information, he is obviously recalcitrant, or stubbornly resistant to authority.

15. **The correct answer is C.** The word *although* contrasts the two parts of the sentence; therefore, the best answer is *elusive*—the solution to the problem evaded all the attempts to find it.

16. **The correct answer is C.** Since the sentence is about the police, *investigation* is the best choice.

17. **The correct answer is B.** The best choice is *effect*, meaning "result." Be careful of *affectation*, which looks like *effect* but actually means "artificial behavior designed to impress others."

18. **The correct answer is D.** The mayor did acknowledge the invitation by sending the letter. Since she politely declined, she did not rebuff, return, or reconsider the invitation.

19. **The correct answer is C.** The phrase *compensate for*, meaning "make up for," best fits the sentence.

20. **The correct answer is B.** A person who has hay fever may be *forced* to stay indoors to reduce their symptoms. *Coerced* (choice A) is not the best fit in this context, as typically this word has a negative connotation involving another person compelling or threatening compliance.

21. **The correct answer is C.** Once the Senate ratifies a treaty, it goes into *effect*, making choice C the best answer. *Distribution* might seem like a good answer, but is not the best choice.

22. **The correct answer is B.** The word *authorized*, meaning "permitted" or "allowed," is the best choice to fill in the blank. The speaker may be *willing* (choice A) or *happy* (choice D) to give out the information but not allowed to by the head of the agency, making these answer choices not the best fit. The word *programmed* (choice C) does not make sense and is therefore incorrect.

23. **The correct answer is C.** The word *when* implies that the second part of the sentence should happen as soon as the first part occurs. In other words, it should happen *automatically*.

24. **The correct answer is B.** The word *but* contrasts the first part of the sentence with the second part; the best fit is *laudable*, or "deserving praise."

25. **The correct answer is D.** *Submit*, or "give," best fits the meaning of the sentence.

SUMMING IT UP

- In a sentence completion question, you are presented with a sentence or passage in which some part has been left blank. Your answer choices consist of several words or phrases that may fit grammatically in the blank, and you are to choose the word or phrase that best completes the meaning of the sentence or passage as a whole.

- Follow these steps to successfully choose the correct answers to sentence completion questions:

  o Read the question carefully and review all the answer choices.

  o Eliminate any answer choices that are obviously incorrect.

  o Select the remaining answer choice that best completes the meaning of the sentence or passage given, even if it is unfamiliar to you.

  o Double-check your answer by reading the sentence or passage again, putting your answer in the blank.

- Be on the lookout for words that look alike but have different meanings. Read each answer choice carefully so that you will not fall into this common trap.

Verbal Analogies

Chapter 8

OVERVIEW

- **What are Verbal Analogy Questions?**
- **Strategies for Answering Verbal Analogy Questions**
- **Exercise 1**
- **Exercise 2**
- **Answer Keys and Explanations**
- **Summing It Up**

WHAT ARE VERBAL ANALOGY QUESTIONS?

A verbal analogy question is made up of four terms in two pairs. You are given the first complete pair, which establishes the relationship. You must then choose a pair of words whose relationship is most similar to the relationship in the given pair.

One type of verbal analogy question presents the first pair of words and the first half of the second pair, followed by a list of possible matches. This type of question looks like this:

CLOCK is to TIME as THERMOMETER is to

The four answer choices are all single words. You must choose the one word that completes a relationship with *thermometer* that is analogous to the relationship between *clock* and *time*.

Or you may just be given the first pair of words, and then a selection of paired terms from which you must find the one that implies the same relationship as the given pair. This type of question looks like this:

CLOCK : TIME ::

The four answer choices are all pairs of words. You must choose the pair that has a relationship analogous to that between *clock* and *time*.

STRATEGIES FOR ANSWERING VERBAL ANALOGY QUESTIONS

To answer verbal analogy questions, look at the given pair of words and decide what the relationship between the words is. Then choose the answer that has the most similar relationship to the given pair of words. Follow these four steps:

1. Read each question carefully.

2. Establish the relationship between the terms in the given pair.

3. Study the selection of possible answers carefully and eliminate any that do not share the same relationship as the given pair.

4. Read the remaining choices through again, this time substituting the key relationship word from the sample pair (CLOCK measures TIME, THERMOMETER measures TEMPERATURE).

Try this question:

SPEEDOMETER is to POINTER as WATCH is to

A. case.

B. hands.

C. dial.

D. numerals.

The correct answer is B. First consider what a *pointer* is used for on a *speedometer*. It indicates speed at a particular moment. A watch uses *hands* (choice B) for the same general function, that is, to indicate something at a particular moment. In this case, the hands indicate time. *Case* (choice A) is incorrect because the watch case has nothing to do with this function. *Dial* and *numerals* (choices C and D) are incorrect because although the dial and the numbers have to do with indicating time, they don't perform the specific function of indicating something at any one particular moment.

Try another sample question:

WINTER is to SUMMER as COLD is to

A. wet.

B. future.

C. warm.

D. freezing.

The correct answer is C. *Winter* and *summer* are opposites, so you should look for an answer choice that means the opposite of cold. *Warm* is the opposite of *cold*.

Now, try the other verbal analogy question type:

SPELLING : PUNCTUATION ::

A. pajamas : fatigue

B. powder : shaving

C. bandage : cut

D. biology : physics

The correct answer is D. Spelling and punctuation are parts of the mechanics of English. Biology and physics are parts of the field of science. Therefore, the pair of words with the most analogous relationship to the given pair is answer choice D. In this type of question, it may help to substitute the colons for words when you read it in your head. For example, read it as, "Spelling is to punctuation as _____ is to _____."

TIP

Remember to choose the correct answer because it is an analogous relationship, not because it relates to the same subject as the given pair of words.

EXERCISE 1

Directions: In each question, the first two words have a certain relationship to each other. Select the answer choice that will create a relationship with the third word similar to that of the given pair.

1. ORATION is to CHAT as BANQUET is to
   A. festival.
   B. party.
   C. wedding.
   D. snack.

2. INCLEMENT is to CLEAR as PERTINENT is to
   A. pert.
   B. cloudy.
   C. irrelevant.
   D. perceptive.

3. WHEAT is to FLOUR as GRAPE is to
   A. vintage.
   B. vine.
   C. wine.
   D. fruit.

4. COMMON is to IRON as RARE is to
   A. steak.
   B. crowd.
   C. humor.
   D. diamond.

5. VICTORY is to CONTEST as KNOWLEDGE is to
   A. professor.
   B. test.
   C. degree.
   D. study.

6. DIAGNOSIS is to ANALYSIS as THESIS is to
   A. antithesis.
   B. research.
   C. paper.
   D. college.

7. MARE is to FILLY as KING is to
   A. throne.
   B. prince.
   C. queen.
   D. kingdom.

8. ARMY is to RECRUIT as RELIGION is to
   A. priest.
   B. worshipper.
   C. convert.
   D. acolyte.

9. OPULENCE is to LUXURY as POVERTY is to
   A. penury.
   B. misery.
   C. charity.
   D. hunger.

10. WILL is to CODICIL as CONSTITUTION is to
    A. preamble.
    B. amendment.
    C. law.
    D. independence.

EXERCISE 2

Directions: In each question, the two capitalized words have a certain relationship to each other. Select the pair of words that are related in the same way as the two capitalized words.

1. INTIMIDATE : FEAR ::
   A. maintain : satisfaction
   B. astonish : wonder
   C. soothe : concern
   D. feed : hunger

2. STOVE : KITCHEN ::
   A. window : bedroom
   B. sink : bathroom
   C. television : living room
   D. trunk : attic

3. CELEBRATE : MARRIAGE ::
   A. announce : birthday
   B. report : injury
   C. lament : bereavement
   D. face : penalty

4. MARGARINE : BUTTER ::
   A. cream : milk
   B. lace : cotton
   C. nylon : silk
   D. egg : chicken

5. NEGLIGENT : REQUIREMENT ::
   A. careful : position
   B. remiss : duty
   C. cautious : injury
   D. cogent : task

6. GAZELLE : SWIFT ::
   A. horse : slow
   B. wolf : hungry
   C. swan : graceful
   D. elephant : gray

7. IGNOMINY : DISLOYALTY ::
   A. fame : heroism
   B. castigation : praise
   C. death : victory
   D. approbation : consecration

8. SATURNINE : MERCURIAL ::
   A. Saturn : Venus
   B. Apennines : Alps
   C. redundant : wordy
   D. crucial : trivial

9. ORANGES : MARMALADE ::
   A. potatoes : vegetable
   B. jelly : jam
   C. tomatoes : ketchup
   D. cake : picnic

10. BANISH : APOSTATE ::
    A. reward : traitor
    B. welcome : ally
    C. remove : result
    D. avoid : truce

11. CIRCLE : SPHERE ::
    A. square : cube
    B. balloon : jet plane
    C. heaven : hell
    D. wheel : orange

12. OPEN : SECRETIVE ::
    A. mystery : detective
    B. tunnel : toll
    C. forthright : dishonest
    D. better : best

13. AFFIRM : HINT ::

    A. say : deny

    B. assert : convince

    C. confirm : reject

    D. charge : insinuate

14. THROW : BALL ::

    A. kill : bullet

    B. shoot : gun

    C. question : answer

    D. hit : run

15. SPEEDY : GREYHOUND ::

    A. innocent : lamb

    B. animate : animal

    C. voracious : tiger

    D. sluggish : sloth

16. TRIANGLE : PYRAMID ::

    A. cone : circle

    B. corner : angle

    C. square : cube

    D. pentagon : quadrilateral

17. IMPEACH : DISMISS ::

    A. arraign : convict

    B. exonerate : charge

    C. imprison : jail

    D. plant : reap

18. EMULATE : MIMIC ::

    A. slander : defame

    B. praise : flatter

    C. aggravate : promote

    D. complain : condemn

19. HAND : NAIL ::

    A. paw : claw

    B. foot : toe

    C. head : hair

    D. ear : nose

20. SQUARE : DIAMOND ::

    A. cube : sugar

    B. circle : ellipse

    C. innocence : jewelry

    D. pentangle : square

ANSWER KEYS AND EXPLANATIONS

Exercise 1

1. D	3. C	5. D	7. B	9. A
2. C	4. D	6. B	8. C	10. B

1. **The correct answer is D.** An oration is a far more elaborate form of speech than a chat; a banquet is a far more elaborate form of meal than a snack.

2. **The correct answer is C.** *Inclement* is the opposite of *clear*; *pertinent* is the opposite of *irrelevant*.

3. **The correct answer is C.** Flour comes from wheat; wine comes from grapes.

4. **The correct answer is D.** A characteristic of iron is that it is common; a characteristic of a diamond is that it is rare.

5. **The correct answer is D.** A contest results in victory; study results in knowledge.

6. **The correct answer is B.** Diagnosis comes after careful analysis; a thesis comes after thorough research.

7. **The correct answer is B.** The mare is a parent of a filly; the king is a parent of a prince.

8. **The correct answer is C.** A recruit is new to the army; a convert is new to a religion.

9. **The correct answer is A.** Opulence is the same as luxury; poverty is the same as penury.

10. **The correct answer is B.** The purpose of a codicil is to change a will; the purpose of an amendment is to change a constitution.

Exercise 2

1. B	5. B	9. C	13. D	17. A
2. B	6. C	10. B	14. B	18. B
3. C	7. A	11. D	15. D	19. A
4. C	8. D	12. C	16. C	20. B

1. **The correct answer is B.** To intimidate is to inspire fear; to astonish is to inspire wonder.

2. **The correct answer is B.** A stove is often part of a kitchen; a sink is often part of a bathroom.

3. **The correct answer is C.** You happily celebrate a marriage; you sorrowfully lament a bereavement.

4. **The correct answer is C.** Margarine is a manufactured substitute for butter; nylon is a manufactured substitute for silk.

5. **The correct answer is B.** A person may be negligent in meeting a requirement; he may similarly be remiss in performing his duty.

6. **The correct answer is C.** A gazelle is known to be swift; a swan is known to be graceful.

7. **The correct answer is A.** One falls into ignominy if one shows disloyalty; one gains fame if one shows heroism.

8. **The correct answer is D.** Saturnine and mercurial are antonyms; so are crucial and trivial.

9. **The correct answer is C.** Marmalade is made from oranges; ketchup is made from tomatoes.

10. **The correct answer is B.** An apostate is banished; an ally is welcomed.

11. **The correct answer is D.** All four—circle, sphere, wheel, and orange—are round.

12. **The correct answer is C.** *Open* is the opposite of *secretive*; *forthright* is the opposite of *dishonest*.

13. **The correct answer is D.** When you affirm, you are direct; when you hint, you are indirect. When you charge, you are direct; when you insinuate, you are indirect.

14. **The correct answer is B.** One throws a ball; one shoots a gun.

15. **The correct answer is D.** A greyhound is proverbially speedy; a sloth is proverbially sluggish.

16. **The correct answer is C.** A triangle (a two-dimensional figure) is the lateral face of a pyramid (a three-dimensional figure); and a square (a two-dimensional figure) is the lateral face of a cube (a three-dimensional figure).

17. **The correct answer is A.** To impeach is to charge or challenge; if the impeachment proceedings are successful, the charged person is dismissed. To arraign is to call into court as a result of accusation; if the accusation is proven, the arraigned person is convicted.

18. **The correct answer is B.** To emulate is to imitate another person's good points; to mimic is to imitate another person. To praise is to speak well of another person; to flatter is to praise another person.

19. **The correct answer is A.** For people, the thin substance at the end of a hand is called a nail; for animals, the horny sheath at the end of a paw is called a claw.

20. **The correct answer is B.** A diamond is a partially compressed square; an ellipse is a partially compressed circle.

answers exercises

SUMMING IT UP

- A verbal analogy question presents four terms in two pairs. The first pair presents a relationship between the words; you are to choose a pair of words whose relationship is most similar to the relationship presented in the given pair. There are two types of verbal analogy question types you may encounter:

    1. The question presents a pair of words and the first half of a second pair, and then asks you to choose the word that completes a relationship that is analogous to the relationship between the first pair.

    2. The question presents a pair of words and then a selection of paired terms as answer choices. You are to choose the set that most nearly matches the relationship between the presented pair.

- Follow these steps to answer verbal analogy questions successfully:

    1. Read each question carefully.

    2. Establish the relationship between the terms in the given pair.

    3. Study the answer choices carefully and eliminate any that you know are incorrect.

    4. Read the remaining choices again, substituting the key relationship word from the sample pair.

Effective Expression

OVERVIEW

- **What Is Being Tested?**
- **Strategies for Answering Effective Expression Questions**
- **Exercise**
- **Answer Key and Explanations**
- **Summing It Up**

WHAT IS BEING TESTED?

Effective expression questions test the entire range of grammatical skills, including knowledge of correct grammar, spelling, word usage, and sentence formation. They also test reading comprehension and writing skills. Everything that you have learned so far will come into play when answering these questions. Even if you do not find effective expression questions on your civil service exam, studying the questions in this chapter will be a great help in preparing for the entire verbal ability portion of your exam.

Before answering any of the practice questions, it will be helpful to turn back to Chapter 4 and review the rules of grammar. If you have time, quickly review the spelling rules listed in Chapter 5 as well.

STRATEGIES FOR ANSWERING EFFECTIVE EXPRESSION QUESTIONS

In the effective expression portion of the exam, you are presented with a long passage. Some portions of the passage are underlined and numbered. Corresponding to each numbered portion are three options to improve or correct the portion and choice A, which is always "NO CHANGE." You must choose the answer that is the best way to phrase the expression, which may be to leave it as it is stated.

Follow these four steps to answer an effective expression question:

1. Read through the passage quickly to determine the sense of the passage.
2. Return to the first underlined portion.
3. Choose the best answer from the following criteria:
   - If you feel that there is an error in grammar, sentence structure, punctuation, or word usage in the underlined portion, mark the correct choice from the answers given.

o If the underlined portion appears to be correct, but you believe that one of the alternatives would be more effective, mark that choice.

o If you feel that the underlined portion is the correct and most effective choice, mark answer choice **A.** NO CHANGE.

4. After answering quickly and to the best of your knowledge, go on to the next underlined portion.

Try a sample passage and question set:

If a <u>person were to try</u> stripping the disguises from actors while they play a
           1

scene upon the stage, showing to the audience <u>there real looks</u> and the faces
                                                   2

they were <u>born with. Would</u> not such a one spoil the whole play? Destroy the
            3

illusion and <u>any play was ruined.</u>
            4

1. **A.** NO CHANGE
   B. Person were to try
   C. Person was to try
   D. person was to try

2. **A.** NO CHANGE
   B. their real looks
   C. there Real Looks
   D. they're "real looks"

3. **A.** NO CHANGE
   B. born to—would
   C. born. Would
   D. born with, would

4. **A.** NO CHANGE
   B. any play was ruined!
   C. any play is ruined?
   D. any play is ruined.

Compare your selections with the correct answers.

1. **The correct answer is A.** The passage is correct as shown; therefore, NO CHANGE is the best selection. The sentence speculates about what could happen hypothetically, so *were*, the subjunctive mood of the verb *to be*, is used correctly here. There is no need to capitalize the common noun *person*.

2. **The correct answer is B.** Be careful when dealing with words that sound alike but are spelled differently and have entirely different meanings. The possessive plural pronoun needed here is spelled *their*. Using the adverb *there* (choices A and C) or the contraction for "they are" (choice D) is incorrect. Capitalizing or putting the words *real looks* in quotes is unnecessary.

3. **The correct answer is D.** The issue that needs correction is the long sentence fragment that starts the sentence. Adding a comma corrects the issue and allows the fragment to act as a dependent clause, modifying the rest of the sentence. None of the other choices corrects the issue.

4. **The correct answer is D.** The present tense *is* consistent with the present tense *destroy*. Choices A and B incorrectly mix verb tenses; the use of an exclamation point (choice B) does not fit with the tone of the passage. The sentence is not asking a question, so the use of a question mark (choice C) is incorrect.

Remember to look for the best, most effective answer. Even if the underlined portion of the passage is technically correct, it may not be the best way to phrase the expression.

EXERCISE

Directions: In each of the following passages, some portions are underlined and numbered. Corresponding to each numbered portion are three different ways of saying the same thing. If you feel that an underlined portion is correct and is stated as well as possible, mark choice **A.** NO CHANGE. If you feel that there is an error in the underlined portion or if one of the alternatives would be more effective, choose the correct answer.

Passage 1

The standardized educational or psychological <u>tests, that are</u> widely used to aid
                                                        1

in selecting, classifying, assigning, or <u>promoting students</u>, employees, and mil-
                                                  2

itary personnel have been the target of recent attacks in books, magazines, and

<u>newspapers that are printed every day</u>. The target is wrong, for in attacking the
        3

tests, critics <u>revert attention from</u> the fault that <u>lays with illinformed</u> or incom-
                        4   5

petent users. The tests themselves are merely <u>tools; with</u> characteristics that can
                                                        6

be <u>assessed reasonably precise</u> under specified conditions. Whether the results
        7

will be valuable, meaningless, or even misleading <u>are dependent partly upon</u> the
                                                            8

tool itself but largely upon the user.

1. **A.** NO CHANGE
   B. tests that are
   C. tests: which are
   D. tests; which are

2. **A.** NO CHANGE
   B. promoting of students
   C. promotion of students
   D. promotion for students

3. **A.** NO CHANGE
   B. the daily press
   C. newspapers that are published daily
   D. the daily newspaper press

4. **A.** NO CHANGE
   B. revert attention to
   C. divert attention from
   D. avert attention from

5. **A.** NO CHANGE
   B. lies with poorly-informed
   C. lays with poor-informed
   D. lies with ill-informed

6. **A.** NO CHANGE
   B. tools with
   C. tools, possessed of
   D. tools; whose

7. **A.** NO CHANGE
   B. assessed as to its reasonable precision
   C. assessed reasonably and with precision
   D. assessed with reasonable precision

8. **A.** NO CHANGE
   B. is dependent partly upon
   C. depend partly upon
   D. depends partly upon

Passage 2

The forces that generate conditions conducive to crime and riots, are stronger in
<u>   </u>
                                                     9
urban communities then in rural areas. Urban living is more anonymous living, it
        <u>   </u>   <u>   </u>
                 10   11
often releases the individual from community restraints more common in

tradition, oriented societies. But more freedom from constraints and controls
<u>   </u> <u></u>
         12   13
also provides greater freedom to deviate from the law. In the more imperson-

alized, formally, controlled urban society regulatory orders of conduct are
        <u>   </u>
                14
often directed by distant bureaucrats. The police are strangers which execute
                                                             <u>   </u>
                                                                  15
these prescriptions on, at worst, an alien sub-community and, at best, an

anonymous and unknown set of subjects. Minor offenses in a small town or
<u>   </u>
          16
village are often handled without resort to official police action. As disputable
                          <u>   </u>
                               17
as such action may seem to be, you will find it results in fewer recorded viola-
                            <u>   </u>
                                  18
tions of the law compared to the city.

9. **A.** NO CHANGE
   B. rioting, are stronger
   C. riots are more strong
   D. riots are stronger

10. **A.** NO CHANGE
    B. then in rural communities
    C. than in rural areas
    D. then they are in the country

11. **A.** NO CHANGE
    B. living. It
    C. living; which
    D. living. Because it

12. **A.** NO CHANGE
    B. traditional oriented societies
    C. traditionally, oriented societies
    D. tradition-oriented societies

13. **A.** NO CHANGE
    B. Moreover
    C. Therefore
    D. Besides

14. **A.** NO CHANGE
    B. formally controlled
    C. formalized controlled
    D. formally-controlled

15. **A.** NO CHANGE
    B. they execute
    C. executing
    D. who conduct executions of

16. **A.** NO CHANGE
    B. anonymously unknown
    C. anonymous
    D. anonymous, unknown

17. **A.** NO CHANGE
    B. without their having to resort to
    C. without
    D. outside the limits of

18. **A.** NO CHANGE
    B. they say it results
    C. you will say, "It results
    D. it nonetheless results

Passage 3

Human beings are born with a desire to <u>communicate with</u> other human
                                                        19

<u>beings, they</u> satisfy this desire in many ways. A smile communicates
        20

<u>a friendly feeling</u>, a clenched <u>fist anger</u>; tears, sorrow. From the first days
        21   22

of life, <u>pain and hunger are expressed by baby's</u> by cries and actions. Gradually
                                        23

they add expressions of pleasure and <u>smiling</u> for a familiar face. Soon they
                                        24

begin to reach out <u>for picking up</u>. <u>Those people who are human beings</u> also use
                        25   26

words to communicate. Babies eventually learn the language of <u>there</u>
                                                            27

parents. If the parents speak English, the baby will learn to speak English.

If the parents speak Spanish, <u>a Spanish-speaking baby will result</u>. An
                                                    28

<u>American baby</u> who is taken from his natural parents and brought up by foster
        29

parents who speak Chinese, Urdu, Swahili, or any other language <u>will talk</u> the
                                                            30

language of the people around him instead of English.

19. **A.** NO CHANGE
    B. communicate to
    C. communicate about
    D. communicate

20. **A.** NO CHANGE
    B. beings. They
    C. beings; and they
    D. beings—who

21. **A.** NO CHANGE
    B. a friendly, feeling;
    C. friendship,
    D. a friendly feeling;

22. **A.** NO CHANGE
    B. fist an angry feeling,
    C. fist, anger;
    D. fist, angriness,

23. **A.** NO CHANGE
    B. babies express pain or hunger
    C. a baby's pain or hunger are expressed
    D. pain and hunger is expressed by babies

24. **A.** NO CHANGE
    B. smiled
    C. smiles
    D. he may smile

25. **A.** NO CHANGE
    B. to pick up
    C. and pick up
    D. to be picked up

26. **A.** NO CHANGE
    B. (BEGIN new paragraph) Those people who are human beings
    C. (BEGIN new paragraph) Human being babies
    D. (BEGIN new paragraph) Human beings

27. **A.** NO CHANGE
    B. their
    C. they're
    D. OMIT

28. **A.** NO CHANGE
    B. their baby will speak Spanish.
    C. the baby will learn spanish.
    D. there baby will speak Spanish.

29. **A.** NO CHANGE
    B American Baby
    C. american baby
    D. american-born baby

30. **A.** NO CHANGE
    B. will be speaking
    C. will speak
    D. will talk of

ANSWER KEY AND EXPLANATIONS

1. B	7. D	13. A	19. A	25. D
2. A	8. D	14. B	20. B	26. D
3. B	9. D	15. C	21. D	27. B
4. C	10. C	16. C	22. C	28. B
5. D	11. B	17. C	23. B	29. A
6. B	12. D	18. D	24. C	30. C

1. **The correct answer is B.** The phrase following *tests* is an essential part of this sentence and should not be set off by commas.

2. **The correct answer is A.** As written, the list (selecting, classifying, assigning, or promoting) is parallel in structure. *Students* correctly acts as the object of this list of verbs and does not require the addition of a preposition.

3. **The correct answer is B.** Choice B is the most concise choice to express what is said by the other, more wordy choices.

4. **The correct answer is C.** *Divert*, meaning "to turn from one course to another," is the most appropriate choice. *Revert* means "to return to," and *avert* means "to turn away or prevent."

5. **The correct answer is D.** The present tense of the verb *lie*, meaning "belonging to," is required here. Also, choice B can't be correct because you don't use a hyphen to combine an adverb ending in *-ly* with the word it modifies (poorly-informed).

6. **The correct answer is B.** It is not necessary to set off the prepositional phrase from the rest of the sentence with any form of punctuation.

7. **The correct answer is D.** This is the clearest and least-awkward choice.

8. **The correct answer is D.** The clause "Whether the results will be valuable, meaningless, or even misleading" is the subject of the predicate, so the verb must be singular.

9. **The correct answer is D.** Do not use a comma to separate a subject and a verb (except when the subject contains a nonessential clause, an appositive, or another phrase that is set off by two commas).

10. **The correct answer is C.** *Than*, a conjunction, is used after the comparative degree of an adjective or adverb. *Then*, an adverb, means "at that time" or "next."

11. **The correct answer is B.** To correct this run-on sentence, it is necessary to add a period after *living*. Beginning the next sentence with *Because* creates a sentence fragment rather than a complete sentence.

12. **The correct answer is D.** Use a hyphen in unit modifiers immediately preceding the word or words modified. *Tradition-oriented* is a unit modifier.

13. **The correct answer is A.** *But* is correct to indicate a contrasting idea. *Moreover* and *besides* mean "in addition to what has been said." *Therefore* means "for that reason."

14. **The correct answer is B.** Do not use a comma to divide an adverb from the word it modifies. In this case, *formally* modifies the adjective *controlled*. Remember that adverbs can modify verbs, adjectives, and other adverbs. The *-ly* ending is a giveaway that *formally* is an adverb.

15. **The correct answer is C.** The participle *executing*—meaning "carrying out," not "putting to death"—is the correct word for this sentence. *Which* refers to things, not to people. Choice B creates a run-on sentence.

16. **The correct answer is C.** *Anonymous* means "unknown."

17. **The correct answer is C.** This is the most concise and correct way to make this statement.

18. **The correct answer is D.** As written, this sentence illustrates a needless shift in subject (from action to you), which results in a dangling modifier.

19. **The correct answer is A.** The simple present tense form of *communicate* is correct.

20. **The correct answer is B.** As written, this is a run-on sentence. To correct it, add a period after *beings* and start a new sentence with *They*.

21. **The correct answer is D.** Use a semicolon to separate sentence parts of equal rank if one or more of these parts is subdivided by commas.

22. **The correct answer is C.** Use a comma to indicate the omission of a word or words. This phrase actually means "a clenched fist (communicates) anger."

23. **The correct answer is B.** Avoid the shift from the active to the passive voice. The possessive *baby's* is incorrectly substituted for the plural *babies*.

24. **The correct answer is C.** *And* is used to connect similar grammatical elements, in this case the noun *expressions* and the noun *smiles*.

25. **The correct answer is D.** The present infinitive is correct, because the action of the infinitive is present or future in relation to the action of the finite verb *begin*.

26. **The correct answer is D.** The introduction of a new topic—the use of words to communicate—indicates the need for a new paragraph. Human beings are people, and so the phrase *Those people who are* is unnecessary.

27. **The correct answer is B.** The possessive pronoun needed here is *their*. *There* refers to place, and *they're* is a contraction for "they are."

28. **The correct answer is B.** A comparison is being drawn between English- and Spanish-speaking families. The two sentences that form the comparison should be parallel in structure. *Spanish* is a proper noun and must begin with a capital letter.

29. **The correct answer is A.** *American* is a proper noun and should be capitalized; *baby* is merely a noun and needs no capital letter.

30. **The correct answer is C.** *Will speak the language* is idiomatically correct.

answers exercise

SUMMING IT UP

- Effective expression questions test your entire range of grammatical skills, including your knowledge of grammar, spelling, word usage, and sentence formation. To practice for these questions, it may be helpful to turn back to Chapters 4 and 5 in this book and review the rules of grammar and spelling.

- In effective expression questions, you are presented with a long passage in which some portions are underlined and numbered. Corresponding to each numbered part are three different ways of saying the same thing and NO CHANGE. You must choose the answer that presents the best way to phrase the expression.

- Follow these steps to answer effective expression questions successfully: Read through the passage quickly to determine its sense; return to the first underlined portion; choose the best answer based on criteria outlined in this chapter; and, after answering, go on to the next underlined portion and do the same.

Reading Comprehension

OVERVIEW

- **Types of Reading Comprehension Questions**
- **Strategies for Answering Reading Comprehension Questions**
- **Exercise**
- **Answer Key and Explanations**
- **Summing It Up**

TYPES OF READING COMPREHENSION QUESTIONS

Some exams present classic reading comprehension questions that provide a passage and then ask questions about the details of the passage and, perhaps, about its meaning. Other exams require candidates to indicate proper behavior based on their reading of printed procedures and regulations. Still another type of reading-based question requires candidates to reason and choose the next steps based on information presented in a passage. There are nearly as many variations of the reading-based question as there are test makers.

In the past few years, the federal government has introduced a new style of reading comprehension question into many of its exams. The reading selection itself is very short, and it is followed by only one question. At first glance, the task is deceptively simple. However, the paragraph is often dense with information and difficult to absorb. The question may be phrased in a circular, oblique, or negative fashion. Total concentration is needed for answering this type of reading question. You will get the opportunity to practice both this type of reading-based question and the classic reading comprehension question at the end of this chapter.

Most often, you will be given a reading passage and then will be asked to answer a series of questions based on the passage. The following are the most common kinds of questions asked:

- **Question of fact or detail.** You may have to mentally rephrase or rearrange information, but you should find the answer stated in the body of the passage.

- **Best title or main idea.** The answer may be obvious, but the incorrect choices for the "main idea" question are often half-truths that are easily confused with the main idea. They may misstate the idea, omit part of the idea, or even offer a supporting idea quoted directly from the text. The correct answer is the one that covers the largest part of the selection.

Chapter 10

- **Interpretation.** This type of question asks you what the selection means, not just what it says. On police exams, questions based on definitions of crimes fall into this category, for example.

- **Vocabulary.** Some civil service reading passages directly or indirectly ask the meanings of certain words used in the passage.

- **Inference.** This is the most difficult type of reading comprehension question. It asks you to go beyond what the passage says and predict what might happen next. Your answer must be based on the information in the passage and your own common sense but not on any other information that you may have about the subject.

Don't worry if you're unfamiliar with the subject discussed in the reading selection. You don't need to have any knowledge about the subject of the passage because the answer to the question is always given in the passage itself.

STRATEGIES FOR ANSWERING READING COMPREHENSION QUESTIONS

Before you begin to devote attention to strategies for dealing with reading-based questions, give some thought to your reading habits and skills. How well do you read? Do you concentrate? Do you get the point on your first reading? Do you notice details?

Between now and test day, resolve to improve your reading concentration and comprehension. A daily newspaper—print or online—provides excellent material for you to practice reading comprehension skills. Here are some tips for using news articles, columns, opinion pieces, and news blogs to improve your reading comprehension:

- Make a point of reading all the way through any article that you begin. Don't be satisfied with the first paragraph or two.

- Notice points of view, arguments, and supporting information. If you're reading a print newspaper, underline details and ideas that seem to be crucial to the meaning. If you're reading an online version, use a pencil and paper to make notes.

- When you finish your reading, summarize the piece for yourself. Do you know what the main idea is? The purpose of the article? The attitude of the writer if it's a blog, column, or opinion piece? The points of view in any controversy? Did you find that you wanted to know more details?

- Skim your notes or parts you underlined. Did you focus on important words and ideas? Did you understand what you read?

Success with reading-based questions depends on more than reading comprehension. You must also know how to draw the answers from the reading selection and be able to distinguish the best answer from a number of answers that all seem to be good ones or from a number of answers that all seem to be wrong.

To answer a reading comprehension question, follow these nine steps:

1. Read the questions—not the answer choices, just the questions themselves—before you read the passage. The questions will alert you to look for certain details, ideas, and points of view in the passage. If you are taking a paper-and-pencil test, underline key words in the questions to help direct your attention as you read.

2. Skim the passage rapidly to get an idea of its subject matter, its organization, and the point being made. If key words or ideas pop out at you, underline them. Don't consciously search out details at this point.

3. Now read the selection again carefully with comprehension as your main goal. Give attention to details and point of view.

4. Return to the questions and read the first question carefully. Determine exactly what is being asked.

5. Read all the answer choices. Don't rush to choose the first answer that might be correct.

6. Eliminate choices that clearly conflict with the paragraph.

7. If you still have two or more choices left, look for the specific section of the passage that covers the information given in each of the choices.

8. Compare the facts carefully until you can eliminate the remaining incorrect choices.

9. Don't spend too much time on any one question. If looking back at the passage doesn't help you find the answer, choose from among the remaining answers and move on to the next question.

Be alert for hints as to what the author of the passage thinks is important. Phrases such as "note that," "it is important that," and "do not overlook" give clues to what the writer is stressing.

A major cause of errors on reading comprehension questions is misreading questions, so read each question carefully and be sure that you understand what it's asking. Watch for negative or all-inclusive words that can greatly affect your answer, like *always, never, all, only, every, absolutely, completely, none, entirely,* and *no*. Be careful of these words in answer choices. Often, these qualifiers make an answer incorrect.

TIP

Avoid inserting your judgments into your answers. Even if you disagree with the author or if you spot a factual error in the passage, you must answer based on what is stated or implied in the passage.

EXERCISE

> **Directions:** Answer each question based on the information stated or implied in the accompanying reading passage.

Questions 1–4 refer to the following passage.

Passage 1

The recipient gains an impression of a business letter before beginning to read the message. Facts that give a good first impres-
Line sion include margins and spacings that are
5 visually pleasing, formal parts of the letter that are correctly placed according to the style of the letter, copy that is free of errors, and transcript that is even and clear. The problem for the typist is how to produce
10 that first, positive impression of her work.

There are several general rules that a typist can follow when she wishes to prepare a properly spaced letter on a sheet of letterhead. The width of a letter should
15 ordinarily not be less than four inches, nor more than six inches. The side margins should also have a proportionate relation to the bottom margin, as well as the space between the letterhead and the body of the
20 letter. Usually the most appealing arrangement is when the side margins are even, and the bottom margin is slightly wider than the side margins. In some offices, however, a standard line length is used for
25 all business letters, and the typist then varies the spacing between the date line and the inside address according to the length of the letter.

1. The best title for the preceding paragraph is
   A. "Writing Office Letters."
   B. "Making Good First Impressions."
   C. "Judging Well-Typed Letters."
   D. "Proper Spacing for Office Letters."

2. Which of the following might be considered the way that people quickly judge the quality of a business letter?
   A. By measuring the margins to see if they are correct
   B. By looking at the placement of elements in the letter for overall visual appeal
   C. By scanning the body of the letter for meaning
   D. By checking for misspelled names in the letter

3. What would be undesirable as the average line length of a typed letter?
   A. Four inches
   B. Five inches
   C. Six inches
   D. Seven inches

4. When the line length is kept standard, the person typing
   A. does not have to vary the spacing at all because this also is standard.
   B. adjusts the spacing between the date line and inside address for different lengths of letters.
   C. uses the longest line as a guideline for spacing between the date line and inside address.
   D. varies the number of spaces between the lines.

Questions 5–9 refer to the following passage.

Passage 2

Cotton fabrics treated with XYZ Process have features that make them far superior to any previously known flame-retardant-
Line treated cotton fabrics. XYZ Process-treated
5 fabrics endure repeated laundering and dry cleaning; they are glow-resistant as well as flame-resistant; when exposed to flames or intense heat they form tough, pliable, and protective chars; they are inert physi-
10 ologically to persons handling or exposed to the fabric; they are only slightly heavier than untreated fabrics and are susceptible to further wet and dry finishing treatments. In addition, the treated fabrics exhibit
15 little or no adverse change in feel, texture, and appearance and are shrink-, rot-, and mildew-resistant. The treatment reduces strength only slightly. Finished fabrics have "easy care" properties in that they are wrin-
20 kle-resistant and dry rapidly.

5. It is most accurate to state that the author in the preceding selection presents
    A. facts but reaches no conclusion concerning the value of the process.
    B. a conclusion concerning the value of the process and facts to support that conclusion.
    C. a conclusion concerning the value of the process unsupported by facts.
    D. neither facts nor conclusions, but merely describes the process.

6. For which of the following articles is the XYZ Process most suitable?
    A. Nylon stockings
    B. Woolen shirt
    C. Silk tie
    D. Cotton bedsheet

7. Of the following aspects of the XYZ Process, which is NOT discussed in the passage?
    A. Cost
    B. Washability
    C. Wearability
    D. The human body

8. The main reason for treating a fabric with XYZ Process is to
    A. prepare the fabric for other wet and dry finishing treatment.
    B. render it shrink-, rot-, and mildew-resistant.
    C. increase its weight and strength.
    D. reduce the chance that it will catch fire.

9. Which of the following would be considered a minor drawback of the XYZ Process?
    A. It forms chars when exposed to flame.
    B. It makes fabrics mildew-resistant.
    C. It adds to the weight of fabrics.
    D. It is compatible with other finishing treatments.

Questions 10–12 refer to the following passage.

Passage 3

Language performs an essentially social function. It helps us communicate and achieve a great measure of concerted action.
Line Words are signs that have significance by
5 convention, and the people who do not adopt the conventions simply fail to communicate. They do not "get along," and a social force arises that encourages them to achieve the correct associations. By *cor-*
10 *rect*, we mean "as used by other members of the social group." Some of the vital points about language are brought home to an English visitor to the United States, and vice versa, because our vocabularies are
15 nearly the same, but not quite.

10. As defined in the passage, usage of a word is "correct" when it is
   A. defined in standard dictionaries.
   B. used by most persons throughout the world who speak the same language.
   C. used by most educated persons who speak the same language.
   D. used by other persons with whom we are associating.

11. The author is concerned primarily with the
   A. meaning of words.
   B. pronunciation of words.
   C. structure of sentences.
   D. origin and development of language.

12. The main language problem of an English visitor to the United States stems from the fact that an English person
   A. uses some words that have different meanings for Americans.
   B. has different social values than the Americans.
   C. has had more exposure to non-English speaking persons than Americans have had.
   D. pronounces words differently from the way Americans do.

Questions 13–18 refer to the following passage.

Passage 4

In applying for a job with the federal government, you will more than likely need to complete a self-assessment of your experi-
Line ence, skills, and abilities. This approach to
5 hiring is part of a reform of the way that the federal government recruits, hires, and retains workers that was started under President Barack Obama in 2010. The purpose is to make hiring more efficient and result
10 in more qualified employees.

The self-assessment tool is also called an occupational questionnaire or a job-specific questionnaire. What exactly is it?

According to the Office of Personnel Management (OPM), "an occupational ques-
15 tionnaire is an assessment method used to screen and rate job applicants." It is composed of a series of questions tailored to the requirements for each specific job. The
20 questionnaire is normally administered online and submitted as part of a candidate's application. The result is a self-rating of the person's training and experience.

The question formats are similar from
25 job to job and department to department within the government. Questions are

typically multiple choice or yes/no and cover a variety of competencies related to the particular position. Typically, a ques-
30 tionnaire will have five to ten items for each competency that is to be measured for the position. Because of the format, occupational questionnaires are a quick and inexpensive way to screen for minimum
35 qualifications while determining the most qualified candidate.

In addition, occupational questionnaires can assess a wide variety of knowledge, skills, abilities, and competencies—once
40 the subject of arduous and time-consuming essays. They are easy to automate, and, unlike traditional civil service exams, test security is not an issue. It doesn't matter who knows what the questions are because
45 there are no right or wrong answers. The concept of measuring training and experience is a familiar one to government agencies that routinely use performance as a measure of employee competence.

13. The **best** title for the preceding selection is
   A. "How to Complete an Occupational Questionnaire."
   B. "How to Write an Occupational Questionnaire."
   C. "Occupational Questionnaires: Their Use and Format."
   D. "Occupational Questionnaires."

14. The federal government switched to the use of occupational questionnaires
   A. to make hiring more efficient and to identify more qualified employees.
   B. to save money.
   C. to help candidates identify their career interests.
   D. because occupational questionnaires are more valid.

15. Implicit in the passage is the idea that
   A. secure testing is too costly.
   B. candidates screened in the past were not always the best candidates.
   C. the government cares more about saving money than taking time to screen candidates.
   D. competencies are more important today than in the past.

16. It is important to revise a general resume to match your self-assessment for a specific job so that
   A. your self-assessment is supported by your experience and education.
   B. your self-assessment and your resume are correlated.
   C. you don't seem to be lying.
   D. you show that you understand the importance of your education and experience in qualifying for a job.

17. Keeping occupational questionnaires secure is unnecessary because they
   A. are administered online.
   B. can be downloaded and printed by candidates to review ahead of completing them.
   C. are not difficult to answer.
   D. are not tests.

18. *Competency* in the sense used in the passage (line 31) means
   A. suitableness.
   B. condition.
   C. adequateness.
   D. ability.

Question 19 refers to the following passage.

Passage 5

The modern conception of the economic role of the public sector (government), as distinct from the private sector, is that
Line every level of government is a link in the
5 economic process. Government's contribution to political and economic welfare must, however, be evaluated not merely in terms of its technical efficiency, but also in the light of its acceptability to a particular
10 society at a particular state of political and economic development. Even in a dictatorship, this principle is formally observed, although the authorities usually destroy the substance by presuming to interpret to the
15 public its collective desires.

19. The paragraph **best** supports the statement that

A. it is not true that some levels of government are not links in the economic process.

B. all dictatorships observe the same economic principles as other governments.

C. all links in the economic process are levels of government.

D. the contributions of some levels of government do not need to be evaluated for technical efficiency and acceptability to society.

E. no links in the economic process are institutions other than levels of government.

Question 20 refers to the following passage.

Passage 6

All property is classified as either personal property or real property, but not both. In general, if something is classified as per-
Line sonal property, it is transient and transport-
5 able in nature, while real property is not. Things such as leaseholds, animals, money, and intangible and other moveable goods are examples of personal property. Permanent buildings and land, on the other hand,
10 are fixed in nature and are not transportable.

20. The paragraph **best** supports the statement that

A. if something is classified as personal property, it is not transient and transportable in nature.

B. some forms of property are considered as both personal property and real property.

C. permanent buildings and land are real property.

D. permanent buildings and land are personal property.

E. tangible goods are considered as real property.

ANSWER KEY AND EXPLANATIONS

1. D	**5.** B	**9.** C	**13.** C	**17.** D
2. B	**6.** D	**10.** D	**14.** A	**18.** D
3. D	**7.** A	**11.** A	**15.** B	**19.** A
4. B	**8.** D	**12.** A	**15.** A	**20.** C

1. **The correct answer is D.** The best title for any selection is the one that takes in all the ideas presented without being too broad or too narrow. Choice D provides the most inclusive title for this passage. A look at the other choices shows you why. Choice A can be eliminated because the passage discusses typing a letter, not writing one. Although the first paragraph states that a letter should make a good first impression, the passage is clearly devoted to the letter, not the first impression, so choice B can be eliminated. Choice C puts the emphasis on the wrong aspect of the word-processed letter. The passage concerns how to prepare a properly spaced letter, not how to judge one.

2. **The correct answer is B.** Both placement of elements and visual appeal are mentioned in the first paragraph as ways to judge the quality of a typed letter. The first paragraph states that the margins should be "visually pleasing" in relation to the body of the letter, but that doesn't imply margins of a specific measure, so choice A is incorrect.

3. **The correct answer is D.** This answer comes from the information provided in the second paragraph, that the width of a letter "should ordinarily not be less than four inches, nor more than six inches." According to this rule, seven inches is an undesirable line length.

4. **The correct answer is B.** The answer to this question is stated in the last sentence of the passage. When a standard line length is used, the typist "varies the spacing between the date line and the inside address according to the length of the letter." The passage offers no support for any other choice.

5. **The correct answer is B.** This is a combination of a main idea and an interpretation question. If you cannot answer this question readily, reread the passage. The author clearly thinks that the XYZ Process is terrific and says so in the first sentence. The rest of the selection presents a wealth of facts to support the initial claim.

6. **The correct answer is D.** At first glance, you might think that this is an inference question requiring you to make a judgment based upon the few drawbacks of the process. Closer reading, however, shows you that there is no contest for the correct answer here. This is a simple question of fact. The XYZ Process is a treatment for cotton fabrics.

7. **The correct answer is A.** Cost is not mentioned; all other aspects of the XYZ Process are. If you are having trouble finding mention of the effect of the XYZ Process on the human body, look up *inert* and *physiologically* in the dictionary.

8. **The correct answer is D.** This is a main idea question. You must distinguish between the main idea and the supporting and incidental facts.

9. **The correct answer is C.** Obviously, a drawback is a negative feature. The passage mentions only two negative features. The treatment reduces strength slightly, and it makes fabrics slightly heavier than untreated fabrics. Only one of these negative features is offered among the answer choices.

10. **The correct answer is D.** The answer to this question is stated in the next-to-last sentence of the passage. Choices B and C are too broad in scope. The passage states that words have significance by convention, not dictionary definitions (choice A).

11. **The correct answer is A.** This main idea question can be answered by looking at sentences 2 and 3, in which the significance and usage of words are discussed. Neither word pronunciation (choice B), sentence structure (choice C), nor language origin and development (choice D) are addressed in the passage.

12. **The correct answer is A.** This is a question of fact. The phrasing of the question is quite different from the phrasing of the last sentence, but the meaning is the same. You may have found this reading selection more difficult to absorb than some of the others, but you should have had no difficulty answering this question by eliminating the wrong answers.

13. **The correct answer is C.** Questions that ask about the best title are really asking for the main idea. The selection has no information about how to complete (choice A) or how to write (choice B) a questionnaire. Choice D might work, but choice C is more specific about the content of the selection, so it's a better choice.

14. **The correct answer is A.** The correct answer is found in the last sentence in paragraph 1. The purpose of the occupational questionnaire is to make hiring more efficient and to identify more qualified employees.

15. **The correct answer is B.** This is the only answer that can be implied from the content. The inexpensiveness of the occupational questionnaire is mentioned as a benefit, but there is no indication that secure testing (choice A) was used prior to the introduction of occupational questionnaires. While it is mentioned that occupational questionnaires can be completed quickly and inexpensively, there is nothing in the passage to suggest that saving money (choice C) was a key factor in the implementation of the occupational questionnaire. There is no mention of past practices in evaluating candidates (choice D). This doesn't mean that candidates weren't evaluated, only that the topic was not discussed in this selection about the new practice.

16. **The correct answer is A.** All the answers appear to be true, but choice A—that your self-assessment is supported by your experience and education—is the best answer because it encompasses the other answers. It is the most complete.

17. **The correct answer is D.** Occupational questionnaires are not tests; they are more like an inventory of one's abilities.

18. **The correct answer is D.** A competency is the ability of an individual to do a job properly.

19. **The correct answer is A.** This answer can be inferred from the first sentence of the paragraph, which states that "every level of government is a link in the economic process." It can be deduced that its contradictory statement, "some levels of government are not links in the economic process," cannot be true.

Choice B isn't supported by the paragraph because it goes beyond the information given. The third sentence of the paragraph states that a dictatorship observes (at least formally) one of the same principles as other governments. It cannot be concluded from this that dictatorships observe more than this one principle in common with other governments.

Choices C and E represent incorrect interpretations of the information given in the first sentence, which states that "every level of government is a link in the economic process." You can't infer from this statement that "all links in the economic process are levels of government," only that some are. We know that the category "all levels of government" is contained in the category "links in the economic process," but we don't know if links in the economic process exist that are not levels of government. With regard to choice E, it cannot be inferred that "no links in the economic process are institutions other than levels of government," because that would be the same as saying that all links in the economic process are levels of government.

Choice D isn't supported by the passage because the second sentence implies that the contributions of all levels of government must be evaluated for technical efficiency and acceptability to society. There is nothing to suggest that the contributions of some levels of society do not need to be evaluated.

Note that in this question, the correct answer follows from one sentence in the paragraph, the first sentence. The rest of the paragraph presents additional information about the public sector and its effects on society that is relevant to the discussion but not necessary to make the inference. Part of your task is to understand what you read and then to discern which conclusions follow logically from statements in the passage. Consequently, you will find some questions necessitate the use of all or most of the statements presented in the paragraph, while others require only one statement to infer the correct answer.

20. **The correct answer is C.** The answer can be inferred from information contained in the first, second, and fourth sentences. The first sentence is a disjunction; that is, it presents two mutually exclusive alternatives—"all property is classified as either personal property or real property, but not both." The second sentence states that "if something is classified as personal property, it is transient and transportable in nature." The fourth sentence states that "permanent buildings and land…are fixed in nature and are not transportable." You can conclude that, since permanent buildings and land are not transient and transportable in nature, they are not personal property. In view of the disjunction in the first sentence, it can be seen that they must be real property.

Choice A is incorrect because it contradicts the information presented in the second sentence. Choice B is incorrect because it contradicts the first sentence, which states that "all property is classified as either personal property or real property, but not both."

Choice D contradicts the information presented in the second and fourth sentences. The second sentence states that "if something is classified as personal property, it is transient and transportable in nature." The fourth sentence indicates that permanent buildings and land don't have these qualities. Therefore, you can conclude that they are not personal property.

Choice E seems to be derived from the third sentence, which says that intangible goods are examples of personal property. However, you can't conclude from this statement that tangible goods are real property. In fact, the third sentence gives examples of tangible goods that are personal property.

SUMMING IT UP

- Reading comprehension questions vary depending on which civil service exam you are taking. Some present classic reading comprehension questions, in which a passage is provided and you are asked questions on the details of the passage. Another type requires you to indicate proper behavior based on your reading of procedures and regulations. A third type asks you to reason and then choose the next steps based on information presented in the passage.

- A newer reading comprehension question type presents a very short passage and then asks you a single question about it. This type of question can seem deceptively easy, but the passage is usually dense and filled with complex information that is not always presented directly.

- The most common types of reading comprehension questions include those that ask you to identify facts or details, to choose the best title or main idea for a passage, to interpret information presented, to determine (directly or indirectly) the meaning of certain words used in the passage, and to go beyond what the passage actually says and predict what might happen next.

- You are not expected to have any knowledge about the subjects in the reading selections, because the answer is always presented somewhere and in some way in the passage itself.

- Before you take your exam, resolve to improve your reading comprehension and concentration skills. Make a point of reading all the way through any article you begin. Read with a pencil handy to mark details and ideas that seem most important, or make notes if you're reading online. Summarize articles after you've finished reading them. Skim your underlinings or notes and determine whether you focused on the main ideas.

- Follow these nine practice strategies to succeed in dealing with reading-based questions:

  1. Read the questions before you read the passage.

  2. Skim the passage to familiarize yourself with its subject matter, organization, and main point. Note any word or thoughts that jump out at you.

  3. Reread the passage with comprehension as the goal.

  4. Return to the first question and determine exactly what is being asked.

  5. Read all the answer choices.

  6. Eliminate all choices that clearly conflict with the paragraph.

  7. If two or more choices remain, look for the specific section of the passage that covers the information given in each of the choices.

  8. Compare facts until you can eliminate the remaining incorrect answer choices.

  9. Don't spend too much time on one question.

PART IV
CLERICAL ABILITY

Judgment, Communication, and Memory

Chapter 11

OVERVIEW

STRATEGIES FOR ANSWERING JUDGMENT QUESTIONS

Good judgment is a necessary skill for many positions in federal, state, and local government. Even the entry-level employee who works under close supervision has occasions when he or she must rely on his or her own good judgment in dealing with an emergency situation—or in choosing priorities when there is no supervisor to consult. Almost all multiple-choice civil service exams include some questions designed to measure judgment, either directly or indirectly. For test-taking purposes, judgment is defined as a process of combining knowledge and understanding with common sense. Even though judgment questions resemble reading comprehension questions, they are different in that you must choose the best answer based on your accumulated knowledge and common sense. The answer will not necessarily be given in the reading passage. Clues to the correct answer, however, may be found in the reading passage, so reading comprehension will play a large part in answering judgment questions correctly.

To recognize judgment questions and understand how to answer them, try the following practice exercises. You must read the passage and choose the best answer for the question asked. The correct answers and explanations of those answers follow the exercise.

175

EXERCISE: JUDGMENT

> **Directions:** Read the passage for each question and choose the best answer.

1. Decisions about handcuffing or restraining inmates are often left up to the corrections officers involved. An officer is legally responsible for exercising good judgment and for taking necessary precautions to prevent harm both to the inmate involved and to others. In which one of the following situations is handcuffing or other physical restraint most likely to be needed?

    A. An inmate seems to have lost control of his senses and is banging his fists repeatedly against the bars of his cell.

    B. During the past two weeks, an inmate has deliberately tried to start three fights with other inmates.

    C. An inmate claims to be sick and refuses to leave his cell for a scheduled meal.

    D. During the night, an inmate begins to shout and sing, disturbing the sleep of other inmates.

2. While you are working on a routine assignment, a coworker asks you to help her for a few minutes so that she can complete an assignment that has top priority and must be completed immediately. Of the following, the best action for you to take should be to

    A. tell her to find somebody else who does not look busy and ask that person for help.

    B. tell her you will help her as soon as you complete your own work.

    C. help her to complete her assignment and then go back to your work.

    D. tell her that your work is as important to you as her work is to her and continue to work on your own assignment.

3. A police officer stationed along the route of a parade has been ordered not to allow cars to cross the route while the parade is in progress. An ambulance driver on an emergency run attempts to drive an ambulance across the route while the parade is passing. Under these circumstances, the officer should

    A. ask the driver to wait while the officer calls headquarters and obtains a decision.

    B. stop the parade long enough to permit the ambulance to cross the street.

    C. direct the ambulance driver to the shortest detour available, which will add at least 10 minutes to the run.

    D. hold up the ambulance in accordance with the order.

4. An office worker frequently complains to the building custodian that her office is poorly lighted. The best action for the building custodian to follow is to

    A. ignore the complaints because they come from a habitual crank.

    B. inform the worker that illumination is a fixed item built into the building originally and evidently is the result of faulty planning by the architect.

    C. request a licensed electrician to install additional ceiling lights.

    D. investigate for faulty illumination features in the room, such as dirty lamp globes and incorrect lamp wattage.

5. Suppose that one of your neighbors walks into the police precinct where you are an administrative aide and asks you to make 100 photocopies of a flyer he intends to distribute in the neighborhood. Of the following, what action should you take in this situation?

    A. Pretend that you do not know the person and order him to leave the building.

    B. Call a police officer and report the person for attempting to make illegal use of police equipment.

    C. Tell the person that you will make the copies when you are off duty.

    D. Explain that you cannot use police equipment for non-police work.

6. A police officer, walking a beat at 3 a.m., notices heavy smoke coming out of a top-floor window of a large apartment building. Out of the following, the action the officer should take first is to

    A. make certain that there really is a fire.

    B. enter the building and warn all the occupants of the apartment building.

    C. attempt to extinguish the fire before it gets out of control.

    D. call the fire department.

7. An elevator inspector on routine inspection for the Building Department notices many dangerous situations in the basement of the building she is in. Of the following conditions that she notices, which is the most dangerous and should be reported immediately?

    A. Gas is leaking from a broken pipe.

    B. The sewer pipe is broken.

    C. Water is seeping into the basement.

    D. The basement is unlighted.

8. There are times when an employee of one city department should notify and seek assistance from employees of another department. A parking enforcement agent is checking meters on a busy one-way street. Of the following situations he notices, which should he report immediately?

    A. A rat runs out of a building and into the storm sewer across the street.

    B. A wire is dangling over the sidewalk, giving off sparks.

    C. A car is parked directly in front of a hydrant.

    D. Two men are sitting on the front steps of a building sharing a marijuana joint.

exercise

ANSWER KEY AND EXPLANATIONS

1. A	**3.** B	**5.** D	**7.** A
2. C	**4.** D	**6.** D	**8.** B

1. **The correct answer is A.** The inmate who repeatedly bangs his fists against the bars of his cell is in immediate danger of causing himself bodily harm. The inmate must be restrained. The other inmates require attention, and their situations must be dealt with, but they do not require physical restraint.

2. **The correct answer is C.** There are a number of points to take into consideration: Your own task is described as routine; the coworker's assignment is described as one that has top priority; and the coworker has asked for only a few minutes of your time. If you were involved in "rush" work yourself, you might refuse to help until you had finished your own task, but under these circumstances, help get the priority work done. A side benefit to be considered here is maintaining a good relationship with the coworker, so that you, too, may request assistance at some time when your job demands it.

3. **The correct answer is B.** Without any knowledge of police rules, common sense dictates that saving lives is the number-one priority. An ambulance on an emergency run is on a mission to save a life. Lifesaving takes precedence over the desire for an uninterrupted parade, despite the officer's prior orders.

4. **The correct answer is D.** The repeated complaints may be quite legitimate if the lighting problem has not been corrected. Do not dismiss the office worker as a "crank." The custodian should check out the fixtures personally before calling in an electrician. Costs can be held down by having house staff perform those tasks for which they are qualified.

5. **The correct answer is D.** When a calm, reasoned explanation is offered as an answer choice, it is nearly always the correct answer. There is no need to be impolite or hostile to the neighbor. He may not even realize that he is asking you to do something that is not permitted. He will respect you for obeying the rules.

6. **The correct answer is D.** A police officer is a police officer and not a firefighter. Eliminate choices A and C at once. It is the job of the firefighters to ascertain whether or not there really is a fire and to put it out. Since the building is a large one and fires spread rapidly, the practical move is to call the fire department immediately rather than running through the building alone trying to rouse all the occupants. Firefighters will have greater manpower to do this efficiently and are trained in nighttime rousing procedures.

7. **The correct answer is A.** Leaking gas can ignite, causing a fire. If a large amount of gas collects in the basement and is ignited, an explosion and fire are likely. This is the greatest hazard. The broken sewer pipe and the water seepage can create health hazards and should be reported and repaired, but these corrections do not represent the same emergency situation as the gas leak. An unlit basement is also a safety hazard but is even less of an emergency.

8. **The correct answer is B.** The most urgent hazard is that caused by the sparking wire. A quick call to the police department will get the area sealed off and a repair crew to attend to the wire. The health department could be notified of rodents in the building, but pest infestation is a chronic problem rather than an emergency. The parking enforcement agent can ticket the illegally parked car. The two men sharing one joint pose no immediate danger.

answers exercise

STRATEGIES FOR ANSWERING COMMUNICATION SKILLS QUESTIONS

No one works entirely alone. Every person must at times communicate information to someone else. The communication may be in the form of written emails, memos, or reports, or it may be oral. No matter what form the communication takes, it must be clear and readily understood. It must convey all necessary information in a usable form.

Most city civil service exams include some measure of a candidate's ability to organize and communicate information. Where the communication is likely to be oral, such as a telephone call to a central post, communication questions offer a set of facts and ask how you would best organize those facts into a clear and accurate report. The following practice questions will help you answer this type of question, which measures your oral communication skills. The correct answers and explanations follow the exercise.

EXERCISE: COMMUNICATION SKILLS

Directions: For the following questions, read the passage and choose the answer that most clearly and accurately expresses the information provided in the question.

1. Police Officer Franks arrives at the scene of a two-family frame house in Brooklyn and observes flames leaping from the door onto the porch. A woman on the sidewalk gives him a description of a man she saw running from the house just before she noticed the fire. The information is:

   - Place of Occurrence: 1520 Clarendon Road, Brooklyn
   - Time of Occurrence: 6:32 a.m.
   - Type of Building: two-family frame dwelling
   - Event: fire, suspected arson
   - Suspect: male, white, approx. 6 ft., wearing blue jeans
   - Witness: Mary Smith of 1523 Clarendon Road, Brooklyn

   Officer Franks is about to radio an alert for the suspect. Which of the following expresses the information *most clearly and accurately*?

   A. At 6:32 a.m., Mary Smith of 1523 Clarendon Road, Brooklyn, saw a white male wearing approximately 6-ft. blue jeans running from the building across the street.

   B. A white male wearing blue jeans ran from the house at 1520 Clarendon Road at 6:32 a.m. Mary Smith saw him.

   C. At 6:32 a.m., a 6-ft. white male wearing blue jeans ran from a burning two-family frame structure at 1520 Clarendon Road, Brooklyn. He was observed by a neighbor, Mary Smith.

   D. A two-family frame house is on fire at 1520 Clarendon Road in Brooklyn. A white male in blue jeans probably did it. Mary Smith saw him run.

2. A woman runs to a clerk at the platform of the subway station to report that her purse was just snatched. She gives the following information to the clerk:

   - Time of Occurrence: 1:22 a.m.
   - Place of Occurrence: uptown-bound platform, 59th Street Station, 7th Avenue line
   - Victim: Juana Martinez
   - Crime: purse-snatching
   - Description of Suspect: unknown, fled down steps to lower platform

   The clerk is about to call for assistance from the transit police. Which of the following expresses the information *most clearly and accurately*?

   A. Juana Martinez had her purse snatched on the subway platform at 59th Street Station. She did not see him.

   B. A purse was just snatched by a man who ran down the steps. This is the 7th Avenue booth at 59th Street Station. Her name is Juana Martinez.

   C. It is 1:22 a.m. The person who snatched Juana Martinez's purse is downstairs at 59th Street Station.

   D. This is the 59th Street Station, uptown-bound 7th Avenue booth. A Juana Martinez reports that her purse was just snatched by a person who fled down the steps to a lower platform.

ANSWER KEY AND EXPLANATIONS

1. C	2. D

1. **The correct answer is C.** This statement tells what happened, where, and when. It gives a brief description of the suspect and identifies the witness. Choices A and B neglect to mention the fire; choice D omits the height of the suspect, which is an important fact, and does not identify the relationship of the witness for later questioning if necessary.

2. **The correct answer is D.** This statement gives the precise location, the event, and a direction in which the suspect might be traced. Since the statement says that the event just occurred, the time is irrelevant. The recipient of the message knows to move quickly. Choice A does not give enough details to be of use. Choice B makes a disjointed statement. Choice C makes a flat statement that is not necessarily true; the purse-snatcher may have exited by another route.

STRATEGIES FOR ANSWERING OBSERVATION AND MEMORY QUESTIONS

Some government positions, such as firefighter, police officer, and corrections officer, require good observation and memory skills. Civil service exams for these and related positions may include questions that measure these skills. Typically, you are presented with a picture and are allowed to study it for a short period of time. Then, the picture is covered, and you must answer questions based on what you remember of the details that you observed in the picture.

The following exercise will help you practice for this type of question. You will need a timer so that you can be aware of the amount of time allowed for studying the picture.

EXERCISE: OBSERVATION AND MEMORY

Directions: You will have 3 minutes to study the following picture, to note details about people, time and place, and activities. Then you will have to answer five questions about the picture without looking back at the picture.

Directions: Answer questions 1–5 on the basis of the picture. Do not look at the picture again.

1. The teller is
   A. wearing a striped tie.
   B. wearing glasses.
   C. making change.
   D. left-handed.

2. The man wearing a hat is
   A. handing money to the teller.
   B. wearing a bow tie.
   C. talking to another man in the line.
   D. smoking a pipe.

3. The teller's name is
   A. R. Smith.
   B. T. Jones.
   C. T. Smith.
   D. R. Jones.

4. The woman in the dark dress is
   A. carrying a handbag.
   B. wearing gloves.
   C. holding a hat.
   D. third in line.

5. The time of day is
   A. early morning.
   B. around noon.
   C. mid-afternoon.
   D. late afternoon.

ANSWER KEY AND EXPLANATIONS

1. B	2. D	3. D	4. B	5. B

1. **The correct answer is B.** The teller is wearing glasses. His tie is solid, and he is holding a pencil in his right hand.

2. **The correct answer is D.** The man wearing a hat is also smoking a pipe. He is not talking to anyone in line and is reading, not handing money to the teller.

3. **The correct answer is D.** The teller's nameplate reads R. Jones.

4. **The correct answer is B.** The woman in the dark dress is wearing gloves. She is neither carrying a handbag nor holding a hat. She is second in line.

5. **The correct answer is B.** The clock indicates it is 12:05, which is around noon.

answers exercise

SUMMING IT UP

- Good judgment is a required skill for most federal, state, and local civil service positions. Almost all multiple-choice civil service exams include questions designed to directly or indirectly assess judgment skills.

- Judgment questions may resemble reading comprehension questions, but they differ in that you must choose the best answer based on your own knowledge and common sense, not on the meaning of the passage. The answer to a judgment question does not necessarily appear in the passage.

- To recognize and understand judgment questions when they appear on your exam, review the exercises in this chapter and review the answer explanations at the end.

- Like good judgment, communication skills are essential to doing your job effectively in the civil service. No matter what form it takes, all of your communication must be clear and easily understood, and it must convey the necessary information.

- Most civil service exams include assessments of your ability to organize and communicate effectively. Review the exercises in this chapter and review the answer explanations at the end to practice answering these types of questions.

- Good observation and memory skills are especially important for certain civil service positions, such as firefighter, police officer, and corrections officer. Civil service exams for these types of positions usually include questions designed to measure these skills. Typically, you're presented with a picture and asked to study it for a short time. Then, without looking at the picture again, you must answer questions based on what you remember of the details you observed.

Alphabetizing and Filing

OVERVIEW

- **Rules of Alphabetic Filing**
- **Strategies for Answering Alphabetizing and Filing Questions**
- **Exercise 1**
- **Exercise 2**
- **Exercise 3**
- **Exercise 4**
- **Answer Keys and Explanations**
- **Summing It Up**

RULES OF ALPHABETIC FILING

The most important rule for putting names in alphabetical order is to consider each letter in the complete name in strict alphabetical order, exactly as it appears, starting with the last name for individuals. However, there are some specific rules that you should understand, and these can differ for names of people and names of organizations. The following sections outline all the rules that you should know to score well on this portion of the clerical ability exam.

Names of Individuals

The following rules apply to the alphabetizing of people's names:

- The names of individuals are filed in strict alphabetical order, first according to last name, then according to first name or initial, and finally according to middle name or initial. For example, *George Allen* comes before *Edward Bell*, and *Leonard P. Reston* comes before *Lucille B. Reston*.

- When last names and first initials are the same, the one with the initial comes before the one with the name written out. For example, *A. Green* comes before *Agnes Green*.

- When first and last names are the same, the name without a middle initial comes before the one with a middle name or initial. For example, *John Doe* comes before both *John A. Doe* and *John Alan Doe*.

- When first and last names are the same, the name with a middle initial comes before the one with a middle name beginning with the same initial. For example, *Jack R. Hertz* comes before *Jack Richard Hertz*.

Chapter 12

- Prefixes like *De, O', Mac, Mc,* and *Van* are filed exactly as written and treated as part of the names they come before. Ignore apostrophes for purposes of filing. For example, *Robert O'Dea* comes before *David Olsen,* and *Gladys McTeague* comes before *Frances Meadows.*

- Foreign names are filed as spelled. Prefixes are not considered separately. Likewise, foreign language articles (such as *Le, La, Les,* and *El*), whether they begin with a lowercase or capital letter, are considered part of the name with which they appear. For example, *Carl Da Costa* is filed before *Ugo D'Agnota.*

- Hyphenated surnames are indexed as though the hyphen joins the two parts, making one. Thus, *Amadeus Lyttonet* is filed before *John Lytton-Strachey.*

- Abbreviated names are treated as if they are spelled out. For example, *Chas.* is filed as *Charles,* and *Thos.* is filed as *Thomas.*

- Titles and designations, such as *Dr., Mr., Prof., Jr.,* or *II,* are given last consideration in filing.

Names of Businesses

The following rules apply to the alphabetizing of business names:

- The names of organizations, institutions, and buildings are filed according to the order in which each word in the name appears, except where these names include the full names of individuals.

- When business names include the full names of individuals, the business names are filed using the rules for filing individual names. For example, *Edward Rice and Sons, Ltd.* is filed as *Rice, Edward, and Sons, Ltd.*

- When *the, of, and,* or an apostrophe are parts of a business name, they are disregarded for purposes of filing.

- Names that include numerals should be filed as if the numerals were spelled out. Thus, *10th Street Bootery* is filed as *Tenth Street Bootery.*

- When the same names appear with different addresses, arrange them alphabetically according to town or city, considering state only when town or city names are duplicated. Example: *American Tobacco Co., Norfolk, VA; American Tobacco Co., Quincy, IL; American Tobacco Co., Quincy, MA.*

- Abbreviations are alphabetized as though the words were spelled out. Thus, *Indus. Bros. of America* is filed as *Industrial Brothers of America.*

- Hyphenated firm names are treated as separate words. For example, Oil-O-Match Heating Co. is filed before Oilimatic Heating Co. because the word Oil falls alphabetically before Oilimatic.

- Compound geographic names written as separate words are always treated as separate words. For example, *West Chester* comes before *Westchester.*

- Bureaus, boards, offices, and government departments are filed under the names of the chief governing body. For example, *Bureau of the Budget* would be filed as if written *Budget, Bureau of the.*

STRATEGIES FOR ANSWERING ALPHABETIZING AND FILING QUESTIONS

There are four different kinds of alphabetizing and filing questions, and any of these may appear on your civil service exam. Therefore, you should read the directions closely and make certain that you mark your answers exactly as specified. Let's take a look at an example of each kind of question.

One type is a simple alphabetizing question. All you have to do is insert the given word into its correct alphabetical position in the list of words and choose the letter of the word it precedes. Try an example:

1. BIOGRAPHY
   A. bible
   B. bibliography
   C. bilge
   D. biology

The correct answer is D. Biography should be filed *before* biology.

Another kind of alphabetizing question tests your knowledge of the rules for filing names of individuals. You are given a name, followed by four names in proper alphabetic order. The spaces between the names are lettered. You must mark the space where the given name should be filed. Try an example:

2. Kessler, Neilson
   A. –
   Kessel, Carl
   B. –
   Kessinger, D. J.
   C. –
   Kessler, Karl
   D. –
   Kessner, Lewis
   E. –

The correct answer is D. According to the rules for alphabetizing names of individuals, when the last names are the same, you should alphabetize by the first name. Thus, *Neilson* falls after *Karl*.

A third type of question tests your ability to alphabetize both individual and business names. One name in a group of names is bold. You must determine where this name should be filed in the entire group: mark **A** if it should be first, mark **B** if it should be second, mark **C** if it should be third, and mark **D** if it should be fourth. Try a question of this type:

3. Albert Brown

James Borenstein

Frieda Albrecht

Samuel Brown

A. First

B. Second

C. Third

D. Fourth

The correct answer is D. The correctly alphabetized group would look like this: Albrecht, Frieda; Borenstein, James; Brown, Albert; **Brown, Samuel**. Because the bold name is fourth in the group, choice D is the correct answer.

The final kind of alphabetizing question also tests your ability to file individual and business names. You are given a group of four names, and you must select the name that would be *third* if the group were correctly alphabetized. Here's an example:

4. A. Herbert Restman

B. H. Restman

C. Harry Restmore

D. H. Restmore

The correct answer is D. The correctly alphabetized group would look like this: Restman, H.; Restman, Herbert; Restmore, H.; Restmore, Harry. Choice D, *H. Restmore*, falls third in this group.

EXERCISE 1

Directions: Each question consists of a CAPITALIZED word that is to be filed correctly among the alphabetized words listed. Choose the word that should come **after** the given word.

1. CATHOLIC
   A. catacombs
   B. catalogs
   C. catechisms
   D. cattle

2. DRAMA
   A. drawing
   B. Drayton
   C. Dreyfus
   D. drugs

3. INQUISITION
   A. industry
   B. insurance
   C. international
   D. intern

4. LUGUBRIOUS
   A. Lucretius
   B. lumber
   C. Luther
   D. Lutheran

5. OCEANIC
   A. occult
   B. Ohio
   C. Oklahoma
   D. optics

6. ENGLAND
   A. engineering
   B. English
   C. engraving
   D. entomology

7. IRRIGATION
   A. Ireland
   B. Irish
   C. iron
   D. Irving

8. MARINE
   A. Margolin
   B. marketing
   C. Mary
   D. Maryland

9. PALEONTOLOGY
   A. Pacific
   B. painting
   C. Palestine
   D. paltry

10. ASIATIC
    A. ascetic
    B. assyriology
    C. astronomy
    D. astrophysics

EXERCISE 2

> **Directions:** In each of the following questions, you are given a name, followed by four names in proper alphabetic order. The spaces between the names are lettered. Decide where the given name belongs in the alphabetic series, and mark the letter of the space.

1. Eatley, Mary
   A. —
      Eagin, John
   B. —
      Eagley, Robert
   C. —
      Ebert, Jack
   D. —
      Eckert, Wallace
   E. —

2. Pinch, Nathaniel
   A. —
      Payne, Briscoe
   B. —
      Pearlman, Abe
   C. —
      Pincus, Harry
   D. —
      Pollaci, Angelina
   E. —

3. Raphan, Max
   A. —
      Rankin, H.
   B. —
      Rappan, Sol
   C. —
      Rascoll, Jon
   D. —
      Rich, Harold
   E. —

4. Schwartz, H.
   A. —
      Scavone, John
   B. —
      Schwartz, Harry
   C. —
      Seiden, Burt
   D. —
      Shields, Vera
   E. —

5. Hakim, Wm.
   A. —
      Hakiel, R.
   B. —
      Hakim, Louis
   C. —
      Hakim, M.
   D. —
      Halabi, Joe
   E. —

6. Horn, Sol
   A. —
      Hormel, Max
   B. —
      Horn, Harold
   C. —
      Horn, Irving
   D. —
      Hornbeck, J. W.
   E. —

7. Krommes, Selma
   A. —
     Kromolitz, J.
   B. —
     Kromowitz, L.
   C. —
     Kromwitz, Abe
   D. —
     Kron, Harold
   E. —

8. Melzer, Max
   A. —
     Meltz, Lena
   B. —
     Meltzer, Abe
   C. —
     Meltzer, Alex
   D. —
     Melzner, L.
   E. —

9. Nesbitt, Carl
   A. —
     Nesbiet, Jerry
   B. —
     Nesbitt, Al
   C. —
     Nesbitt, Gloria
   D. —
     Nesci, Jas.
   E. —

10. Perron, Homer
   A. —
     Perrin, Larry
   B. —
     Perron, Lewis
   C. —
     Perrone, James
   D. —
     Perrotta, Chas.
   E. —

EXERCISE 3

Directions: Consider each group of names as a unit. Determine where the name printed in boldface would be if the names in the group were correctly alphabetized. If the name in boldface is first, mark **A**; if second, mark **B**; if third, mark **C**; and if fourth, mark **D**.

1. Hugh F. Martenson
A. S. Martinson
Albert Martinsen
Albert S. Martinson
A. First
B. Second
C. Third
D. Fourth

2. Arthur Roberts
James Robin
J. B. Robin
Arnold Robinson
A. First
B. Second
C. Third
D. Fourth

3. **Eugene Thompkins**
Alice Thompson
Arnold G. Thomas
B. Thomas
A. First
B. Second
C. Third
D. Fourth

4. Albert Green
Wm. Greenfield
A. B. Green
Frank E. Green
A. First
B. Second
C. Third
D. Fourth

5. Dr. Francis Karell
John Joseph Karelsen Jr.
John J. Karelson Sr.
Mrs. Jeanette Kelly
A. First
B. Second
C. Third
D. Fourth

6. Norman Fitzgibbons
Charles F. Franklin
Jas. Fitzgerald
Andrew Fitzsimmons
A. First
B. Second
C. Third
D. Fourth

7. **Chas. R. Connolly**
Frank Conlon
Charles S. Connolly
Abraham Cohen
A. First
B. Second
C. Third
D. Fourth

8. **The 5th Ave. Bus Co.**
The Baltimore and Ohio Railroad
3rd Ave. Elevated Co.
Pennsylvania Railroad
A. First
B. Second
C. Third
D. Fourth

9. The Jane Miller Shop
   Joseph Millard Corp.
   John Muller & Co.
   Jean Mullins, Inc.
   - **A.** First
   - **B.** Second
   - **C.** Third
   - **D.** Fourth

10. **Anthony Delaney**
    A. De Landri
    A. M. D'Elia
    Alfred De Monte
    - **A.** First
    - **B.** Second
    - **C.** Third
    - **D.** Fourth

EXERCISE 4

Directions: Each question consists of four names. For each question, select the name that should be **third** if the four names were arranged in alphabetical order in accordance with the rules for alphabetical filing.

1. **A.** Elm Trading Co.
    B. El Dorado Trucking Corp.
    C. James Eldred Jewelry Store
    D. Eldridge Printing, Inc.

2. **A.** Fifth Avenue Book Shop
    B. Mr. Wm. A. Fifner
    C. 52nd Street Association
    D. Robert B. Fiffner

3. **A.** Timothy Macalan
    B. Fred McAlden
    C. Tomas MacAllister
    D. Mrs. Frank McAllen

4. **A.** Peter La Vance
    B. George Van Meer
    C. Wallace De Vance
    D. Leonard Vance

5. **A.** 71st Street Theater
    B. The Seven Seas Corp.
    C. 7th Ave. Service Co.
    D. Walter R. Sevan and Co.

6. **A.** Dr. Chas. D. Peterson
    B. Miss Irene F. Petersen
    C. Lawrence E. Peterson
    D. Prof. N. A. Petersen

7. **A.** Edward La Gabriel
    B. Marie Doris Gabriel
    C. Marjorie N. Gabriel
    D. Mrs. Marian Gabriel

8. **A.** Adam Dunn
    B. E. Dunn
    C. A. Duncan
    D. Edward Robert Dunn

9. **A.** Paul Moore
    B. William Moore
    C. Paul A. Moore
    D. William Allen Moore

10. **A.** George Peters
    B. Eric Petersen
    C. G. Peters
    D. E. Petersen

ANSWER KEYS AND EXPLANATIONS

Exercise 1

1. D	**3.** B	**5.** B	**7.** D	**9.** C
2. A	**4.** B	**6.** B	**8.** B	**10.** B

1. **The correct answer is D.** *Cattle* should be filed after *catholic*.

2. **The correct answer is A.** *Drawing* should be filed after *drama*.

3. **The correct answer is B.** *Insurance* should be filed after *inquisition*.

4. **The correct answer is B.** *Lumber* should be filed after *lugubrious*.

5. **The correct answer is B.** *Ohio* should be filed after *oceanic*.

6. **The correct answer is B.** *English* should be filed after *England*.

7. **The correct answer is D.** *Irving* should be filed after *irrigation*.

8. **The correct answer is B.** *Marketing* should be filed after *marine*.

9. **The correct answer is C.** *Palestine* should be filed after *paleontology*.

10. **The correct answer is B.** *Assyriology* should be filed after *Asiatic*.

Exercise 2

1. C	**3.** B	**5.** D	**7.** A	**9.** C
2. C	**4.** B	**6.** D	**8.** D	**10.** B

1. **The correct answer is C.** *Eatley, Mary* belongs between *Eagley, Robert* and *Ebert, Jack*.

2. **The correct answer is C.** *Pinch, Nathaniel* belongs between *Pearlman, Abe* and *Pincus, Harry*.

3. **The correct answer is B.** *Raphan, Max* belongs between *Rankin, H.* and *Rappan, Sol*.

4. **The correct answer is B.** *Schwartz, H.* belongs between *Scavone, John* and *Schwartz, Harry*.

5. **The correct answer is D.** *Hakim, Wm.* belongs between *Hakim, M.* and *Halabi, Joe*.

6. **The correct answer is D.** *Horn, Sol* belongs between *Horn, Irving* and *Hornbeck, J. W.*

7. **The correct answer is A.** *Krommes, Selma.* belongs before *Kromolitz, J.*

8. **The correct answer is D.** *Melzer, Max* belongs between *Meltzer, Alex* and *Melzner, L.*

9. **The correct answer is C.** *Nesbitt, Carl* belongs between *Nesbitt, Al* and *Nesbitt, Gloria*.

10. **The correct answer is B.** *Perron, Homer* belongs between *Perrin, Larry* and *Perron, Lewis*.

answers exercises

Exercise 3

1. D	3. C	5. B	7. C	9. A
2. C	4. A	6. A	8. B	10. B

1. **The correct answer is D.** Martenson, Hugh F.; Martinsen, Albert; Martinson, A. S.; **Martinson, Albert S.**

2. **The correct answer is C.** Roberts, Arthur; Robin, J. B.; **Robin, James**; Robinson, Arnold

3. **The correct answer is C.** Thomas, Arnold G.; Thomas, B.; **Thompkins, Eugene**; Thompson, Alice

4. **The correct answer is A.** Green, A. B.; Green, Albert; Green, Frank E.; Greenfield, Wm.

5. **The correct answer is B.** Karell, Francis, Dr.; **Karelsen, John Joseph, Jr.**; Karelson, John J., Sr.; Kelly, Jeanette, Mrs.

6. **The correct answer is A. Fitzgerald, Jas.**; Fitzgibbons, Norman; Fitzsimmons, Andrew; Franklin, Charles F.

7. **The correct answer is C.** Cohen, Abraham; Conlon, Frank; **Connolly, Chas. R.**; Connolly, Charles S.

8. **The correct answer is B.** Baltimore and Ohio Railroad, The; **5th (Fifth) Ave. Bus Co., The;** Pennsylvania Railroad; 3rd (Third) Ave. Elevated Co.

9. **The correct answer is A. Millard, Joseph**, Corp.; Miller, Jane, Shop, The; Muller, John & Co.; Mullins, Jean, Inc.

10. **The correct answer is B.** De Landri, A.; **Delaney, Anthony**; D'Elia, A. M.; De Monte, Alfred

Exercise 4

1. D	3. B	5. C	7. C	9. B
2. A	4. D	6. A	8. B	10. D

1. **The correct answer is D.** El Dorado Trucking Corp.; Eldred, James, Jewelry Store; Eldridge Printing, Inc.; Elm Trading Co.

2. **The correct answer is A.** Fiffner, Robert B.; Fifner, Wm. A., Mr.; Fifth Avenue Book Shop; 52nd (Fifty-second) Street Association

3. **The correct answer is B.** Macalan, Timothy; MacAllister, Tomas; McAlden, Fred; McAllen, Frank, Mrs.

4. **The correct answer is D.** De Vance, Wallace; La Vance, Peter; Vance, Leonard; Van Meer, George

5. **The correct answer is C.** Sevan, Walter R. and Co.; Seven Seas Corp., The; 7th (Seventh) Ave. Service Co.; 71st (Seventy-first) Street Theater

6. **The correct answer is A.** Petersen, Irene F., Miss; Petersen, N. A., Prof.; Peterson, Chas. D., Dr.; Peterson, Lawrence E.

7. **The correct answer is C.** Gabriel, Marian, Mrs.; Gabriel, Marie Doris; Gabriel, Marjorie N.; La Gabriel, Edward

8. **The correct answer is B.** Duncan, A.; Dunn, Adam; Dunn, E.; Dunn, Edward Robert

9. **The correct answer is B.** Moore, Paul; Moore, Paul A.; Moore, William; Moore, William Allen

10. **The correct answer is D.** Peters, G.; Peters, George; Petersen, E.; Petersen, Eric

SUMMING IT UP

- The most important rule of alphabetical filing is to consider each letter in the complete name or phrase in strict alphabetical order, exactly as it appears. Review this chapter for more specific rules on alphabetizing names of individuals and names of businesses.

- Civil service exams present four types of questions about alphabetizing and filing. One type requires simple alphabetizing. Another type tests your knowledge of alphabetizing rules. A third type requires you to alphabetize both individual and business names, and a fourth tests your ability to correctly file individual and business names. Read all directions carefully and make sure you know what the question is asking you to do.

Clerical Speed and Accuracy

OVERVIEW

ANSWERING TIMED QUESTIONS

Generally, time is a crucial factor in comparison questions. You'll probably find that there are more questions than you can answer in the time allowed. Since accuracy is of prime importance, you should follow these rules:

- Work steadily until time is called.
- Don't rush beyond your ability to focus on words and numbers.
- Don't guess.
- Don't randomly answer the remaining questions when time is called.

Tests of clerical speed and accuracy put such a premium on accuracy that the scoring formula is sometimes "score equals the correct answers minus the wrong answers." Don't allow the fear of making errors to slow you down so that you plod along and answer very few questions; speed is important. You must work steadily until time is called.

Chapter 13

STRATEGIES FOR ANSWERING COMPARISON QUESTIONS

In comparison questions, you are given several sets of names or numbers. You must quickly compare them to find which is different or inaccurate. Lots of practice with various forms of comparison questions should improve your skills in this area.

In answering comparison questions, look for differences in one area at a time. If you narrow your focus to compare only short numbers, abbreviations, or just the words, you're more likely to notice differences and less apt to see what you expect to see rather than what is actually printed on the page.

Start with length of line, number of digits, middle initials, or small words. Once you spot any *difference* at all, you know that the two items being compared are different. If, while concentrating on one area, you happen to catch a difference in another area, consider the items to be different and go on to the next comparison. A system may be useful, but don't stick to it slavishly.

The best way to read names, numbers, and addresses being compared is to read exactly what you see and to sound out words by syllables. For example:

- If you see *St*, read "es-tee" not "street."
- If you see *NH*, read "en-aitch," not "New Hampshire."
- If you see *1035*, read "one-zero-three-five" not "one thousand thirty-five."
- Read *sassafras* as "sas-sa-fras."

Psychologists have discovered that the human mind always tries to complete a figure. If you read "Pky" as "Parkway," you'll probably read "Pkwy" as "Parkway" and never notice the difference between the two. Your mind will complete the word without allowing you to focus on the letters. If, however, you read the abbreviation as an abbreviation, you'll notice that the two are different.

Remember that although one type of question asks you to identify the *difference* between the given word or string of numbers and the answer choices, another type asks you to identify the answer that is the *same* as the given words or set of numbers. Directions for the third type of question ask you to identify mistakes; this is the same as finding the differences. You have to read the directions carefully.

Finally, trust yourself. Once you've decided that an answer is the same or there is no mistake, don't second guess yourself.

EXERCISE 1

> **Directions:** Each question lists four names or numbers. The names or numbers may or may not be exactly the same. Compare the four names or numbers in each question, and choose your answer as follows:
>
> Choose **A** if all four names or numbers are DIFFERENT.
> Choose **B** if TWO of the names or numbers are exactly the same.
> Choose **C** if THREE of the names or numbers are exactly the same.
> Choose **D** if all FOUR names or numbers are exactly the same.

1. W.E. Johnston
   W.E. Johnson
   W.E. Johnson
   W.B. Johnson
   - **A.** All four names are DIFFERENT.
   - **B.** TWO of the names are exactly the same.
   - **C.** THREE of the names are exactly the same.
   - **D.** All FOUR names are exactly the same.

2. Vergil L. Muller
   Vergil L. Muller
   Vergil L. Muller
   Vergil L. Muller
   - **A.** All four names are DIFFERENT.
   - **B.** TWO of the names are exactly the same.
   - **C.** THREE of the names are exactly the same.
   - **D.** All FOUR names are exactly the same.

3. 5261383
   5263183
   5263183
   5623183
   - **A.** All four numbers are DIFFERENT.
   - **B.** TWO of the numbers are exactly the same.
   - **C.** THREE of the numbers are exactly the same.
   - **D.** All FOUR numbers are exactly the same.

4. Atherton R. Warde
   Asheton R. Warde
   Atherton P. Warde
   Athertin P. Warde
   - **A.** All four names are DIFFERENT.
   - **B.** TWO of the names are exactly the same.
   - **C.** THREE of the names are exactly the same.
   - **D.** All FOUR names are exactly the same.

5. 8125690
   8126690
   8125609
   8125609
   - **A.** All four numbers are DIFFERENT.
   - **B.** TWO of the numbers are exactly the same.
   - **C.** THREE of the numbers are exactly the same.
   - **D.** All FOUR numbers are exactly the same.

6. E. Owens McVey
   E. Owen McVey
   E. Owen McVay
   E. Owen McVey
   - **A.** All four names are DIFFERENT.
   - **B.** TWO of the names are exactly the same.
   - **C.** THREE of the names are exactly the same.
   - **D.** All FOUR names are exactly the same.

exercises

> **NOTE**
>
> In lieu of including an answer sheet, throughout this chapter we've added answer choices for you to select from in the exercises. On the actual test, only the lists will appear.

7. Emily Neal Rouse
Emily Neal Rowse
Emily Neal Roose
Emily Neal Rowse
   A. All four names are DIFFERENT.
   B. TWO of the names are exactly the same.
   C. THREE of the names are exactly the same.
   D. All FOUR names are exactly the same.

8. Francis Ramsdell
Francis Ransdell
Francis Ramsdell
Francis Ramsdell
   A. All four names are DIFFERENT.
   B. TWO of the names are exactly the same.
   C. THREE of the names are exactly the same.
   D. All FOUR names are exactly the same.

9. 2395890
2395890
2395890
2395890
   A. All four numbers are DIFFERENT.
   B. TWO of the numbers are exactly the same.
   C. THREE of the numbers are exactly the same.
   D. All FOUR numbers are exactly the same.

10. 1926341
1962341
1963241
1926341
   A. All four numbers are DIFFERENT.
   B. TWO of the numbers are exactly the same.
   C. THREE of the numbers are exactly the same.
   D. All FOUR numbers are exactly the same.

EXERCISE 2

Directions: Each question gives the name and identification number of an employee. You are to choose the one answer that has exactly the same identification number and name as those given in the question.

1. 176823   Katherine Blau
   A. 176823   Catherine Blau
   B. 176283   Katherine Blau
   C. 176823   Katherine Blau
   D. 176823   Katherine Blaw

2. 673403   Boris T. Frame
   A. 673403   Boris P. Frame
   B. 673403   Boris T. Frame
   C. 673403   Boris T. Fraim
   D. 673430   Boris T. Frame

3. 498832   Hyman Ziebart
   A. 498832   Hyman Zeibart
   B. 498832   Hiram Ziebart
   C. 498832   Hyman Ziebardt
   D. 498832   Hyman Ziebart

4. 506745   Barbara O'Dey
   A. 507645   Barbara O'Day
   B. 506745   Barbara O'Day
   C. 506475   Barbara O'Day
   D. 506745   Barbara O'Dey

5. 344223   Morton Sklar

   A. 344223   Morton Sklar

   B. 344332   Norton Sklar

   C. 344332   Morton Sklaar

   D. 343322   Morton Sklar

6. 816040   Betsy B. Voight

   A. 816404   Betsy B. Voight

   B. 814060   Betsy B. Voight

   C. 816040   Betsy B. Voight

   D. 816040   Betsey B. Voight

7. 913576   Harold Howritz

   A. 913576   Harold Horwitz

   B. 913576   Harold Howritz

   C. 913756   Harold Howritz

   D. 913576   Harald Howritz

8. 621190   Jayne T. Downs

   A. 621990   Janie T. Downs

   B. 621190   Janie T. Downs

   C. 622190   Janie T. Downs

   D. 621190   Jayne T. Downs

9. 004620   George McBoyd

   A. 006420   George McBoyd

   B. 006420   George MacBoyd

   C. 006420   George McBoid

   D. 004620   George McBoyd

10. 723495   Alice Appleton

   A. 723495   Alice Appleton

   B. 723594   Alica Appleton

   C. 723459   Alice Appleton

   D. 732495   Alice Appleton

EXERCISE 3

Directions: Each of the following questions consists of three sets of names and name codes. In each question, the two names and name codes on the same line are supposed to be exactly the same. Look carefully at each set of names and codes, and choose your answer as follows:

     Choose **A** if there are mistakes in all THREE sets.

     Choose **B** if there are mistakes in TWO of the sets.

     Choose **C** if there are mistakes in only ONE set.

     Choose **D** if there are NO MISTAKES in any of the sets.

---

1. Macabe, John N.   V 53162   Macade, John N.   V 53162

   Howard, Joan S.   J 24791   Howard, Joan S.   J 24791

   Ware, Susan B.   A 45068   Ware, Susan B.   A 45968

   A. There are mistakes in all THREE sets.

   B. There are mistakes in TWO of the sets.

   C. There are mistakes in only ONE set.

   D. There are NO MISTAKES in any of the sets.

2. Powell, Michael C.   78537 F   Powell, Michael C.   78537 F
Martinez, Pablo J.   24435 P   Martinez, Pablo J.   24435 P
MacBane, Eliot M.   98674 E   MacBane, Eliot M.   98674 E

   A. There are mistakes in all THREE sets.

   B. There are mistakes in TWO of the sets.

   C. There are mistakes in only ONE set.

   D. There are NO MISTAKES in any of the sets.

3. Fitz-Kramer Machines Inc.   259090   Fitz-Kramer Machines Inc.   259090
Marvel Cleaning Service   482657   Marvel Cleaning Service   482657
Donato, Carl G.   637418   Danato, Carl G.   687418

   A. There are mistakes in all THREE sets.

   B. There are mistakes in TWO of the sets.

   C. There are mistakes in only ONE set.

   D. There are NO MISTAKES in any of the sets.

4. M. Davison Trading Corp.   43108 T   M. Davidson Trading Corp.   43108 T
Cotwald Lighting Fixtures   76065 L   Cotwald Lighting Fixtures   70056 L
R. Crawford Plumbers   23157 C   R. Crawford Plumbers   23157 G

   A. There are mistakes in all THREE sets.

   B. There are mistakes in TWO of the sets.

   C. There are mistakes in only ONE set.

   D. There are NO MISTAKES in any of the sets.

5. Fraiman Engineering Corp.   M4773   Friaman Engineering Corp.   M4773
Neuman, Walter B.   N7745   Neumen, Walter B.   N7745
Pierce, Eric M.   W6304   Pierce, Eric M.   W6304

   A. There are mistakes in all THREE sets.

   B. There are mistakes in TWO of the sets.

   C. There are mistakes in only ONE set.

   D. There are NO MISTAKES in any of the sets.

6. Constable, Eugene   B 64837   Comstable, Eugene   B 64837
Derrick, Paul   H 27119   Derrik, Paul   H 27119
Scalsi Office Furniture   R 36742   Scalsi Office Furniture   R 36742

   A. There are mistakes in all THREE sets.

   B. There are mistakes in TWO of the sets.

   C. There are mistakes in only ONE set.

   D. There are NO MISTAKES in any of the sets.

7. | H. Delivery Service Co. | D 7456 | H. Delivery Service Co. | D 7456 |
   | Barettz Electrical Supplies | N 5392 | Barettz Electrical Supplies | N 5392 |
   | Tanner, Abraham | M 4798 | Tanner, Abraham | M 4798 |

   A. There are mistakes in all THREE sets.

   B. There are mistakes in TWO of the sets.

   C. There are mistakes in only ONE set.

   D. There are NO MISTAKES in any of the sets.

8. | Kalin Associates | R 38641 | Kaline Associates | R 38641 |
   | Sealey, Robert E. | P 63533 | Sealey, Robert E. | P 63553 |
   | Scalsi Office Furniture | R 3674 | Scalsi Office Furniture | R 36742 |

   A. There are mistakes in all THREE sets.

   B. There are mistakes in TWO of the sets.

   C. There are mistakes in only ONE set.

   D. There are NO MISTAKES in any of the sets.

9. | Janowsky, Philip M. | 742213 | Janowsky, Philip M. | 742213 |
   | Hansen, Thomas H. | 934816 | Hanson, Thomas H. | 934816 |
   | L. Lester and Son Inc. | 294568 | L. Lester and Son Inc. | 294568 |

   A. There are mistakes in all THREE sets.

   B. There are mistakes in TWO of the sets.

   C. There are mistakes in only ONE set.

   D. There are NO MISTAKES in any of the sets.

10. | Majthenyi, Alexander | P 4802 | Majthenyi, Alexander | B 4802 |
    | Prisco Pools, Inc. | W 3641 | Frisco Pools, Inc. | W 3641 |
    | DePaso, Nancy G. | X 4464 | DePaso, Nancy G. | X 4464 |

    A. There are mistakes in all THREE sets.

    B. There are mistakes in TWO of the sets.

    C. There are mistakes in only ONE set.

    D. There are NO MISTAKES in any of the sets.

ANSWER KEYS AND EXPLANATIONS

Exercise 1

1. B	**3.** B	**5.** B	**7.** B	**9.** D
2. D	**4.** A	**6.** B	**8.** C	**10.** B

1. **The correct answer is B.** The second and third names are the same.

2. **The correct answer is D.** All four names are the same.

3. **The correct answer is B.** The second and third numbers are the same.

4. **The correct answer is A.** All the names are different.

5. **The correct answer is B.** The third and fourth numbers are the same.

6. **The correct answer is B.** The second and fourth names are the same.

7. **The correct answer is B.** The second and fourth names are the same.

8. **The correct answer is C.** The first, third, and fourth names are the same.

9. **The correct answer is D.** All four numbers are the same.

10. **The correct answer is B.** The first and fourth numbers are the same.

Exercise 2

1. C	**3.** D	**5.** A	**7.** B	**9.** D
2. B	**4.** D	**6.** C	**8.** D	**10.** A

1. **The correct answer is C.** Choices A and D contain spelling errors; choice B contains a number order error.

2. **The correct answer is B.** Choices A and C contain spelling errors; choice D contains a number order error.

3. **The correct answer is D.** Choices A, B, and C contain spelling errors.

4. **The correct answer is D.** Choices A and C contain both spelling and number order errors; choice B contains a spelling error.

5. **The correct answer is A.** Choices B and C contain both spelling and number order errors; choice D contains a number order error.

6. **The correct answer is C.** Choices A and B contain number order errors; choice D contains a spelling error.

7. **The correct answer is B.** Choices A and D contain spelling errors; choice C contains both a spelling and number order error.

8. **The correct answer is D.** Choices A and C contain both spelling and number order errors; choice B contains a spelling error.

9. **The correct answer is D.** Choices B and C contain both spelling and number order errors; choice A contains a number order error.

10. **The correct answer is A.** Choice B contains both spelling and number order errors; choices C and D contain number order errors.

Exercise 3

1. B	**3.** C	**5.** B	**7.** D	**9.** C
2. D	**4.** A	**6.** B	**8.** A	**10.** B

1. **The correct answer is B.** There are mistakes in the first and third sets.

2. **The correct answer is D.** There are no mistakes.

3. **The correct answer is C.** There are mistakes in the third set.

4. **The correct answer is A.** There are mistakes in all three sets.

5. **The correct answer is B.** There are mistakes in the first and second sets.

6. **The correct answer is B.** There are mistakes in the first and second sets.

7. **The correct answer is D.** There are no mistakes.

8. **The correct answer is A.** There are mistakes in all three sets.

9. **The correct answer is C.** There is a mistake in the second set.

10. **The correct answer is B.** There are mistakes in the first and second sets.

CODING QUESTIONS

The most common variety of coding questions found on civil service exams consists of a coding table (which need not be memorized) and a series of questions that requires you to demonstrate your understanding of the use of the code and your ability to follow directions in answering the questions. From one exam to another, the chief variations in coding questions tend to be in the number of digits and letters in each question line and in the directions. The best way to learn how to answer coding questions is to practice with some examples.

EXERCISE 1

Directions: Each letter should be matched with its number in accordance with the following table:

Letter	P	S	B	O	Q	K	A	M	E	Y
Number	0	1	2	3	4	5	6	7	8	9

For each question, compare each line of letters and numbers carefully to see if each letter is matched correctly to its corresponding number. Choose your answer according to the number of lines in which all the letters and numbers are matched correctly:

Choose **A** if NONE of the lines are matched correctly.
Choose **B** if only ONE of the lines is matched correctly.
Choose **C** if TWO of the lines are matched correctly.
Choose **D** if all THREE lines are matched correctly.

1. SEOB   1732
   YMQA   9756
   BEPM   2806

    A. NONE of the lines are matched correctly.

    B. ONE of the lines is matched correctly.

    C. TWO of the lines are matched correctly.

    D. All THREE lines are matched correctly.

2. AOSY   6319
   EKQM   8547
   YBOP   9230

    A. NONE of the lines are matched correctly.

    B. ONE of the lines is matched correctly.

    C. TWO of the lines are matched correctly.

    D. All THREE lines are matched correctly.

3. QABS   3621
   PKEO   0583
   SEYO   1983

    A. NONE of the lines are matched correctly.

    B. ONE of the lines is matched correctly.

    C. TWO of the lines are matched correctly.

    D. All THREE lines are matched correctly.

4. AQOB   6432
   YSAP   9061
   BAKM   2657

    A. NONE of the lines are matched correctly.

    B. ONE of the lines is matched correctly.

    C. TWO of the lines are matched correctly.

    D. All THREE lines are matched correctly.

5. SBOK   1234

    YEAQ   9854

    MPES   7081

  A. NONE of the lines are matched correctly.

  B. ONE of the lines is matched correctly.

  C. TWO of the lines are matched correctly.

  D. All THREE lines are matched correctly.

EXERCISE 2

Directions: Each question contains three lines of letters and numbers. The numbers in each line should correspond with the code letters in this table:

Code Letter	M	Q	O	H	B	C	I	N	Y	V
Number	0	1	2	3	4	5	6	7	8	9

In some of the lines below, an error exists in the coding. Compare the numbers and letters in each question very carefully. Choose your answers according to the number of lines in which you find an error as follows:

        Choose **A** if only ONE line contains an error.

        Choose **B** if TWO lines contain errors.

        Choose **C** if all THREE lines contain errors.

        Choose **D** if NONE of the lines contains an error.

1. BCMHIOB   4503624

   VYBQNCO   8941752

   MHBCNIV   0345869

  A. ONE line contains an error.

  B. TWO lines contain errors.

  C. All THREE lines contain errors.

  D. NONE of the lines contains an error.

2. HYVNOQM   3987210

   NCOMHYQ   7520481

   QBCHIYN   1463687

  A. ONE line contains an error.

  B. TWO lines contain errors.

  C. All THREE lines contain errors.

  D. NONE of the lines contains an error.

3. MHBNYQO   0347812

   CONBMYH   5274083

   QBHNOMV   1430279

  A. ONE line contains an error.

  B. TWO lines contain errors.

  C. All THREE lines contain errors.

  D. NONE of the lines contains an error.

ANSWER KEYS AND EXPLANATIONS

Exercise 1

1. A	2. D	3. B	4. C	5. B

1. **The correct answer is A.** None of the lines is matched correctly. In the first set, E is incorrectly matched with 7. In the second set, Q is incorrectly matched with 5. In the third set, M is incorrectly matched with 6.

2. **The correct answer is D.** All three lines are matched correctly.

3. **The correct answer is B.** Only the second set is matched correctly. In the first set, Q is incorrectly matched with 3. In the third set, E is incorrectly matched with 9, and Y is incorrectly matched with 8.

4. **The correct answer is C.** The first and third sets are matched correctly. In the second set, S is incorrectly matched with 0, and P is incorrectly matched with 1.

5. **The correct answer is B.** Only the last set is matched correctly. In the first set, K is incorrectly matched with 4. In the second set, A is incorrectly matched with 5.

Exercise 2

1. B	2. C	3. A

1. **The correct answer is B.** The first line contains no errors. On the second line, V is incorrectly coded as 8, and Y is incorrectly coded as 9. On the third line, N is incorrectly coded as 8.

2. **The correct answer is C.** All three lines contain errors. In the first line, Y is incorrectly coded as 9, and V is incorrectly coded as 8. In the second line, H is incorrectly coded as 4. In the third line, C is incorrectly coded as 6.

3. **The correct answer is A.** The first and second lines contain no errors. In the third line, N is incorrectly coded as 0, and M is incorrectly coded as 7.

SUMMING IT UP

- Comparison questions measure speed and accuracy by presenting several sets of names or numbers and asking you to quickly compare them to identify which one is the same, or which contain an error (or errors). Be sure to practice with various forms of this question type to improve your ability to work quickly and accurately.

- Time is crucial in answering comparison questions. To be sure you're as accurate as possible, follow these rules: Work steadily until time is called, don't rush beyond your ability to focus on words and numbers, don't guess at answers, and don't randomly answer remaining questions when time is called.

- A good strategy for answering comparison questions is to look for differences in one area at a time, so you're more likely to notice differences or errors. Once you spot any difference at all, you know that the two items being compared are different.

- An essential tip for reading names, numbers, and addresses being compared is to read them phonetically, syllable by syllable. If you see "St," don't read it as "street" but as "ess tee." You're more likely to notice differences this way.

- The directions for coding questions include a coding table that shows letters paired with numbers. You don't have to memorize the table; it will be available for you to refer to as you answer questions. The questions require that you identify any errors in the matching of the letters and numbers.

Typing and Stenography

OVERVIEW

THE TYPING TEST

For jobs in which typing is a very important skill, the typing test may be competitively scored. In those cases, the score on the typing test is part of the overall civil service exam score and affects hiring decisions. If typing is a requirement of the job, the job announcement will tell you the minimum number of words per minute an applicant must be able to input.

In the typing test, you're faced with a single task: copying material exactly as it is presented. You must demonstrate how rapidly you can do so and with what degree of accuracy.

What to Expect on the Typing Test

The typing test consists of a passage that you must copy exactly as it is presented to you. You'll have a specified length of time in which to type, and your score will be based upon the number of words per minute that you type within that time and upon the number of errors that you make.

You'll also be given a practice exercise before the test itself. The practice exercise, usually about ten lines in length, enables you to warm up. It is not scored.

How the Typing Test Is Scored

The length of the typing test varies from one governmental jurisdiction to another. Most typing tests last 5 minutes. The minimum performance standards also vary. For some positions, a minimum speed of 30 words per minute (wpm) is adequate; for others 35 wpm, 40 wpm, or even greater speeds are required. Likewise, the number of errors permitted varies according to department and the position for which you're applying.

The basic principles in charging typing errors are as follows:

- WORD or PUNCTUATION MARK incorrectly typed. (An error in spacing that follows an incorrect word or punctuation mark is not further charged.)

- SERIES of consecutive words omitted, repeated, inserted, transposed, or erased. (A charge is made for errors within such series, but the total charge cannot exceed the number of words.)

- LINE or part of a line typed in all capitals or apparently typed with the fingers on the wrong keys.

- CHANGE from the MARGIN where most lines are begun by the candidate or from the PARAGRAPH INDENTION most frequently used by the candidate.

Strategies for Taking the Typing Test

Assuming that you already know how to type, the best preparation for any typing test is typing. Choose any material at all and practice copying it line for line, exactly as you see it. As on the actual typing test, spell, capitalize, punctuate, and begin and end lines exactly as they appear on the page that you're copying. Try to balance yourself to meet speed requirements while maintaining a very high level of accuracy.

EXERCISE

Directions: Type the copy exactly as it is given below. Spell, space, begin and end each line and paragraph, punctuate, and capitalize precisely as shown. Make no insertions or other corrections in the copy. Keep on typing even though you detect an error in your copy. If you finish typing the passage before the time limit is up, simply double space once and continue typing from the beginning of the passage.

TIME: 5 minutes

Line

1   Under President Bill Clinton, the federal government underwent its own
    process of rationalization and consolidation. President Clinton appointed Vice
3   President Al Gore to trim the federal government through a program known
    as "The National Performance Review." Known as reinventing government, the
5   program undertook a broad review of departments, agencies, and personnel.
    The goal was to cut inefficient, unnecessary, and redundant programs, thereby
7   saving the federal government and taxpayers millions of dollars. The reinvention
    of government was also intended to restore people's faith in government by pro-
9   viding improving service to people.

      President George W. Bush consolidated a number of programs and
11   agencies related to the nation's defense under a new Department of Homeland
    Security. This department, which includes the Federal Emergency Management
13   Agency, is also responsible for preparedness, response, and recovery to natural
    disasters.

EACH TIME YOU REACH THIS POINT, DOUBLE SPACE ONCE AND BEGIN AGAIN.

TYPING SPEED ATTAINED: _____ words per minute

NUMBER OF ERRORS: _____

THE STENOGRAPHY TEST

Only stenographer candidates take a stenography test. You will be expected to take dictation at the rate of 80 words per minute. You must then consult your notes to fill in the missing words of a transcript from an alphabetic word list. The sample stenography test given in this section shows the length of the dictated material and will help you prepare if your exam includes a stenography test.

To take the practice stenography test, sit down with your pencil and notebook, and hand this book to a friend or family member. Have that person dictate the passage to you. Each pair of lines is dictated in 10 seconds. Your friend should dictate periods, but not commas, and should read the exercise with the expression that the punctuation indicates. Have your friend use a watch with a second hand or a stopwatch to read the sentences at the proper pace.

EXERCISE 1

Directions: Exactly on a minute, start dictating. Finish reading each line at the number of seconds indicated below.

I realize that this practice dictation	
is not a part of the examination	10 sec.
proper and is not to be scored. (Period)	
When making a study of the defined	20 sec.
contribution plan and its influence,	
the most striking feature of it is its	30 sec.
youth. (Period) As has been shown, the time	
of greatest growth began just a few years	40 sec.
ago. (Period) The influence that this	
growth has had on the labor market and	50 sec.
worker attitudes is hard to assess,	
partly because the effects have not yet fully	**1 min.**
evolved and many are still in the	
growing stage. (Period) Even so, most pension	10 sec.
plans continue to be defined benefit plans,	
which pay a specified amount of money regularly	20 sec.
to retirees. (Period) But the newer defined	
contribution plans specify only the amount	30 sec.
contributed by the employee and usually by the	
employer. (Period) Employees whose	40 sec.
plans have been changed from a defined	
benefit to a defined contribution plan	50 sec.
find that they do not have the guaranteed	
retirement payments that they thought they	**2 min.**
would. (Period) This has angered many	
employees and raised concerns among workers'	10 sec.
advocates. (Period) As informal and formal	
information on these pension plans spreads,	20 sec.
workers will become more aware of the plans	
and their provisions. (Period) Their impact	30 sec.
on employee attitudes will no doubt become	
stronger. (Period) Each year, more and more workers	40 sec.
will be retiring and, as they do, those with defined	
contribution plans will be sounding the alarm for	50 sec.
younger workers. (Period) So, active workers may	
begin to pay more attention to their pensions. (Period)	**3 min.**

EXERCISE 2

> **Directions:** The following transcript and word list are taken from the previous dictation. Many words have been omitted from the transcript. Compare your notes with it. When you come to a blank space in the transcript, decide what word (or words) belongs there. Look for the missing word in the word list. Notice which letter (A, B, C, or D) is printed beside the word. Write that letter in the blank. **B** is written in blank 1 to show how you are to record your choice. Write **E** if the exact answer is not in the word list. You may also write the word (or words) or the shorthand for it, if you wish. The same choice may belong in more than one blank.

Alphabetic Word List

> Write **E** if the answer is not listed.

a — (D)	labor — (C)
attitudes — (C)	main — (B)
be — (B)	make — (A)
been — (C)	making — (B)
began — (D)	market — (B)
being — (A)	markets — (D)
completely — (A)	marking — (D)
contribution — (C)	never — (B)
defined — (D)	not — (D)
examination — (A)	over — (C)
examine — (B)	part — (C)
examining — (D)	partly — (D)
feat — (A)	plan — (D)
feature — (C)	practical — (C)
full — (B)	practice — (B)
fully — (D)	proper — (C)
greater — (D)	section — (D)
grow — (B)	so — (B)
growing — (C)	still — (A)
had — (D)	striking — (B)
has — (C)	to — (D)
has been — (B)	to be — (C)
has had — (A)	trial — (A)
has made — (A)	turn — (D)
in — (C)	values — (A)
in part — (B)	yet — (C)
influence — (A)	

Transcript

I realize that this <u>B</u> dictation is __ a __ of the __ __ and is __ __ scored. When __
                1   2   3   4 5   6 7   8

a __ of the __ __ __ and its __, the most __ __ is its youth. As __ shown, the
 9   10 11 12   13   14 15   16

time of __ growth began just a few years ago. The __ that this growth __ on
       17   18   19

the labor __ and worker __ is hard to assess, __ because the effects have not yet __
      20   21   22   23

evolved and many are __ in the __ stage.
                  24   25

ANSWER KEY AND EXPLANATIONS

Exercise 2

1. B	**6.** D	**11.** C	**16.** B	**21.** C
2. D	**7.** C	**12.** D	**17.** E	**22.** D
3. C	**8.** B	**13.** A	**18.** A	**23.** D
4. A	**9.** E	**14.** B	**19.** A	**24.** A
5. C	**10.** D	**15.** C	**20.** B	**25.** C

1. **The correct answer is B.** practice (filled in for you)

2. **The correct answer is D.** not

3. **The correct answer is C.** part

4. **The correct answer is A.** examination

5. **The correct answer is C.** proper

6. **The correct answer is D.** not

7. **The correct answer is C.** to be

8. **The correct answer is B.** making

9. **The correct answer is E.** study (not given)

10. **The correct answer is D.** defined

11. **The correct answer is C.** contribution

12. **The correct answer is D.** plan

13. **The correct answer is A.** influence

14. **The correct answer is B.** striking

15. **The correct answer is C.** feature

16. **The correct answer is B.** has been

17. **The correct answer is E.** greatest (not given)

18. **The correct answer is A.** influence

19. **The correct answer is A.** has had

20. **The correct answer is B.** market

21. **The correct answer is C.** attitudes

22. **The correct answer is D.** partly

23. **The correct answer is D.** fully

24. **The correct answer is A.** still

25. **The correct answer is C.** growing

SUMMING IT UP

- The typing test consists of one task: Copying material exactly as it is presented within a specified period of time. Your score is based on the number of words per minute that you type minus the number of errors you make. Before the actual timed test, you'll be given an unscored practice test that allows you to warm up.

- The best preparation for any typing test is simply to practice typing. Choose any material and practice copying it exactly as it's presented, with the same punctuation, line breaks, capitalization, and spelling. Try timing yourself and aim for speed balanced with accuracy.

- Stenography tests are given only to those who are seeking a position as a stenographer. You are expected to take dictation at 80 words per minute or better. You must then consult your notes and fill in the missing words of a transcript from an alphabetic word list.

PART V
ARITHMETIC ABILITY

Fractions and Decimals

OVERVIEW

FRACTIONS AND MIXED NUMBERS

Before going over the rules for solving arithmetic problems involving fractions and mixed numbers, let's review what fractions and mixed numbers are:

- A **fraction** is part of a unit. The two parts of the fraction are the **numerator** and the **denominator**. In the fraction $\frac{3}{4}$, 3 is the numerator and 4 is the denominator. In any fraction, the numerator is being divided by the denominator. So in the previous example, 3 is being divided by 4.

- A **mixed number** is an integer together with a fraction, such as $2\frac{3}{5}$. The integer is the integral part, and the fraction is the fractional part.

- An **improper fraction** is one in which the numerator is equal to or greater than the denominator, such as $\frac{19}{6}$, $\frac{25}{4}$, or $\frac{10}{10}$.

In a fraction problem, the whole quantity is 1, which can be expressed by a fraction in which the numerator and denominator are the same number. For example, if a problem involves $\frac{1}{8}$ of a quantity, the whole quantity is $\frac{8}{8}$, or 1.

Rules to Know: Fractions and Mixed Numbers

If you understand the rules outlined in this section, you'll be able to solve any arithmetic problem that involves fractions and mixed numbers. Study the rules and example problems, and be sure that you understand each rule before moving on to the practice exercises.

227

Chapter 15

Converting Mixed Numbers and Improper Fractions

To solve fraction problems, it's often helpful to convert mixed numbers to improper fractions. To do so, follow these three steps:

1. Multiply the denominator of the fraction by the integer.
2. Add the numerator to this product.
3. Place this sum over the denominator.

Change $3\frac{4}{7}$ to an improper fraction using these steps:

- 7 (denominator) × 3 (integer) = 21
- 21 (product) + 4 (numerator) = 25
- The answer is $\frac{25}{7}$.

To convert an improper fraction to a mixed number, reverse the process and follow these two steps:

1. Divide the numerator by the denominator. The quotient, disregarding the remainder, is the integral part of the mixed number.
2. Place the remainder, if any, over the denominator. This is the fractional part of the mixed number.

Change $\frac{36}{13}$ to a mixed number using these steps:

- 36 (numerator) ÷ 13 (denominator) = 2 with a remainder of 10
- The answer is $2\frac{10}{13}$.

Reducing Fractions

The numerator and denominator of a fraction can be changed by dividing both by the same number, without affecting the value of the fraction. This process is called **reducing the fraction**. A fraction that has been reduced as much as possible is said to be in **lowest terms.**

For example, the value of the fraction $\frac{3}{12}$ is not altered if both the numerator and denominator are divided by 3, resulting in $\frac{1}{4}$. Likewise, if $\frac{6}{30}$ is reduced to lowest terms (by dividing both the numerator and denominator by 6), the result is $\frac{1}{5}$.

Finding the Least Common Denominator

Fractions can't be added or subtracted unless the denominators are all the same. To convert all fractions to have the same denominator, you must first find the least common denominator. The **least common denominator** (LCD) is the lowest number that can be divided evenly by all the given denominators. If no two of the given denominators can be divided by the same number, the LCD is the product of all the denominators.

To find the LCD when two or more of the given denominators can be divided by the same number, follow these five steps:

1. Write down all the denominators.

2. Select the smallest number (other than 1) by which two or more of the denominators can be divided evenly.

3. Divide the denominators by this number, copying down those that cannot be divided evenly. Write this number to one side.

4. Repeat this process, writing each divisor to one side until there are no longer any denominators that can be divided evenly by the same number.

5. Multiply all the divisors to find the LCD.

Find the LCD of $\frac{1}{5}$, $\frac{1}{7}$, $\frac{1}{10}$, and $\frac{3}{14}$ using these steps:

- Write down the denominators: 5, 7, 10, 14

- 10 and 14 can be divided by 2: 5, 7, 5, 7

- 5 and 5 can be divided by 5: 1, 7, 1, 7

- 7 and 7 can be divided by 7: 1, 1, 1, 1

- None of the denominators can be divided any further.
  Multiply the divisors: $2 \times 5 \times 7 = 70$.

70 is the least common denominator.

If two fractions have the same denominator, the one with the larger numerator is the greater fraction. If two fractions have the same numerator, the one with the larger denominator is the smaller fraction. To compare fractions with different numerators and denominators, change them to equivalent fractions by finding the LCD.

Adding Fractions

Now that you know how to find the LCD, you can add any fractions by following these four steps:

1. Find the LCD of the denominators.

2. Convert each fraction to an equivalent fraction with the LCD as its denominator.

3. Add all the numerators and place this sum over the common denominator.

4. Reduce the answer as far as possible. Change improper fractions to mixed numbers.

Add $\frac{1}{4}$, $\frac{3}{10}$, and $\frac{2}{5}$ using these steps:

- Find the LCD; your answer should be 20.

- Convert each fraction to one having a denominator of 20: $\frac{1}{4} \times \frac{5}{5} = \frac{5}{20}$
  $\frac{3}{10} \times \frac{2}{2} = \frac{6}{20}$; $\frac{2}{5} \times \frac{4}{4} = \frac{8}{20}$

- Add all the numerators: $5 + 6 + 8 = 19$

- Place the sum over the common denominator: $\frac{19}{20}$. This is not an improper fraction and it cannot be reduced, so it is the final answer.

- If the problem contains any mixed numbers, add the fractions first, and then add the integers. You don't need to convert the mixed numbers to improper fractions.

Subtracting Fractions

Finding the LCD is also the first step when subtracting fractions. You can subtract fractions by following these four steps:

1. Find the LCD of the denominators.

2. Convert each fraction to an equivalent fraction with the LCD as its denominator.

3. Subtract the numerators and place the difference over the common denominator.

4. Reduce the answer as far as possible. Change improper fractions to mixed numbers.

Subtract $\frac{1}{4}$ from $\frac{3}{10}$ using these steps:

- Find the LCD; your answer should be 20.

- Convert the fractions so they each have a denominator of 20: $\frac{3}{10} \times \frac{2}{2} = \frac{6}{20}$; $\frac{1}{4} \times \frac{5}{5} = \frac{5}{20}$

- Subtract the numerators: $6 - 5 = 1$

- Place the difference over the common denominator: $\frac{1}{20}$. This is not an improper fraction and it cannot be reduced, so it is the final answer.

If the problem contains any mixed numbers, find the LCD and convert the fractions first. If you need to, borrow from the integer, subtract the fractions, and then subtract the integers. You don't need to convert the mixed numbers to improper fractions.

Solve $7\frac{1}{12} - 3\frac{3}{4}$ using these steps:

- Find the LCD; your answer should be 12.

- Convert the fractions so they each have a denominator of 12: $7\frac{1}{12} - 3\frac{9}{12}$

- Borrow from the integer: $6\frac{13}{12} - 3\frac{9}{12}$

- Subtract the numerators: $13 - 9 = 4$.

- Place the difference over the common denominator: $\frac{4}{12}$. This is an improper fraction and can be reduced.

- Reduce the fraction and subtract the integers to get the final answer: $3\frac{1}{3}$

Multiplying Fractions

Fractions don't need to have the same denominators to be multiplied. Follow these five steps to multiply fractions:

1. Change the mixed numbers, if any, to improper fractions.
2. Multiply all the numerators.
3. Multiply all the denominators.
4. Place the product of the numerators over the product of the denominators.
5. Reduce, if possible, and convert improper fractions to mixed numbers.

Multiply $\frac{2}{3} \times 2\frac{4}{7} \times \frac{5}{9}$ using these steps:

- Convert $2\frac{4}{7}$ to an improper fraction: $\frac{18}{7}$
- Multiply the numerators and denominators; put the products on top of each other:
  $$\frac{2}{3} \times \frac{18}{7} \times \frac{5}{9} = \frac{180}{189}$$
- Reduce as much as possible: $\frac{180}{189} \div \frac{9}{9} = \frac{20}{21}$

A whole number has an understood denominator of 1. To multiply a whole number by a mixed number, first multiply the fractional part of the mixed number by the whole number, and then the integral part of the mixed number; then add both products.

For example, to multiply $23\frac{3}{4}$ by 95, first multiply $\frac{3}{4}$ by $\frac{95}{1}$, then multiply 23 by 95, and then add the results of each. You should get $2,256\frac{1}{4}$.

Dividing Fractions

To divide two fractions, multiply one fraction by the other's **reciprocal**. The reciprocal of a fraction is its invert; for example, the reciprocal of $\frac{3}{8}$ is $\frac{8}{3}$. Since every whole number has an understood denominator of 1, the reciprocal of a whole number has 1 as the numerator and the whole number as the denominator; for example, the reciprocal of 5 is $\frac{1}{5}$.

Follow these three steps to divide two fractions:

1. Convert all mixed numbers, if any, to improper fractions.
2. Invert the second fraction and multiply the two.
3. Reduce the answer, if possible. Convert improper fractions to mixed numbers.

Divide $\frac{2}{3}$ by $2\frac{1}{4}$ using these steps:

- Convert $2\frac{1}{4}$ to an improper fraction: $\frac{9}{4}$
- Invert the second fraction and multiply the two: $\frac{2}{3} \div \frac{9}{4} = \frac{2}{3} \times \frac{4}{9}$
- The answer is $\frac{8}{27}$.

A complex fraction has a fraction as the numerator and/or the denominator, such as $\dfrac{\frac{2}{3}}{\frac{5}{14}}$.

To clear (or simplify) a complex fraction, divide the numerator by the denominator and reduce:

$$\frac{2}{3} \times \frac{14}{5} = \frac{28}{15} = 1\frac{14}{15}$$

TACKLING FRACTION PROBLEMS

Most fraction problems can be arranged in the form, "What fraction of a number is another number?" This form contains three important parts: the fractional part; the number following *of*; and the number following *is*. Follow these three rules to find the answer:

1. If the fraction and the *of* number are given, multiply them to find the *is* number. For example, if asked, "What is $\frac{3}{4}$ of 20?" rewrite the question as "$\frac{3}{4}$ of 20 is what number?" Then multiply $\frac{3}{4}$ (the fraction) by 20 (the *of* number) to get $\frac{60}{4}$, which can be reduced to 15.

2. If the fraction and the *is* number are given, divide the *is* number by the fraction to find the *of* number. For example, if asked, "$\frac{4}{5}$ of what number is 40?" divide 40 (the *is* number) by $\frac{4}{5}$ (the fraction) to get $\frac{200}{4}$, which can be reduced to 50.

3. To find the fraction when the other two numbers are known, divide the *is* number by the *of* number. For example, if asked, "What part of 12 is 9?" divide 9 (the *is* number) by 12 (the *of* number). The answer is $\frac{9}{12}$, which can be reduced to $\frac{3}{4}$.

It's time to practice using the rules you've learned about fractions. Work through the exercises carefully and then compare your answers with the answer keys and explanations that follow.

EXERCISE 1

Directions: Solve the following fraction problems as directed and select the correct answer from the answer choices provided.

1. Reduce to lowest terms: $\frac{60}{108}$

   SHOW YOUR WORK HERE

   A. $\frac{1}{48}$

   B. $\frac{1}{3}$

   C. $\frac{5}{9}$

   D. $\frac{10}{18}$

2. Change $\frac{27}{7}$ to a mixed number.

   A. $2\frac{1}{7}$

   B. $3\frac{6}{7}$

   C. $6\frac{1}{3}$

   D. $7\frac{1}{2}$

3. Find the LCD of $\frac{1}{6}, \frac{1}{10}, \frac{1}{18}$, and $\frac{1}{21}$.

   A. 160

   B. 330

   C. 630

   D. 1,260

4. Add $16\frac{3}{8}, 4\frac{4}{5}, 12\frac{3}{4}$, and $23\frac{5}{6}$.

   A. $57\frac{91}{120}$

   B. $57\frac{1}{4}$

   C. 58

   D. 59

SHOW YOUR WORK HERE

5. Subtract $27\frac{5}{14}$ from $43\frac{1}{6}$.
   A. 15
   B. 16
   C. $15\frac{8}{21}$
   D. $15\frac{17}{21}$

6. Multiply $17\frac{5}{8}$ by 128.
   A. 2,200
   B. 2,305
   C. 2,356
   D. 2,256

7. Divide $1\frac{2}{3}$ by $1\frac{1}{9}$.
   A. $\frac{2}{3}$
   B. $1\frac{1}{2}$
   C. $1\frac{23}{27}$
   D. 6

EXERCISE 2

Directions: Solve the following word problems using the operations with fractions discussed in this chapter. Select the correct answer from the answer choices provided.

1. The number of half-pound packages of tea that can be weighed out of a box that holds $10\frac{1}{2}$ pounds of tea is

   SHOW YOUR WORK HERE

   A. 5

   B. $10\frac{1}{2}$

   C. $20\frac{1}{2}$

   D. 21

2. If each bag of tokens weighs $5\frac{3}{4}$ pounds, how many pounds do three bags weigh?

   A. $7\frac{1}{4}$

   B. $15\frac{3}{4}$

   C. $16\frac{1}{2}$

   D. $17\frac{1}{4}$

3. During one week, a man traveled $3\frac{1}{2}, 1\frac{1}{4}, 1\frac{1}{16},$ and $2\frac{3}{8}$ miles.
   The next week he traveled $\frac{1}{4}, \frac{3}{8}, \frac{9}{16}, 3\frac{1}{16}, 2\frac{5}{8},$ and $3\frac{3}{16}$ miles.
   How many more miles did he travel the second week than the first week?

   A. $1\frac{7}{8}$

   B. $1\frac{1}{2}$

   C. $1\frac{3}{4}$

   D. 1

4. A certain type of board is sold only in lengths of multiples of 2 feet. The shortest board sold is 6 feet and the longest is 24 feet. A builder needs a large quantity of this type of board in $5\frac{1}{2}$ -foot lengths. For minimum waste, the lengths to be ordered should be
   A. 6 feet
   B. 12 feet
   C. 22 feet
   D. 24 feet

5. A man spent $\frac{15}{16}$ of his assets in buying a car for $7,500. How much money did the man originally have?
   A. $6,000
   B. $6,500
   C. $7,000
   D. $8,000

6. The population of a town was 54,000 in the last census. It has increased $\frac{2}{3}$ since then. Its present population is
   A. 18,000
   B. 36,000
   C. 72,000
   D. 90,000

7. If one-third of the liquid contents of a can evaporates on the first day, and three-fourths of the remainder evaporates on the second day, the part of the original contents remaining at the close of the second day is
   A. $\frac{5}{12}$
   B. $\frac{7}{12}$
   C. $\frac{1}{6}$
   D. $\frac{1}{2}$

SHOW YOUR WORK HERE

8. A car is run until the gas tank is $\frac{1}{8}$ full. The tank is then filled to capacity by putting in 14 gallons. The capacity of the gas tank of the car is

A. 14 gal.

B. 15 gal.

C. 16 gal.

D. 17 gal.

SHOW YOUR WORK HERE

ANSWER KEYS AND EXPLANATIONS

Exercise 1

1. C	3. C	5. D	6. D	7. B
2. B	4. A			

1. **The correct answer is C.** Divide the numerator and denominator by 12 to get $\frac{5}{9}$.

2. **The correct answer is B.** Divide the numerator (27) by the denominator (7) to get 3 with a remainder of 6; the answer is $3\frac{6}{7}$.

3. **The correct answer is C.** You can divide the denominators by 2, 3, 3, 5, and 7. Multiply these divisors to find 630.

4. **The correct answer is A.** The LCD is 120, so the mixed numbers convert to $16\frac{45}{120} + 4\frac{96}{120} + 12\frac{90}{120} + 23\frac{100}{120}$.

   Add the numerators and the integers: $55\frac{331}{120}$.

   Change the improper fraction to a mixed number: $57\frac{91}{120}$.

5. **The correct answer is D.** The LCD is 42, so the mixed numbers convert to $43\frac{7}{42} - 27\frac{15}{42}$.

   Borrow to make the first numerator greater than the second: $42\frac{49}{42} - 27\frac{15}{42}$.

   Subtract the integers and numerators: $15\frac{34}{42}$.

   Reduce: $15\frac{17}{21}$.

6. **The correct answer is D.**

   Convert $17\frac{5}{8}$ to an improper fraction: $\frac{141}{8}$.

   Multiply the numerators and denominators: $\frac{141}{8} \times \frac{128}{1} = \frac{18,048}{8}$.

   Reduce: 2,256.

7. **The correct answer is B.** Convert the mixed numbers to improper fractions: $\frac{5}{3} \div \frac{10}{9}$.

   Invert the second fraction and multiply: $\frac{5}{3} \times \frac{9}{10} = \frac{45}{30}$. Reduce: $\frac{3}{2}$. Convert to a mixed number: $1\frac{1}{2}$.

Exercise 2

1. D	3. A	5. D	7. C	8. C
2. D	4. C	6. D		

1. **The correct answer is D.**

   Divide $10\frac{1}{2}$ pounds by $\frac{1}{2}$ pound:

   $\frac{21}{2} \div \frac{1}{2} = \frac{21}{2} \times \frac{2}{1} = \frac{42}{2} = 21$.

2. **The correct answer is D.** Multiply $5\frac{3}{4}$ pounds by 3: $\frac{23}{4} \times \frac{3}{1} = \frac{69}{4} = 17\frac{1}{4}$.

3. **The correct answer is A.** For the first week, the LCD is 16; add all the fractions to get $8\frac{3}{16}$ miles. For the second week, the LCD is 16; add all the fractions to get $10\frac{1}{16}$ miles.

   Subtract $8\frac{3}{16}$ from $10\frac{1}{16}$. Borrow to make the first numerator greater than the second: $9\frac{17}{16} - 8\frac{3}{16} = 1\frac{14}{16}$. Reduce to $1\frac{7}{8}$.

4. **The correct answer is C.** Consider each choice. Each 6-foot board yields one $5\frac{1}{2}$-foot board with $\frac{1}{2}$ foot waste. Each 12-foot board yields two $5\frac{1}{2}$-foot boards with 1 foot waste ($2 \times 5 = 11$; $12 - 11 = 1$). Each 24-foot board yields four $5\frac{1}{2}$-foot boards with 2 feet waste ($4 \times 5\frac{1}{2} = 22$; $24 - 22 = 2$). Each 22-foot board yields four $5\frac{1}{2}$-foot boards with no waste ($4 \times 5\frac{1}{2} = 22$ exactly). So 22 feet is the best choice.

5. **The correct answer is D.** $\frac{15}{16}$ of the assets is $7,500. Therefore, the amount is $7,500 \div \frac{15}{16}$, or $8,000.

6. **The correct answer is D.** The increase equals $\frac{2}{3}$ of 54,000. Therefore, the increase is $\frac{2}{3} \times \frac{54,000}{1}$, or 36,000. The present population is 54,000 + 36,000, or 90,000.

7. **The correct answer is C.** On the first day, $\frac{1}{3}$ evaporates and $\frac{2}{3}$ remains. On the second day, $\frac{3}{4}$ of $\frac{2}{3}$ evaporates, and $\frac{1}{4}$ of $\frac{2}{3}$ remains. The amount remaining is $\frac{1}{4} \times \frac{2}{3}$, or $\frac{1}{6}$ of the original contents.

8. **The correct answer is C.** $\frac{7}{8}$ of capacity equals 14 gal. Therefore, the capacity is $14 \div \frac{7}{8}$, or 16 gal.

DECIMALS

A **decimal** is actually a fraction, the denominator of which is understood to be a power of 10. The number of digits, or places, after a decimal point determines which power of 10 the denominator is. If there is one digit, the denominator is 10; if there are two digits, the denominator is 100, and so on. For example, $0.3 = \frac{3}{10}$, $0.57 = \frac{57}{100}$, and $0.643 = \frac{643}{1,000}$.

To convert a mixed number containing a decimal to a fraction by dividing the mixed number by the power of 10 indicated by its number of decimal places. The fraction doesn't count as a decimal place. For example, to convert $0.25\frac{1}{3}$ to a fraction, divide $25\frac{1}{3}$ by 100.

Rules to Know: Decimals

Study the rules outlined in this section to learn how to solve any arithmetic problem that involves decimals. Be sure that you understand the rules before moving on to the practice problems.

Adding and Subtracting Decimals

Decimals are added and subtracted in the same way as whole numbers. However, decimal points must be kept in a vertical line to determine the place of the decimal point in the answer:

$$
\begin{array}{r}
2.3100 \\
0.0370 \\
4.0000 \\
+\ 5.0017 \\
\hline
11.3487
\end{array}
\qquad
\begin{array}{r}
15.3000 \\
-\ 4.0037 \\
\hline
11.2963
\end{array}
$$

Multiplying Decimals

Decimals are multiplied the same way as whole numbers. The number of decimal places in the product equals the sum of the decimal places in the multiplicand and the multiplier. If there are fewer places in the product than this sum, then a sufficient number of zeros must be added in front of the product to equal the number of places required, and the decimal point is placed in front of the zeros. For example, 2.372 (three decimal places) × 0.012 (three decimal places) = 0.028464 (six decimal places).

Dividing Decimals

There are four types of division involving decimals:

1. **When only the dividend is a decimal**, the division is the same as that of whole numbers; the number of decimal places in the answer must equal that in the dividend:

$$12.864 \div 32 = 0.402.$$

2. **When only the divisor is a decimal**, the decimal point in the divisor is omitted, and as many zeros are placed to the right of the dividend as there are decimal points in the divisor:

$$211{,}327 \div 6.817 = 211{,}327{,}000 \div 6{,}817 = 31{,}000.$$

3. **When both divisor and divided are decimals**, the decimal point in the divisor is omitted, and the decimal point in the dividend is moved to the right as many decimal places as there are in the divisor. If there aren't enough places in the dividend, zeros must be added to make up the difference:

$$2.62 \div 0.131 = 2{,}620 \div 131 = 20.$$

4. **When neither the divisor nor the dividend is a decimal**, the problem may still involve decimals. This occurs when the dividend is a smaller number than the divisor, and when you must work out a division to a certain number of decimal places. In either case, write in a decimal point after the dividend, add as many zeros as necessary, and then divide:

$$7 \div 50 = 7.00 \div 50 = 0.14.$$

Converting Fractions to Decimals

A fraction can be changed to a decimal by dividing the numerator by the denominator and working out the division to as many decimal points as required. For example, to change $\frac{5}{11}$ to a decimal of two places, divide 5.00 by 11, which equals 0.45.

Because decimal equivalents of fractions are often used, it's helpful to be familiar with the most common conversions (the decimal values have been rounded to the nearest ten-thousandth):

$$\frac{1}{2} = 0.5$$

$$\frac{1}{3} = 0.3333$$

$$\frac{2}{3} = 0.6667$$

$$\frac{1}{4} = 0.25$$

$$\frac{3}{4} = 0.75$$

$$\frac{1}{5} = 0.2$$

$$\frac{1}{8} = 0.125$$

It's time to practice using the rules you've learned about decimals. Work through the exercises carefully and then compare your answers with the answer keys and explanations that follow.

EXERCISE 1

> **Directions:** Each question has four suggested answers. Select the correct one.

1. Add 37.03; 11.5627; 3.4005; 3,423; and 1.141.

   SHOW YOUR WORK HERE

   A. 3,476.1342
   B. 3,500
   C. 3,524.4322
   D. 3,424.1342

2. Subtract 4.64324 from 7.
   A. 3.35676
   B. 2.35676
   C. 2.45676
   D. 2.36676

3. Multiply 27.34 by 16.943.
   A. 463.22162
   B. 453.52162
   C. 462.52162
   D. 462.53162

4. How much is 19.6 divided by 3.2 carried out to three decimal places?
   A. 6.125
   B. 6.124
   C. 6.123
   D. 5.123

5. What is $\frac{5}{11}$ in decimal form (to the nearest hundredth)?
   A. 0.44
   B. 0.55
   C. 0.40
   D. 0.45

6. What is $0.64\frac{2}{3}$ in fraction form?

   SHOW YOUR WORK HERE

   A. $\frac{97}{120}$

   B. $\frac{97}{150}$

   C. $\frac{97}{130}$

   D. $\frac{98}{130}$

7. What is the difference between $\frac{9}{8}$ and $\frac{3}{5}$ expressed decimally?

   A. 0.525

   B. 0.425

   C. 0.520

   D. 0.500

exercises

EXERCISE 2

Directions: Each question has four suggested answers. Select the correct one.

1. A boy saved up $4.56 the first month, $3.82 the second month, and $5.06 the third month. How much did he save in total?

    A. $12.56

    B. $13.28

    C. $13.44

    D. $14.02

2. The diameter of a certain rod is required to be 1.51 ± 0.015 inches. The rod would NOT be acceptable if the diameter measured

    A. 1.490 inches.

    B. 1.500 inches.

    C. 1.510 inches.

    D. 1.525 inches.

3. After an employer figures out an employee's salary of $190.57, he deducts $3.05 for Social Security and $5.68 for pension. What is the amount of the check after these deductions?

    A. $181.84

    B. $181.92

    C. $181.93

    D. $181.99

4. If the outer diameter of a metal pipe is 2.84 inches and the inner diameter is 1.94 inches, the thickness of the metal is

    A. 0.45 inch.

    B. 0.90 inch.

    C. 1.94 inches.

    D. 2.39 inches.

SHOW YOUR WORK HERE

5. A boy earns $20.56 on Monday, $32.90 on Tuesday, and $20.78 on Wednesday. He spends half of all that he earned during the three days. How much does he have left?

   A. $29.19

   B. $31.23

   C. $34.27

   D. $37.12

SHOW YOUR WORK HERE

6. To the nearest cent, what will be the total cost of $3\frac{1}{2}$ pounds of meat at $1.69 a pound and 20 lemons at $0.60 a dozen?

   A. $6.00

   B. $6.40

   C. $6.52

   D. $6.92

7. A reel of cable weighs 1,279 pounds. If the empty reel weighs 285 pounds and the cable weighs 7.1 pounds per foot, the number of feet of cable on the reel is

   A. 220.

   B. 180.

   C. 140.

   D. 100.

8. To the nearest cent, what will 345 fasteners at $4.15 per hundred cost?

   A. $0.14

   B. $1.43

   C. $14.32

   D. $143.20

ANSWER KEYS AND EXPLANATIONS

Exercise 1

1. A	**3.** A	**5.** D	**6.** B	**7.** A
2. B	**4.** A			

1. **The correct answer is A.** Line up the decimal points one under the other before adding.

2. **The correct answer is B.** Add a decimal point and five zeros to the 7 before subtracting.

3. **The correct answer is A.** Because two decimal places are in the multiplicand and three decimal places are in the multiplier, there should be five decimal places in the product.

4. **The correct answer is A.** Omit the decimal point in the divisor by moving it one place to the right. Move the decimal point in the dividend one place to the right and add three zeros to carry your answer out to three decimal places:

$$196.000 \div 32 = 6.125.$$

5. **The correct answer is D.** Divide the numerator by the denominator:

$5.000 \div 11 = 0.45$ to the nearest hundredth.

6. **The correct answer is B.** Divide by the power of 10 indicated by the number of decimal places. (The fraction doesn't count as a decimal place.)

$$64\frac{2}{3} \div 100 = \frac{97}{150}$$

7. **The correct answer is A.** Convert each fraction to a decimal and subtract to find the difference:

$\frac{9}{8} = 1.125; \frac{3}{5} = 0.60; 1.125 - 0.60 = 0.525.$

Exercise 2

1. C	3. A	5. D	7. C	8. C
2. A	4. A	6. D		

1. **The correct answer is C.** Add the savings for each month: $4.56 + $3.82 + $5.06 = $13.44.

2. **The correct answer is A.** The rod may have a diameter of 1.495 inches to 1.525 inches: 1.51 + 0.015 = 1.525; 1.510 − 0.015 = 1.495. Therefore, 1.490 inches is not acceptable.

3. **The correct answer is A.** Add to find the total deductions: $3.05 + $5.68 = $8.73. Subtract total deductions from salary to find the amount of the check:

   $$\$190.57 - \$8.73 = \$181.84.$$

4. **The correct answer is A.** The difference of the two diameters equals the total thickness of the metal. Find the difference of the two diameters, and then divide by 2: 2.84 − 1.94 = 0.90; 0.90 ÷ 2 = 0.45 in. (the thickness of the metal).

5. **The correct answer is D.** Add the daily earnings to find the total earnings: $20.56 + $32.90 + $20.78 = $74.24. Divide the total earnings by 2 (the inverse of $\frac{1}{2}$) to find what he has left: $74.24 ÷ 2 = $37.12.

6. **The correct answer is D.** Find the cost of $3\frac{1}{2}$ pounds of meat: $1.69 × 3.5 = $5.92 (to the nearest cent). Find the cost of 20 lemons: 0.60 ÷ 12 = $0.05 (for one lemon); $0.05 × 20 = $1.00 (for 20 lemons). Add the cost of the meat and the cost of the lemons: $5.92 + $1.00 = $6.92.

7. **The correct answer is C.** Subtract the weight of the empty reel from the total weight to find the weight of the cable: 1,279 pounds − 285 pounds = 994 pounds. Each foot of cable weighs 7.1 pounds; therefore, to find the number of feet of cable on the reel, divide 994 by 7.1 = 140.

8. **The correct answer is C.** Each fastener costs $4.15 ÷ 100 = $0.0415. 345 fasteners cost 345 × 0.0415 = $14.32 (rounded to the nearest cent).

SUMMING IT UP

- Knowing what fractions and mixed numbers are and how to work with them is key to performing well on arithmetic problems on your civil service exam. Study the ways to convert mixed numbers and improper fractions; reduce fractions; and add, subtract, multiply, and divide fractions.

- Most fraction questions can be arranged in the form, "What fraction of a number is another number?" This question type contains three important parts: the fractional part, the number following *of*, and the number following *is*. Any one of these three parts may be missing and what you need to find. Follow the rules outlined in this chapter and take the practice exercises to successfully and correctly answer this type of question on your exam.

- You can consider decimal questions as a type of fraction question. The denominator is understood to be a power of 10. The number of digits after the decimal point determines the power of the 10 of the denominator. To convert a mixed number containing a decimal to a fraction, divide the mixed number by the power of 10, which is indicated by the number of decimal points in the number. Follow the rules outlined in this chapter for adding, subtracting, multiplying, and dividing decimals and for converting fractions to decimals and vice versa.

Percentages, Ratios, and Proportions

OVERVIEW

PERCENTAGES

The percent sign (%) means "parts of a hundred." Some problems require you to express a fraction, mixed number, or a decimal as a percentage. In other problems, you must convert a percentage to a fraction, mixed number, or a decimal to perform the calculations.

Rules to Know: Percentages

To answer percentage problems, it's important to understand the following rules for making these conversions.

Decimal–Percentage Conversions

Follow these two steps to convert a whole number or decimal to a percentage:

1. Multiply the number by 100.
2. Affix a percent sign to the product.

For example, to convert 3 to a percentage, multiply 3 by 100 and affix a percent sign: 300%. To convert 0.67 to a percentage, multiply 0.67 by 100 and affix a percent sign: 67%.

To convert a percentage to a decimal or whole number, divide the percentage by 100. For example, 0.5% equals 0.005. You can then convert the resulting decimal to a fraction, if necessary: $\frac{1}{200}$.

Fraction–Percentage Conversions

Follow these three steps to convert a fraction or mixed number to a percentage:

1. Multiply the fraction or mixed number by 100.

2. Reduce, if possible, and convert improper fractions to mixed numbers.

3. Affix a percent sign to the result.

Convert $4\frac{2}{3}$ to a percentage using these steps:

- Multiply $4\frac{2}{3}$ by 100: $\frac{14}{3} \times 100 = \frac{1,400}{3}$.

- Convert the improper fraction to a mixed number: $466\frac{2}{3}$.

- Affix a percent sign: $466\frac{2}{3}\%$.

Some fraction–percent equivalents are used so frequently that it's helpful to be familiar with them:

$$\frac{1}{25} = 4\%$$

$$\frac{1}{20} = 5\%$$

$$\frac{1}{10} = 10\%$$

$$\frac{1}{5} = 20\%$$

$$\frac{1}{4} = 25\%$$

$$\frac{1}{2} = 50\%$$

$$\frac{3}{4} = 75\%$$

To convert a fractional percentage to a fraction, divide the fractional percentage by 100 and reduce, if possible. For example, $\frac{3}{4}\% \div 100 = \frac{3}{400}$. You can then convert the resulting fraction to a decimal, if necessary: 0.075.

Tackling Percentage Problems

Most percentage problems involve three quantities:

- The rate (R), which is followed by a percent sign

- The base (B), which follows the word *of*

- The amount of percentage (P), which usually follows the word *is*

Depending on which two quantities you know, you can easily find the third quantity by following a formula:

- If the rate and the base are known, then $P = R \times B$.

- If the rate and the percentage are known, then $B = \frac{P}{R}$.

- If the percentage and the base are known, then $R = \frac{P}{B}$.

Try an example of each kind of problem:

- Find 15% of 50.

  In this problem, you know the rate (15%) and the base (50). To find the percentage, multiply 15% by 50: $0.15 \times 50 = 7.5$.

- 7% of what number is 35?

  In this problem, you know the rate (7%) and the percentage (35). To find the base, divide 35 by 7%: $35 \div 0.07 = 500$.

- There are 96 men in a group of 150 people. What percentage of the group are men?

  Here you know the base (150) and the amount, or percentage, (96). To find the rate, divide 96 by 150: $96 \div 150 = 0.64$, or 64%.

In all percentage problems, the whole is always 100%. Knowing this, you can often deduce a solution to a problem. If a problem involves 10% of a quantity, the rest of the quantity is 90%; if a quantity has been decreased by 15%, the new amount is 85% of the original quantity; or if a quantity has been increased by 5%, the new amount is 105% of the original quantity.

It's time to practice using the rules you've learned about percentages. Work through the exercises carefully and then compare your answers with the answer keys and explanations that follow.

EXERCISE 1

Directions: Choose the correct answer to the following percentage conversion problems.

1. 10% written as a decimal is: SHOW YOUR WORK HERE
   A. 1.0
   B. 0.01
   C. 0.001
   D. 0.1

2. What is 5.37% in fraction form?

   A. $\dfrac{537}{10,000}$

   B. $5\dfrac{37}{10,000}$

   C. $\dfrac{537}{1,000}$

   D. $5\dfrac{37}{100}$

3. What percent of $\dfrac{5}{6}$ is $\dfrac{3}{4}$?
   A. 75%
   B. 60%
   C. 80%
   D. 90%

4. What percent is 14 of 24?

   A. $62\dfrac{1}{4}\%$

   B. $58\dfrac{1}{3}\%$

   C. $41\dfrac{2}{3}\%$

   D. $33\dfrac{3}{5}\%$

5. 200% of 800 =
   A. 2,500
   B. 16
   C. 1,600
   D. 4

EXERCISE 2

Directions: Choose the correct answer to the following percentage conversion problems.

1. If John must have a mark of 80% to pass a test of 35 items, the number of items he may miss and still pass the test is:

   A. 7

   B. 8

   C. 11

   D. 28

   SHOW YOUR WORK HERE

2. A television set sold for $118.80 at a 20% reduction sale. What is the regular price of the television set?

   A. $148.50

   B. $142.60

   C. $138.84

   D. $95.04

3. A circle graph of a budget shows the expenditure of 26.2% for housing, 28.4% for food, 12% for clothing, 12.7% for taxes, and the balance for miscellaneous items. What is the percentage for miscellaneous items?

   A. 31.5

   B. 79.3

   C. 20.7

   D. 68.5

4. Two dozen shuttlecocks and four badminton rackets are to be purchased for a playground. The shuttlecocks are priced at $0.35 each and the rackets at $2.75 each. The playground receives a discount of 30% from these prices. What is the total cost of this equipment?

   A. $7.29

   B. $11.43

   C. $13.58

   D. $18.60

5. A piece of wood weighing 10 ounces is found to have a weight of 8 ounces after drying. The moisture content was

    A. 25%.

    B. $33\frac{1}{3}\%$.

    C. 20%.

    D. 40%.

6. A bag contains 800 coins. Of these, 10 percent are dimes, 30 percent are nickels, and the rest are quarters. The amount of money in the bag is

    A. less than $150.

    B. between $150 and $300.

    C. between $301 and $450.

    D. more than $450.

7. Six quarts of a 20% solution of alcohol in water are mixed with four quarts of a 60% solution of alcohol in water. What is the alcoholic strength of the mixture?

    A. 80%

    B. 40%

    C. 36%

    D. 72%

8. A man insures 80% of his property and pays a $2\frac{1}{2}\%$ premium amounting to $348. What is the total value of his property?

    A. $17,000

    B. $18,000

    C. $18,400

    D. $17,400

SHOW YOUR WORK HERE

9. A clerk divided his 35-hour workweek as follows: $\frac{1}{5}$ of his time was spent in sorting mail; $\frac{1}{2}$ of his time in filing letters; and $\frac{1}{7}$ of his time in reception work. The rest of his time was devoted to messenger work. The percent of time spent on messenger work by the clerk during the week was most nearly

   A. 6%.

   B. 10%.

   C. 14%.

   D. 16%.

10. In a school in which 40% of the enrolled students are boys, 80% of the boys are present on a certain day. If 1,152 boys are present, what is the total school enrollment?

    A. 1,440

    B. 2,880

    C. 3,600

    D. 5,400

SHOW YOUR WORK HERE

ANSWER KEYS AND EXPLANATIONS

Exercise 1

1. D	2. A	3. D	4. B	5. C

1. **The correct answer is D.** $10\% \div 100 = 0.1$

2. **The correct answer is A.**

    $5.37\% \div 100 = 0.0537 = \dfrac{537}{10,000}$.

3. **The correct answer is D.**

    Base (number following *of*) = $\dfrac{5}{6}$

    Percentage (number following *is*) = $\dfrac{3}{4}$

    Rate = Percentage ÷ Base =

    $\dfrac{3}{4} \div \dfrac{5}{6} = \dfrac{9}{10} = 0.9 = 90\%$

4. **The correct answer is B.**

    Base (number following *of*) = 24

    Percentage (number following *is*) = 14

    Rate = Percentage ÷ Base = $14 \div 24 =$

    $0.58\dfrac{1}{3} = 58\dfrac{1}{3}\%$

5. **The correct answer is C.**

    Percentage = 200

    Base = 800

    Rate = Percentage × Base = $2.00 \times 800 = 1,600$

Exercise 2

1. A	3. C	5. C	7. C	9. D
2. A	4. C	6. A	8. D	10. C

1. **The correct answer is A.** He must answer 80% of 35 correctly. Therefore, he can miss 20% of 35. 20% of 35 (percentage) = 0.20 (rate) × 35 (base) = 7.

2. **The correct answer is A.** Since $118.80 represents a 20% reduction, $118.80 equals 80% of the regular price. The regular price (base) = $118.80 (percentage) ÷ 80% (rate) = 118.80 ÷ 0.80 = $148.50.

3. **The correct answer is C.** All the items in a circle graph total 100%. Add the figures given for housing, food, clothing, and taxes: 26.2 + 28.4 + 12 + 12.7 = 79.3%. Subtract this total from 100% to find the percentage for miscellaneous items: 100 − 79.3 = 20.7%.

4. **The correct answer is C.** The price of the shuttlecocks: 24 × $.35 = $8.40. The price of the rackets: 4 × $2.75 = $11.00. The total price: $8.40 + $11.00 = $19.40. The discount is 30%, and 100% minus 30% equals 70%. So the actual cost is 70% of $19.40: 0.70 (rate) × 19.40 (base) = $13.58 (percentage).

5. **The correct answer is C.** Subtract the weight of the wood after drying from the original weight of the wood to find the amount of moisture in the wood: 10 − 8 = 2 ounces of moisture in the wood. The moisture content (rate) equals 2 ounces (percentage) divided by 10 ounces (base): 2 ÷ 10 = 0.2 = 20%.

6. **The correct answer is A.** Find the number of each kind of coin: 10% of 800 = 0.10 × 800 = 80 dimes; 30% of 800 = 0.30 × 800 = 240 nickels; 60% of 800 = 0.60 × 800 = 480 quarters. Find the value of the coins: 80 dimes = 80 × 0.10 = $8.00; 240 nickels = 240 × 0.05 = $12.00; 480 quarters = 480 × 0.25 = $120.00; $8.00 + $12.00 + $120.00 = $140.00. So there is less than $150 in the bag.

7. **The correct answer is C.** The first solution contains 20% of 6 quarts of alcohol; the alcohol content is 0.20 × 6 = 1.2 quarts. The second solution contains 60% of 4 quarts of alcohol; the alcohol content is 0.60 × 4 = 2.4 quarts. The mixture contains 1.2 + 2.4 = 3.6 quarts alcohol, and 6 + 4 = 10 quarts liquid. So the alcoholic strength of the mixture (rate) = 3.6 (percentage) ÷ 10 (base) = 36%.

8. **The correct answer is D.** $2\frac{1}{2}$%, or 2.5%, of the insured value = $348; the insured value (base) = 348 (percentage) ÷ 2.5% (rate): 348 ÷ 0.025 = $13,920. The insured value ($13,920) is 80% of the total value; the total value (base) = $13,920 (percentage) ÷ 80% (rate): 13,290 ÷ 0.80 = $17,400.

9. **The correct answer is D.** The workweek is 35 hours long. $\frac{1}{5} \times 35 = 7$ hours sorting mail; $\frac{1}{2} \times 35 = 17\frac{1}{2}$ hours filing; $\frac{1}{7} \times 35 = 5$ hours reception. $7 + 17\frac{1}{2} + 5 = 29\frac{1}{2}$ hours accounted for. $35 - 29\frac{1}{2} = 5\frac{1}{2}$ hours left for messenger work. The percentage time spent on messenger work (rate) = $5\frac{1}{2}$ (percentage) ÷ 35 (base) = $\frac{11}{70} = 15\frac{5}{7}$ = most nearly 16%.

10. **The correct answer is C.** 80% of the boys equals 1,152; the total number of boys (base) = 1,152 (percentage) ÷ 80% (rate) = 1,152 ÷ 0.80 = 1,440 boys. 40% of the students = 1,440, so the total number of students (base) = 1,440 (percentage) ÷ 40% (rate) = 1,440 ÷ 0.40 = 3,600 students.

RATIOS AND PROPORTIONS

Ratio and proportion questions have long been a popular type of arithmetic problem given on civil service exams. This section will help you understand the rules governing ratio and proportion problems.

A **ratio** expresses the relationship between two (or more) quantities in terms of numbers. The mark used to indicate ratio is the colon (:) and is read "to." For example, the ratio 2:3 is read "2 to 3."

A ratio also represents division. Therefore, any ratio of two terms can be written as a fraction, and any fraction can be written as a ratio. For example, $3:4 = \frac{3}{4}$.

Solving Ratio Problems

Follow these three steps to solve problems in which the ratio is given:

1. Add the terms in the ratio.

2. Divide the total amount that is to be put into a ratio by this sum.

3. Multiply each term in the ratio by this quotient.

For example, the sum of $360 is to be divided among three people according to the ratio 3:4:5. How much does each one receive? Follow these steps:

- Add the terms in the ratio: 3 + 4 + 5 = 12.

- Divide the total amount to be put into the ratio by this sum: $360 ÷ 12 = $30.

- Multiply each term in the ratio by this quotient: $30 × 3 = $90; 30 × 4 = $120; $30 × 5 = $150.

The money is divided thus: $90, $120, and $150.

To simplify any complicated ratio of two terms containing fractions, decimals, or percents, you only need to divide the first term by the second. Reduce the answer to its lowest terms, and write the fraction as a ratio. For example, simplify the ratio $\frac{5}{6} : \frac{7}{8}$.

$$\frac{5}{6} : \frac{7}{8} \rightarrow \frac{5}{6} \div \frac{7}{8} = \frac{20}{21} = 20 : 21$$

Solving Proportion Problems

A proportion indicates the equality of two ratios. For example, 2:4 = 5:10 is a proportion. This is read, "2 is to 4 as 5 is to 10." The two outside terms (2 and 10) are the extremes, and the two inside terms (4 and 5) are the means. Proportions are often written in fractional form. For example, the proportion 2:4 = 5:10 can be written as $\frac{2}{4} = \frac{5}{10}$.

In any proportion, the product of the means equals the product of the extremes. If the proportion is in fractional form, the products can be found by cross-multiplication. For example, in the proportion $\frac{2}{4} = \frac{5}{10}$, 4 × 5 = 2 × 10.

Many problems in which three terms are given and one term is unknown can be solved using proportions. To solve such problems, follow these three steps:

1. Formulate the proportion very carefully according to the facts given. (If any term is misplaced, the solution will be incorrect.) Any symbol can be written in place of the missing term.

2. Determine by inspection whether the means or the extremes are known. Multiply the pair that has both terms given.

3. Divide this product by the third term given to find the unknown term.

Try this example problem:

> The scale on a map shows that 2 centimeters represent 30 miles of actual length. What is the actual length of a road that is represented by 7 centimeters on the map?

In this problem, the map lengths and the actual lengths are in proportion; that is, they have equal ratios. If m stands for the unknown length, the proportion is $\frac{2}{7} = \frac{30}{m}$. As the proportion is written, m is an extreme and is equal to the product of the means, divided by the other extreme:

$$m = 7 \times 30 \div 2 = 210 \div 2 = 105.$$

Therefore, 7 cm on the map represent 105 miles.

It's time to practice using the rules you've learned about ratios and proportions. Work through the exercises carefully and then compare your answers with the answer keys and explanations that follow.

EXERCISE 1

> **Directions:** Choose the correct answer to the following ratio and proportion problems.

1. The ratio of 24 to 64 is   **SHOW YOUR WORK HERE**
    A. 8:3
    B. 24:100
    C. 3:8
    D. 64:100

2. A football team won 8 games and lost 3.
    The ratio of games won to games played is
    A. 8:11
    B. 3:11
    C. 8:3
    D. 3:8

3. The ratio of $\frac{1}{4}$ to $\frac{3}{5}$ is
    A. 1 to 3
    B. 3 to 20
    C. 5 to 12
    D. 3 to 4

4. If there are 16 boys and 12 girls in a class,
    the ratio of the number of girls to the
    number of children in the class is
    A. 3 to 4
    B. 3 to 7
    C. 4 to 7
    D. 4 to 3

5. 259 is to 37 as
    A. 5 is to 1
    B. 63 is to 441
    C. 84 is to 12
    D. 130 is to 19

EXERCISE 2

Directions: Choose the correct answer to the following ratio and proportion problems.

1. Two dozen cans of dog food at the rate of three cans for $1.45 would cost how much?

   A. $10.05
   B. $11.20
   C. $11.60
   D. $11.75

   SHOW YOUR WORK HERE

2. A snapshot measures $2\frac{1}{2}$ inches by $1\frac{7}{8}$ inches. It is to be enlarged so that the longer dimension will be 4 inches. The length of the enlarged shorter dimension will be

   A. $2\frac{1}{2}$ inches

   B. 3 inches

   C. $3\frac{3}{8}$ inches

   D. None of these

3. Packs of tissues cost $2.29 for three. The cost per a dozen packs is

   A. $27.48.
   B. $13.74.
   C. $9.16.
   D. $6.87.

4. A certain pole casts a shadow 24 feet long. Another pole 3 feet high casts a shadow 4 feet long. How high is the first pole, given that the heights and shadows are in proportion?

   A. 18 feet
   B. 19 feet
   C. 20 feet
   D. 21 feet

5. The actual length represented by $3\frac{1}{2}$ inches on a drawing having a scale of $\frac{1}{8}$ inch to the foot is
   A. 3.75 ft.
   B. 28 ft.
   C. 360 ft.
   D. 120 ft.

SHOW YOUR WORK HERE

6. Aluminum bronze consists of copper and aluminum, usually in the ratio of 10:1 by weight. If an object made of this alloy weighs 77 pounds, how many pounds of aluminum does it contain?
   A. 7.7
   B. 7.0
   C. 70.0
   D. 62.3

7. It costs 31 cents a square foot to lay vinyl flooring. How much will it cost to lay 180 square feet of flooring?
   A. $16.20
   B. $18.60
   C. $55.80
   D. $62.00

8. If a temp worker earns $352 in 16 days, the amount that he will earn in 117 days is most nearly
   A. $3,050
   B. $2,574
   C. $2,285
   D. $2,080

9. Assuming that on a blueprint $\frac{1}{8}$ inch equals 12 inches of actual length, what is the actual length in inches of a steel bar represented on the blueprint by a line $3\frac{3}{4}$ inches long?

   A. 3

   B. 30

   C. 450

   D. 360

10. Alan, Bonnie, and Chris invested $9,000, $7,000, and $6,000, respectively. Their profits were to be divided according to the ratio of their investments. If Bonnie uses her share of the firm's profit of $825 to pay a personal debt of $230, how much will she have left?

    A. $30.50

    B. $32.50

    C. $34.50

    D. $36.50

SHOW YOUR WORK HERE

ANSWER KEYS AND EXPLANATIONS

Exercise 1

1. C	2. A	3. C	4. B	5. C

1. **The correct answer is C.** The ratio 24 to 64 can be written 24:64, or $\frac{24}{64}$. In fraction form, the ratio can be reduced to $\frac{3}{8}$, or 3:8.

2. **The correct answer is A.** The number of games played was 3 + 8 = 11. The ratio of games won to games played is 8:11.

3. **The correct answer is C.**
$$\frac{1}{4} : \frac{3}{5} = \frac{1}{4} \div \frac{3}{5} = \frac{5}{12} = 5 : 12$$

4. **The correct answer is B.** There are 16 + 12 = 28 children in the class. The ratio of number of girls to number of children is 12:28, which can be reduced to 3:7.

5. **The correct answer is C.** The ratio $\frac{259}{37}$ reduces by 37 to $\frac{7}{1}$. The ratio $\frac{84}{12}$ also reduces to $\frac{7}{1}$. Therefore, $\frac{259}{37} = \frac{84}{12}$ is a proportion.

Exercise 2

| 1. C | 3. C | 5. B | 7. C | 9. D |
| 2. B | 4. A | 6. B | 8. B | 10. B |

1. **The correct answer is C.** The number of cans is proportional to the price. Let p represent the unknown price:

$$\frac{3}{24} = \frac{1.45}{p}.$$

$p = 1.45 \times 24 \div 3 = 34.80 \div 3 = \$11.60.$

2. **The correct answer is B.** Let s represent the unknown shorter dimension: $\frac{2\frac{1}{2}}{4} = \frac{1\frac{7}{8}}{s}.$

$s = 4 \times 1\frac{7}{8} \div 2\frac{1}{2} = \frac{15}{2} \div 2\frac{1}{2} = 3$ inches

3. **The correct answer is C.** If p is the cost per dozen (12), the proportion is: $\frac{3}{12} = \frac{2.29}{p}.$
$p = 12 \times 2.29 \div 3 = \$9.16.$

4. **The correct answer is A.** If f is the height of the first pole, the proportion is $\frac{f}{24} = \frac{3}{4}.$
$f = 24 \times 3 \div 4 = 18$ ft.

5. **The correct answer is B.** If y is the unknown length, the proportion is $\frac{3\frac{1}{2}}{\frac{1}{8}} = \frac{y}{1}.$

$y = 3\frac{1}{2} \times 1 \div \frac{1}{8} = 28$ ft.

6. **The correct answer is B.** Because only two parts of a proportion are known (77 pounds is the total weight), the problem must be solved by the ratio method. The ratio of 10:1 means that if the alloy were separated into equal parts, 10 of those parts would be copper and 1 would be aluminum, for a total of 11 parts. $77 \div 11 = 7$ pounds per part. The alloy has 1 part aluminum: $7 \times 1 = 7$ pounds of aluminum.

7. **The correct answer is C.** The cost (c) is proportional to the number of square feet:

$$\frac{0.31}{c} = \frac{1}{180}.$$

$c = 0.31 \times 180 \div 1 = \$55.80$

8. **The correct answer is B.** The amount earned is proportional to the number of days worked. If a is the unknown amount, the proportion is $\frac{\$352}{a} = \frac{16}{117}.$

$a = 352 \times 117 \div 16 = \$2,574.$

9. **The correct answer is D.** If n is the unknown length, the proportion is $\frac{\frac{1}{8}}{3\frac{3}{4}} = \frac{12}{n}.$

$n = 12 \times 3\frac{3}{4} \div \frac{1}{8} = 360.$

10. **The correct answer is B.** The ratio of investment is: 9,000:7,000:6,000, or 9:7:6. $9 + 7 + 6 = 22.$ Each share of the profit is $\$825 \div 22 = \$37.50.$ Bonnie's share of the profit is $7 \times 37.50 = \$262.50.$ The amount Bonnie has left is $\$262.50 - \$230.00 = \$32.50.$

SUMMING IT UP

- Percentage questions often require you to change a fraction, mixed number, or decimal to a percentage, or vice versa, so be sure you understand the rules for making these conversions.

- Remember that in all percentage problems, the whole is always 100%. Keeping this in mind may help you figure out the answer to a question. For example, if a problem involves 40% of a quantity, you know for certain that the rest of the quantity must be 60%.

- A ratio expresses the relationship between two or more quantities in terms of numbers. A ratio also represents division.

- A proportion indicates the equality of two ratios. Remember that the product of the means (inner numbers) equals the products of the extremes (outer numbers) in a proportion.

Graphs and Tables

OVERVIEW

- **Graphs**
- **Exercise**
- **Answer Key and Explanations**
- **Tabular Completions**
- **Exercise**
- **Answer Key and Explanations**
- **Summing It Up**

GRAPHS

A graph is a picture that illustrates comparisons and trends in statistical information. This section will prepare you to see the "complete picture" in a graph and supply the correct answers based on the data. The following are the most commonly used graphs:

- Bar graphs
- Line graphs
- Circle graphs
- Pictographs

Understanding Bar Graphs

Bar graphs compare various quantities using either horizontal or vertical bars. Each bar may represent a single quantity or may be divided to represent several quantities. See Figure 17.1 for an example of a bar graph. The questions following the graph are typical of the kinds of questions found on the civil service exam.

Chapter 17

Figure 17.1

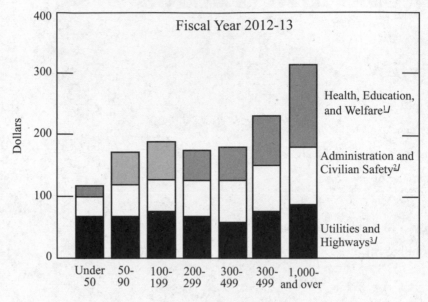

Municipal Expenditures, Per Capita

1. Public welfare, education, hospitals, health, libraries, and housing and urban renewal.
2. Police and fire protection, file administration, general control, general public buildings, interest on general debt, and other.
3. Highway, sewage, sanitation, parks and recreation, and utilities.

Source: Department of Commerce

- What was the approximate municipal expenditure per capita in cities having populations of 200,000 to 299,000?

  o The middle bar represents cities having populations from 200,000 to 299,000. This bar reaches above halfway between 100 and 200. Therefore, the per capita expenditure is approximately $175.

- Which cities spent the most per capita on health, education, and welfare?

  o The bar for cities having populations of 1 million and over has a larger gray section than the other bars. Therefore, those cities spent the most.

- Of the three categories of expenditures, which was least dependent on city size?

  o The expenditures for utilities and highways, the darkest part of each bar, varied least as city size increased.

Understanding Line Graphs

Line graphs illustrate trends, often over a period of time. A line graph may include more than one line, with each line representing a different item. Study the line graph in Figure 17.2 and answer the questions following the graph.

Figure 17.2

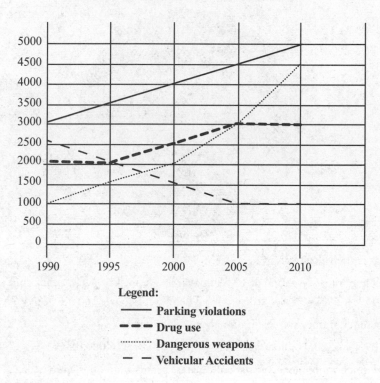

- Over the 20-year period, which offense shows an average rate of increase of more than 150 citations per year?
  - ○ Dangerous weapons citations increased from 1,000 in 1990 to 4,500 in 2010. The average increase over the 20-year period is $\frac{3,500}{20}$ = 175.
- Over the 20-year period, which offense shows a constant rate of increase or decrease?
  - ○ A straight line indicates a constant rate of increase or decrease. Of the four lines, the one representing parking violations is the only straight one.
- Which offense shows a total increase or decrease of 50% for the full 20-year period?
  - ○ Drug use citations increased from 2,000 in 1990 to 3,000 in 2010, an increase of 50%.

Understanding Circle Graphs

Circle graphs (also called **pie charts**) show the relationship of various parts of a quantity to each other and to the whole quantity. Each part of a circle graph is called a **sector**.

Study the circle graph in Figure 17.3 and answer the questions following the graph.

Figure 17.3

How the Federal Budget of $300.4 Billion Was Spent

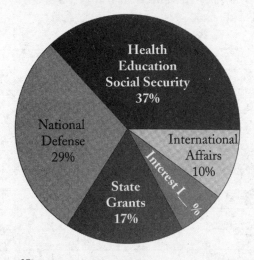

- What is the value of I?
  - There must be a total of 100% in a circle graph. The sum of the other sections is: 17% + 29% + 37% + 10% = 93%. Therefore, I equals 100% − 93% = 7%.
- How much money was spent on national defense?
  - 29% × $300.4 billion = $87.116 billion, or $87,116,000,000.
- How much more money was spent on state grants than on interest?
  - 17% − 7% = 10%; 10% × $300.4 billion = $30.04 billion, or $30,040,000,000.

Understanding Pictographs

Pictographs compare quantities using symbols. Each symbol represents a given number of a particular item. Take a look at the pictograph in Figure 17.4 and answer the questions following the graph.

Figure 17.4

The Number of New Houses Built in XYZ Town, 1995–2010

- How many more new houses were built in 2000 than in 2005?
  - There are two more symbols for 2000 than for 2005. Each symbol represents 100 houses. Therefore, 200 more houses were built in 2000.
- How many new houses were built in 1995?
  - There are $3\frac{1}{2}$ symbols shown for 1995: $3\frac{1}{2} \times 100 = 350$ houses.
- In which year were half as many houses built as in 2005?
  - In 2005, $3 \times 100 = 300$ houses were built. Half of 300, or 150 houses, were built in 2010.

It's time to practice using the rules you've learned about graphs. Work through the exercises carefully and then compare your answers with the answer keys and explanations that follow.

EXERCISE

Directions: Choose the correct answer to the following graph problems.

Questions 1–4 refer to the following graph.

Yearly Incidence of Major Crimes for Community Z 2010–12

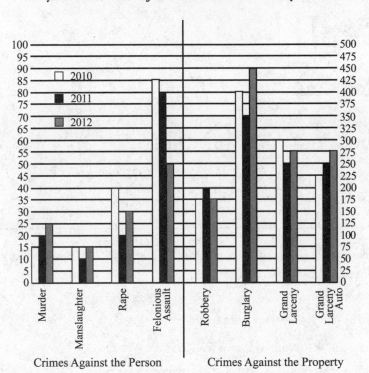

1. In 2012, the incidence of which of the following crimes was greater than in the previous two years?
   A. Grand larceny
   B. Murder
   C. Rape
   D. Robbery

2. If the incidence of burglary in 2013 had increased over 2012 by the same number as it had increased in 2012 over 2011, then the average incidences for this crime for the period from 2010 to 2013 would be most nearly
   A. 100.
   B. 100.
   C. 425.
   D. 440.

3. The graph indicates that the percentage increase in grand larceny auto from 2011 to 2012 was
   A. 5%.
   B. 10%.
   C. 15%.
   D. 20%.

4. Which of the following cannot be determined because there is NOT enough information in the graph to do so?
   A. For the three-year period, what percentage of all "Crimes Against the Person" involved murders committed in 2011?
   B. For the three-year period, what percentage of all major crimes was committed in the first six months of 2011?
   C. Which major crimes followed a pattern of continuing yearly increases for the three-year period?
   D. For 2012, what was the ratio of robbery, burglary, and grand larceny crimes?

exercise

Questions 5–7 refer to the following graph.

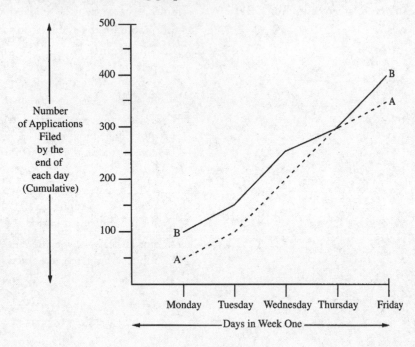

Directions: In the graph above, the lines labeled "A" and "B" represent the cumulative progress in the work of two file clerks, each of whom was given 500 consecutively numbered applications to file in the proper cabinets over a five-day workweek.

5. The day during which the largest number of applications was filed by both clerks was
   A. Monday.
   B. Tuesday.
   C. Wednesday.
   D. Friday.

6. At the end of the second day, the percentage of applications still to be filed was
   A. 25%.
   B. 50%.
   C. 66%.
   D. 75%.

7. Assuming that the production pattern continues during the following week as though there had been no days off, the day on which Clerk B will finish this assignment will be
   A. Monday.
   B. Tuesday.
   C. Wednesday.
   D. Friday.

Questions 8–11 refer to the following graphs.

Age
1.3 Million = 100%

**Characteristics of
U.S. Travelers Abroad...**
Based on Passports Issued
and Renewed in 2012

Occupation*
1.2 Million = 100%

A. Skilled, Clerical, Technical
   or Sales Workers
B. Others
C. Retired
D. Civilian, Government and Military

* Based on nine months only

Note: Due to rounding, figures may not add up to 100%

Residence
1.3 Million = 100%

▲ Mountain

8. Approximately how many persons aged 29 or younger traveled abroad in 2012?

   A. 175,000
   B. 245,000
   C. 385,000
   D. 450,000

9. Of the people who did NOT live in the Northeast, what percentage came from the North Central states?

   A. 19.2%
   B. 19.9%
   C. 26.5%
   D. 31.6%

10. The fraction of travelers from the four smallest occupation groups is most nearly equal to the fraction of travelers

   A. under age 20, and 65 and over, combined.
   B. from the North Central and Mountain states.
   C. between 45 and 64 years of age.
   D. from the Housewife and Other categories.

11. If the South Central, Mountain, and Pacific sections were considered as a single classification, how many degrees would its sector include?

   A. 30°
   B. 67°
   C. 108°
   D. 120°

Questions 12–15 refer to the following graph.

**Vehicles Crossing
the Hudson Bridge**

Each symbol represents 500 vehicles

Passenger car

Truck

12. What percentage of the total number of vehicles on Wednesday were cars?

    A. 30%

    B. 60%

    C. 20%

    D. 50%

13. What was the total number of vehicles crossing the bridge on Tuesday?

    A. 7

    B. 700

    C. 1,100

    D. 3,500

14. How many more trucks crossed on Monday than on Saturday?

    A. 200

    B. 1,000

    C. 1,500

    D. 2,000

15. If trucks paid a toll of $1.00 and cars paid a toll of $0.50, how much money was collected in tolls on Friday?

    A. $400

    B. $600

    C. $2,000

    D. $2,500

ANSWER KEY AND EXPLANATIONS

1. B	4. B	7. B	10. A	13. D
2. D	5. C	8. D	11. C	14. B
3. B	6. D	9. D	12. B	15. C

1. **The correct answer is B.** The incidence of murder increased from 15 in 2010 to 20 in 2011 to 25 in 2012.

2. **The correct answer is D.** The incidence of burglary in 2010 was 400; in 2011, it was 350; and in 2012, it was 450. The increase from 2011 to 2012 was 100. If there is the same increase of 100 from 2012 to 2013, the incidence of burglary would be 550 in 2013. The average of 400, 350, 450, and 550 is: 400 + 350 + 450 + 550 = 1,750 ÷ 4 = 437.5, which rounds up to 440.

3. **The correct answer is B.** The incidence of grand larceny auto went from 250 in 2011 to 275 in 2012, an increase of 25. The percentage increase is 25 ÷ 250 = 0.10 = 10%.

4. **The correct answer is B.** This graph gives information by year, not month. It's impossible to determine from the graph the percentage of crimes committed during the first six months of any year.

5. **The correct answer is C.** For Clerks A and B, the greatest increase in the cumulative totals occurred from the end of Tuesday until the end of Wednesday. Therefore, the largest number of applications was filed on Wednesday.

6. **The correct answer is D.** By the end of Tuesday, Clerk A had filed 100 applications and Clerk B had filed 150, for a total of 250. This left 750 of the original 1,000 applications: 750 ÷ 1000 = 0.75 = 75%.

7. **The correct answer is B.** During Week One, Clerk B filed 100 applications on Monday, 50 on Tuesday, 100 on Wednesday, 50 on Thursday, and 100 on Friday. If he follows this pattern, he will file 50 on the Monday of Week Two, for a total of 450, and the remaining 50 during Tuesday.

8. **The correct answer is D.** 20−29 yrs. = 19.9%; under 20 yrs. = 14.8%; 19.9% + 14.8% = 34.7%; 34.7% × 1.3 million = 0.4511 million = 451,100, which rounds down to 450,000.

9. **The correct answer is D.** 100% − 39.2% = 60.8% did not live in the Northeast. 19.2% lived in the North Central states. 19.2 ÷ 60.8 = approximately 0.316, or 31.6%.

10. **The correct answer is A.** The four smallest groups of occupation: 7.9 + 6.9 + 5.8 + 5.7 = 26.3. Age groups under 20 and over 65: 14.8 + 11.4 = 26.2. Therefore, these two groups are most nearly equal.

11. **The correct answer is C.** South Central: 8.2%; Mountain: 3.1%; Pacific: 18.7%; 8.2 + 3.1 + 18.7 = 30.0%; 30% × 360° = 108°.

12. **The correct answer is B.** There are five vehicle symbols, of which three are cars: 3 ÷ 5 = 60%.

13. **The correct answer is D.** On Tuesday, there were 3 × 500 = 1,500 cars and 4 × 500 = 2,000 trucks. The total number of vehicles was 3,500.

14. **The correct answer is B.** The graph shows two more truck symbols on Monday than on Saturday. Each symbol represents 500 trucks, so there were 2 × 500 = 1,000 more trucks on Monday.

15. **The correct answer is C.** On Friday there were 4 × 500 = 2,000 cars and 2 × 500 = 1,000 trucks; car tolls: 2,000 × $0.50 = $1,000; truck tolls: 1,000 × $1.00 = $1,000; total tolls: $1,000 + $1,000 = $2,000.

TABULAR COMPLETIONS

Numerically, tabular completion items are among the easiest questions. The arithmetic involved is limited to addition and subtraction. The numbers may be large, but the process itself is simple.

Answering Tabular Completion Questions

The difficulty of answering tabular completion questions lies in choosing which numbers to add or subtract. The tables demand careful reading. For example, if a question calls for you to add the entry for "Utilities" and the entry for "Transportation," don't make the mistake of adding (or subtracting) the major category "Utilities" and its subcategories. The subcategories are already included in the major category. For example:

Utilities	4,665,170
Gas-powered	1,065,080
Coal-powered	3,600,090

The category "Utilities" is the sum of its two subcategories.

In answering these questions, you must first determine which entries combine to create each total and subtotal. If you're unclear about how to arrive at a number, you may have to look at a completed column to determine how certain figures were determined. Then move over into the column with the unknown that you're seeking, and calculate it by combining the appropriate entries.

Note that the directions for tabular completion questions give you five options. The final answer choice always is "**E.** None of the above." The directions state that the exact answer may not always be among the answer choices. In that case, you should choose "**E.** None of the above."

It's time to practice using the rules you've learned about tables. Work through the exercises carefully and then compare your answers with the answer key and explanations that follow.

EXERCISE

Directions: These questions are based on information presented in tables. You must calculate the unknown values by using the known values given in the table. In some questions, the exact answer will not be given as one of the response choices. In such cases, you should select "**E.** None of the above."

Questions 1–5 refer to the following table.

**Local Government Expenditures of Finances
2009 to 2012 (in millions of dollars)**

Item	2009	2010	2011	2012	Total Percent*
Expenditures	I	432,328	485,174	520,966	100.0
Direct General Expenditures	326,024	367,340	405,576	IV	83.2
Utility and Liquor Stores	30,846	II	43,016	47,970	9.2
Water and electric	20,734	24,244	28,453	31,499	6.0
Transit and others	10,112	11,947	14,563	16,471	3.2
Insurance Trust Expenditures	23,504	28,797	36,582	39,466	V
Employee retirement	12,273	14,008	III	17,835	3.4
Unemployment compensation	11,231	14,789	20,887	21,631	4.2

*Rounded to one decimal place

1. What is the value of I in millions of dollars?
   - **A.** 380,374
   - **B.** 377,604
   - **C.** 356,870
   - **D.** 349,528
   - **E.** None of the above

2. What is the value of II in millions of dollars?
   - **A.** 338,543
   - **B.** 64,988
   - **C.** 53,041
   - **D.** 40,744
   - **E.** None of the above

3. What is the value of III in millions of dollars?
   - **A.** 57,469
   - **B.** 52,277
   - **C.** 20,887
   - **D.** 15,695
   - **E.** None of the above

4. What is the value of IV in millions of dollars?
   - **A.** 472,996
   - **B.** 433,530
   - **C.** 425,026
   - **D.** 134,807
   - **E.** None of the above

5. What is the percent value of V?
   - **A.** 7.6
   - **B.** 7.4
   - **C.** 6.7
   - **D.** 3.3
   - **E.** None of the above

Questions 6–10 refer to the following table.

Revenue of All Governments By Source and Level of Government
Fiscal Year 2012 (in millions of dollars)*

Source	Total	Federal	State	Local
Total Revenue	1,259,421	660,759	310.828	V
Intergovernmental	184,033	1,804	70,786	111,443
From Federal Government	90,295	—	III	22,427
From state or local government	93,738	1,804	2,918	89,016
Revenue from Own Sources	1,075,388	II	240,042	176,391
General	820,814	487,706	187,373	145,735
Taxes	I	405,714	149,738	94,776
Property	74,969	—	2,949	72,020
Individual and corporate income	407,257	346,688	55,039	5,530
Sales and gross receipts	134,532	48,561	72,751	13,220
Other	33,470	10,465	18,999	4,006
Charges and miscellaneous	170,586	81,992	37,635	50,959
Utility and liquor stores	29,896	—	4,628	25,268
Insurance trust	224,678	171,249	48,041	5,388
Employee and railroad retirement	36,962	6,580	IV	5,260
Unemployment compensation	18,733	162	18,443	128
Old age, disability, and health insurance	168,983	164,507	4,476	—

Hypothetical data.

6. What is the value of I in millions of dollars?
   - A. 695,097
   - B. 616,758
   - C. 555,452
   - D. 254,574
   - E. None of the above

7. What is the value of II in millions of dollars?
   - A. 835,346
   - B. 662,563
   - C. 658,955
   - D. 417,433
   - E. None of the above

8. What is the value of III in millions of dollars?
   - A. 73,704
   - B. 68,868
   - C. 67,868
   - D. 67,978
   - E. None of the above

9. What is the value of IV in millions of dollars?
   - A. 43,565
   - B. 29,598
   - C. 25,122
   - D. 22,919
   - E. None of the above

10. What is the value of V in millions of dollars?
    - A. 821,567
    - B. 464,175
    - C. 318,490
    - D. 287,834
    - E. None of the above

Questions 11–15 refer to the following table.

Finance Companies—Assets and Liabilities
2002 to 2012 (in millions of dollars)*

Item	2002	2007	2012
Total Receivables	I	85,994	183,341
Consumer Receivables	31,773	40,814	77,460
Retail passenger car paper and others	11,577	13,399	31,950
Retail consumer goods and loans	20,196	27,415	IV
Business Receivables	22,999	39,286	86,067
Wholesale paper and others	14,084	22,012	48,059
Lease paper and others	8,915	17,274	38,008
Other Receivables	2,341	5,894	19,814
Total Liabilities	60,577	III	175,025
Loans and Notes Payable to Banks	7,551	8,617	15,458
Short-term	II	7,900	7,885
Long-term	969	717	7,573
Commercial Paper	22,073	25,905	52,328
Other Debt	30,953	54,194	V

Hypothetical data.

11. What is the value of I in millions of dollars?

    A. 54,772

    B. 57,113

    C. 63,546

    D. 68,856

    E. None of the above

12. What is the value of II in millions of dollars?

    A. 6,582

    B. 14,522

    C. 53,026

    D. 58,236

    E. None of the above

13. What is the value of III in millions of dollars?

    A. 62,811

    B. 88,716

    C. 94,610

    D. 97,333

    E. None of the above

14. What is the value of IV in millions of dollars?

    A. 45,610

    B. 47,610

    C. 47,611

    D. 54,117

    E. None of the above

15. What is the value of V in millions of dollars?

    A. 67,786

    B. 85,147

    C. 107,239

    D. 107,259

    E. None of the above

ANSWER KEY AND EXPLANATIONS

1. A	**4.** B	**7.** C	**10.** D	**13.** B
2. E	**5.** A	**8.** C	**11.** B	**14.** E
3. D	**6.** E	**9.** C	**12.** A	**15.** C

1. **The correct answer is A.** To calculate the total 2009 Expenditures, add the 2009 values for Direct General Expenditures, Utility and Liquor Stores, and Insurance Trust Expenditures: 326,024 + 30,846 + 23,504 = 380,374.

2. **The correct answer is E.** The correct value (not given as an answer) is calculated by adding the value for Water and electric and the value for Transit and others:

    24,244 + 11,947 = 36,191.

3. **The correct answer is D.** To calculate the 2011 Employee retirement costs, subtract the 2011 value of Unemployment compensation from the total Insurance Trust Expenditures: 36,582 − 20,887 = 15,695.

4. **The correct answer is B.** To calculate the value of 2012 Direct General Expenditures, add the 2012 values of Utility and Liquor Stores and Insurance Trust Expenditures, and subtract that sum from the total of 2012 Expenditures:

    520,966 − (47,970 + 39,466) = 433,530.

5. **The correct answer is A.** To calculate the percent of total 2012 Expenditures represented by Insurance Trust Expenditures, add the percentages represented by Direct General Expenditures and Utility and Liquor Stores, and subtract from 100%: 100% − (83.2% + 9.2%) = 7.6%. Alternatively, add the two components of Insurance Trust Expenditures (Employee retirement and Unemployment compensation):

    3.4% + 4.2% = 7.6%.

6. **The correct answer is E.** The correct value (not given as an answer) is calculated by subtracting the value for Charges and miscellaneous in the Total column from the value for General under Revenue from Own Sources: 820,814 − 170,586 = 650,228.

7. **The correct answer is C.** Federal Revenue from Own Sources can be calculated by subtracting the value for Intergovernmental in the Federal column from the value for Total Revenue in the Federal column:

    660,759 − 1,804 = 658,955.

8. **The correct answer is C.** Calculate the value of state revenues From Federal Government by subtracting the value of revenues From state or local government in the State column from the value of Intergovernmental revenues in the State column:

    70,786 − 2,918 = 67,868.

9. **The correct answer is C.** Calculate the value of state revenues from Employee and railroad retirement by subtracting the combined values of Unemployment compensation and Old age, disability, and health insurance in the State column from the value of Insurance trust: 48,041 − (18,443 + 4,476) = 25,122.

10. **The correct answer is D.** To calculate total local revenue, add together Local Intergovernmental revenue and Revenue from Own Sources in the Local column:

    111,443 + 176,391 = 287,834.

11. **The correct answer is B.** Total 2002 Receivables can be calculated by adding the values for 2002 Consumer Receivables, Business Receivables, and Other Receivables:

    31,773 + 22,999 + 2,341 = 57,113.

12. **The correct answer is A.** The value of 2002 Short-term can be calculated by subtracting the value for Long-term from the value for Loans and Notes Payable to Banks: 7,551 − 969 = 6,582.

13. **The correct answer is B.** Calculate total 2007 liabilities by adding the value of 2007 Loans and Notes Payable to Banks, Commercial Paper, and Other Debt: 8,617 + 25,905 + 54,194 = 88,716.

14. **The correct answer is E.** The correct answer (45,510) was not among the choices provided. To calculate the value of the 2012 Retail consumer goods and loans, subtract the 2012 Retail passenger car paper and others value from the 2012 Consumer Receivables value: 77,460 − 31,950 = 45,510.

15. **The correct answer is C.** Calculate the value of 2012 Other Debt by subtracting the sum of the values of Loans and Notes Payable to Banks and Commercial Paper from 2012 Total Liabilities: 175,025 − (15,458 + 52,328) = 107,239.

answers exercise

SUMMING IT UP

- Graphs are pictures that illustrate comparisons and trends in statistical information. On your civil service exam, you're likely to encounter the most commonly used types of graphs: bar graphs, line graphs, circle graphs (pie charts), and pictographs.

- A bar graph compares various quantities using either horizontal or vertical bars, each of which represents a single quantity (or is divided to represent several linked quantities).

- Line graphs illustrate trends over periods of time. Such a graph may include more than one line, each representing a different item.

- Circle graphs, sometimes called pie charts, show the relationship of various related parts to each other and to a whole. Each part of a circle graph is called a sector.

- Pictographs, as the name implies, compare quantities using pictures or symbols, each of which represents a given number of a particular item of data.

- Tabular completion items are among the easiest question types, but the difficulty in answering these questions lies in choosing which numbers to add or subtract. You must read the tables carefully to ensure you're working with the correct information.

Reasoning

OVERVIEW

WORK PROBLEMS

In work problems, three factors are involved: the number of people (or machines) working; the time to complete the job, expressed in minutes, hours, or days; and the amount of work done. Work problems follow these rules:

- The number of people or machines working is directly proportional to the amount of work done. The more people or machines on the job, the more work will be done, and vice versa.

- The number of people or machines working is inversely proportional to the time. The more people or machines on the job, the less time it will take to finish it, and vice versa.

- The time expended on a job is directly proportional to the amount of work done. The more time expended on a job, the more work that is done, and vice versa.

Tackling Work Problems

In work problems, you are asked to find a rate, time, or number of workers. Depending on what information you have, you can solve the problem using various formulas, as outlined in this section.

Chapter 18

Solving Problems Using Equal Rates

The rate at which a person works is the amount of work he or she can do in a unit of time. If all the workers work at equal rates to complete a job, you can easily find how long it will take any number of workers to finish the job. Follow these two steps:

1. Multiply the number of people by the time to find the amount of time required by one person to complete the job.

2. Divide this time by the number of people required to complete the job to find how long it will take them to finish it.

If four workers each working at the same rate can do a job in 48 days, how long will it take to finish the same job if only three of these workers are able to work on the job?

- Multiply the number of people by the time: 48 × 4 = 192 days. So one worker can do the job in 192 days.

- Divide this amount by three, the number of workers able to work: 192 ÷ 3 = 64. So three workers can finish the job in 64 days.

In some work problems, the rates, though unequal, can be equalized by comparison. Follow these three steps to solve such problems:

1. Determine from the facts how many equal rates there are.

2. Multiply the number of equal rates by the time given.

3. Divide this time by the number of equal rates.

Three workers can do a job in 12 days. Two of the workers work twice as fast as the third. How long would it take one of the faster workers to do the job himself? Follow the steps:

- There are two fast workers and one slow worker, so there are actually five slow workers working at equal rates.

- One slow worker will take 12 days × 5 slow workers = 60 days to complete the job.

- One fast worker equals two slow workers; therefore, he will take 60 ÷ 2 = 30 days to complete the job.

Solving Problems Using Time

If you're given the various times at which each person in a group can complete a job, you can find the time it will take to do the job if all work together by following these three steps:

1. Invert the time of each person to find how much work each person can do in one unit of time.

2. Add these reciprocals to find which part of the job all the workers working together can complete in one unit of time.

3. Invert this sum to find the time it will take all the workers to finish the entire job.

If it takes A three days to dig a ditch, whereas B can dig it in six days and C in twelve, how long would it take all three to do the job? Follow the steps:

- A can complete the job in three days; therefore, he can finish $\frac{1}{3}$ of the job in one day. B can complete the job in six days; therefore, he can finish $\frac{1}{6}$ of the job in one day. C can complete the job in 12 days; therefore, he can finish $\frac{1}{12}$ of the job in one day.

- $\frac{1}{3} + \frac{1}{6} + \frac{1}{12} = \frac{7}{12}$

- A, B, and C can finish $\frac{7}{12}$ of the work in one day; therefore, it will take them $\frac{12}{7}$, or $1\frac{5}{7}$, days to complete the job working together.

When given the time it will take one person to finish a job, the reciprocal of that time is how much of the job can be completed in one particular unit of time. For example, if a worker can finish a job in six days, then she can finish $\frac{1}{6}$ of the job in one day. Conversely, the reciprocal of the work done in one unit of time is the time it will take to finish the entire job. For example, if a worker can complete $\frac{3}{7}$ of the work in one day, then she can finish the whole job in $\frac{7}{3}$, or $2\frac{1}{3}$, days.

If you're given the total time it requires a number of people working together to complete a job, and the times of all but one are known, follow these four steps to find the missing time:

1. Invert the given times to find how much of the job each worker can complete in one unit of time.

2. Add these reciprocals to find how much of the job can be completed in one unit of time by those workers whose rates are known.

3. Subtract this sum from the reciprocal of the total time to complete the job to find the missing rate.

4. Invert this rate to find the unknown time.

A, B, and C can finish a job in two days. B can finish it in five days, and C can finish it in four days. How long would it take A to finish the job by himself? Follow the steps:

- B can finish the job in five days; therefore, he can complete $\frac{1}{5}$ of the job in one day. C can finish the job in four days; therefore, he can complete $\frac{1}{4}$ of the job in one day.

- The part of the job that can be completed by B and C together in one day is $\frac{1}{5} + \frac{1}{4} = \frac{9}{20}$. The total time to complete the job is two days; therefore, all the workers can complete $\frac{1}{2}$ job in 1 day: $\frac{1}{2} - \frac{9}{20} = \frac{1}{20}$.

- A can complete $\frac{1}{20}$ of the job in one day; therefore, he can finish the whole job in 20 days.

Solving Problems Using All Factors

In some work problems, certain values are given for the three factors: the number of workers, the amount of work done, and the time. Usually you must find the changes that occur when one or two of the factors are given different values.

The best way to solve such problems is to directly make the necessary cancellations, divisions, and multiplications. Try this problem:

> If 60 workers can build four houses in twelve months, how many workers, working at the same rate, would be required to build six houses in four months?

In this problem, you can easily see that more workers would be required because more houses must be built in a shorter time:

- To build six houses instead of four in the same amount of time requires $\frac{6}{4}$ of the number of workers: $\frac{6}{4} \times 60 = 90$.

- Because you have four months to complete the job where previously twelve were required, you must triple $(12 \div 4 = 3)$ the number of workers: $90 \times 3 = 270$. Therefore, 270 workers are needed to build six houses in four months.

EXERCISE

> **Directions:** Choose the correct answer to the following work problems.

1. If 314 clerks filed 6,594 papers in 10 minutes, what is the number filed per minute by the average clerk?

    A. 2

    B. 2.4

    C. 2.1

    D. 2.5

2. Four men working together can dig a ditch in 42 days. They begin, but one man works only half-days. How long will it take to complete the job?

    A. 48 days

    B. 45 days

    C. 43 days

    D. 44 days

3. A clerk is requested to file 800 cards. If he can file cards at the rate of 80 cards an hour, the number of cards remaining to be filed after seven hours of work is

    A. 140.

    B. 240.

    C. 260.

    D. 560.

4. If it takes four days for three machines to do a certain job, it will take two machines

    A. 6 days.

    B. $5\frac{1}{2}$ days.

    C. 5 days.

    D. $4\frac{1}{2}$ days.

SHOW YOUR WORK HERE

5. A stenographer has been assigned to place entries on 500 forms. She places entries on 25 forms by the end of half an hour when she is joined by another stenographer. The second stenographer places entries at the rate of 45 an hour. Assuming that both stenographers continue to work at their respective rates of speed, the total number of hours required to carry out the entire assignment is

A. 5.

B. $5\frac{1}{2}$.

C. $6\frac{1}{2}$.

D. 7.

6. If in five days a clerk can copy 125 pages, 36 lines each, 11 words to the line, how many pages of 30 lines each and 12 words to the line can he copy in six days?

A. 145

B. 155

C. 160

D. 165

7. A and B do a job together in 2 hours. Working alone, A does the job in 5 hours. How long will it take B to do the job alone?

A. $3\frac{1}{3}$ hr.

B. $2\frac{1}{4}$ hr.

C. 3 hr.

D. 2 hr.

SHOW YOUR WORK HERE

8. A stenographer transcribes her notes at the rate of one line typed in 10 seconds. At this rate, how long (in minutes and seconds) will it take her to transcribe notes that require seven pages of typing, 25 lines to the page?

   A. 29 min. and 10 sec.

   B. 17 min. and 50 sec.

   C. 40 min. and 10 sec.

   D. 20 min. and 30 sec.

9. A group of five clerks has been assigned to insert 24,000 letters into envelopes. The clerks perform this work at the following rates of speed: Clerk A, 1,100 letters an hour; Clerk B, 1,450 letters an hour; Clerk C, 1,200 letters an hour; Clerk D, 1,300 letters an hour; Clerk E, 1,250 letters an hour. At the end of two hours of work, Clerks C and D are assigned to another task. From the time that Clerks C and D were taken off the assignment, the number of hours required for the remaining clerks to complete this assignment is

   A. less than 3 hours.

   B. 3 hours.

   C. between 3 and 4 hours.

   D. more than 4 hours.

10. If a certain job can be performed by 18 workers in 26 days, the number of workers needed to perform the job in 12 days is

   A. 24.

   B. 30.

   C. 39.

   D. 52.

ANSWER KEY AND EXPLANATIONS

1. C	3. B	5. B	7. A	9. B
2. A	4. A	6. D	8. A	10. C

1. **The correct answer is C.** 6,594 papers ÷ 314 clerks = 21 papers filed by each clerk in 10 minutes; 21 papers ÷ 10 minutes = 2.1 papers per minute filed by the average clerk.

2. **The correct answer is A.** It takes one man 42 × 4 = 168 days to complete the job, working alone. If 3 1/2 men are working (one man works half-days, the other three work full days), the job takes $168 ÷ 3\frac{1}{2}$ = 48 days.

3. **The correct answer is B.** In seven hours, the clerk files 7 × 80 = 560 cards. Because 800 cards must be filed, there are 800 − 560 = 240 remaining.

4. **The correct answer is A.** It takes one machine 3 × 4 = 12 days to complete the job. Two machines can do the job in 12 ÷ 2 = 6 days.

5. **The correct answer is B.** At the end of the first half-hour, there are 500 − 25 = 475 forms remaining. If the first stenographer completed 25 forms in half an hour, her rate is 25 × 2 = 50 forms per hour. The combined rate of the two stenographers is 50 + 45 = 95 forms per hour. The remaining forms can be completed in 475 ÷ 95 = 5 hours. Adding the first half-hour, the entire job requires $5\frac{1}{2}$ hours.

6. **The correct answer is D.** 36 lines × 11 words = 396 words on each page; 125 pages × 396 words = 49,500 words copied in five days; 49,500 ÷ 5 = 9,900 words copied in one day. 12 words × 30 lines = 360 words on each page; 9,900 ÷ 360 = $27\frac{1}{2}$ pages copied in one day; $27\frac{1}{2}$ × 6 = 165 pages copied in six days.

7. **The correct answer is A.** If A can finish the job alone in 5 hours, A can do $\frac{1}{5}$ of the job in one hour. Working together, A and B can complete the job in 2 hours; therefore, in one hour, they finish half the job. In one hour, B alone completes $\frac{1}{2} - \frac{1}{5} = \frac{3}{10}$ of the job. It would take B $\frac{10}{3}$ hours, or $3\frac{1}{3}$ hours, to finish the whole job alone.

8. **The correct answer is A.** She must type 7 × 25 = 175 lines. At the rate of one line per 10 seconds, the job takes 175 × 10 = 1,750 seconds. 1,750 seconds ÷ 60 = $29\frac{1}{6}$ minutes, or 29 minutes and 10 seconds.

9. **The correct answer is B.** All five clerks working together process a total of 1,100 + 1,450 + 1,200 + 1,300 + 1,250 = 6,300 letters per hour. After two hours, they process 6,300 × 2 = 12,600 letters. Of the original 24,000 letters, there are 24,000 − 12,600 = 11,400 letters remaining. Clerks A, B, and E working together process a total of 1,100 + 1,450 + 1,250 = 3,800 letters per hour. It takes them 11,400 ÷ 3,800 = 3 hours to process the remaining letters.

10. **The correct answer is C.** The job could be completed by one worker in 18 × 26 = 468 days. Completing the job in 12 days requires 468 ÷ 12 = 39 workers.

ARITHMETIC REASONING PROBLEMS

Arithmetic reasoning problems are word problems that require you to reason out the answer based on the information given. No set formulas must be followed, other than the ones that you've already learned, so the best way to prepare is to practice with several different kinds of reasoning problems.

Arithmetic reasoning problems often require you to solve problems involving fractions, decimals, percents, ratios, and proportions. Turn back to Chapters 15, "Fractions and Decimals," and 16, "Percentages, Ratios, and Proportions," to review the rules governing these problems.

Note that the five answer choices for this type of problem include "**E.** None of the above." The directions state that the exact answer may not be given as one of the choices, so don't be surprised if, after you do your calculations, you don't see the answer you arrived at. In that case, choose **E**.

EXERCISE

Directions: These questions require you to solve problems formulated in both verbal and numeric form. You will have to analyze a paragraph in order to set up the problem and then solve it. If the exact answer is not given as one of the response choices, you should select "**E.** None of the above."

1. An investigator rented a car for four days and was charged $200. The car rental company charged $10 per day plus $0.20 per mile driven. How many miles did the investigator drive the car?

   A. 800
   B. 950
   C. 1,000
   D. 1,200
   E. None of the above

SHOW YOUR WORK HERE

2. In one federal office, $\frac{1}{6}$ of the employees favored abandoning a flexible work schedule system. In a second office that had the same number of employees, $\frac{1}{4}$ of the workers favored abandoning it. What is the average of the fractions of the workers in the two offices who favored abandoning the system?

   A. $\frac{1}{10}$

   B. $\frac{1}{5}$

   C. $\frac{5}{24}$

   D. $\frac{5}{12}$

   E. None of the above

3. A federal agency had a personal computer repaired at a cost of $49.20. This amount included a charge of $22 per hour for labor and a charge for a new switch that cost $18 before a 10% government discount was applied. How long did the repair job take?

   A. 1 hr. and 6 min.
   B. 1 hr. and 11 min.
   C. 1 hr. and 22 min.
   D. 1 hr. and 30 min.
   E. None of the above

4. In a large agency where mail is delivered in motorized carts, two tires were replaced on a cart at a cost of $34 per tire. If the agency had expected to pay $80 for a pair of tires, what percent of its expected cost did it save?

   A. 7.5%
   B. 17.6%
   C. 57.5%
   D. 75.0%
   E. None of the above

5. An interagency task force has representatives from three different agencies. Half of the task force members represent Agency A, one third represent Agency B, and three represent Agency C. How many people are on the task force?

   A. 12
   B. 15
   C. 18
   D. 24
   E. None of the above

SHOW YOUR WORK HERE

exercise

6. It has been established in recent productivity studies that, on the average, it takes a filing clerk 2 hours and 12 minutes to fill four drawers of a filing cabinet. At this rate, how long would it take two clerks to fill 16 drawers?

   A. 4 hrs.

   B. 4 hrs. and 20 min.

   C. 8 hrs.

   D. 8 hrs. and 40 min.

   E. None of the above

7. It costs $60,000 per month to maintain a small medical facility. The basic charge per person for treatment is $40, but 50% of those seeking treatment require laboratory work at an additional average charge of $20 per person. How many patients per month would the facility have to serve to cover its costs?

   A. 1,000

   B. 1,200

   C. 1,500

   D. 2,000

   E. None of the above

8. An experimental anti-pollution vehicle powered by electricity traveled 33 kilometers (km) at a constant speed of 110 kilometers per hour (km/h). How many minutes did it take this vehicle to complete its experimental run?

   A. 3

   B. 10

   C. 18

   D. 20

   E. None of the above

9. It takes two typists three 8-hour work days to type a report on a word processor. How many typists would be needed to type two reports of the same length in one 8-hour work day?

   A. 4
   B. 6
   C. 8
   D. 12
   E. None of the above

10. A clerk is able to process 40 unemployment compensation claims in one hour. After deductions of 18% for benefits and taxes, the clerk's net pay is $6.97 per hour. If the clerk processed 1,200 claims, how much would the government have to pay for the work, based on the clerk's hourly wage before deductions?

    A. $278.80
    B. $255.00
    C. $246.74
    D. $209.10
    E. None of the above

SHOW YOUR WORK HERE

ANSWER KEY AND EXPLANATIONS

1. A	3. D	5. C	7. B	9. D
2. C	4. E	6. E	8. C	10. B

1. **The correct answer is A.** The investigator rented the car for four days at $10 per day, which is $40; the portion of the total charge expended for miles driven is $200 − $40 = $160. The number of miles driven by the investigator is $160 ÷ $0.20 = 800.

2. **The correct answer is C.** The average of the two fractions is $\left(\frac{1}{6} + \frac{1}{4}\right) \div 2 = \frac{5}{24}$.

3. **The correct answer is D.** The government discount is $18 × 10% = $1.80. The cost of the switch is $18.00 − $1.80 = $16.20. The charge for labor is $49.20 − $16.20 = $33. The number of hours worked is $33 ÷ $22 = 1.5 hours, or 1 hour and 30 minutes.

4. **The correct answer is E.** The correct answer is not given. The difference between the actual cost of $34 per tire and the expected cost of $40 per tire ($80 ÷ 2) is $6: $6 ÷ $40 = 0.15, or 15% of the expected cost.

5. **The correct answer is C.** Obtain the correct answer by computing $\frac{1}{2}x + \frac{1}{3}x + 3 = x$, where x is the total number of task force members; $\frac{1}{2}x$ is the number from Agency A; $\frac{1}{3}x$ is the number from Agency B; and 3 is the number from Agency C. Add the two fractions: $\frac{1}{2}x + \frac{1}{3}x = \frac{5}{6}x$. $x\left(\text{or }\frac{6}{6}x\right) - \frac{5}{6}x = \frac{1}{6}x = 3$. $\frac{1}{6} \times 18 = 3$, so the number of people on the task force is 18.

6. **The correct answer is E.** The correct answer is not given. First, convert two hours and 12 minutes to 2.2 hours, and then set up a simple proportion: $\frac{2.2}{4} = \frac{x}{16}$. The number of hours it takes one filing clerk to do the job is 2.2 × 16 ÷ 4 = 8.8 hours. If two clerks are filling 16

drawers, the job would be completed in half that time: 4.4 hours, or 4 hours, 24 minutes.

7. **The correct answer is B.** The basic charge of $40 applies to all patients (x); the additional average charge of $20 applies to only 50% $\left(\text{or }\frac{1}{2}\right)$ of them (0.5x). The combined charges—$40 times the total number of patients (40x) plus $20 times the total number of patients (20 × 0.5x, or 10x)—must equal $60,000, the cost of maintaining the medical facility: 40x + 10x = 60,000. Solve for x: 60,000 ÷ 50 = 1,200, the number of patients who must be served per month.

8. **The correct answer is C.** Obtain the correct answer by setting up a simple proportion:

$$\frac{110 \text{ km}}{60 \text{ min}} = \frac{33 \text{ km}}{x \text{ min}}$$

$$33 \times 60 \div 110 = 18 \text{ min}$$

9. **The correct answer is D.** The total number of 8-hour work days of typing required for the two reports is 3 days × 2 typists × 2 reports = 12 eight-hour work days of typing. If all of this had to be accomplished in one 8-hour work day, 12 typists would be needed to do the job.

10. **The correct answer is B.** The clerk's net pay of $6.97 per hour represents 82% of his gross pay (100% − 18% = 82%). The clerk's hourly salary before deductions is $6.97 ÷ 82% = $8.50. The total number of hours of work involved is 1,200 forms ÷ 40 forms per hour = 30 hours. The amount the government would have to pay for the work is 30 hours × $8.50 = $255.

SUMMING IT UP

- Three factors are involved in work problems:
    1. The number of people or machines working
    2. The time required to complete a job
    3. The amount of work completed

- Work problem questions ask you to find a rate, time, or number of workers. Depending on the information you're presented with, you must solve the problem using one or more of several formulas. Follow the tips in this chapter to solve using equal rates, time, or all three factors.

- Arithmetic reasoning problems require you to reason out an answer based on the information presented in the question. The formulas that you've already reviewed in Chapters 16 and 17, and in the first part of this chapter, are all you'll need to know to understand and solve the problems on the test.

- The best way to prepare for this section of your exam is to practice answering a variety of arithmetic reasoning questions. Because they often involve calculating fractions, decimals, percentages, ratios, and proportions, you may wish to review Chapters 15 and 16 for the rules on these types of calculations.

PART VI
FOUR PRACTICE TESTS

ANSWER SHEET PRACTICE TEST 2

Verbal Ability

1. Ⓐ Ⓑ Ⓒ Ⓓ
2. Ⓐ Ⓑ Ⓒ Ⓓ
3. Ⓐ Ⓑ Ⓒ Ⓓ
4. Ⓐ Ⓑ Ⓒ Ⓓ
5. Ⓐ Ⓑ Ⓒ Ⓓ
6. Ⓐ Ⓑ Ⓒ Ⓓ
7. Ⓐ Ⓑ Ⓒ Ⓓ
8. Ⓐ Ⓑ Ⓒ Ⓓ
9. Ⓐ Ⓑ Ⓒ Ⓓ
10. Ⓐ Ⓑ Ⓒ Ⓓ
11. Ⓐ Ⓑ Ⓒ Ⓓ
12. Ⓐ Ⓑ Ⓒ Ⓓ
13. Ⓐ Ⓑ Ⓒ Ⓓ
14. Ⓐ Ⓑ Ⓒ Ⓓ
15. Ⓐ Ⓑ Ⓒ Ⓓ
16. Ⓐ Ⓑ Ⓒ Ⓓ
17. Ⓐ Ⓑ Ⓒ Ⓓ
18. Ⓐ Ⓑ Ⓒ Ⓓ
19. Ⓐ Ⓑ Ⓒ Ⓓ
20. Ⓐ Ⓑ Ⓒ Ⓓ
21. Ⓐ Ⓑ Ⓒ Ⓓ
22. Ⓐ Ⓑ Ⓒ Ⓓ

23. Ⓐ Ⓑ Ⓒ Ⓓ
24. Ⓐ Ⓑ Ⓒ Ⓓ
25. Ⓐ Ⓑ Ⓒ Ⓓ
26. Ⓐ Ⓑ Ⓒ Ⓓ
27. Ⓐ Ⓑ Ⓒ Ⓓ
28. Ⓐ Ⓑ Ⓒ Ⓓ
29. Ⓐ Ⓑ Ⓒ Ⓓ
30. Ⓐ Ⓑ Ⓒ Ⓓ
31. Ⓐ Ⓑ Ⓒ Ⓓ
32. Ⓐ Ⓑ Ⓒ Ⓓ
33. Ⓐ Ⓑ Ⓒ Ⓓ
34. Ⓐ Ⓑ Ⓒ Ⓓ
35. Ⓐ Ⓑ Ⓒ Ⓓ
36. Ⓐ Ⓑ Ⓒ Ⓓ
37. Ⓐ Ⓑ Ⓒ Ⓓ
38. Ⓐ Ⓑ Ⓒ Ⓓ
39. Ⓐ Ⓑ Ⓒ Ⓓ
40. Ⓐ Ⓑ Ⓒ Ⓓ
41. Ⓐ Ⓑ Ⓒ Ⓓ
42. Ⓐ Ⓑ Ⓒ Ⓓ
43. Ⓐ Ⓑ Ⓒ Ⓓ

44. Ⓐ Ⓑ Ⓒ Ⓓ
45. Ⓐ Ⓑ Ⓒ Ⓓ
46. Ⓐ Ⓑ Ⓒ Ⓓ
47. Ⓐ Ⓑ Ⓒ Ⓓ
48. Ⓐ Ⓑ Ⓒ Ⓓ
49. Ⓐ Ⓑ Ⓒ Ⓓ
50. Ⓐ Ⓑ Ⓒ Ⓓ
51. Ⓐ Ⓑ Ⓒ Ⓓ
52. Ⓐ Ⓑ Ⓒ Ⓓ
53. Ⓐ Ⓑ Ⓒ Ⓓ
54. Ⓐ Ⓑ Ⓒ Ⓓ
55. Ⓐ Ⓑ Ⓒ Ⓓ
56. Ⓐ Ⓑ Ⓒ Ⓓ
57. Ⓐ Ⓑ Ⓒ Ⓓ
58. Ⓐ Ⓑ Ⓒ Ⓓ
59. Ⓐ Ⓑ Ⓒ Ⓓ
60. Ⓐ Ⓑ Ⓒ Ⓓ
61. Ⓐ Ⓑ Ⓒ Ⓓ
62. Ⓐ Ⓑ Ⓒ Ⓓ
63. Ⓐ Ⓑ Ⓒ Ⓓ
64. Ⓐ Ⓑ Ⓒ Ⓓ

65. Ⓐ Ⓑ Ⓒ Ⓓ
66. Ⓐ Ⓑ Ⓒ Ⓓ
67. Ⓐ Ⓑ Ⓒ Ⓓ
68. Ⓐ Ⓑ Ⓒ Ⓓ
69. Ⓐ Ⓑ Ⓒ Ⓓ
70. Ⓐ Ⓑ Ⓒ Ⓓ
71. Ⓐ Ⓑ Ⓒ Ⓓ
72. Ⓐ Ⓑ Ⓒ Ⓓ
73. Ⓐ Ⓑ Ⓒ Ⓓ
74. Ⓐ Ⓑ Ⓒ Ⓓ
75. Ⓐ Ⓑ Ⓒ Ⓓ
76. Ⓐ Ⓑ Ⓒ Ⓓ
77. Ⓐ Ⓑ Ⓒ Ⓓ
78. Ⓐ Ⓑ Ⓒ Ⓓ
79. Ⓐ Ⓑ Ⓒ Ⓓ
80. Ⓐ Ⓑ Ⓒ Ⓓ
81. Ⓐ Ⓑ Ⓒ Ⓓ
82. Ⓐ Ⓑ Ⓒ Ⓓ
83. Ⓐ Ⓑ Ⓒ Ⓓ
84. Ⓐ Ⓑ Ⓒ Ⓓ
85. Ⓐ Ⓑ Ⓒ Ⓓ

answer sheet

Clerical Ability

1. Ⓐ Ⓑ Ⓒ Ⓓ	31. Ⓐ Ⓑ Ⓒ Ⓓ Ⓔ	61. Ⓐ Ⓑ Ⓒ Ⓓ Ⓔ	91. Ⓐ Ⓑ Ⓒ Ⓓ Ⓔ
2. Ⓐ Ⓑ Ⓒ Ⓓ	32. Ⓐ Ⓑ Ⓒ Ⓓ Ⓔ	62. Ⓐ Ⓑ Ⓒ Ⓓ Ⓔ	92. Ⓐ Ⓑ Ⓒ Ⓓ Ⓔ
3. Ⓐ Ⓑ Ⓒ Ⓓ Ⓔ	33. Ⓐ Ⓑ Ⓒ Ⓓ Ⓔ	63. Ⓐ Ⓑ Ⓒ Ⓓ Ⓔ	93. Ⓐ Ⓑ Ⓒ Ⓓ Ⓔ
4. Ⓐ Ⓑ Ⓒ Ⓓ Ⓔ	34. Ⓐ Ⓑ Ⓒ Ⓓ Ⓔ	64. Ⓐ Ⓑ Ⓒ Ⓓ Ⓔ	94. Ⓐ Ⓑ Ⓒ Ⓓ Ⓔ
5. Ⓐ Ⓑ Ⓒ Ⓓ Ⓔ	35. Ⓐ Ⓑ Ⓒ Ⓓ Ⓔ	65. Ⓐ Ⓑ Ⓒ Ⓓ Ⓔ	95. Ⓐ Ⓑ Ⓒ Ⓓ Ⓔ
6. Ⓐ Ⓑ Ⓒ Ⓓ Ⓔ	36. Ⓐ Ⓑ Ⓒ Ⓓ Ⓔ	66. Ⓐ Ⓑ Ⓒ Ⓓ Ⓔ	96. Ⓐ Ⓑ Ⓒ Ⓓ Ⓔ
7. Ⓐ Ⓑ Ⓒ Ⓓ Ⓔ	37. Ⓐ Ⓑ Ⓒ Ⓓ Ⓔ	67. Ⓐ Ⓑ Ⓒ Ⓓ Ⓔ	97. Ⓐ Ⓑ Ⓒ Ⓓ Ⓔ
8. Ⓐ Ⓑ Ⓒ Ⓓ Ⓔ	38. Ⓐ Ⓑ Ⓒ Ⓓ Ⓔ	68. Ⓐ Ⓑ Ⓒ Ⓓ Ⓔ	98. Ⓐ Ⓑ Ⓒ Ⓓ Ⓔ
9. Ⓐ Ⓑ Ⓒ Ⓓ Ⓔ	39. Ⓐ Ⓑ Ⓒ Ⓓ Ⓔ	69. Ⓐ Ⓑ Ⓒ Ⓓ Ⓔ	99. Ⓐ Ⓑ Ⓒ Ⓓ Ⓔ
10. Ⓐ Ⓑ Ⓒ Ⓓ Ⓔ	40. Ⓐ Ⓑ Ⓒ Ⓓ Ⓔ	70. Ⓐ Ⓑ Ⓒ Ⓓ Ⓔ	100. Ⓐ Ⓑ Ⓒ Ⓓ Ⓔ
11. Ⓐ Ⓑ Ⓒ Ⓓ Ⓔ	41. Ⓐ Ⓑ Ⓒ Ⓓ Ⓔ	71. Ⓐ Ⓑ Ⓒ Ⓓ Ⓔ	101. Ⓐ Ⓑ Ⓒ Ⓓ Ⓔ
12. Ⓐ Ⓑ Ⓒ Ⓓ Ⓔ	42. Ⓐ Ⓑ Ⓒ Ⓓ Ⓔ	72. Ⓐ Ⓑ Ⓒ Ⓓ Ⓔ	102. Ⓐ Ⓑ Ⓒ Ⓓ Ⓔ
13. Ⓐ Ⓑ Ⓒ Ⓓ Ⓔ	43. Ⓐ Ⓑ Ⓒ Ⓓ Ⓔ	73. Ⓐ Ⓑ Ⓒ Ⓓ Ⓔ	103. Ⓐ Ⓑ Ⓒ Ⓓ Ⓔ
14. Ⓐ Ⓑ Ⓒ Ⓓ Ⓔ	44. Ⓐ Ⓑ Ⓒ Ⓓ Ⓔ	74. Ⓐ Ⓑ Ⓒ Ⓓ Ⓔ	104. Ⓐ Ⓑ Ⓒ Ⓓ Ⓔ
15. Ⓐ Ⓑ Ⓒ Ⓓ Ⓔ	45. Ⓐ Ⓑ Ⓒ Ⓓ Ⓔ	75. Ⓐ Ⓑ Ⓒ Ⓓ Ⓔ	105. Ⓐ Ⓑ Ⓒ Ⓓ Ⓔ
16. Ⓐ Ⓑ Ⓒ Ⓓ Ⓔ	46. Ⓐ Ⓑ Ⓒ Ⓓ Ⓔ	76. Ⓐ Ⓑ Ⓒ Ⓓ Ⓔ	106. Ⓐ Ⓑ Ⓒ Ⓓ Ⓔ
17. Ⓐ Ⓑ Ⓒ Ⓓ Ⓔ	47. Ⓐ Ⓑ Ⓒ Ⓓ Ⓔ	77. Ⓐ Ⓑ Ⓒ Ⓓ Ⓔ	107. Ⓐ Ⓑ Ⓒ Ⓓ Ⓔ
18. Ⓐ Ⓑ Ⓒ Ⓓ Ⓔ	48. Ⓐ Ⓑ Ⓒ Ⓓ Ⓔ	78. Ⓐ Ⓑ Ⓒ Ⓓ Ⓔ	108. Ⓐ Ⓑ Ⓒ Ⓓ Ⓔ
19. Ⓐ Ⓑ Ⓒ Ⓓ Ⓔ	49. Ⓐ Ⓑ Ⓒ Ⓓ Ⓔ	79. Ⓐ Ⓑ Ⓒ Ⓓ Ⓔ	109. Ⓐ Ⓑ Ⓒ Ⓓ Ⓔ
20. Ⓐ Ⓑ Ⓒ Ⓓ Ⓔ	50. Ⓐ Ⓑ Ⓒ Ⓓ Ⓔ	80. Ⓐ Ⓑ Ⓒ Ⓓ Ⓔ	110. Ⓐ Ⓑ Ⓒ Ⓓ Ⓔ
21. Ⓐ Ⓑ Ⓒ Ⓓ Ⓔ	51. Ⓐ Ⓑ Ⓒ Ⓓ Ⓔ	81. Ⓐ Ⓑ Ⓒ Ⓓ Ⓔ	111. Ⓐ Ⓑ Ⓒ Ⓓ
22. Ⓐ Ⓑ Ⓒ Ⓓ Ⓔ	52. Ⓐ Ⓑ Ⓒ Ⓓ Ⓔ	82. Ⓐ Ⓑ Ⓒ Ⓓ Ⓔ	112. Ⓐ Ⓑ Ⓒ Ⓓ
23. Ⓐ Ⓑ Ⓒ Ⓓ Ⓔ	53. Ⓐ Ⓑ Ⓒ Ⓓ	83. Ⓐ Ⓑ Ⓒ Ⓓ Ⓔ	113. Ⓐ Ⓑ Ⓒ Ⓓ
24. Ⓐ Ⓑ Ⓒ Ⓓ Ⓔ	54. Ⓐ Ⓑ Ⓒ Ⓓ	84. Ⓐ Ⓑ Ⓒ Ⓓ Ⓔ	114. Ⓐ Ⓑ Ⓒ Ⓓ
25. Ⓐ Ⓑ Ⓒ Ⓓ Ⓔ	55. Ⓐ Ⓑ Ⓒ Ⓓ	85. Ⓐ Ⓑ Ⓒ Ⓓ Ⓔ	115. Ⓐ Ⓑ Ⓒ Ⓓ
26. Ⓐ Ⓑ Ⓒ Ⓓ Ⓔ	56. Ⓐ Ⓑ Ⓒ Ⓓ	86. Ⓐ Ⓑ Ⓒ Ⓓ Ⓔ	116. Ⓐ Ⓑ Ⓒ Ⓓ
27. Ⓐ Ⓑ Ⓒ Ⓓ Ⓔ	57. Ⓐ Ⓑ Ⓒ Ⓓ Ⓔ	87. Ⓐ Ⓑ Ⓒ Ⓓ Ⓔ	117. Ⓐ Ⓑ Ⓒ Ⓓ
28. Ⓐ Ⓑ Ⓒ Ⓓ Ⓔ	58. Ⓐ Ⓑ Ⓒ Ⓓ Ⓔ	88. Ⓐ Ⓑ Ⓒ Ⓓ Ⓔ	118. Ⓐ Ⓑ Ⓒ Ⓓ
29. Ⓐ Ⓑ Ⓒ Ⓓ Ⓔ	59. Ⓐ Ⓑ Ⓒ Ⓓ Ⓔ	89. Ⓐ Ⓑ Ⓒ Ⓓ Ⓔ	119. Ⓐ Ⓑ Ⓒ Ⓓ
30. Ⓐ Ⓑ Ⓒ Ⓓ Ⓔ	60. Ⓐ Ⓑ Ⓒ Ⓓ Ⓔ	90. Ⓐ Ⓑ Ⓒ Ⓓ Ⓔ	120. Ⓐ Ⓑ Ⓒ Ⓓ

Practice Test 2

VERBAL ABILITY

85 Questions • 40 Minutes

Directions: For questions 1–15, choose the word closest in meaning to the word given.

1. *Enthrall* most nearly means:
   A. shrink
   B. enchant
   C. tire
   D. capture

2. To *verify* most nearly means:
   A. examine
   B. explain
   C. confirm
   D. guarantee

3. *Impede* most nearly means:
   A. hinder
   B. help
   C. lift
   D. release

4. *Beseech* most nearly means:
   A. ignore
   B. console
   C. fight
   D. plead

5. *Boisterous* most nearly means:
   A. relaxed
   B. rowdy
   C. tall
   D. heavy

6. *Despondent* most nearly means:
   A. confused
   B. lost
   C. tired
   D. hopeless

7. *Divulge* most nearly means:
   A. reveal
   B. disguise
   C. trick
   D. lift

8. *Fallacy* most nearly means:
   A. truth
   B. fancy
   C. fear
   D. falsehood

9. *Tumultuous* most nearly means:
   A. peaceful
   B. turbulent
   C. unaware
   D. hilarious

10. *Flourish* most nearly means:
    A. struggle
    B. shrink
    C. thrive
    D. fly

11. *Pulverize* most nearly means:
    A. construct
    B. demolish
    C. connect
    D. invent

12. *Tranquil* most nearly means:
    A. quiet
    B. noisy
    C. lengthy
    D. boring

13. *Opaque* most nearly means:
    A. invisible
    B. shiny
    C. not clear
    D. obvious

14. *Inevitable* most nearly means:
    A. unavoidable
    B. unlikely
    C. envied
    D. difficult

15. *Persistent* most nearly means:
    A. picky
    B. common
    C. cruel
    D. stubborn

NOTE

The directions stated here pertain to taking the exam in a paper-and-pencil format. If you will be taking the exam on a computer, each section will have directions specific to answering questions on a computer.

Directions: In questions 16–35, identify the statement that is most clearly written and grammatically correct.

16. A. The client's contract will award the effective building to the design from the most architect.
    B. The architect with the most effective building design will be awarded the client contract.
    C. The most effective client contract will be awarded to the building of the architect who wins.
    D. The architect with the client award will contract to be building an effective design.

17. A. The package contents was removed and scattered around the floor.
    B. Removed and scattered around the floor, were the package's contents.
    C. The contents of the package were removed and scattered around the floor.
    D. The removed contents of the package were taken out and scattered around the floor.

18. A. Taking into account the existing population of the neighborhood, it's likely that rezoning could displace up to a thousand people.
    B. The rezoning will take into account the existing population of the neighborhood, except for a thousand people.
    C. Rezoning may displace the existing population of the neighborhood. A thousand people.
    D. As a result of displacement, rezoning may affect up to a thousand people in the neighborhood.

19. A. Its clear that Mr. Simon is not up to the stated requirements of the job.
    B. Mr. Simon is clearly not up to the clearly stated requirements of the job.
    C. The job is clear that Mr. Simon is not up to the stated requirements.
    D. Mr. Simon is clearly not up to the stated requirements of the job.

20. **A.** The environmental study shows that if left unchecked, the local population of field grouse will be gone by 2030.

B. The environmental study, shows that if left unchecked, the local population of field grouse will be gone by, 2030.

C. The environmental study shows (that if left unchecked), the local population of field grouse will be gone by 2030.

D. The environmental study shows that if—left unchecked—the local population of field grouse will be gone by 2030.

21. **A.** MS Jenkins used to live at 311 Fairview Court until November of 1999.

B. Until November 1999, Ms. Jenkins lived at 311 Fairview Court.

C. 311 Fairview Court that's where Ms. Jenkins lived until November of 1999.

D. 311 Fairview Court, Ms. Jenkins's address until November of 1999.

22. **A.** At current rates' the department staff will need to grow by 35 on the next five years to keep up with demand.

B. The department's staff will need to grow by 35 percent over the next five years, if we want to keep up with demand.

C. The demand that we need to keep up with calls for 35percent department staff growth over the next five years.

D. If we want to keep up with demand, it will need to grow by 35 percent over the next five years.

23. **A.** Any safety violations, the floor manager should be reported to.

B. If you notice any safety violations, the floor manager should report them.

C. You should report any safety violations to the floor manager.

D. The floor manager receives any safety violations.

24. **A.** This restaurant have been closed down four times for health code violations.

B. Four times this restaurant has been closed down for health code violations.

C. Those violations have closed the restaurant four times.

D. Due to health code violations, this restaurant has been closed down four times.

25. **A.** Gifts should never be accepted from clients, as they can create a conflict of interest.

B. Gifts from clients create a conflict of interest, so…don't accept them.

C. Gifts from clients can create a conflict of interest, should never be accepted.

D. Gifts from clients accepted create conflicts of interest.

26. **A.** Renewing your license requires an $80 annual fee and you pass a standardized test.

B. Requirements for renewing your license include paying an $80 annual fee and passing a standardized test.

C. Passing a standardized test and paying an $80 fee = license renewal requirements.

D. An $80 annual fee renews your license and you are required to pass a standardized test.

27. **A.** There is a zero-tolerance policy for employees who fail a random drug test.

    B. Random drug test failures have a zero-tolerance policy for employees.

    C. Failing a random drug test is a zero-tolerance policy for employees.

    D. Employees have a zero tolerance policy for failing a random drug test.

28. **A.** The Parks Department picnic budgeted at $500 this year.

    B. This year, there is $500 budgeted for the Parks Department picnic.

    C. Parks Department picnic: $500.

    D. There are $500 dollars budgeted for the Parks Department this year picnic.

29. **A.** The price as of January for stamps is scheduled to be 72 cents.

    B. The price scheduled for stamps for January is 72 cents.

    C. As of January, the price of stamps is scheduled to be 72 cents.

    D. Per January, the price of stamps is scheduled to be 72 cents.

30. **A.** Check it out: office hours will be changing from 9:00 a.m. to 6:00 p.m.

    B. Oh and: office hours will be changing from 9:00 a.m. to 6:00 p.m.

    C. Please: office hours will be changing from 9:00 a.m. to 6:00 p.m.

    D. Please note: office hours will be changing from 9:00 a.m. to 6:00 p.m.

31. **A.** Volunteers will be needed to distribute water and basic supplies in the event of a hurricane.

    B. Water and basic supplies will be needed to distribute by volunteers in the event of a hurricane.

    C. In the event of a hurricane, water and basic supplies will be needed by volunteers.

    D. Water will be distributed, and basic supplies, by volunteers in the event of a hurricane.

32. **A.** The suspect appeared unstable potentially dangerous and possibly armed.

    B. The suspect appeared, unstable, potentially dangerous, and possibly armed.

    C. The suspect appeared; unstable, potentially dangerous, and possibly armed.

    D. The suspect appeared unstable, potentially dangerous, and possibly armed.

33. **A.** We will save $10,000 in the first year alone, the cost savings will be enormous.

    B. The cost savings will be enormous; in just the first year alone, we will save $10,000.

    C. In just one year, the cost savings alone, will be an enormous $10,000.

    D. Cost savings in the first year alone were to be $10,000, which is enormous.

34. **A.** Every year requires that all employees take part in an emergency situation drill.

    B. Each year there is an emergency situation drill required by all employees.

    C. Each year there is an emergency situation drill required for all employees.

    D. Every year employees require to take part in an emergency situation drill.

35. **A.** Final report: there were four major safety violations, ten minor safety violations, and one case of improper data handling.

    B. There were four major safety violations included in the final report. Ten minor safety violations. One case of improper data handling.

    C. Four major safety violations, ten minor safety violations, and one case of improper data handling in the final report.

    D. In the final report, there were four major safety violations, ten minor safety violations, and one case of improper data handling.

Directions: In questions 36–55, identify the correct spelling of each word. If no suggested spelling is correct, choose choice D.

36. **A.** scintillate
    B. sintillate
    C. scintilate
    D. None of the above

37. **A.** joodishus
    B. judisheus
    C. judicious
    D. None of the above

38. **A.** rehspiration
    B. respiration
    C. resparation
    D. None of the above

39. **A.** omenous
    B. ahminus
    C. ominous
    D. None of the above

40. **A.** conceivable
    B. conseeveable
    C. cunsievible
    D. None of the above

41. **A.** noosants
    B. newcents
    C. nuisance
    D. None of the above

42. **A.** association
    B. associashun
    C. ahsoceation
    D. None of the above

43. **A.** queschunair
    B. questionnaire
    C. quistionnair
    D. None of the above

44. **A.** comemorate
    B. commemorate
    C. commemmorate
    D. None of the above

45. **A.** misspelled
    B. mispelled
    C. misspelld
    D. None of the above

46. **A.** gratefull
    B. greatful
    C. grateful
    D. None of the above

47. **A.** complience
    B. compliance
    C. commpliance
    D. None of the above

48. **A.** victorious
    B. victorious
    C. victorius
    D. None of the above

49. **A.** evaluashun
    B. evaluaition
    C. evaluation
    D. None of the above

50. **A.** annial
    B. annule
    C. annual
    D. None of the above

51. **A.** denial
    B. denile
    C. deenial
    D. None of the above

52. **A.** callender

    B. calender

    C. calendar

    D. None of the above

53. **A.** arguement

    B. argument

    C. argumente

    D. None of the above

54. **A.** sufficient

    B. suffiscient

    C. suficient

    D. None of the above

55. **A.** develope

    B. develup

    C. divelop

    D. None of the above

Directions: In questions 56–60, read each paragraph and answer the question that follows.

---

56. In order to prevent accidents, safety devices must be used to guard exposed machinery. In addition, mechanics must be instructed in safety rules that they must follow for their own protection. Finally, the lighting in the plant must be adequate.

The paragraph best supports the statement that industrial accidents

    A. may be due to lack of knowledge.

    B. are always avoidable.

    C. usually result from inadequate machinery.

    D. cannot be entirely overcome.

57. In the election on Tuesday, the incumbent Mayor Tilden received 14,987 votes. City Councilwoman Angie Franklin received 12,983 votes, and Joe Anderson received 8,765 votes. The results have been certified, and the swearing-in ceremony is scheduled for next month.

The paragraph best supports the statement that

    A. Angie Franklin is the incumbent.

    B. the election results are under dispute.

    C. Joe Anderson received a lot of local support.

    D. Mayor Tilden will remain in office.

58. Anyone who would like to join the car sharing program will need to start by submitting an application online, including a photocopy of a valid driver's license. After the applicant passes a background check of his or her driving history and is approved, the applicant will then be charged a $40 processing and membership fee.

The paragraph best supports the statement that

    A. The applicant will pay a $40 fee even if the application is denied.

    B. Only applicants with a spotless driving record will be approved.

    C. Applicants must be licensed drivers in order to join the program.

    D. Only 100 new applicants per year are considered for membership.

59. To keep up with a fast-paced news cycle, news media organizations often "prewrite" obituaries for celebrities and other notable public figures. It may sound morbid, but it allows TV, radio, print, and online editors to be ready to go when the time comes. The shell story will often be pre-written with the person's lifetime accomplishments, with final details added as necessary.

The paragraph best supports the statement that

A. Pre-written obituaries save time for news outlets.

B. Pre-written obituaries save money for news outlets.

C. Celebrities object to being eulogized before they're gone.

D. Celebrity obituaries are not accurate stories.

60. Those short online cooking tutorial videos make cooking look so easy, but there is plenty you don't see. Remember: these videos are edited to get rid of spills, chef errors, burned dishes, and just about every bit of human error involved in the cooking process. Your real-life product may not be as pretty, but it is certainly more real. Enjoy!

The paragraph best supports the statement that

A. home cooks will never be as good as internet chefs.

B. authentic food is just as good as attractive food.

C. the internet has ruined the way we cook.

D. mistakes happen when you try to copy what others do.

Directions: For questions 61–70, read the passage and answer each question on the basis of the information stated or implied in the passage.

Passage 1

Today more than ever, people are looking for nontraditional options to complete their education. Standard four-year colleges and universities, as well as community colleges, are still going strong (especially for people straight out of
Line high school), but for students who have made different life choices, a flexible,
5   affordable option is key. Not everyone has the time or money to become a full-time student in pursuit of a bachelor's degree. This is where distance learning and online colleges come in.

These less traditional schools allow people to work toward their degrees with live or digital professors, "attending" lectures by logging in, chat with
10   fellow students who might live three states away, and do coursework on a flexible schedule. For people with jobs or family obligations, or who need to work at their own pace, this setup can be ideal for completing their degrees. And these online courses are often far less expensive than the exorbitant loans oftennecessary to attend traditional schools.
15   Still, there are factors that students should be aware of before applying to these schools. Some online colleges and universities have less than stellar reputations, and even shadier financial practices, with a trail of scammed students in their wakes. It's important that anyone considering these courses as an option to invest in their future do as much research as possible to make sure that any
20   potential school program is accredited and legitimate, and that it meets their needs.

61. The best title for this passage is

A. Avoiding Scam Colleges

B. Is Online College Right for You?

C. Why College Isn't Necessary

D. College Student Handbook

62. According to the passage, which of the following is NOT a characteristic of online colleges?

A. Free tuition

B. Flexible classes

C. Digital lectures

D. Bachelor's degrees

63. Which of the following does the author consider a problem when considering an online college?

A. Too much homework

B. Distant professors

C. Illegitimate costs

D. Non-traditional students

64. According to the passage, online colleges can be a good option for students who

A. want to attend school full-time.

B. do not have day jobs.

C. are just out of high school.

D. have limited time.

65. Which of the following would the author of this passage likely say is true?

A. In ten years, very few people will attend traditional colleges.

B. Online college administrators are nothing but scammers.

C. Online colleges can help improve the likelihood of completing a degree.

D. People learn better when they can read and watch information online.

Passage 2

If you open the app store on your smartphone or tablet, you see plenty of tempting free apps, just waiting for you to download and enjoy them. But these "free" apps often come with a hidden price tag. Sure, that game or useful tool is

Line free to download, and maybe even to use some of its features. But before long,

5 you may see the dreaded pop-up: "Like this app? We know you'll love it more if you pay $0.99 to see more of the game!" Or, in the case of some popular games, it waits until you reach an impossible level, and suddenly a convenient booster appears…for just $1.99.

These apps often prey upon our human nature to sell their product. We like

10 to win games, and we like to feel like we're getting a lot for our money. When a relatively small cost pops up, the apps are designed to get us to think that this tiny amount of money isn't a big deal, just this once. In reality, it's conditioning us to do this over and over. It's an insidious way to get us to spend more than we were planning to spend originally, and I believe that there should be more

15 explicit warnings when you download apps from the store.

66. The main idea of the passage is that
    A. people don't want to download expensive apps.
    B. the only good app is a free app.
    C. apps that are not free should be banned.
    D. people should be aware of what they're downloading.

67. The author of the passage is likely a(n)
    A. app developer.
    B. app user.
    C. politician.
    D. sales representative.

68. Which of the following supporting details would best fit with the author's argument?
    A. The number of "free" apps available in the store at any given time
    B. That some kids' apps allow children to buy premium content without parents knowing
    C. How much it costs to get extra lives in a particular game
    D. The name of the first app ever to be downloaded

69. In the second paragraph, the word *insidious* (line 13) most nearly means:
    A. appropriate
    B. smart
    C. straightforward
    D. sneaky

70. From the passage, you can infer that the author believes that
    A. the app store bears responsibility for deceptive app costs.
    B. games should always be free, practical apps should cost money.
    C. kids should be barred from downloading apps.
    D. app stores should charge more for premium content.

Directions: For questions 71–85, some portions of the passage are underlined and numbered. Corresponding to each numbered portion are three different ways of saying the same thing. If you feel that an underlined portion is correct and is stated as well as possible, mark choice **A.** NO CHANGE. If you feel that there is an error in the underlined portion or if one of the alternatives would be more effective, choose the correct answer.

If you're having trouble sleeping, experts that recommend you try to improve
        71   72

your "sleep hygiene." This means saying regular bed and wakeup times for
                               73

yourself, as well as limiting distractions before going to sleep. For many people,
                                            74

this means putting away phones and tablets which have been found to emit
                                        75

"blue light" that triggers wakefulness and upsets the circadian rhythms

that helps us sleep and wake on a normal schedule. Although phone companies
76

are trying to find ways to limit this blue light for consumers, sleep experts say

that the only way to truly avoid blue light sleep problems is two shut off your
                                                        77

devices and stop looking at them for at least a half an hour before you'd like to
                      78

go to sleep.

71. **A.** NO CHANGE
    B. you've having
    C. your having
    D. you'd having

72. **A.** NO CHANGE
    B. recommend that you
    C. you recommend that
    D. recommend you that

73. **A.** NO CHANGE
    B. doing
    C. saving
    D. setting

74. **A.** NO CHANGE
    B. gone to sleep
    C. going to go to sleep
    D. went to sleep

75. **A.** NO CHANGE
    B. tablets; which
    C. tablets, which
    D. tablets. Which

76. **A.** NO CHANGE
    B. that help
    C. what help
    D. which helps

77. A. NO CHANGE
   B. too
   C. tow
   D. to

78. A. NO CHANGE
   B. at it
   C. at its
   D. at they

"Stop and frisk policies have become a controversial method in local policing
      79

behind the last few years. Supports of the practice think that when police have
   80   81

the power to stop; and investigate people they deem suspicious, it lead to more
            82   83

criminals caught and cleanest streets. On the other side, you have people who
                84

believe that the policy can unfairly target people from socially disadvantaged

groups in a disproportionate way, leading to an endless unbreakable cycle of
                                  85

arrest, jail, and recidivism.

79. A. NO CHANGE
   B. Stop and frisk"
   C. "Stop and frisk"
   D. Stop And Frisk

80. A. NO CHANGE
   B. ahead of
   C. over
   D. on

81. A. NO CHANGE
   B. Supporters
   C. The supports
   D. The support

82. A. NO CHANGE
   B. stop, and investigate
   C. stop—and investigate
   D. stop and investigate

83. A. NO CHANGE
   B. it led
   C. they lead
   D. it leads

84. A. NO CHANGE
   B. cleaner
   C. most clean
   D. the clean

85. A. NO CHANGE
   B. endless, unbreakable, cycle
   C. endless, unbreakable cycle
   D. endless…unbreakable cycle

CLERICAL ABILITY

120 Questions • 60 Minutes

Directions: Questions 1 and 2 consist of a CAPITALIZED word that is to be filed correctly among the alphabetized words listed. Choose the word that should come after the capitalized word.

---

1. HEIFERS
   - A. heathens
   - B. hedges
   - C. hegemonies
   - D. heirs

2. COLONIALS
   - A. colonels
   - B. colonists
   - C. colonies
   - D. colors

Directions: For questions 3–26, find the correct place for the given name.

---

3. Bobbitt, Olivier E.
   - A. –
     Bobbitt, D. Olivier
   - B. –
     Bobbitt, Olive B.
   - C. –
     Bobbitt, Olivia H.
   - D. –
     Bobbitt, R. Olivia
   - E. –

4. Mosely, Werner
   - A. –
     Mosely, Albert J.
   - B. –
     Mosley, Alvin
   - C. –
     Mosley, S. M.
   - D. –
     Mosley, Vinson N.
   - E. –

5. Youmuns, Frank L.
   - A. –
     Youmons, Frank G.
   - B. –
     Youmons, Frank H.
   - C. –
     Youmons, Frank K.
   - D. –
     Youmons, Frank M.
   - E. –

6. Watters, N. O.
   - A –
     Waters, Charles L.
   - B. –
     Waterson, Nina P.
   - C. –
     Watson, Nora J.
   - D. –
     Wattwood, Paul A.
   - E. –

7. Johnston, Edward

A. –

Johnston, Edgar R.

B. –

Johnston, Edmond

C. –

Johnston, Edmund

D. –

Johnstone, Edmund A.

E. –

8. Rensch, Adeline

A. –

Ramsay, Amos

B. –

Remschel, Augusta

C. –

Renshaw, Austin

D. –

Rentzel, Becky

E. –

9. DeMattia, Jessica

A. –

DeLong, Jesse

B. –

DeMatteo, Jessie

C. –

Derby, Jessie S.

D. –

DeShazo, L. M.

E. –

10. Theriault, Louis

A. –

Therien, Annette

B. –

Therien, Elaine

C. –

Thibeault, Gerald

D. –

Thiebeault, Pierre

E. –

11. Gaston, M. Hubert

A. –

Gaston, Dorothy M.

B. –

Gaston, Henry N.

C. –

Gaston, Isabel

D. –

Gaston, M. Melvin

E. –

12. SanMiguel, Carlos

A. –

San-Luis, Juana

B. –

Santilli, Laura

C. –

Stinnett, Nellie

D. –

Stoddard, Victor

E. –

13. DeLaTour, Hall F.

A. –

   Delargy, Harold

B. –

   De-Lathouder, Hilda

C. –

   Lathrop, Hillary

D. –

   LaTour, Hulbert E.

E. –

14. O'Bannon, M. J.

A. –

   O'Beirne, B. B.

B. –

   Oberlin, E. L.

C. –

   Oberneir, L. P.

D. –

   O'Brian, S. F.

E. –

15. Entsminger, Jacob

A. –

   Ensminger, J.

B. –

   Entsminger, J. A.

C. –

   Entsminger, Jack

D. –

   Entsminger, James

E. –

16. Iacone, Pete R.

A. –

   Iacone, Pedro

B. –

   Iacone, Pedro M.

C. –

   Iacone, Peter F.

D. –

   Iascone, Peter W.

E. –

17. Dunlavey, M. Hilary

A. –

   Dunleavy, Hilary G.

B. –

   Dunleavy, Hilary K.

C. –

   Dunleavy, Hilary S.

D. –

   Dunleavy, Hilery W.

E. –

18. Yarbrough, Maria

A. –

   Yabroudy, Margy

B. –

   Yarboro, Marie

C. –

   Yarborough, Marina

D. –

   Yarborough, Mary

E. –

19. Prouty, Martha

A. –

Proutey, Margaret

B. –

Proutey, Maude

C. –

Prouty, Myra

D. –

Prouty, Naomi

E. –

20. Pawlowicz, Ruth M.

A. –

Pawalek, Edward

B. –

Pawelek, Flora G.

C. –

Pawlowski, Joan M.

D. –

Pawtowski, Wanda

E. –

21. Vanstory, George

A. –

Vanover, Eva

B. –

VanSwinderen, Floyd

C. –

VanSyckle, Harry

D. –

Vanture, Laurence

E. –

22. Fitzsimmons, Hugh

A. –

Fitts, Harold

B. –

Fitzgerald, June

C. –

FitzGibbon, Junius

D. –

FitzSimons, Martin

E. –

23. D'Amato, Vincent

A. –

Daly, Steven

B. –

D'Amboise, S. Vincent

C. –

Daniel, Vail

D. –

DeAlba, Valentina

E. –

24. Schaeffer, Roger D.

A. –

Schaffert, Evelyn M.

B. –

Schaffner, Margaret M.

C. –

Schafhirt, Milton G.

D.–

Shafer, Richard E.

E. –

25. White-Lewis, Cecil

   A. –

      Whitelaw, Cordelia

   B. –

      White-Leigh, Nancy

   C. –

      Whitely, Rodney

   D. –

      Whitlock, Warren

   E. –

26. VanDerHeggen, Don

   A. –

      VanDemark, Doris

   B. –

      Vandenberg, H. E.

   C. –

      VanDercook, Marie

   D. –

      VanderLinden, Robert

   E. –

Directions: In questions 27–52, perform the computation and mark the corresponding correct answer on your answer sheet.

---

27.   43

      + 32

   A. 55

   B. 65

   C. 66

   D. 75

   E. None of the above

28.   83

      − 4

   A. 73

   B. 79

   C. 80

   D. 90

   E. None of the above

29.   41

      × 7

   A. 281

   B. 287

   C. 291

   D. 297

   E. None of the above

SHOW YOUR WORK HERE

30.   306
         $\div 6$

- A. 44
- B. 51
- C. 52
- D. 60
- E. None of the above

31.   37
         $+ 15$

- A. 42
- B. 52
- C. 53
- D. 62
- E. None of the above

32. Subtract: 68 − 47
- A. 10
- B. 11
- C. 20
- D. 22
- E. None of the above

33. Multiply: 50 • 8
- A. 400
- B. 408
- C. 450
- D. 458
- E. None of the above

34. Divide: 180 ÷ 9
- A. 20
- B. 29
- C. 30
- D. 39
- E. None of the above

35. Add: 78 + 63
- A. 131
- B. 140
- C. 141
- D. 151
- E. None of the above

36. Subtract: 89 − 70

    A. 9

    B. 18

    C. 19

    D. 29

    E. None of the above

37. Multiply: 62 • 5

    A. 300

    B. 310

    C. 315

    D. 360

    E. None of the above

38. Divide: 153 ÷ 3

    A. 41

    B. 43

    C. 51

    D. 53

    E. None of the above

39. Add: 47 + 21

    A. 58

    B. 59

    C. 67

    D. 68

    E. None of the above

40. Subtract: 87 − 42

    A. 34

    B. 35

    C. 44

    D. 45

    E. None of the above

41. Multiply: 37 • 3

    A. 91

    B. 101

    C. 104

    D. 114

    E. None of the above

SHOW YOUR WORK HERE

42. Divide: 357 ÷ 7

   A. 51

   B. 52

   C. 53

   D. 54

   E. None of the above

43. Add: 58 + 27

   A. 75

   B. 84

   C. 85

   D. 95

   E. None of the above

44. Subtract: 86 − 57

   A. 18

   B. 29

   C. 38

   D. 39

   E. None of the above

45. Multiply: 68 · 4

   A. 242

   B. 264

   C. 272

   D. 274

   E. None of the above

46. Divide: 639 ÷ 9

   A. 71

   B. 73

   C. 81

   D. 83

   E. None of the above

47. Add: 28 + 35

   A. 53

   B. 62

   C. 64

   D. 73

   E. None of the above

SHOW YOUR WORK HERE

48. Subtract: 78 − 69
  A. 7
  B. 8
  C. 18
  D. 19
  E. None of the above

49. Multiply: 86 · 6
  A. 492
  B. 506
  C. 516
  D. 526
  E. None of the above

50. Divide: 648 ÷ 8
  A. 71
  B. 76
  C. 81
  D. 89
  E. None of the above

51. Add: 97 + 34
  A. 131
  B. 132
  C. 140
  D. 141
  E. None of the above

52. Add: 75 + 49
  A. 124
  B. 125
  C. 134
  D. 225
  E. None of the above

Directions: You will have three minutes to study the following picture, to note details about people, time and place, and activities. Then answer questions 53 and 54 without looking back at the picture.

https://www.pexels.com/photo/people-gathering-inside-room-1345085/

53. What is the man who is wearing glasses holding in his hand?

   A. A phone

   B. A piece of paper

   C. A laptop

   D. Nothing

54. How many people are seated in the photo?

   A. One

   B. Two

   C. Three

   D. Four

Directions: For questions 55 and 56, read the passage and choose the best answer for the question asked.

---

55. You overhear a conversation in which a supervisor tells her employee that he won't be promoted unless he runs personal errands for her. Of the following, the best action for you to take would be to

   A. Loudly confront the supervisor right then and there.

   B. Pretend you didn't hear anything.

   C. Go to your department's Human Resources rep to let them know.

   D. See if you can get a promotion by running errands for your boss.

56. A health inspector is inspecting a restaurant kitchen. Which of the following conditions should she report immediately?

   A. Evidence of roaches in the back corner of the pantry

   B. A slight smell of gas throughout the kitchen

   C. A freezer set slightly above the proper temperature

   D. A small rat running along the edge of the wall

Directions: For questions 57–61, find which one of the suggested answers is completely found within each question.

Suggested Answers

57. 6 2 5 K 4 P T G   **A** = 4, 5, K, T

58. L 4 7 2 T 6 V K   **B** = 4, 7, G, K

59. 3 5 4 L 9 V T G   **C** = 2, 5, G, L

60. G 4 K 7 L 3 5 Z   **D** = 2, 7, L, T

61. 4 K 2 9 N 5 T G   **E** = None of the above

62. 9 G Z 3 L 4 6 N   **A** = 4, 9, L, V

63. L 5 N K 4 3 9 V   **B** = 4, 5, N, Z

64. 8 2 V P 9 L Z 5   **C** = 5, 8, L, Z

65. V P 9 Z 5 L 8 7   **D** = 8, 9, N, V

66. 5 T 8 N 2 9 V L   **E** = None of the above

Suggested Answers

67. N   5   4   7   T   K   3   Z   **A** = 3, 8, K, N

68. 8   5   3   V   L   2   Z   N   **B** = 5, 8, N, V

69. 7   2   5   N   9   K   L   V   **C** = 3, 9, V, Z

70. 9   8   L   2   5   Z   K   V   **D** = 5, 9, K, Z

71. Z   6   5   V   9   3   P   N   **E** = None of the above

72. 6   Z   T   N   8   7   4   V   **A** = 2, 7, L, N

73. V   7   8   6   N   5   P   L   **B** = 2, 8, T, V

74. N   7   P   V   8   4   2   L   **C** = 6, 8, L, T

75. 7   8   G   4   3   V   L   T   **D** = 6, 7, N, V

76. 4   8   G   2   T   N   6   L   **E** = None of the above

77. V   5   7   Z   N   9   4   T   **A** = 2, 5, N, Z

78. 4   6   P   T   2   N   K   9   **B** = 4, 5, N, P

79. 6   4   N   2   P   8   Z   K   **C** = 2, 9, P, T

80. 7   P   5   2   4   N   K   T   **D** = 4, 9, T, Z

81. K   T   8   5   4   N   2   P   **E** = None of the above

82. Z   3   N   P   G   5   4   2   **A** = 2, 3, G, N

83. 6   N   2   8   G   4   P   T   **B** = 2, 6, N, T

84. 6   N   4   T   V   G   8   2   **C** = 3, 4, G, K

85. T   3   P   4   N   8   G   2   **D** = 4, 6, K, T

86. 6   7   K   G   N   2   L   5   **E** = None of the above

> **Directions:** In questions 87–110, compare the three names or numbers, and choose:
>   **A** if ALL THREE names or numbers are exactly ALIKE.
>   **B** if only the FIRST and SECOND names or numbers are exactly ALIKE.
>   **C** if only the FIRST and THIRD names or numbers are exactly ALIKE.
>   **D** if only the SECOND and THIRD names or numbers are exactly ALIKE.
>   **E** if ALL THREE names or numbers are DIFFERENT.

87.	5261383	5261383	5261338
88.	8125690	8126690	8125609
89.	W. E. Johnston	W. E. Johnson	W. E. Johnson
90.	2395890	2395890	2395890
91.	1926341	1926347	1926314
92.	E. Owens McVey	E. Owen McVey	E. Owen McVay
93.	Emily Neal Rouse	Emily Neal Rowse	Emily Neal Rowse
94.	H. Merritt Audubon	H. Merriott Audubon	H. Merritt Audubon
95.	6219354	6219354	6219354
96.	2311.2793	2312793	2312793
97.	1065407	1065407	1065047
98.	6452054	6452654	6452054
99.	8501268	8501268	8501286
100.	Ella Burk Newham	Ella Burk Newnham	Elena Burk Newnham
101.	Jno. K. Ravencroft	Jno. H. Ravencroft	Jno. H. Ravencroft
102.	Martin Wills Pullen	Martin Wills Pulen	Martin Wills Pullen
103.	3457988	3457986	3457986
104.	4695682	4695862	4695682
105.	Sticklund Kanedy	Stricklund Kanedy	Stricklund Kanedy
106.	1592514	1592574	1592574
107.	2010202	2010202	2010220
108.	6177396	6177936	6177396
109.	Drusilla S. Ridgeley	Drusilla S. Ridgeley	Drusilla S. Ridgeley
110.	Andrei I. Toumantzev	Andrei I. Tourmantzev	Andrei I. Toumantzov

Directions: In questions 111 and 112, consider each group of names as a unit. Determine where the name printed in boldface would appear if the names in the group were correctly alphabetized. If the name in boldface is first, mark **A**; if second, mark **B**; if third, mark **C**; and if fourth, mark **D**.

111. 1st Division Automotive
1st Street Shopping Mall
First Level Furnishings
The First Florist, LTD.

112. Mindy L. Moon
Mindy Moone
Mandy Moone
Mandy W. Moon

Directions: In questions 113 and 114, there are four names listed. For each question, select the name that should be third if the four names were arranged in alphabetical order in accordance with the rules for alphabetical filing.

113. A. Dr. Zelda Gilroy, DDS
B. 2 Dewdrop Lane Brewery
C. Ms. Z. A. Ferrara
D. Toothsome Dentistry, Inc.

114. A. Dr. Roz Thurman
B. Vice President Joe Biden
C. Mr. Yohji Yamamoto
D. VP Andrew Rodriguez

Directions: In questions 115 and 116, each question gives the name and identification number of an employee. You are to choose the one answer that has exactly the same identification number and name as those given in the question.

115. 6553-D Bernard K. Rhodes
A. 6553-D Bernard Rhodes
B. 6553-D Bernard K. Rodes
C. 6553 Bernard K. Rhodes
D. 6553-D Bernard K. Rhodes

116. 221390-J Jean Battye
A. 221390 Jean Battye
B. 221390-J Jean Battye
C. 221390-J Jean Batty
D. 221390-J Jean J. Battye

Directions: Questions 117–120 consist of three sets of names and name codes. In each question, the two names and name codes on the same line are supposed to be exactly the same. Look carefully at each set of names and codes, and choose your answer as follows:

Choose **A** if there are mistakes in all THREE sets.

Choose **B** if there are mistakes in TWO of the sets.

Choose **C** if there are mistakes in only ONE set.

Choose **D** if there are NO MISTAKES in any of the sets.

117. Mr. Marc J. Lourd   H 86758   Mr. Marc J. Lourde   H 86758
     Mr. Al Partridge   O 98076   Mr. Al Partridge   98076
     Ms. Bernice Bakshi   Y 765746   Ms. Bernice Bakshi   Y-765746

118. ABC Taxi Co.   T 64758   ABC Taxi Co   T 64758
     Bertrum Bus Company   45936 G   Bertrum Bus Company   45936 G
     Lorenzo Limousines Inc.   45367 F   Lorenzo Limousines Inc.   4536 F

119. Balloonatix Party Supplies   87763 B   Balloonatix Party Supplies   87763 B
     Classic Catering   F 67565   Classic Catering   F 67565
     Dapper DJs   G-95432   Dapper DJs   G-95432

120. Mr. Joaquin Claddending   J-50097   Mr. Joaquin Claddening   J-50097
     Mrs. Celestine Arbothnot   596388 O   Mrs. Celestine Arbothnot   596388 O
     Mr. Bertram Wilem-Gilles   76440-6   Mr. Bertram Wilem-Gilles   76440-6

ANSWER KEYS AND EXPLANATIONS

Verbal

1. B	18. A	35. D	52. C	69. D
2. C	19. D	36. A	53. B	70. A
3. A	20. A	37. C	54. A	71. A
4. D	21. B	38. B	55. D	72. B
5. B	22. B	39. C	56. A	73. D
6. D	23. C	40. A	57. D	74. A
7. A	24. D	41. C	58. C	75. C
8. D	25. A	42. A	59. A	76. B
9. B	26. B	43. B	60. B	77. D
10. C	27. A	44. B	61. B	78. A
11. B	28. B	45. A	62. A	79. B
12. A	29. C	46. C	63. C	80. C
13. C	30. D	47. B	64. D	81. B
14. A	31. A	48. A	65. C	82. D
15. D	32. D	49. C	66. D	83. D
16. B	33. B	50. C	67. B	84. B
17. C	34. C	51. A	68. B	85. C

1. **The correct answer is B.** To *enthrall* means "to enchant."

2. **The correct answer is C.** To *verify* is to check the accuracy of or to confirm.

3. **The correct answer is A.** To *impede* means "to hinder."

4. **The correct answer is D.** To *beseech* means "to plead."

5. **The correct answer is B.** *Boisterous* means "rowdy."

6. **The correct answer is D.** *Despondent* means "hopeless."

7. **The correct answer is A.** To *divulge* means to "reveal."

8. **The correct answer is D.** A *fallacy* means a "falsehood."

9. **The correct answer is B.** *Tumultuous* means "turbulent."

10. **The correct answer is C.** To *flourish* means to "thrive."

11. **The correct answer is B.** To *pulverize* means to "demolish."

12. **The correct answer is A.** *Tranquil* means "quiet."

13. **The correct answer is C.** *Opaque* means that something is not clear, or not see-through.

14. **The correct answer is A.** The prefix *in-* frequently means "un-," so you should be on the lookout for similar words that carry that prefix. In this case, *unavoidable* (choice A) comes closest in meaning.

15. **The correct answer is D.** To *persist* means to be stubborn, or to keep going.

16. **The correct answer is B.** This version represents the clearest and best written version of the ideas expressed. The other choices are awkward and confusing with grammatical errors.

17. **The correct answer is C.** In choice A, the verb *was* does not match the plural subject (*package contents*). Choice B is awkwardly phrased, with two incomplete clauses. Choice D includes awkward phrasing (*removed contents of the package*). Choice C is the clearest sentence of the options.

18. **The correct answer is A.** Choice B has a misplaced clause, suggesting that the rezoning is evaluating the situation. Choice C creates a sentence fragment by separating the sentences. Choice D is incorrect because it changes the meaning of the sentence, suggesting that the displacement is responsible for the rezoning, not vice versa.

19. **The correct answer is D.** Choice A is incorrect because *its* is missing an apostrophe. Choice B is incorrect because it uses *clearly* twice, creating redundancy. Choice C is incorrect because it changes the meaning of the sentence, suggesting that the job (and not *it*) is the subject of the sentence.

20. **The correct answer is A.** Choice B is incorrect because of the extra comma inserted before *2030*. Choice C is incorrect because there is no need to use parentheses to set off this phrase, because it is essential information for the sentence to make sense. Choice C is incorrect because setting this phrase off with em dashes suggests that it's a subordinate clause, and it's not.

21. **The correct answer is B.** Choice A is incorrect because it improperly capitalizes and does not punctuate the title

Ms. Choice C is incorrect because it is an incomplete thought without punctuation. Choice D is incorrect because it is missing connecting information to make it a complete sentence. As it stands, it is an incomplete thought.

22. **The correct answer is B.** Choice A is incorrect because *rates* is plural, and should not be possessive. Choice C is incorrect because it is worded very awkwardly. Choice D is incorrect because *it* is unclear—it could refer to *demand*, or something else.

23. **The correct answer is C.** There is no additional punctuation needed for this short sentence. Choice A is incorrect because *any safety violations* is not subordinate to any other clause, but it is presented as a subordinate or dependent clause. Choice B is incorrect because it makes it look like the floor manager should report the violations, not you. Choice D is incorrect because it changes the sentence altogether, removing the part about you reporting violations.

24. **The correct answer is D.** Choice A is incorrect because the plural verb phrase *have been* does not match the singular noun *restaurant*. Choice B is incorrect because it creates an incomplete sentence. Choice C is incorrect because it is unclear which, or how many violations, the sentence is describing, so it removes necessary information that is contained in the other answer choices.

25. **The correct answer is A.** Choice B is incorrect because the tone is less formal, and an ellipsis should not be used for conversational emphasis in a formal report. Choice C is incorrect because the pronoun *they* is missing from the second part of the sentence. Choice D is incorrect because the phrasing is too ambiguous, and it needs to be made clear what is being accepted, and

what creates the conflict of interest. As it stands, the sentence is incomplete.

26. **The correct answer is B.** Choice A is incorrect because the list items are not phrased in a parallel way. Choice C is incorrect because it is a casual, incomplete sentence, and does not fit the formal tone of a report. Choice D is incorrect because it makes the subject of the sentence appear to be *an $80 annual fee*, while creating a confusing compound sentence with *and you are required to pass…*

27. **The correct answer is A.** Choice B is incorrect because it falsely suggests that the drug test failures have the policy. Choice C is incorrect because it suggests that the act of failing a drug test is the policy. Choice D is incorrect because it looks like the policy is set by employees, not for employees.

28. **The correct answer is B.** Choice A is incorrect because there is a missing helper verb between the noun *picnic* and the verb *budgeted*. Choice C is incorrect because it is an incomplete thought, and more of a brief note. Choice D is incorrect because it unnecessarily uses both a dollar sign and *dollars*, and breaks up the noun phrase *Parks Department picnic* with a confusing qualifier (*this year*).

29. **The correct answer is C.** Both choices A and B are confusingly written. Choice D is incorrect because it uses *per*, which suggests that January is making the decision, and is not just an indication of timing. Choice C states the information clearly and with correct punctuation.

30. **The correct answer is D.** The issue here is one of tone. In a formal report, *check it out* (choice A) or *oh and* (choice B) are too conversational, and inappropriate for the format. Choice C is incorrect because it seems like the speaker/writer is asking

for something or making a request, not making a statement.

31. **The correct answer is A.** Choice B is incorrect because there is confusion about what is being distributed, and by whom. Choice C suggests that it is the volunteers who need the supplies, not that they will be handing them out. Choice D is incorrect because it breaks up the thought, unnecessarily splitting up *water* and *basic supplies*, even though they are a compound subject.

32. **The correct answer is D.** The issue in this sentence is punctuation. Choice A creates an incredibly confusing sentence by leaving out punctuation altogether. It's not clear what is happening. Choice B adds an unnecessary comma after *appeared*. Choice C incorrectly adds a semi-colon, when there is no punctuation necessary to set off the suspect's three qualities.

33. **The correct answer is B.** Choice A is a comma splice, with two complete sentences on either side of the comma. Choice C adds an incorrect comma after *savings alone*. Choice D incorrectly uses the past tense *were*, when the sentence is talking about future savings.

34. **The correct answer is C.** Choice A is incorrect because it suggests that the year is requiring the drills. Choice B is incorrect because it reads as though the employees are requiring the drill, not required to take part. Choice D is incorrect because there is a verb missing that tells the reader who is required, and what they're supposed to do.

35. **The correct answer is D.** Choice A is incorrect because it is an incomplete sentence; there is only a noun phrase before the colon. Choice B is incorrect because it unnecessarily creates more than one sentence, and only the first one is a complete sentence. Choice C is incorrect because it

is an incomplete thought. There is no verb in the sentence.

36. **The correct answer is A.** The correct spelling is *scintillate*.

37. **The correct answer is C.** The correct spelling is *judicious*.

38. **The correct answer is B.** The correct spelling is *respiration*.

39. **The correct answer is C.** The correct spelling is *ominous*.

40. **The correct answer is A.** The correct spelling is *conceivable*.

41. **The correct answer is C.** The correct spelling is *nuisance*.

42. **The correct answer is A.** The correct spelling is *association*.

43. **The correct answer is B.** The correct spelling is *questionnaire*.

44. **The correct answer is B.** The correct spelling is *commemorate*.

45. **The correct answer is A.** The correct spelling is *misspelled*.

46. **The correct answer is C.** The correct spelling is *grateful*.

47. **The correct answer is B.** The correct spelling is *compliance*.

48. **The correct answer is A.** The correct spelling is *victorious*.

49. **The correct answer is C.** The correct spelling is *evaluation*.

50. **The correct answer is C.** The correct spelling is *annual*.

51. **The correct answer is A.** The correct spelling is *denial*.

52. **The correct answer is C.** The correct spelling is *calendar*.

53. **The correct answer is B.** The correct spelling is *argument*.

54. **The correct answer is A.** The correct spelling is *sufficient*.

55. **The correct answer is D.** The correct spelling is *develop*.

56. **The correct answer is A.** If instruction in safety rules will help to prevent accidents, some accidents must occur because of lack of knowledge.

57. **The correct answer is D.** Mayor Tilden has the highest number of votes, so he or she will win the election.

58. **The correct answer is C.** According to the paragraph, the application must include a photocopy of a valid driver's license. None of the other options are supported by the paragraph.

59. **The correct answer is A.** The phrase *ready to go* suggests that time is an issue, and that the pre-written obituaries are used for that reason.

60. **The correct answer is B.** The paragraph refers to the food cooked at home as "real," so it can be inferred that the author values authenticity as much as the "pretty."

61. **The correct answer is B.** Choice A suggests that the entire passage is about colleges with bad financial practices, and this is not the case. Choice C is incorrect because the passage describes different college options for students. Choice D is incorrect because this is not a handbook, but rather an informational passage about some of the pros and cons of online colleges.

62. **The correct answer is A.** There is no information in the passage which suggests that online colleges offer free tuition.

63. **The correct answer is C.** Paragraph 3 describes how some online colleges scam

their students. There is no indication that the author thinks there is too much work (choice A). Paragraph 2 suggests that choices B and D are benefits of an online college, not a problem.

64. **The correct answer is D.** The passage focuses on students who fall outside of the traditional student who goes straight to college from high school, and graduates with a degree in four years. All three of the other options describe that traditional student.

65. **The correct answer is C.** The passage does not speculate on what the future of any colleges are, so choice A is not supported. The passage describes benefits of online college as well as potential drawbacks, so choice B is not supported either. Choice D is incorrect because there is no information given about how students learn personally.

66. **The correct answer is D.** The passage does not take a specific stance on whether or not people want expensive apps (choice A), that only free apps are acceptable (choice B), or that paid apps should be banned (choice C). Choice D is the only option supported by the full passage.

67. **The correct answer is B.** Because the author is critical of how apps are marketed and sold, it is unlikely that he or she works in that field (choices A and D)—or at least there is not enough information to support that. There is also not enough information to support the idea that the writer is a politician (choice C), even though the opinionated tone could be interpreted that way. With reading comprehension questions, it's important to make sure that your answer is fully supported by information in the passage.

68. **The correct answer is B.** Although the passage does not specifically mention children using apps, this is information that could support the author's main point. Choices A, C, and D would all be presenting information that is not tied to any of the author's specific points.

69. **The correct answer is D.** From the context of the passage, you can infer that *insidious* is not a positive word, given that the author is using it to criticize hidden costs in apps. If you insert each choice into the sentence, only choice D makes sense.

70. **The correct answer is A.** In paragraph 2, the author ends by calling for warnings when apps are downloaded, suggesting that it's the store's responsibility to let customers know what they're getting. None of the other options are supported by specific statements or information in the passage.

71. **The correct answer is A.** The sentence is correct as written. Choices B and D use incorrect contractions for *you*. Choice C incorrectly uses a possessive, not a contraction.

72. **The correct answer is B.** In this case, *that* should be used as a conjunction used to explain what the experts are recommending.

73. **The correct answer is D.** *Setting* is the appropriate word choice in this sentence. If you try plugging the other verbs into the sentence, they don't match the context of the sentence.

74. **The correct answer is A.** The verb tense of *to go* is correct as its written.

75. **The correct answer is C.** The comma correctly sets off the descriptive clause.

76. **The correct answer is B.** This phrase is modifying the plural noun *rhythms*, and the verb should be plural as well.

77. **The correct answer is D.** *To* is the correct word as part of the verb phrase.

78. **The correct answer is A.** The pronoun *them* is used in place of the plural noun *devices*, so it should be plural as well.

79. **The correct answer is B.** This specific phrase should have opening and closing quotation marks. No additional capitalization is needed.

80. **The correct answer is C.** The correct preposition to describe years in the past is *over*.

81. **The correct answer is B.** The noun used here should refer to people. *Supports* and *support* suggest inanimate objects and ideas, so *supporters* is the best choice.

82. **The correct answer is D.** No additional punctuation is needed here. Adding a comma, em dash, or semicolon incorrectly breaks up the sentence.

83. **The correct answer is D.** The pronoun *it* is singular, so the matching verb should be singular as well.

84. **The correct answer is B.** There are no clear comparisons to determine whether the streets are cleanest, so superlatives don't work here.

85. **The correct answer is C.** Both *endless* and *unbreakable* are adjectives modifying *cycle*, so it's appropriate to separate them with a comma.

Clerical Ability

1. D	25. C	49. C	73. D	97. B
2. B	26. D	50. C	74. A	98. C
3. D	27. D	51. A	75. E	99. B
4. B	28. B	52. A	76. C	100. E
5. E	29. B	53. B	77. D	101. D
6. D	30. B	54. D	78. C	102. C
7. D	31. B	55. C	79. E	103. D
8. C	32. E	56. B	80. B	104. C
9. C	33. A	57. A	81. B	105. D
10. A	34. A	58. D	82. A	106. D
11. D	35. C	59. E	83. B	107. B
12. B	36. C	60. B	84. B	108. C
13. C	37. B	61. A	85. A	109. A
14. A	38. C	62. E	86. E	110. E
15. D	39. D	63. A	87. B	111. D
16. C	40. D	64. C	88. E	112. A
17. A	41. E	65. C	89. D	113. D
18. E	42. A	66. D	90. A	114. A
19. C	43. C	67. E	91. E	115. D
20. C	44. B	68. B	92. E	116. B
21. B	45. C	69. E	93. D	117. A
22. D	46. A	70. D	94. C	118. B
23. B	47. E	71. C	95. A	119. D
24. A	48. E	72. D	96. D	210. C

1. **The correct answer is D.** In alphabetical order, *heifers* comes after *hegemonies* and before *heirs*.

2. **The correct answer is B.** In alphabetical order, *colonials* come after *colonels* and before *colonists*.

3. **The correct answer is D.** Bobbitt, Olivia H.; Bobbitt, Olivier E.; Bobbitt, R. Olivia

4. **The correct answer is B.** Mosely, Albert J.; Mosely, Werner; Mosley, Alvin.

5. **The correct answer is E.** Youmons; Youmuns

6. **The correct answer is D.** Watson; Watters; Wattwood

7. **The correct answer is D.** Johnston, Edmund; Johnston, Edward; Johnstone, Edmund A.

8. **The correct answer is C.** Remschel; Rensch; Renshaw

9. **The correct answer is C.** DeMatteo; DeMattia; Derby

10. **The correct answer is A.** Theriault; Therien

11. **The correct answer is D.** Gaston, Isabel; Gaston, M. Hubert; Gaston, M. Melvin

12. **The correct answer is B.** San-Luis; San-Miguel; Santilli

13. **The correct answer is C.** De-Lathouder; DeLaTour; Lathrop

14. **The correct answer is A.** O'Bannon; O'Beirne

15. **The correct answer is D.** Entsminger, Jack; Entsminger, Jacob; Entsminger, James

16. **The correct answer is C.** Iacone, Pedro M.; Iacone, Pete R.; Iacone, Peter F.

17. **The correct answer is A.** Dunlavey; Dunleavy

18. **The correct answer is E.** Yarborough; Yarbrough

19. **The correct answer is C.** Proutey, Maude; Prouty, Martha; Prouty, Myra

20. **The correct answer is C.** Pawalek; Pawlowicz; Pawlowski

21. **The correct answer is B.** Vanover; Vanstory; VanSwinderen

22. **The correct answer is D.** FitzGibbon; Fitzsimmons; FitzSimons

23. **The correct answer is B.** Daly; D'Amato; D'Amboise

24. **The correct answer is A.** Schaeffer; Schaffert

25. **The correct answer is C.** White-Leigh; White-Lewis; Whitely

26. **The correct answer is D.** VanDercook; VanDerHeggen; VanderLinden

27. **The correct answer is D.** 75

28. **The correct answer is B.** 79

29. **The correct answer is B.** 287

30. **The correct answer is B.** 51

31. **The correct answer is B.** 52

32. **The correct answer is E.** 21

33. **The correct answer is A.** 400

34. **The correct answer is A.** 20

35. **The correct answer is C.** 141

36. **The correct answer is C.** 19

37. **The correct answer is B.** 310

38. **The correct answer is C.** 51

39. **The correct answer is D.** 68

40. **The correct answer is D.** 45

41. **The correct answer is E.** 111

42. **The correct answer is A.** 51

43. **The correct answer is C.** 85

44. **The correct answer is B.** 29

45. **The correct answer is C.** 272

46. **The correct answer is A.** 71

47. **The correct answer is E.** 63

48. **The correct answer is E.** 9

49. **The correct answer is C.** 516

50. **The correct answer is C.** 81

51. **The correct answer is A.** 131

52. **The correct answer is A.** 124

53. **The correct answer is B.** The man who is wearing glasses has a laptop computer on the table in front of him, but in his hand he is holding a piece of paper.

54. **The correct answer is D.** One woman is standing, but the four other people in the photo are all sitting.

55. **The correct answer is C.** Because you're not one of the people directly in the conversation, it may not be appropriate to insert yourself into the situation (choice A). However, it is unethical for a supervisor to demand personal favors in exchange for professional benefits, and could actually be harassment. So it would not be appropriate to try to use the same tactic to get a promotion for yourself (choice D) or to stay silent and let the employee continue to be harassed (choice C).

56. The correct answer is B. Although all of the options are likely violations, only one presents an urgent potential danger. If the inspector smells gas, she should report it to the fire department immediately, rather than handling it through the standard violation paperwork process—which is how the others should be handled.

57. The correct answer is A. 6 2 5 K 4 P T G

58. The correct answer is D. L 4 7 2 T 6 V K

59. The correct answer is E. The answer cannot be choice A or B because there is no **K**; it cannot be choice C or D because there is no **2**.

60. The correct answer is B. G 4 K 7 L 3 5 Z

61. The correct answer is A. 4 K 2 9 N 5 T G

62. The correct answer is E. The answer cannot be choice A because there is no **V**; it cannot be choice B or C because there is no **5**; it cannot be choice D because there is no **8** or **V**.

63. The correct answer is A. L 5 N K 4 3 9 V

64. The correct answer is C. 8 2 V P 9 L Z 5

65. The correct answer is C. V P 9 Z 5 L 8 7

66. The correct answer is D. 5 T 8 N 2 9 V L

67. The correct answer is E. The answer cannot be choice A or B because there is no **8**; it cannot be choice C or D because there is no **9**.

68. The correct answer is B. 8 5 3 V L 2 Z N

69. The correct answer is E. The answer cannot be choice A or B because there is no **8**; it cannot be choice C or D because there is no **Z**.

70. The correct answer is D. 9 8 L 2 5 Z K V

71. The correct answer is C. Z 6 5 V 9 3 P N

72. The correct answer is D. 6 Z T N 8 7 4 V

73. The correct answer is D. V 7 8 6 N 5 P L

74. The correct answer is A. N 7 P V 8 4 2 L

75. The correct answer is E. The answer cannot be choice A or B because there is no **2**; it cannot be choice C or D because there is no **6**.

76. The correct answer is C. 4 8 G 2 T N 6 L

77. The correct answer is D. V 5 7 Z N 9 4 T

78. The correct answer is C. 4 6 P T 2 N K 9

79. The correct answer is E. The answer cannot be choice A or B because there is no **5**; it cannot be choice C or D because there is no **9**.

80. The correct answer is B. 7 P 5 2 4 N K T

81. The correct answer is B. K T 8 5 4 N 2 P

82. The correct answer is A. Z 3 N P G 5 4 2

83. The correct answer is B. 6 N 2 8 G 4 P T

84. The correct answer is B. 6 N 4 T V G 8 2

85. The correct answer is A. T 3 P 4 N 8 G 2

86. The correct answer is E. The answer cannot be choice A or C because there is no **3**; it cannot be choice B or D because there is no **T**.

87. The correct answer is B. The third number is different.

88. The correct answer is E. All three numbers are different.

89. The correct answer is D. The first name is different.

90. The correct answer is A. All three numbers are exactly alike.

91. The correct answer is E. All three numbers are different.

92. The correct answer is E. All three names are different.

93. **The correct answer is D.** The first name is different.

94. **The correct answer is C.** The second name is different.

95. **The correct answer is A.** All three numbers are exactly alike.

96. **The correct answer is D.** The first number is different.

97. **The correct answer is B.** The third number is different.

98. **The correct answer is C.** The second number is different.

99. **The correct answer is B.** The third number is different.

100. **The correct answer is E.** All three names are different.

101. **The correct answer is D.** The first name is different.

102. **The correct answer is C.** The second name is different.

103. **The correct answer is D.** The first number is different.

104. **The correct answer is C.** The second number is different.

105. **The correct answer is D.** All three names are exactly alike.

106. **The correct answer is D.** The first number is different.

107. **The correct answer is B.** The third number is different.

108. **The correct answer is C.** The second number is different.

109. **The correct answer is A.** All three names are exactly alike.

110. **The correct answer is E.** All three names are different.

111. **The correct answer is D.** Business names that begin with numerals should be alphabetized as if the numerals are spelled out. Articles such as *the* are disregarded when alphabetizing business names. Therefore, the correct order is: 1st Division Automotive, The First Florist, LTD., First Level Furnishings, **1st Street Shopping Mall.**

112. **The correct answer is A.** Names are alphabetized with importance placed on the last name first, the first name or initial second, and the middle name or initial last. Since *Mandy* would be alphabetized before *Mindy*, and *Moon* would be alphabetized before *Moone*, correct alphabetical order is: **Mandy W. Moon,** Mindy L. Moon, Mandy Moone, Mindy Moone.

113. **The correct answer is D.** Business names that begin with numerals should be alphabetized as if the numerals are spelled out. Titles such as *Dr.* and *Ms.* are disregarded when alphabetizing names. Therefore, correct alphabetical order is: Ms. Z. A. Ferrara; Dr. Zelda Gilroy; Toothsome Dentistry, Inc.; 21 Dewdrop Lane Brewery. Choice D is the correct answer because Toothsome Dentistry, Inc. is third in the order.

114. **The correct answer is A.** Titles such as *Dr., VP, Vice President* and *Mr.* are disregarded when alphabetizing names. Therefore, correct alphabetical order is: Vice President Joe Biden; VP Andrew Rodriguez; Dr. Roz Thurman; Mr. Yohji Yamamoto. Choice A is the correct answer because Dr. Roz Thurman is third in the order.

115. **The correct answer is D.** Only choice D is written correctly. Choice A is missing the employee's middle initial. In choice B, *Rhodes* is missing its *h*. The *D* is missing from the identification number in choice C.

116. **The correct answer is B.** Only choice B is written correctly. The *J* is missing from the identification number in choice A. The letter *e* is missing from the end of the employee's last name in choice C. Choice D adds a middle initial to the employee's name.

117. **The correct answer is A.** There are mistakes in all three sets. In the first set, *Lourd* is spelled differently in each column. In the second set, the letter *O* is missing from the code in the second column. In the third set, there is a hyphen in the second-column code name only.

118. **The correct answer is B.** There are mistakes in the first and third sets. In the second column of the first set, a period is missing after *Co*. In the second column of the third set, a *7* is missing from the code.

119. **The correct answer is D.** There are no mistakes in any of the sets.

120. **The correct answer is C.** In the second column of the first set, *Claddending* is spelled differently in each column.

SELF-EVALUATION

On your answer sheet, mark the numbers of the questions that you answered incorrectly and check them against the following charts. If you missed several of any question type, you need more practice with that kind of question. Return to the appropriate chapter and review the rules and practice exercises before moving on to the next sample exam.

SELF-EVALUATION CHART: VERBAL ABILITY TEST

Question Type	Question Numbers	Chapter to Review
English Grammar and Usage	16–35	4
Spelling	36–55	5
Synonyms	1–15	6
Effective Expression	71-85	9
Reading Comprehension	56–70	10

SELF-EVALUATION CHART: CLERICAL ABILITY TEST

Question Type	Question Numbers	Chapter to Review
Alphabetizing and Filing	1–26; 111-114	12
Speed and Accuracy	57-110, 115-120	13
Simple Arithmetic	27–52	NA
Judgment, Communication, and Memory	53–56	11

ANSWER SHEET PRACTICE TEST 3

Clerical Ability

1. Ⓐ Ⓑ Ⓒ Ⓓ Ⓔ 20. Ⓐ Ⓑ Ⓒ Ⓓ 39. Ⓐ Ⓑ Ⓒ Ⓓ Ⓔ 58. Ⓐ Ⓑ Ⓒ Ⓓ Ⓔ
2. Ⓐ Ⓑ Ⓒ Ⓓ Ⓔ 21. Ⓐ Ⓑ Ⓒ Ⓓ Ⓔ 40. Ⓐ Ⓑ Ⓒ Ⓓ Ⓔ 59. Ⓐ Ⓑ Ⓒ Ⓓ Ⓔ
3. Ⓐ Ⓑ Ⓒ Ⓓ Ⓔ 22. Ⓐ Ⓑ Ⓒ Ⓓ Ⓔ 41. Ⓐ Ⓑ Ⓒ Ⓓ Ⓔ 60. Ⓐ Ⓑ Ⓒ Ⓓ Ⓔ
4. Ⓐ Ⓑ Ⓒ Ⓓ Ⓔ 23. Ⓐ Ⓑ Ⓒ Ⓓ Ⓔ 42. Ⓐ Ⓑ Ⓒ Ⓓ Ⓔ 61. Ⓐ Ⓑ Ⓒ Ⓓ Ⓔ
5. Ⓐ Ⓑ Ⓒ Ⓓ Ⓔ 24. Ⓐ Ⓑ Ⓒ Ⓓ Ⓔ 43. Ⓐ Ⓑ Ⓒ Ⓓ Ⓔ 62. Ⓐ Ⓑ Ⓒ Ⓓ Ⓔ
6. Ⓐ Ⓑ Ⓒ Ⓓ Ⓔ 25. Ⓐ Ⓑ Ⓒ Ⓓ Ⓔ 44. Ⓐ Ⓑ Ⓒ Ⓓ Ⓔ 63. Ⓐ Ⓑ Ⓒ Ⓓ Ⓔ
7. Ⓐ Ⓑ Ⓒ Ⓓ Ⓔ 26. Ⓐ Ⓑ Ⓒ Ⓓ Ⓔ 45. Ⓐ Ⓑ Ⓒ Ⓓ 64. Ⓐ Ⓑ Ⓒ Ⓓ Ⓔ
8. Ⓐ Ⓑ Ⓒ Ⓓ Ⓔ 27. Ⓐ Ⓑ Ⓒ Ⓓ Ⓔ 46. Ⓐ Ⓑ Ⓒ Ⓓ 65. Ⓐ Ⓑ Ⓒ Ⓓ Ⓔ
9. Ⓐ Ⓑ Ⓒ Ⓓ Ⓔ 28. Ⓐ Ⓑ Ⓒ Ⓓ Ⓔ 47. Ⓐ Ⓑ Ⓒ Ⓓ 66. Ⓐ Ⓑ Ⓒ Ⓓ
10. Ⓐ Ⓑ Ⓒ Ⓓ Ⓔ 29. Ⓐ Ⓑ Ⓒ Ⓓ Ⓔ 48. Ⓐ Ⓑ Ⓒ Ⓓ 67. Ⓐ Ⓑ Ⓒ Ⓓ
11. Ⓐ Ⓑ Ⓒ Ⓓ Ⓔ 30. Ⓐ Ⓑ Ⓒ Ⓓ Ⓔ 49. Ⓐ Ⓑ Ⓒ Ⓓ 68. Ⓐ Ⓑ Ⓒ Ⓓ
12. Ⓐ Ⓑ Ⓒ Ⓓ Ⓔ 31. Ⓐ Ⓑ Ⓒ Ⓓ Ⓔ 50. Ⓐ Ⓑ Ⓒ Ⓓ 69. Ⓐ Ⓑ Ⓒ Ⓓ
13. Ⓐ Ⓑ Ⓒ Ⓓ Ⓔ 32. Ⓐ Ⓑ Ⓒ Ⓓ Ⓔ 51. Ⓐ Ⓑ Ⓒ Ⓓ Ⓔ 70. Ⓐ Ⓑ Ⓒ Ⓓ
14. Ⓐ Ⓑ Ⓒ Ⓓ Ⓔ 33. Ⓐ Ⓑ Ⓒ Ⓓ Ⓔ 52. Ⓐ Ⓑ Ⓒ Ⓓ Ⓔ 71. Ⓐ Ⓑ Ⓒ Ⓓ
15. Ⓐ Ⓑ Ⓒ Ⓓ Ⓔ 34. Ⓐ Ⓑ Ⓒ Ⓓ Ⓔ 53. Ⓐ Ⓑ Ⓒ Ⓓ Ⓔ 72. Ⓐ Ⓑ Ⓒ Ⓓ
16. Ⓐ Ⓑ Ⓒ Ⓓ Ⓔ 35. Ⓐ Ⓑ Ⓒ Ⓓ Ⓔ 54. Ⓐ Ⓑ Ⓒ Ⓓ Ⓔ 73. Ⓐ Ⓑ Ⓒ Ⓓ
17. Ⓐ Ⓑ Ⓒ Ⓓ 36. Ⓐ Ⓑ Ⓒ Ⓓ Ⓔ 55. Ⓐ Ⓑ Ⓒ Ⓓ Ⓔ 74. Ⓐ Ⓑ Ⓒ Ⓓ
18. Ⓐ Ⓑ Ⓒ Ⓓ 37. Ⓐ Ⓑ Ⓒ Ⓓ Ⓔ 56. Ⓐ Ⓑ Ⓒ Ⓓ Ⓔ 75. Ⓐ Ⓑ Ⓒ Ⓓ
19. Ⓐ Ⓑ Ⓒ Ⓓ 38. Ⓐ Ⓑ Ⓒ Ⓓ Ⓔ 57. Ⓐ Ⓑ Ⓒ Ⓓ Ⓔ

answer sheet

Verbal Ability

1. Ⓐ Ⓑ Ⓒ Ⓓ	20. Ⓐ Ⓑ Ⓒ Ⓓ	39. Ⓐ Ⓑ Ⓒ Ⓓ	58. Ⓐ Ⓑ Ⓒ Ⓓ
2. Ⓐ Ⓑ Ⓒ Ⓓ	21. Ⓐ Ⓑ Ⓒ Ⓓ	40. Ⓐ Ⓑ Ⓒ Ⓓ	59. Ⓐ Ⓑ Ⓒ Ⓓ
3. Ⓐ Ⓑ Ⓒ Ⓓ	22. Ⓐ Ⓑ Ⓒ Ⓓ	41. Ⓐ Ⓑ Ⓒ Ⓓ	60. Ⓐ Ⓑ Ⓒ Ⓓ
4. Ⓐ Ⓑ Ⓒ Ⓓ	23. Ⓐ Ⓑ Ⓒ Ⓓ	42. Ⓐ Ⓑ Ⓒ Ⓓ	61. Ⓐ Ⓑ Ⓒ Ⓓ
5. Ⓐ Ⓑ Ⓒ Ⓓ	24. Ⓐ Ⓑ Ⓒ Ⓓ	43. Ⓐ Ⓑ Ⓒ Ⓓ	62. Ⓐ Ⓑ Ⓒ Ⓓ
6. Ⓐ Ⓑ Ⓒ Ⓓ	25. Ⓐ Ⓑ Ⓒ Ⓓ	44. Ⓐ Ⓑ Ⓒ Ⓓ	63. Ⓐ Ⓑ Ⓒ Ⓓ
7. Ⓐ Ⓑ Ⓒ Ⓓ	26. Ⓐ Ⓑ Ⓒ Ⓓ	45. Ⓐ Ⓑ Ⓒ Ⓓ	64. Ⓐ Ⓑ Ⓒ Ⓓ
8. Ⓐ Ⓑ Ⓒ Ⓓ	27. Ⓐ Ⓑ Ⓒ Ⓓ	46. Ⓐ Ⓑ Ⓒ Ⓓ	65. Ⓐ Ⓑ Ⓒ Ⓓ
9. Ⓐ Ⓑ Ⓒ Ⓓ	28. Ⓐ Ⓑ Ⓒ Ⓓ	47. Ⓐ Ⓑ Ⓒ Ⓓ	66. Ⓐ Ⓑ Ⓒ Ⓓ
10. Ⓐ Ⓑ Ⓒ Ⓓ	29. Ⓐ Ⓑ Ⓒ Ⓓ	48. Ⓐ Ⓑ Ⓒ Ⓓ	67. Ⓐ Ⓑ Ⓒ Ⓓ
11. Ⓐ Ⓑ Ⓒ Ⓓ	30. Ⓐ Ⓑ Ⓒ Ⓓ	49. Ⓐ Ⓑ Ⓒ Ⓓ	68. Ⓐ Ⓑ Ⓒ Ⓓ
12. Ⓐ Ⓑ Ⓒ Ⓓ	31. Ⓐ Ⓑ Ⓒ Ⓓ	50. Ⓐ Ⓑ Ⓒ Ⓓ	69. Ⓐ Ⓑ Ⓒ Ⓓ
13. Ⓐ Ⓑ Ⓒ Ⓓ	32. Ⓐ Ⓑ Ⓒ Ⓓ	51. Ⓐ Ⓑ Ⓒ Ⓓ	70. Ⓐ Ⓑ Ⓒ Ⓓ
14. Ⓐ Ⓑ Ⓒ Ⓓ	33. Ⓐ Ⓑ Ⓒ Ⓓ	52. Ⓐ Ⓑ Ⓒ Ⓓ	71. Ⓐ Ⓑ Ⓒ Ⓓ
15. Ⓐ Ⓑ Ⓒ Ⓓ	34. Ⓐ Ⓑ Ⓒ Ⓓ	53. Ⓐ Ⓑ Ⓒ Ⓓ	72. Ⓐ Ⓑ Ⓒ Ⓓ
16. Ⓐ Ⓑ Ⓒ Ⓓ	35. Ⓐ Ⓑ Ⓒ Ⓓ	54. Ⓐ Ⓑ Ⓒ Ⓓ	73. Ⓐ Ⓑ Ⓒ Ⓓ
17. Ⓐ Ⓑ Ⓒ Ⓓ	36. Ⓐ Ⓑ Ⓒ Ⓓ	55. Ⓐ Ⓑ Ⓒ Ⓓ	74. Ⓐ Ⓑ Ⓒ Ⓓ
18. Ⓐ Ⓑ Ⓒ Ⓓ	37. Ⓐ Ⓑ Ⓒ Ⓓ	56. Ⓐ Ⓑ Ⓒ Ⓓ	75. Ⓐ Ⓑ Ⓒ Ⓓ
19. Ⓐ Ⓑ Ⓒ Ⓓ	38. Ⓐ Ⓑ Ⓒ Ⓓ	57. Ⓐ Ⓑ Ⓒ Ⓓ	

Practice Test 3

CLERICAL ABILITY

75 Questions • 38 Minutes

> **Directions:** For questions 1–16, you are given a name, number, or code, followed by four other names or codes in alphabetical or numerical order. Find the correct space for the given name or number so that it will be in alphabetical and/or numerical order with the others.

1. Mathison, J. John

   A –

   Mathers, Doris

   B –

   Matherson, Judy

   C –

   Mathews, J. R.

   D –

   Mathewson, Jerome

   E –

2. 59233362

   A –

   58146020

   B –

   59233162

   C –

   59233262

   D –

   59233662

   E –

3. MYP-6734

   A –

   NYP-6733

   B –

   NYS-7412

   C –

   NZT-4899

   D –

   PYZ-3636

   E –

4. Morin, Jose

   A –

   Morin, J. B.

   B –

   Morin, J. James

   C –

   Morin, James J.

   D –

   Morin, Joseph F.

   E –

NOTE

The directions are stated as if you are taking the exam in a paper-and-pencil format. If you will be taking the exam on a computer, each section will have directions specific to how to answer questions on a computer.

5. 00102032

A –

    00120312

B –

    00120323

C –

    00120324

D –

    00200303

E –

6. LPD-6100

A –

    LPD-5865

B –

    LPD-6001

C –

    LPD-6101

D –

    LPD-6106

E –

7. Vonbrunner, Carl

A –

    Von Alton, Karl

B –

    Vonderson, Michael

C –

    Von Lolhoffel, Darlene

D –

    Vonlolhoffel, M. E.

E –

8. Sanchez, R. R.

A –

    Sanchez, Alvira

B –

    Sanchez, Juanita

C –

    Sanchez, R. Juanita

D –

    Sanchez, S. Robert

E –

9. 01066010

A –

    01006040

B –

    01006051

C –

    01016053

D –

    01016060

E –

10. AAZ-2687

A –

    AAA-2132

B –

    AAS-4623

C –

    ASA-3216

D –

    ASZ-5490

E –

11. Kowalski, Raymond M.

A –

Kawalski, Raymond M.

B –

Kawalski, Robert

C –

Kowalsky, Robert S.

D –

Kowolsky, S.T., Jr.

E –

12. NCD-7834

A –

NBJ-4682

B –

NBT-5066

C –

NCD-7710

D –

NCD-7868

E –

13. 36270013

A –

36260006

B –

36270000

C –

36270030

D –

36670012

E –

14. Ketchener, Glen

A –

Ketchner, Alan

B –

Ketchum, George

C –

Kichner, A. George

D –

Kitchiner, Samuel

E –

15. Figuaro, Estevanico

A –

Figaro, Fernando

B –

Figaro, Francis

C –

Figuaro, Francisco

D –

Figurao, Geraldo

E –

16. 58006021

A –

58006130

B –

58097222

C –

59000599

D –

59909000

E –

Directions: Questions 17 and 18 consist of a CAPITALIZED word that is to be filed correctly among the alphabetized words listed. Choose the word that should come after the capitalized word.

17. IMPRINTS
    A. imports
    B. imposters
    C. impressions
    D. improvements

18. BACON
    A. bachelors
    B. bacteria
    C. badges
    D. badgers

Directions: For questions 19 and 20, consider each group of names as a unit. Determine where the name printed in boldface would appear if the names in the group were correctly alphabetized. If the name in boldface should appear first, mark **A** on your answer sheet; if second, mark **B**; if third, mark **C**; and if fourth, mark **D**.

19. Anne Jamie and Associates
    Larson Haulers, Inc.
    Bronson Brothers Trucking, LLC
    1st National Bank

20. T.T. Carmichael
    Carmine Tito
    Ted Carmine
    Dr. Tera Carmichael

Directions: For questions 21–44, there are three names, addresses, or codes that are very much alike. Compare the three and on your answer sheet, mark:
    A. if ALL THREE names, addresses, or codes are exactly ALIKE.
    B. if only the FIRST and SECOND names, addresses, or codes are exactly ALIKE.
    C. if only the FIRST and THIRD names, addresses, or codes are exactly ALIKE.
    D. if only the SECOND and THIRD names, addresses, or codes are exactly ALIKE.
    E. if ALL THREE names, addresses, or codes are DIFFERENT.

21. Rickard E. VonHofstadter | Rickard E. VonHofstadter | Rickard E. VonHofstadter
22. Sergei Kuznets | Serge Kusnetz | Sergei Kuznetts
23. 6-78912-e3e42 | 6-78912-3e3e42 | 6-78912-e3e42
24. 86529 Dunwoodie Drive | 86529 Dunwoodie Drive | 85629 Dunwoodie Drive
25. 9566110 | 9565101 | 9565101
26. Becca Katherine Hines | Becca Catherine Hanes | Becca Catharine Hane
27. 5416R-1952TZ-op | 5416R-1952TZ-op | 5416R-1952TZ-op
28. 60646 West Touhy Ave. | 60646 West Touhy Ave. | 60646 West Touhey Ave.
29. Mardikian & Moore, Inc. | Mardikian and Moore, Inc. | Mardikian & Moore, Inc.

30. 9670243	9670423	9670423
31. Eduardo Ingles	Eduardo Inglese	Eduardo Inglese
32. Roger T. DeAngelis	Roger T. D'Angelis	Roger T. DeAngeles
33. 7692138	7692138	7692138
34. 2695 East 3435 South	2695 East 3435 South	2695 East 3435 South
35. 63qs5-95YT3-001	63qs5-95YT3-001	62qs5-95YT3-001
36. 2789350	2789350	2798350
37. Helmut V. Lochner	Helmut V. Lockner	Helmut W. Lochner
38. 2454803	2548403	2454803
39. Lemberger, WA 28094	Lemberger, VA 28094	Lemberger, VA 28094
40. 4168-GNP-78852	4168-GNP-78852	4168-GNP-78852
41. Yoshihito Saito	Yoshihito Saito	Yoshihito Saito
42. 5927681	5927861	5927681
43. O'Reilly Bay, LA 56212	O'Reillys Bay, LA 56212	O'Reilly Bay, LA 56212
44. Myra Simpson	Myra Sampson	Myra Simpson

Directions: For questions 45 and 46, select the name that should be third if the four names were arranged in alphabetical order in accordance with the rules for alphabetical filing.

45. A. 1 Zanuck Avenue Catering
  B. 25 Sheridan Street Gymnasium
  C. 52 Pick-Up Playing Cards Manufacturing
  D. 75th Anniversary Films

46. A. Endless Possibilities Arts
  B. Thirteen Lucky Cats, LLC.
  C. Ms. T. Anderson
  D. Mr. B. A. Tonnely

Directions: Questions 47 and 48 give the name and identification number of an employee. Choose the answer that has exactly the same identification number and name as those given in the question.

47. 445321 William Szymczyk

- **A.** 445321 William Szymczik
- **B.** 45321 William Szymczyk
- **C.** 445321 William Szymcizyk
- **D.** 445321 William Szymczyk

48. L-75689 Sandra M. Rickenbacker

- **A.** L-75689 Sandra M. Rickenbacker
- **B.** M-75689 Sandra L. Rickenbacker
- **C.** L-75689 Sandra M. Rickenbackar
- **D.** L-75689 Sandra M. Rickenbaker

Directions: Questions 49 and 50 consist of three sets of names and name codes. In each question, the two names and name codes on the same line are supposed to be exactly the same. Look carefully at each set of names and codes, and choose your answer as follows:

Choose **A** if there are mistakes in all THREE sets.

Choose **B** if there are mistakes in TWO of the sets.

Choose **C** if there are mistakes in only ONE set.

Choose **D** if there are NO MISTAKES in any of the sets.

49.

Sampson Sporting Goods	D 75689	Sampson Sporting Goods	D 75689
Shoreline Boating	F 76859	Shoreline Boating	F 76859
Salice Skiing Supplies	V 86758	Salice Skiing Supplies	V86758

50.

Jane Newton-Travolta	F 64578	Jane N. Newton-Travolta	F 64578
Patricia A. Marquant	D 86970	Patricia A. Narquant	D 86970
Cecily D. Zelazny	T 87960	Cecily T. Zelazny	D 87960

Directions: For questions 51–65, perform the computation as indicated in the question, and find the answer among the choices listed. If the correct answer is not given among the choices, choose choice **E**.

51.   83
      − 56   SHOW YOUR WORK HERE

   A. 23
   B. 29
   C. 33
   D. 37
   E. None of the above

52.   15
      + 17

   A. 22
   B. 32
   C. 39
   D. 42
   E. None of the above

53.   32
      × 7

   A. 224
   B. 234
   C. 324
   D. 334
   E. None of the above

54.   39
      × 2

   A. 77
   B. 78
   C. 79
   D. 81
   E. None of the above

55.   43
       − 15   SHOW YOUR WORK HERE

   A. 23
   B. 32
   C. 33
   D. 35
   E. None of the above

56.   50
       + 49

   A. 89
   B. 90
   C. 99
   D. 109
   E. None of the above

57.   366
       ÷ 6

   A. 11
   B. 31
   C. 36
   D. 66
   E. None of the above

58.   38
       × 3

   A. 111
   B. 113
   C. 115
   D. 117
   E. None of the above

59.   19
      + 21

SHOW YOUR WORK HERE

   A. 20
   B. 30
   C. 40
   D. 50
   E. None of the above

60.   13
      − 6

   A. 5
   B. 7
   C. 9
   D. 11
   E. None of the above

61.   180
      ÷ 6

   A. 29
   B. 31
   C. 33
   D. 39
   E. None of the above

62.   10
      × 1

   A. 0
   B. 1
   C. 10
   D. 100
   E. None of the above

63.   287
       ÷ 7

    A.   21
    B.   27
    C.   31
    D.   37
    E.   None of the above

64.   12
       + 11

    A.   21
    B.   22
    C.   23
    D.   24
    E.   None of the above

65.   85
       − 64

    A.   19
    B.   21
    C.   29
    D.   31
    E.   None of the above

Directions: You will have three minutes to study the following picture, to note details about people, time and place, and activities. Then you will have to answer two questions about the picture without looking back at the picture.

https://www.pexels.com/photo/athletes-baseball-dirt-field-260635/

> **Directions:** Answer questions 66 and 67 on the basis of the picture. Do not look at the picture again.

66. The team name on the front of the uniforms is
- **A.** Tigers.
- **B.** Rice.
- **C.** Baylor.
- **D.** Texas.

67. How many players shown are NOT wearing a hat or helmet?
- **A.** Zero
- **B.** One
- **C.** Three
- **D.** Five

> **Directions:** For questions 68–72, read the passage and choose the best answer.

68. You are late to a meeting with a key person visiting from another department because a previous company meeting run by another department ran late. In front of the meeting guest, your manager scolds you for your lateness and tells you to better manage your time. Of the following, which is the best action to take in this situation?
- **A.** Explain in detail to your manager and the guest that you were not late.
- **B.** Apologize and discuss your scheduling conflict with your manager after the meeting.
- **C.** Call the person who ran the other meeting to explain why the meeting ran over.
- **D.** Say, "Let's just move on," and start with the current meeting agenda.

69. You are on a key deadline for an assignment your team is working on together. One of your teammates is constantly posting on social media sites instead of doing their share, and you are in danger of not completing your work on time. What is the best first course of action you should take?
- **A.** Go directly to your supervisor to let them know you are doing all the work alone.
- **B.** Discuss your concerns directly with your teammate to let them know you will not finish on time due to their lack of work.
- **C.** Stay overtime to do all of the work yourself so you will meet the deadline.
- **D.** Talk to your other coworkers about the issue so the news gets back to your teammate that you are dissatisfied.

70. After being at an agency for a year, your supervisor has made you the lead team member on a new project that is very important to the company. You have many responsibilities, and after a few weeks, you realize you are running behind and will not be able to finish on time by the following Monday. Of the following, which is the best action to take in this situation?

A. Assess your schedule to see if there are tasks you can ask be put on hold until this assignment is completed.

B. Finish the project when you are able to and let your supervisor know you will have to shift the deadline.

C. Ask your supervisor about shifting the deadline to a later date.

D. Ask your team to come in over the weekend to help make your deadline.

71. Your sister is curious about one of her coworkers, and asks you to look up the coworker's information in a confidential database to which you have access. Of the following, the best action for you to take would be to

A. look up the coworker as a one-time favor, but tell your sister that it can never happen again.

B. turn your sister in to your manager for asking you to do this.

C. firmly tell your sister that you can't use the database for this kind of activity.

D. look up the coworker and give your sister the information, but make sure it can't be traced to you.

72. A traffic officer sees an unmarked car parked illegally in front of a fire hydrant. The officer sees that on the dashboard, there is a note that says "be right back" and a t-shirt that suggests that the driver is a member of the same precinct as the officer. The best action for the traffic officer would be to

A. let it slide and pretend that the officer never saw the illegally parked car. After all, the note says the driver will be back soon.

B. call a friend in the precinct to see what she would do in this situation.

C. wait around for as long as it takes for the driver to come back.

D. write a ticket or arrange for a tow, according to the policy for any other car parked in front of a hydrant.

Directions: You will have three minutes to study the following picture, to note details about people, time and place, and activities. Then you will have to answer two questions about the picture without looking back at the picture.

Directions: Answer questions 73–75 on the basis of the picture. Do not look at the picture again.

73. What does the man wearing the black T-shirt with white printing on it have on his face?
    A. A beard
    B. Eyeglasses
    C. Sunglasses
    D. You cannot see his face.

74. What is the man wearing the striped shirt holding in his hands?
    A. One bag
    B. Two bags
    C. The hand of a child
    D. He is not holding anything in his hands.

75. The woman in the lower right corner is
    A. looking at her smartphone.
    B. holding her child's arm.
    C. wearing a scarf around her neck.
    D. sitting on a bench.

VERBAL ABILITY

75 Questions • 38 Minutes

Directions: Each question from 1–20 consists of a sentence written in four different ways. Choose the sentence that is most appropriate with respect to grammar, usage, and punctuation.

---

1. A. After reading the book, the movie seemed less successful.

B. The movie, after reading the book, was less successful it seemed.

C. After the movie read the book, it seemed less successful.

D. After Sheila read the book, she felt that the movie seemed less successful.

2. A. This is entirely among you and he.

B. This is completely among him and you.

C. This is between you and him.

D. This is between he and you.

3. A. The "confused tourist" walked over to the "information desk" and asked, Where's the nearest bus station?

B. The confused tourist walked over to the information desk and asked, "Where's the nearest bus station?"

C. "Where's the nearest bus station?" asking at the information desk said the confused tourist.

D. Only a confused tourist would ask where, to the information desk, is the nearest bus station.

4. A. A promotion means more responsibility and more money, but not everyone wants one.

B. A promotion means more responsibility and more money, not everyone wants one.

C. More responsibility comes with a promotion and more harder work.

D. Not every one wants be promoted even the more money that comes with it.

5. A. Some folks would argue that the keys to a happy life are good friends a satisfying job and a supportive family.

B. Some folks would argue that the keys to a happy life are good, friends a satisfying, job and a supportive family.

C. Some folks would argue that the keys to a happy life are good friends, a satisfying job, and a supportive family.

D. Some folks would argue that the keys to a happy life are good; friends a satisfying job and; a supportive family.

6. A. Having been told that she had interviewed well, she left feeling confident.

B. Feeling confident, the interview went well.

C. She felt the interview went good and left confident.

D. She felt confident, and it went well.

7. **A.** His document was misfiled so they were more difficult to find then hers.

 B. Someone mis-filed his document, hers were filed okay.

 C. His document was misfiled so it was more difficult to find than hers.

 D. Because of filing his document in the wrong place, his file was misplaced.

8. **A.** The final report was input in less than four hours by three typists and whom should be thanked for their hard work.

 B. If the three typists had know they'd be working four hours to finish the report.

 C. The three typists who input the final report in less than four hours should be thanked.

 D. To who should the thanks be given for inputting the final report in less than four hours.

9. **A.** "Are you absolutely certain, she asked, that you are right?"

 B. "Are you absolutely certain," she asked, "that you are right?"

 C. "Are you absolutely certain," she asked, "That you are right"?

 D. "Are you absolutely certain", she asked, "That you are right?"

10. **A.** In agreeing to a deadline, her and me negotiated an extra day just in case.

 B. Our supervisor worked with her and I to set a realistic deadline.

 C. No one asked she and I if we thought we could the work done in two days.

 D. She and I negotiated an extra day for finishing the work in case there was a problem.

11. **A.** Most all these statements have been supported by persons who are reliable and can be depended upon.

 B. The persons which have guaranteed these statements are reliable.

 C. Reliable persons guarantee the facts with regards to the truth of these statements.

 D. These statements can be depended on, for their truth has been guaranteed by reliable persons.

12. **A.** Neither the department head nor the agency head realized the problem was so severe.

 B. Noone realized the severity of the problem.

 C. Both the department head and they was unaware of the problems severity.

 D. The department head was as unaware of the problem as them.

13. **A.** The number of applications for that position has declined greatly over the last three years.

 B. In the last three years the application's numbers have declined greatly.

 C. The number of applications for that position have declined greatly over the last three years.

 D. The applications for that particular position shows a trend downward.

14. **A.** Every carrier should always have something to throw; not something to throw at the dog but something what will divert its attention.

 B. Every carrier should have something to throw—not something to throw at the dog, but something to divert its attention.

 C. Every carrier should always carry something to throw not something to throw at the dog but something that will divert it's attention.

 D. Every carrier should always carry something to throw, not something to throw at the dog, but, something that will divert its' attention.

15. A. O'Brien's and Associates are hiring five lawyers.

B. O'Brien and Associates is taking on several new cases and hiring more lawyers.

C. O'Brien and Associates must be doing good because they have hired five more lawyers.

D. O'Brien and Associates have hired five more lawyers in the recently month.

16. A. He couldn't find his family in all the chaos of the storm around himself.

B. He never felt himself was in danger, it was his family he worried about.

C. Worrying about his family, his own self was not a concern.

D. He never felt himself in danger, but he couldn't find his family.

17. A. One of us have to make the reply before tomorrow.

B. Making the reply before tomorrow will have to be done by one of us.

C. One of us has to reply before tomorrow.

D. Anyone has to reply before tomorrow.

18. A. You have got to get rid of some of these people if you expect to have the quality of the work improve.

B. The quality of the work would improve if they would leave fewer people do it.

C. I believe it would be desirable to have fewer persons doing this work.

D. If you had planned on employing fewer people than this to do the work, this situation would not have arose.

19. A. The paper we use for this purpose must be light, glossy, and stand hard usage as well.

B. Only a light and a glossy, but durable, paper must be used for this purpose.

C. For this purpose, we want a paper that is light, glossy, but that will stand hard wear.

D. For this purpose, paper that is light, glossy, and durable is essential.

20. A. This letter, together with the reports, are to be sent to the postmaster.

B. The reports, together with this letter, is to be sent to the postmaster.

C. The reports and this letter is to be sent to the postmaster.

D. This letter, together with the reports, is to be sent to the postmaster.

Directions: Each question from 21–35 consists of a sentence containing a word in boldface type. Choose the best meaning for the word in boldface type.

---

21. The campers brought their gear to the edge of the forest, and were eager to **embark** upon their hiking adventure.

Embark most nearly means:

A. avoid

B. plan

C. conclude

D. begin

22. The tourist group gasped at the breathtakingly **ornate** design of the church's stained glass ceiling.

Ornate most nearly means:

A. ugly

B. invisible

C. elaborate

D. distant

23. Julia's new coworker seemed **aloof**, and she wondered if he was just uncomfortable and shy.

Aloof most nearly means:

A. distant

B. helpful

C. irresponsible

D. kind

24. Terrence began to **succumb** to the effects of the long day and needed to take a nap.

Succumb most nearly means:

A. submit

B. fight

C. attract

D. repel

25. Shana looked forward to the potentially **lucrative** notion of selling the mobile app she just finished developing.

Lucrative most nearly means:

A. dangerous

B. complicated

C. avoidable

D. profitable

26. After waiting over an hour for his meal, the **disgruntled** restaurant customer stormed out and swore he'd never dine there again.

Disgruntled most nearly means:

A. happy

B. full

C. dissatisfied

D. busy

27. Jeremy was especially **susceptible** to the cold germs in the classroom and found himself sick quite often.

Susceptible most nearly means:

A. sensitive

B. covered

C. ignorant

D. secured

28. The science lecture today was especially **tedious**, and many of the students found it hard to stay focused throughout.

Tedious most nearly means:

A. exciting

B. boring

C. difficult

D. surprising

29. The discussion was a **combative** one, with Steve and Mae each arguing passionately for their sides.

Combative most nearly means:

A. calm

B. agreeable

C. confrontational

D. unproductive

30. The students were expected to know the spelling words by **rote** ahead of this Friday's test.

Rote most nearly means:

A. memorization

B. alphabetical order

C. sound

D. tomorrow

31. There were still many votes to be counted, but the governor's victory seemed **inevitable** based on the exit polls.

Inevitable most nearly means:

A. unlikely

B. unproven

C. unpopular

D. unavoidable

32. On the department's organizational chart, Kelly is **subordinate** to Evelyn, even though Kelly has worked here longer.

Subordinate most nearly means:

A. junior

B. senior

C. aggressive

D. better

33. The assembly instructions seemed very **convoluted** to Ben, with 45 steps and six different tools necessary to put together a simple bookcase.

Convoluted most nearly means:

A. straightforward

B. complex

C. short

D. impossible

34. Ivan struggles sometimes with time management and paperwork, but he has **intangible** people skills that make him one of our best customer service representatives.

Intangible most nearly means:

A. inferior

B. educated

C. indefinable

D. zero

35. The concertgoers began to get **agitated** when the band was still not on stage, more than two hours after the scheduled start time.

Agitated most nearly means:

A. restless

B. soothed

C. joyful

D. inattentive

Directions: For questions 36–42, read each passage and choose the best answer.

36. A survey to determine the subjects that have helped students most in their jobs shows that typing leads all other subjects in the business group. It also leads among the subjects college students consider most valuable and would take again if they were to return to high school.

    The paragraph best supports the statement that

    A. the ability to type is an asset in business and in school.

    B. students who return to night school take typing.

    C. students with a knowledge of typing do superior work in college.

    D. success in business is assured those who can type.

37. The Supreme Court's power to invalidate legislation that violates the Constitution is a strong restriction on the powers of Congress. If an act of Congress is deemed unconstitutional by the Supreme Court, then the act is voided. Unlike a presidential veto, which can be overridden by a two-thirds vote of the House and the Senate, a constitutional ruling by the Supreme Court must be accepted by the Congress.

    The paragraph best supports the statement that

    A. if an act of Congress is voided, then it has been deemed unconstitutional by the Supreme Court.

    B. if an act of Congress has not been voided, then it has not been deemed unconstitutional by the Supreme Court.

    C. if an act of Congress has not been deemed unconstitutional by the Supreme Court, then it is voided.

    D. if an act of Congress is deemed unconstitutional by the Supreme Court, then it is not voided.

38. Since the government can spend only what it obtains from the people, and this amount is ultimately limited by their capacity and willingness to pay taxes, it is very important that the people be given full information about the full work of the government.

    The paragraph best supports the statement that

    A. governmental employees should be trained not only in their own work, but also in how to perform the duties of other employees in their agency.

    B. taxation by the government rests upon the consent of the people.

    C. the release of full information on the work of the government will increase the efficiency of governmental operations.

    D. the work of the government, in recent years, has been restricted because of reduced tax collection.

39. Both high schools and colleges should take responsibility for preparing students to get jobs. Since the ability to write a good application letter is one of the first steps toward this goal, every teacher should be willing to do what he or she can to help the student learn to write such letters.

    The paragraph best supports the statement that

    A. the inability to write a good letter often reduces one's job prospects.

    B. the major responsibility of the school is to obtain jobs for its students.

    C. success is largely a matter of the kind of work the student applies for first.

    D. every teacher should teach a course in the writing of application letters.

40. Direct lighting is the least satisfactory lighting arrangement. A desk or ceiling light with a reflector that diffuses all the rays downward is sure to cause a glare on the work surface.

The paragraph best supports the statement that direct lighting is LEAST satisfactory as a method of lighting chiefly because

- **A.** the light is diffused, causing eyestrain.
- **B.** the shade on the individual desk lamp is not constructed along scientific lines.
- **C.** the working surface is usually obscured by the glare.
- **D.** direct lighting is injurious to the eyes.

41. White collar is a term used to describe one of the largest groups of workers in U.S. industry and trade. It distinguishes those who work in offices in professional, managerial, and administrative functions from those who depend for their living on their hands and large-scale machinery. The term suggests occupations in which physical exertion and handling of materials are not primary job features.

The paragraph best supports the statement that "white collar" workers are

- **A.** not as strong physically as those who work with their hands.
- **B.** those who supervise workers handling materials.
- **C.** all whose work is entirely indoors.
- **D.** not likely to use machines as much as are other groups of workers.

42. In large organizations, a standardized, simple, inexpensive method of giving employees information about company policies and rules, as well as specific instructions regarding their duties, is practically essential. This is the purpose of all office manuals of whatever type.

The paragraph best supports the statement that office manuals

- **A.** are all about the same.
- **B.** should be simple enough for the average employee to understand.
- **C.** are necessary to large organizations.
- **D.** act as constant reminders to the employee of his or her duties.

Directions: For questions 43–48, read the following passage and answer the questions that follow.

As you prepare for a job interview, it's important to keep these factors in mind: appearance and body language. You will, of course, need to know what qualifies you for the job on paper—but no matter how qualified you may be,

Line getting the job may also come down to whether or not you impress the inter-
5 viewer on all levels.

Well before the interview, make sure your go-to interview outfit is ready. That means ensuring that your clothes are wrinkle-free and in good condition. You don't want to be picking things up from the dry cleaner on your way to the interview! Looking neat and clean is a must. Even if the workplace isn't formal,
10 you'll want to show your aspirational ambition by dressing professionally for your interview. If you're wearing a skirt, it should be knee-length. Pants should be tailored to your height; not too long or too short. For shoes, three inches or shorter is ideal.

Your body language should also be on point. The night before the
15 interview, spend some time looking in the mirror and practicing different smiles or nodding along with what someone is saying. If you have an expressive face, you want to make sure that you're able to control your emotions. Your interview smile should look genuine, but not *too* eager.

And don't neglect your handshake! You can't practice that one alone, of
20 course, but if you can find a trusted friend or family member to try out your best handshakes, you'll be ready to go on interview day. The ideal handshake is firm, but not too firm—this isn't an arm wrestling competition, after all. You should also ensure that you make eye contact while shaking someone's hand—but be sure to break off the eye contact after a few seconds, because some interviewers
25 might find it strange or aggressive if they feel like you're staring them down.

43. The best title for the preceding passage is
   A. "How to Get a Job Interview"
   B. "Creating the Best Resume"
   C. "Getting to Know Your Interviewer"
   D. "Preparing for a Job Interview"

44. Which of the following would likely considered a good practice by the author?
   A. Waiting until the last minute to prepare for your interview
   B. Choosing your outfit a week before the interview
   C. Wearing your favorite weekend outfit to the interview
   D. Waiting until the day before to have your clothes cleaned

45. In addition to professional dress, which of the following is necessary for a successful job interview, according to the passage?
   A. Good eye contact
   B. A spell-checked resume
   C. Expensive shoes
   D. A serious facial expression

46. Interview skirts should be
   A. one inch above the knee.
   B. at the knee.
   C. below the knee.
   D. floor-length.

47. The main reason for breaking off eye contact after a short time is to

    A. make your handshake seem stronger.

    B. show respect to the interviewer.

    C. signify that you're ready to sit down.

    D. avoid intimidating the interviewer.

48. The main idea of the passage is that

    A. your resume is the most important part of getting a job.

    B. you can skip other kinds of preparation if your handshake is good.

    C. job interviews are about more than just your qualifications on paper.

    D. job interviews are all about style, not substance.

Directions: For questions 49–56, some portions of the passage are underlined and numbered. Corresponding to each numbered portion are three different ways of saying the same thing. If you feel that an underlined portion is correct and is stated as well as possible, mark choice **A**. NO CHANGE. If you feel that there is an error in the underlined portion or if one of the alternatives would be more effective, choose the correct answer.

Many people dream of going to the Olympics as <u>an elite athlete</u>, but <u>more few</u>
                                                        49   50

ever achieve that goal. Since the <u>first modern Olympics were</u> held in Greece
                                    51

in 1896, <u>137000</u> athletes combined have competed in the Winter and Summer
            52

Olympic Games. And even once they get to the Olympics, relatively few ath-

letes make it to <u>another, only</u> about 37,000 athletes have competed in more
            53

<u>than one</u> Olympics. The record for <u>Repeat Olympics</u> is held by Canadian
   54   55

equestrian athlete <u>Ian Millar who</u> competed in horse show jumping events in
                   56

ten different Olympics (1972–2012).

---

49. A. NO CHANGE

    B. a elite athlete

    C. elite athlete

    D. one elite athlete

50. A. NO CHANGE

    B. few

    C. fewest

    D. fewer

51. A. NO CHANGE

    B. was

    C. would be

    D. are

52. A. NO CHANGE

    B. 13,7000

    C. 137,000

    D. 1,37,000

53. **A.** NO CHANGE
    B. another only
    C. another. . . only
    D. another; only

54. **A.** NO CHANGE
    B. more then one
    C. more of one
    D. more in one

55. **A.** NO CHANGE
    B. repeat olympics
    C. repeat Olympics
    D. Repeat Olympics

56. **A.** NO CHANGE
    B. Ian Millar whom
    C. Ian Millar, whom
    D. Ian Millar, who

Directions: For questions 57–75, find the correct spelling of the word and mark the appropriate space on the answer sheet. If none of the spellings are correct, select choice **D**.

57. **A.** anticipate
    B. antisipate
    C. anticapate
    D. None of the above

58. **A.** similiar
    B. simmilar
    C. similar
    D. None of the above

59. **A.** sufficiantly
    B. suficeintly
    C. sufficiently
    D. None of the above

60. **A.** intelligence
    B. inteligence
    C. intellegence
    D. None of the above

61. **A.** referance
    B. referrence
    C. referense
    D. None of the above

62. **A.** conscious
    B. consious
    C. conscius
    D. None of the above

63. **A.** paralell
    B. parellel
    C. parellell
    D. None of the above

64. **A.** abundence
    B. abundance
    C. abundants
    D. None of the above

65. **A.** corregated
    B. corrigated
    C. corrugated
    D. None of the above

66. **A.** accumalation
    B. accumulation
    C. accumullation
    D. None of the above

67. **A.** resonance
    B. resonence
    C. resonnance
    D. None of the above

68. **A.** benaficial
    B. benefitial
    C. beneficial
    D. None of the above

69. A. spesifically
    B. specificially
    C. specifically
    D. None of the above

70. A. elemanate
    B. elimenate
    C. elliminate
    D. None of the above

71. A. collosal
    B. colosal
    C. collossal
    D. None of the above

72. A. auxillary
    B. auxilliary
    C. auxiliary
    D. None of the above

73. A. inimitable
    B. inimitible
    C. inimatable
    D. None of the above

74. A. disapearance
    B. dissapearance
    C. disappearence
    D. None of the above

75. A. coaltion
    B. coalition
    C. co-alition
    D. None of the above

ANSWER KEYS AND EXPLANATIONS

Clerical Ability

1. E	16. A	31. D	46. B	61. E
2. D	17. D	32. E	47. D	62. C
3. A	18. B	33. A	48. A	63. E
4. D	19. A	34. A	49. C	64. C
5. A	20. C	35. B	50. A	65. B
6. C	21. A	36. B	51. E	66. B
7. B	22. E	37. E	52. B	67. B
8. D	23. C	38. C	53. A	68. B
9. E	24. B	39. D	54. B	69. B
10. C	25. D	40. A	55. E	70. A
11. C	26. E	41. A	56. C	71. C
12. D	27. A	42. C	57. E	72. D
13. C	28. B	43. C	58. E	73. C
14. A	29. C	44. C	59. C	74. B
15. C	30. D	45. D	60. B	75. C

1. **The correct answer is E.** Mathers, Matherson, Mathews, Mathewson, *Mathison.*

2. **The correct answer is D.** 58146020, 59233162, 59233262, *59233362,* 59233662.

3. **The correct answer is A.** *MYP-6734,* NYP-6733, NYS-7412, NZT-4899, PYZ-3636.

4. **The correct answer is D.** Morin, J.B.; Morin, J. James; Morin, James J.; *Morin, Jose*; Morin, Joseph F.

5. **The correct answer is A.** *00102032,* 00120312, 00120323, 00120324, 00200303.

6. **The correct answer is C.** LPD-5865, LPD-6001, *LPD-6100,* LPD-6101, LPD-6106.

7. **The correct answer is B.** Von Alton, Karl; *Vonbrunner, Carl*; Vonderson, Michael; Von Lolhoffel, Darlene; Vonlolhoffel, M. E.

8. **The correct answer is D.** Sanchez, Alvira; Sanchez, Juanita; Sanchez, R. Juanita; *Sanchez, R.R.*; Sanchez, S. Robert.

9. **The correct answer is E.** 01006040, 01006051, 01016053, 01016060, *01066010.*

10. **The correct answer is C.** AAA-2132, AAS-4623, *AAZ-2687,* ASA-3216, ASZ-5490.

11. **The correct answer is C.** Kawalski, Raymond M.; Kawalski, Robert; *Kowalski, Raymond M.*; Kowalsky, Robert S.; Kowolsky, S.T., Jr.

12. **The correct answer is D.** NBJ-4682, NBT-5066, NCD-7710, *NCD-7834,* NCD-7868.

13. **The correct answer is C.** 36260006, 36270000, *36270013,* 36270030, 36670012.

14. The correct answer is A. *Ketchener, Glen*; Ketchner, Alan; Ketchum, George; Kichner, A. George; Kitchiner, Samuel.

15. The correct answer is C. Figaro, Fernando; Figaro, Francis; *Figuaro, Estevanico*; Figuaro, Francisco; Figurao, Geraldo.

16. The correct answer is A. *58006021*, 58006130, 58097222, 59000599, 59909000.

17. The correct answer is D. In alphabetical order, *imprints* comes after *impressions* and before *improvements*.

18. The correct answer is B. In alphabetical order, *bacon* comes after *bachelors* and before *bacteria*.

19. The correct answer is A. Business names that begin with numerals should be alphabetized as if the numerals are spelled out. Furthermore, the names of organizations, institutions, and buildings are filed according to the order in which each word in the name appears, except where these names include the full names of individuals. In such cases, the last name of the person is filed first. Therefore, the correct order is: **Bronson Brothers Trucking, LLC**, 1st National Bank, Anne Jamie and Associates, Larson Haulers, Inc.

20. The correct answer is C. First initials come before spelled out first names and titles such as *Dr.* are disregarded when alphabetizing. Therefore, the correct alphabetical order is: T.T. Carmichael, Dr. Tera Carmichael, **Ted Carmine**, Carmine Tito.

21. The correct answer is A. All three names are exactly alike.

22. The correct answer is E. Sergei Kuznets, Serge Kusnetz, Sergei Kuznetts are all different names.

23. The correct answer is C. The first and third numbers are exactly alike. The middle number (6-78912-3e3e42) is different.

24. The correct answer is B. The first and second addresses are exactly alike and the last address (85629 Dunwoodie Drive) is different.

25. The correct answer is D. The second and third numbers are exactly alike and the first number (9566110) is different.

26. The correct answer is E. All three names are different: Becca Katherine Hines; Becca Catherine Hanes, Becca Catharine Hane.

27. The correct answer is A. All three codes are exactly alike.

28. The correct answer is B. The last address (60646 West Touhey Avenue) is different. The first and second addresses are exactly alike.

29. The correct answer is C. The second name (Mardikian and Moore, Inc.) is different. The first and third names are exactly the same.

30. The correct answer is D. The second and third numbers are exactly alike. The first number (9670243) is different.

31. The correct answer is D. The first name is different: Ingles (missing the final *e*). The second and third names are exactly alike.

32. The correct answer is E. All three names are different: DeAngelis; D'Angelis; DeAngeles.

33. The correct answer is A. All three numbers are exactly alike.

34. The correct answer is A. All three addresses are exactly alike.

35. The correct answer is B. The third code (62qs5-95yT3-001) is different. The first and second codes are exactly the same.

36. The correct answer is B. The first and second numbers are exactly the same. The last number (2798350) is different.

37. **The correct answer is E.** All three names are different: Helmut V. Lochner; Helmut V. Lockner; Helmut W. Lochner.

38. **The correct answer is C.** The first and third numbers are exactly alike. The second number (2548403) is different.

39. **The correct answer is D.** The first address (Lemberger, WA 28094-9182) is different. The second and third addresses are exactly the same.

40. **The correct answer is A.** All three codes are exactly alike.

41. **The correct answer is A.** All three names are exactly alike.

42. **The correct answer is C.** The second number (5927861) is different. The first and third numbers are the same.

43. **The correct answer is C.** The second address (O'Reillys Bay, LA 56212) is different. The first and third addresses are the same.

44. **The correct answer is C.** The second name (Myra Sampson) is different. The first and third names are the same.

45. **The correct answer is D.** Numerals should be alphabetized as if they are spelled out. So correct alphabetical order is: 52 Pick-Up Playing Cards Manufacturing; 1 Zanuck Avenue Catering; 75th Anniversary Films; 25 Sheridan Street Gymnasium. Choice D is the correct answer because 75th Anniversary Films is third in the order.

46. **The correct answer is B.** Titles such as *Mr.* and *Ms.* are disregarded when alphabetizing names. Therefore, correct alphabetical order is: Ms. T. Anderson; Endless Possibilities Arts; Thirteen Lucky Cats, LLC; Mr. B. A. Tonnely. Choice B is the correct answer because Thirteen Lucky Cats, LLC is third in the order.

47. **The correct answer is D.** Only choice D is written correctly. Choice A replaces the second *y* in the employee's last name with an *i*. The first *4* is missing from the identification number in choice B. Choice C adds an *i* to the employee's last name.

48. **The correct answer is A.** Only choice A is written correctly. Choice B mixes up the *L* in the identification number with the employee's middle initial. Choice C replaces an *e* in the employee's last name with an *a*. In choice D, the employee's last name is missing a *c*.

49. **The correct answer is C.** There is a mistake in the third set only. There should be a space between the letter *V* and the numbers in the code.

50. **The correct answer is A.** There are mistakes in all three sets. In the second column of the first set, there is a middle initial that does not appear in the first column. In the second set, the name is spelled differently in each column. In the second column of the third set, the middle initial and the letter *T* in the code are reversed.

51. **The correct answer is E.** 27

52. **The correct answer is B.** 32

53. **The correct answer is A.** 224

54. **The correct answer is B.** 78

55. **The correct answer is E.** 28

56. **The correct answer is C.** 99

57. **The correct answer is E.** 61

58. **The correct answer is E.** 114

59. **The correct answer is C.** 40

60. **The correct answer is B.** 7

61. **The correct answer is E.** 30

62. **The correct answer is C.** 10

63. **The correct answer is E.** 41

64. The correct answer is C. 23

65. The correct answer is B. 21

66. The correct answer is B. Only one player (number 12) has the front of his uniform showing, and the team name is *Rice*.

67. The correct answer is B. There are seven players shown in the picture. Five of them are wearing hats, and the catcher is wearing a helmet. Only one player (number 20) is not wearing a hat or helmet.

68. The correct answer is B. The most important thing is to remain professional and polite and keep the meeting moving along without wasting any more time, which is why choice A is incorrect. Choice C also wastes time—both the time of the current meeting and the other manager. Choice D is impolite and unprofessional— even if the lateness was not your fault, you should apologize.

69. The correct answer is B. The most professional and adult course of action is to go directly to your teammate to let them know your concerns. This is the first course of action you should take. Choice A is more drastic and should not be your first course of action. Try to resolve the problem within your team before notifying a supervisor, which could have lasting consequences. Choice C is unfair—you should not bear the brunt of the work before you try to discuss the problem with your teammate. Choice D is unprofessional, as gossip is not an effective form of communication.

70. The correct answer is A. You should take charge of your schedule, assess what can be deprioritized, and ask if these less-important tasks can be put on hold until your project is finished. Choice B is incorrect because the assignment is important and it is not up to you whether

or not a deadline can shift. Choice C is also incorrect—choice A is a better and more professional way to deal with the situation. Choice D is incorrect because you are not in a position to ask your team to come in on weekends, for which they will likely not be paid.

71. The correct answer is C. Firmly telling your sister that you can't use the database for this kind of activity (choice C) is a professional, ethical way to approach the situation. Choice A is problematic because you would potentially be violating the rules of your job by looking up information for personal, non-work reasons. Choice B goes too far in the other direction; if nothing took place and no confidentiality is breached, there is likely no need to involve your manager, so this is not the best option. Choice D is incorrect because even if no one can trace it to you, it is still unethical to look up the information and use it for personal purposes.

72. The correct answer is D. There is no proof that the driver is truly another officer and that they are parked in front of the fire hydrant for legitimate reasons. The only evidence is that a car is parked illegally, and this should be treated accordingly. The traffic officer should act as he would be required to act for any non-emergency vehicle parked illegally. Therefore, choice D is the best answer.

73. The correct answer is C. The man wearing the black T-shirt with white printing is wearing sunglasses.

74. The correct answer is B. The man wearing the striped shirt has a bag in each hand.

75. The correct answer is C. The woman in the lower right corner is wearing a scarf around her neck.

Verbal Ability

1. D	**16.** D	**31.** D	**46.** B	**61.** D
2. C	**17.** C	**32.** A	**47.** D	**62.** A
3. B	**18.** C	**33.** B	**48.** C	**63.** D
4. A	**19.** D	**34.** C	**49.** A	**64.** B
5. C	**20.** D	**35.** A	**50.** B	**65.** C
6. A	**21.** D	**36.** A	**51.** A	**66.** B
7. C	**22.** C	**37.** B	**52.** C	**67.** A
8. C	**23.** A	**38.** B	**53.** D	**68.** C
9. B	**24.** A	**39.** A	**54.** A	**69.** C
10. D	**25.** D	**40.** C	**55.** C	**70.** D
11. D	**26.** C	**41.** D	**56.** D	**71.** D
12. A	**27.** A	**42.** C	**57.** A	**72.** C
13. A	**28.** B	**43.** D	**58.** C	**73.** A
14. B	**29.** C	**44.** B	**59.** C	**74.** D
15. B	**30.** A	**45.** A	**60.** A	**75.** B

1. **The correct answer is D.** The incorrect answer choices all contain a dangling modifier—it's not clear who read the book. Choice D fixes the mistake and makes it clear that Sheila read the book.

2. **The correct answer is C.** Choices A and B are incorrect because only two persons are involved. The word *between* should be used when there are only two people, and *among* is reserved for three or more. Choices A and D incorrectly use the pronoun *he* instead of *him*. In other words, the object of a preposition (in this case *between*) must be in the objective case (*him*).

3. **The correct answer is B.** This choice is the only version to make correct use of quotation marks, which should appear around any dialogue that's spoken. The other choices either make incorrect use of quotation marks or introduce awkwardness or other grammatical errors into the sentence.

4. **The correct answer is A.** Choice B is a run-on sentence; to be grammatically correct, it needs a period or a semicolon, or it needs a conjunction, such as but. The

correct way to form the comparative of a one-syllable adjective (or adverb) is to add *-er*; for words of more than one syllable, add the word *more*. You don't need both so choice C is incorrect. Choice D is incorrect because *every one* should be one word, and the second part of the sentence doesn't make sense because it has a word or words missing.

5. **The correct answer is C.** Items in a list need to be separated by commas, and choice C is the only version to correctly do this.

6. **The correct answer is A.** As written, choice B is incorrect because it says that the interview felt confident and left. Choice C uses the adjective *good* when the word that is needed is the adverb *well*. Choice D doesn't make sense because there is no antecedent for *it* so you don't know what went well.

7. **The correct answer is C.** There are two errors in choice A. *Document* is singular so the pronoun referring to it should be *it*, not *they*. In addition, *then* should be *than*, which is used for comparisons. Choice B

also has two errors. It's a run-on sentence, and the word *okay* is too informal for writing related to a work situation. Choice D has a misplaced location problem of its own. There is no antecedent for the phrase "Because of filing his document in the wrong place." His file didn't misfile itself.

8. **The correct answer is C.** The error in choice A is *whom*. The sentence requires the subject form *who*. Choice D has the opposite problem. The correct form here should be *whom* because the relative pronoun is the object of the preposition *to*. Choice B is a dependent clause with no main sentence to attach itself to. In addition, the incorrect form of *to know* is used. The clause requires the past participle, *known*.

9. **The correct answer is B.** Only the quoted material should be enclosed by quotation marks, so choice A is incorrect. Only the first word of a sentence should begin with a capital letter, so choices C and D are incorrect. Choice C also has an incorrectly placed question mark. The question mark must be placed inside the quotes as only the quoted material itself is a question. Choice D is also incorrect because the first comma should be placed after *certain* and inside the closing quote.

10. **The correct answer is D.** The misuse of the personal pronouns is a common error in spoken and written English. Fix the rules in your mind now. *Her* and *me* are object pronouns; choice A requires the subject pronouns *she* and *I* . In choice B, *her* is correct because it's the object of the preposition, and *I* is incorrect because the object form *me* is required. Choice C requires *her* and *me* as objects of the predicate asked.

11. **The correct answer is D.** Choice A is incorrect because either *most* or *all* should be used, not both. Choice B should read

"The persons *who. . .*" not "The persons *which. . .*" Choice C should read with *regard* to . . .

12. **The correct answer is A.** *No one* is always two words, so eliminate choice B. Choice C has multiple problems. If *they* is the correct pronoun, then *both* and *was* are incorrect. Also, if there is single problem, then the singular possessive *problem's* should be used; if there are several problems, then *problems'* is correct. You need to finish choice D in order to see that *them* is incorrect: ". . . as unaware of the problem as *they* were," not "*them* were."

13. **The correct answer is A.** Choice B says that there has been only one application, which makes no sense. Choice C is incorrect because number is a collective noun, and the context in which a collective noun is used indicates whether it should take a singular or plural verb. In this case, because number relates to a single type of thing (an application), it is considered singular and should take the singular form of the verb. This also explains why choice A is correct. Choice D is incorrect because it puts a phrase between the subject and verb. The noun closest to the verb is plural, but the subject is singular so the verb should be *show*.

14. **The correct answer is B.** Choice A incorrectly uses a semicolon to separate a complete clause from a sentence fragment; it also incorrectly uses *what* in place of *that*. Choice C is a run-on sentence that also misuses an apostrophe—*it's* is the contraction for *it is*, not the possessive of *it*. Choice D uses commas indiscriminately; it also misuses the apostrophe.

15. **The correct answer is B.** In choice A, the placement of the apostrophe is inappropriate. Choice C uses the adjective *good* when it should use the adverb *well*. Choice

C also uses the plural pronoun *they* when the pronoun should be *it* because the firm is considered a single thing. Choice D has the same error and also introduces the use of the adverb *recently* to modify a noun; adverbs modify verbs, adjectives, and other adverbs.

16. **The correct answer is D.** There is no reason to use the reflexive pronoun *himself*; the pronoun *him* would have been sufficient in choice A. Choice B has the same problem and is also a run-on sentence. Having one's self worrying doesn't make sense, so choice C is incorrect.

17. **The correct answer is C.** Choice A incorrectly uses the plural verb form *have* with the singular subject *one*. Choice B is awkward and wordy. Choice D incorrectly changes the subject from *one of us* to *anyone*.

18. **The correct answer is C.** Choice A is wordy. In choice B, the correct verb should be *have* in place of *leave*. In choice D, the word *arose* should be *arisen*.

19. **The correct answer is D.** The first three sentences lack parallel construction. All of the words that modify paper must appear in the same form.

20. **The correct answer is D.** The phrase *together with. . .* is extra information and not a part of the sentence; therefore, choices A and B contain errors of agreement. Choice C also presents subject-verb disagreement, but in this case, the compound subject, indicated by the conjunction *and*, requires a plural verb.

21. **The correct answer is D.** To *embark* means to "begin."

22. **The correct answer is C.** *Ornate* means "elaborate."

23. **The correct answer is A.** *Aloof* means "distant."

24. **The correct answer is A.** To *succumb* means to "submit."

25. **The correct answer is D.** *Lucrative* means "profitable."

26. **The correct answer is C.** *Disgruntled* means "dissatisfied."

27. **The correct answer is A.** *Susceptible* means "sensitive."

28. **The correct answer is B.** *Tedious* means "boring."

29. **The correct answer is C.** "Combat" should tip you off that the word suggests conflict. *Confrontational* (choice C) is the only option that fits.

30. **The correct answer is A.** To learn something "by rote" is to memorize it. The context of the sentence suggests that students are expected to learn the spelling words by Friday. Therefore, *rote* means "memorization."

31. **The correct answer is D.** The word *but* in the sentence suggests that the word *inevitable* is in contrast to the first part of the sentence (that there are still votes to be counted). That means the outcome is likely already decided, and *unavoidable* (choice D) is the only option that fits this context.

32. **The correct answer is A.** *Subordinate* means that someone (or something) is junior or lesser than someone or something else. The prefix *sub-* is the key clue, but you can also tell from the context of the sentence. The sentence suggests that the speaker is surprised that Kelly is _____ to Evelyn even though she's been there longer. If you plug the other options into the sentence, none make sense the way *junior* (choice A) does.

33. The correct answer is B. The number of steps and tools needed to assemble the bookcase tell you that the word *simple* must be misleading. The word *complex* (choice B) is the closest in meaning to *convoluted*.

34. The correct answer is C. The skills Ivan has are presented in contrast with specific skills like time management and paperwork, suggesting that the skills are less specific, or different. If you put each option into the sentence, only *indefinable* (choice C) shows why Ivan would be a good customer service representative.

35. The correct answer is A. From the context of the sentence, you can tell that the crowd is unlikely to be calm or happy, because they'd been waiting for more than two hours. *Restless* (choice A) best fits the mood of the sentence.

36. The correct answer is A. The survey showed that of all subjects, typing helped most in business. The ability to type was also considered valuable by college students in their schoolwork.

37. The correct answer is B. You can infer the answer from the information in the second sentence, which states that if an act of Congress has been deemed unconstitutional, then it is voided. In choice B, we are told that an act of Congress is not voided; therefore, we can conclude that it has not been deemed unconstitutional by the Supreme Court.

38. The correct answer is B. According to the paragraph, the government can spend only what it obtains from the people. The government obtains money from the people by taxation. If the people are unwilling to pay taxes, the government has no source of funds.

39. The correct answer is A. Step one in the job application process is often the application letter. If the letter is not effective, the applicant will not move on to the next step, and job prospects will be greatly lessened.

40. The correct answer is C. The second sentence of the paragraph states that direct lighting causes glare on the working surface.

41. The correct answer is D. While all of the answer choices are likely to be true, the answer suggested by the paragraph is that "white collar" workers work with their pencils and their minds, rather than with their hands and machines.

42. The correct answer is C. All the paragraph says is that office manuals are a necessity in large organizations, so choice C is the best answer.

43. The correct answer is D. Choice D is specific to the passage, which discusses how to get ready for a job interview. The passage tells readers what to do after they've already scheduled an interview, so choice A doesn't fit. The passage doesn't discuss resumes in any detail, so choice B doesn't work. The passage is about the interviewee's preparations, not the interviewer, so choice C doesn't fit either.

44. The correct answer is B. The author explicitly warns not to wait to dry clean clothes at the last minute before an interview, so you can infer that the author does not think it is a good idea to do anything last-minute, making choices A and D incorrect. The author also discusses wearing nice, professional clothes, so a "weekend outfit" is unlikely to be formal enough (choice C). Therefore, it is reasonable to conclude that the author would consider choosing your outfit a week before the interview a good practice.

45. The correct answer is A. The passage mentions to make sure you make eye contact while shaking someone's hand so choice A is the best answer. The passage does not give best practices for writing your resume, so choice B is incorrect. It also does not recommend any specific kind of shoes, so choice C can be eliminated. The passage recommends that you work on your smile, so a serious facial expression (choice D) is not necessary for a successful job interview.

46. **The correct answer is B.** In paragraph 2, the author recommends a "knee-length" skirt.

47. **The correct answer is D.** In paragraph 4, the author characterizes too-long eye contact as "strange or aggressive."

48. **The correct answer is C.** The main idea of the passage is that job interviews are about more than just your qualifications on paper. The passage does not discuss resumes beyond a single brief mention, so choice A is incorrect. The passage suggests that professional clothes and body language are also important, so choice B is too specific. Although the author contrasts qualifications with things like clothes and body language, the passage also suggests that qualifications are important as well, so choice D is not accurate.

49. **The correct answer is A.** The article *an* should precede a word that starts with a vowel (*elite* in this case) so the underlined phrase is correct as is. Choice B is incorrect because it uses *a*, which should pair with a word that starts with a consonant. Choice C is incorrect because it eliminates the article altogether, making the sentence incomplete. Choice D is incorrect because *one* is very specific, and that is not the author's intent here.

50. **The correct answer is B.** *More few* is incorrect because *few* itself is a quantifier;

you don't need an additional qualifier like *more*. *Fewest* (choice C) and *fewer* (choice D) don't work here because the author is not making direct comparisons, just making a general statement about the number.

51. **The correct answer is A.** The verb here should be plural (because of *Olympics*) and past tense, because the sentence describes an event from 1896. That eliminates *was* (choice B), which is past-tense, but singular; *would be* (choice C), which is future tense; and *are* (choice D), which is plural but present-tense.

52. **The correct answer is C.** When punctuating numbers, commas should be placed every three digits. Only choice C does this correctly.

53. **The correct answer is D.** The comma creates a comma splice. Leaving out any punctuation at all (choice B) creates one very long, incomplete sentence. Ellipses (choice C) should only be used when information is omitted in a sentence, and that does not appear to be the case here. Therefore, a semicolon should be used, making choice D the best answer.

54. **The correct answer is A.** Choices C and D create phrases that don't really make sense with the sentence, so it's really a choice between *then* and *than*. When comparing numbers like *one* or *more* in this passage, *than* is the correct choice.

55. **The correct answer is C.** This one is tricky because you need to decide what is a proper noun in this sentence, and what is not. *Olympics* is a specific, named event so that should be a proper noun. There's no indication that "repeat Olympics" is a specific term, and *repeat* should be a common noun.

56. **The correct answer is D.** This answer actually has two parts. In the first part, you need to decide which pronoun to use:

who or whom? *Whom* should be used when describing the object of a sentence; *who* should be used when describing the subject of a sentence. *Ian Millar* is the subject, so the correct usage here is *who*. In the second part, you need to decide how to punctuate it correctly. *Who competed in horse show jumping events in ten different Olympics* is a dependent clause, so it should be set off with a comma here.

57. The correct answer is A. The correct spelling is *anticipate*.

58. The correct answer is C. The correct spelling is *similar*.

59. The correct answer is C. The correct spelling is *sufficiently*.

60. The correct answer is A. The correct spelling is *intelligence*.

61. The correct answer is D. The correct spelling is *reference*.

62. The correct answer is A. The correct spelling is *conscious*.

63. The correct answer is D. The correct spelling is *parallel*.

64. The correct answer is B. The correct spelling is *abundance*.

65. The correct answer is C. The correct spelling is *corrugated*.

66. The correct answer is B. The correct spelling is *accumulation*.

67. The correct answer is A. The correct spelling is *resonance*.

68. The correct answer is C. The correct spelling is *beneficial*.

69. The correct answer is C. The correct spelling is *specifically*.

70. The correct answer is D. The correct spelling is *eliminate*.

71. The correct answer is D. The correct spelling is *colossal*.

72. The correct answer is C. The correct spelling is *auxiliary*.

73. The correct answer is A. The correct spelling is *inimitable*.

74. The correct answer is D. The correct spelling is *disappearance*.

75. The correct answer is B. The correct spelling is *coalition*.

SELF-EVALUATION

On your answer sheet, mark the numbers of the questions that you answered incorrectly and check them against the following charts. If you missed several of any question type, you need more practice with that kind of question. Return to the appropriate chapter and review the rules and practice exercises before moving on to the next sample exam.

SELF-EVALUATION CHART: CLERICAL ABILITY TEST

Question Type	Question Numbers	Chapter to Review
Alphabetizing and Filing	1–20, 45–46	12
Judgment, Communication, and Memory	66–75	11
Speed and Accuracy	21–44, 47–50	13
Simple Arithmetic	51–65	NA

SELF-EVALUATION CHART: VERBAL ABILITY TEST

Question Type	Question Numbers	Chapter to Review
English Grammar and Usage	1–20	4
Effective Expression	49–56	9
Spelling	57–75	5
Reading Comprehension	36–48	10
Synonyms	21–35	6

ANSWER SHEET PRACTICE TEST 4

Municipal Office Aide

1. Ⓐ Ⓑ Ⓒ Ⓓ
2. Ⓐ Ⓑ Ⓒ Ⓓ
3. Ⓐ Ⓑ Ⓒ Ⓓ
4. Ⓐ Ⓑ Ⓒ Ⓓ
5. Ⓐ Ⓑ Ⓒ Ⓓ
6. Ⓐ Ⓑ Ⓒ Ⓓ
7. Ⓐ Ⓑ Ⓒ Ⓓ
8. Ⓐ Ⓑ Ⓒ Ⓓ
9. Ⓐ Ⓑ Ⓒ Ⓓ
10. Ⓐ Ⓑ Ⓒ Ⓓ
11. Ⓐ Ⓑ Ⓒ Ⓓ
12. Ⓐ Ⓑ Ⓒ Ⓓ
13. Ⓐ Ⓑ Ⓒ Ⓓ

14. Ⓐ Ⓑ Ⓒ Ⓓ
15. Ⓐ Ⓑ Ⓒ Ⓓ
16. Ⓐ Ⓑ Ⓒ Ⓓ
17. Ⓐ Ⓑ Ⓒ Ⓓ
18. Ⓐ Ⓑ Ⓒ Ⓓ
19. Ⓐ Ⓑ Ⓒ Ⓓ
20. Ⓐ Ⓑ Ⓒ Ⓓ
21. Ⓐ Ⓑ Ⓒ Ⓓ
22. Ⓐ Ⓑ Ⓒ Ⓓ
23. Ⓐ Ⓑ Ⓒ Ⓓ
24. Ⓐ Ⓑ Ⓒ Ⓓ
25. Ⓐ Ⓑ Ⓒ Ⓓ
26. Ⓐ Ⓑ Ⓒ Ⓓ

27. Ⓐ Ⓑ Ⓒ Ⓓ
28. Ⓐ Ⓑ Ⓒ Ⓓ
29. Ⓐ Ⓑ Ⓒ Ⓓ
30. Ⓐ Ⓑ Ⓒ Ⓓ
31. Ⓐ Ⓑ Ⓒ Ⓓ
32. Ⓐ Ⓑ Ⓒ Ⓓ
33. Ⓐ Ⓑ Ⓒ Ⓓ
34. Ⓐ Ⓑ Ⓒ Ⓓ
35. Ⓐ Ⓑ Ⓒ Ⓓ
36. Ⓐ Ⓑ Ⓒ Ⓓ
37. Ⓐ Ⓑ Ⓒ Ⓓ
38. Ⓐ Ⓑ Ⓒ Ⓓ
39. Ⓐ Ⓑ Ⓒ Ⓓ

40. Ⓐ Ⓑ Ⓒ Ⓓ
41. Ⓐ Ⓑ Ⓒ Ⓓ
42. Ⓐ Ⓑ Ⓒ Ⓓ
43. Ⓐ Ⓑ Ⓒ Ⓓ
44. Ⓐ Ⓑ Ⓒ Ⓓ
45. Ⓐ Ⓑ Ⓒ Ⓓ
46. Ⓐ Ⓑ Ⓒ Ⓓ
47. Ⓐ Ⓑ Ⓒ Ⓓ
48. Ⓐ Ⓑ Ⓒ Ⓓ
49. Ⓐ Ⓑ Ⓒ Ⓓ
50. Ⓐ Ⓑ Ⓒ Ⓓ

answer sheet

Practice Test 4

MUNICIPAL OFFICE AIDE

50 Questions • 60 Minutes

Directions: For questions 1–3, choose the best answer to each question and mark its letter on the answer sheet.

1. In order to maintain office coverage during working hours, your supervisor has scheduled your lunch hour from 1 p.m. to 2 p.m., and your coworker's lunch hour is from 12 p.m. to 1 p.m. Lately, your coworker has been returning late from lunch each day. As a result, you do not get a full hour, since you must return to the office by 2 p.m. Of the following, the best action for you to take first is to

   A. explain to your coworker in a courteous manner that their lateness is interfering with your right to a full hour for lunch.

   B. tell your coworker that their lateness must stop, or you will report them to your supervisor.

   C. report your coworker's lateness to your supervisor.

   D. leave at 1 p.m. for lunch, whether your coworker has returned or not.

2. Assume that, as an office worker, one of your jobs is to open mail sent to your unit, read the mail for content, and send the mail to the appropriate person for handling. You accidentally open and begin to read a letter marked "personal" addressed to a coworker. Of

the following, the best action for you to take is

   A. report to your supervisor that your coworker is receiving personal mail at the office.

   B. destroy the letter so that your coworker doesn't know you saw it.

   C. reseal the letter and place it on the coworker's desk without saying anything.

   D. bring the letter to your coworker and explain that you opened it by accident.

3. Suppose that in evaluating your work, your supervisor gives you an overall good rating, but states that you sometimes turn in work with careless errors. The best action for you to take would be to

   A. ask a coworker who is good at details to proofread your work.

   B. take time to do a careful job, paying more attention to detail.

   C. continue working as usual since occasional errors are to be expected.

   D. ask your supervisor if they would mind correcting your errors.

Directions: Questions 4–8 consist of a sentence that may or may not be grammatically correct. Examine the underlined parts of each sentence, considering grammar, punctuation, spelling, and capitalization. Choose A if the sentence is correct as written. If the changes suggested in choices B, C, or D would make the sentence grammatically correct, choose the appropriate correct answer choice. Do not choose an option that will change the meaning of the sentence.

4. This manual <u>discribes the duties performed</u> by an office aide.
   A. Correct as is
   B. describe the duties performed
   C. discribe the duties performed
   D. describes the duties performed

5. There <u>weren't no</u> paper in the supply closet.
   A. Correct as is
   B. weren't any
   C. wasn't any
   D. wasn't no

6. The new employees left <u>there</u> office to attend a meeting.
   A. Correct as is
   B. they're
   C. their
   D. thier

7. The office worker started working at <u>8;30 a.m.</u>
   A. Correct as is
   B. 8:30 a.m.
   C. 8;30 A,M.
   D. 8:30 AM.

8. The <u>alphabet, or A to Z sequence are</u> the basis of most filing systems.
   A. Correct as is
   B. alphabet, or A to Z sequence, is
   C. alphabet, or A to Z, sequence are
   D. alphabet, or A too Z sequence, is

Directions: Questions 9–13 have two lists of numbers. Each list contains three sets of numbers. Check each of the three sets in the list on the right to see if they are the same as the corresponding set in the list on the left. Choose your answers as follows:

A if NONE of the sets in the right list is the SAME as those in the left list.

B if ONLY ONE of the sets in the right list is the SAME as those in the left list.

C if ONLY TWO of the sets in the right list are the SAME as those in the left list.

D if ALL THREE sets in the right list are the SAME as those in the left list.

9. 8563327651   8563327651
   4144682253   4146842253
   6467988553   6467988553

10. 5158635578   5158365788
   2119786384   2119687384
   7189836624   7189836624

11. 1344678986   1344768986
   4778633843   4778638343
   3398765578   3397665578

12. 4223768894   4223768894
   2336650975   2336650975
   1124867532   1124867532

13. 5576889043   5576889043
   0086349252   0086347252
   4478875534   4478775534

Directions: Questions 14–16 have two lists of addresses. Each list contains three sets of addresses. Check each of the three sets in the list on the right to see if they are the same as the corresponding set in the list on the left. Choose your answers as follows:

A if NONE of the sets in the right list is the SAME as those in the left list.

B if ONLY ONE of the sets in the right list is the SAME as those in the left list.

C if ONLY TWO of the sets in the right list are the SAME as those in the left list.

D if ALL THREE sets in the right list are the SAME as those in the left list.

14. Roy T. Halloway   Roy T. Halloway
   1746 Arroyo Road   1746 Arroyo Road
   Austin, TX 23357   Austin, TX 23357

   Damia Santiago   Damia Santiago
   4332 10th Avenue   4323 10th Avenue
   Birmingham, AL 37184   Birmingham, AL 37884

   Stephanie Bastian   Stephanie Bastian
   87 Willowville Terrace   87 Willowville Terrace
   Grass Plains, WI 13786   Grass Plains, WI 13736

15. Cyril Blankenship
1434 Palmetto Ln.
Lincoln, NE 29981

Jessica Perrado
72 Oxnard Pla
Lemoine, IA 43327

Shar Jameson
431 Emerald St.
Sanford, NC 11982

16. Abigail Marnsey
902 Sailburg Blvd.
Armingdale, VA 41122

Garrett Sandario
12 Shrub Ct.
Seneca, WI 88325

Aubrey Daniello
389 Pym Village
Coltsville, PA 16678

Cyril Blankenship
1434 Palmetto Ln.
Lincoln, NE 29981

Lincoln, NE 29981
72 Oxnard Pla.
Lemoine, IA 43327

Shar Jameson
431 Emerald St.
Sanford, NC 11982

Abigail Marsney
902 Sailburg Blvd.
Armingdale, VA 41122

Garrett Sandario
12 Shrub Ct.
Seneca, WI 88325

Aubrey Daniello
389 Pym Village
Coltsville, PA 16678

Directions: Answer questions 17–20 solely on the basis of the information contained in the following passage.

In a survey of U.S. businesses, the American Management Association and the ePolicy Institute found that 66 percent of companies monitored their employees' use of the internet, and 65 percent blocked access to websites that the companies considered inappropriate. It's not only private business that limits use of the internet by employees. Federal, state, and local governments also have internet policies. The following is an excerpt from the Executive Branch of the federal government's policy/guidance on "Limited Personal Use" of information technology:

General Policy

Federal employees are permitted limited use of government office equipment for personal needs if the use does not interfere with official business.... This limited personal use of government office equipment should take place during the employee's non-work time.... .

C. Inappropriate Personal Use

Any personal use that could cause congestion, delay, or disruption of service to any government system or equipment. For example, greeting cards, video, sound, or other large file attachments can degrade the performance of the entire network.... .

1. The creation, copying, transmission, or retransmission of chain letters or other unauthorized mass mailings regardless of the subject matter.

2. Using government office equipment for activities that are illegal, inappropriate, or offensive to fellow employees or the public. Such activities include, but are not limited to: hate speech or material that ridicules others on the basis of race, creed, religion, color, sex, disability, national origin, or sexual orientation.

3. The creation, download, viewing, storage, copying, or transmission of sexually explicit or sexually oriented materials.

4. The creation, download, viewing, storage, copying, or transmission of materials related to illegal gambling, illegal weapons, terrorist activities, and any other illegal activities otherwise prohibited, etc.

5. Use for commercial purposes or in support of "for-profit" activities or in support of other outside employment or business activity (e.g., consulting for pay, sales or administration of business transactions, sale of goods or services).

6. Engaging in any outside fundraising activity, endorsing any product or service, participating in any lobbying activity, or engaging in any prohibited partisan political activity.

7. Use for posting agency information to external newsgroups, bulletin boards, or other public forums without authority.

17. Which point refers to terrorist activities?
   A. Statement 5
   B. Statement 7
   C. Statement 4
   D. Statement 2

18. The abbreviation *e.g.* (statement 5) means
   A. indeed
   B. for example
   C. that is
   D. the following

19. Which of the following is NOT mentioned as restricted?
   A. Creating a chain letter
   B. Checking personal email
   C. Signing an online petition in support of school reform
   D. Retransmitting a cartoon that makes fun of a politician

20. Which of the following is NOT listed as covered under statement 2?
   A. Race
   B. Age
   C. Disability
   D. Religion

Directions: For questions 21–23, select the answer choice that is closest in meaning to the underlined word.

21. A central file eliminates the need to <u>retain</u> duplicate material.

   Retain most nearly means:
   A. keep
   B. change
   C. locate
   D. process

22. Filing is a <u>routine</u> office task.

   Routine most nearly means:
   A. proper
   B. regular
   C. simple
   D. difficult

23. Sometimes a word, phrase, or sentence must be <u>deleted</u> to correct an error.

Deleted most nearly means:

A. removed

B. added

C. expanded

D. improved

Directions: The code table below shows 10 letters with matching numbers. For questions 24–28, there are three sets of letters. Each set of letters is followed by a set of numbers that may or may not match their correct letters according to the code table. For each question, check all three sets of letters and numbers and choose your answer as follows:

    A if NO PAIRS are CORRECTLY MATCHED.

    B if only ONE PAIR is CORRECTLY MATCHED.

    C if only TWO PAIRS are CORRECTLY MATCHED.

    D if ALL THREE PAIRS are CORRECTLY MATCHED.

Code Table

T	M	V	D	S	P	R	G	B	H
1	2	3	4	5	6	7	8	9	0

24. DSPRGM   456782

       MVDBHT   234902

       HPMDBT   062491

25. BVPTRD   936184

       GDPHMB   807029

       GMRHMV   827032

26. MGVRSH   283750

       TRDMBS   174295

       SPRMGV   567283

27. SGBSDM   489542

       MGHPTM   290612

       MPBMHT   269301

28. TDPBHM   146902

       VPBMRS   369275

       GDMBHM   842902

Directions: For questions 29–32, choose the name that should be filed first according to the usual system of alphabetical filing of names.

---

29. A. Howard J. Black

    B. Howard Black

    C. J. Howard Black

    D. John H. Black

30. A. Theodora Garth Kingston

    B. Theadore Barth Kingston

    C. Thomas Kingston

    D. Thomas T. Kingston

31. **A.** Paulette Mary Huerta
    B. Paul M. Huerta
    C. Paulette L. Huerta
    D. Peter A. Huerta

32. **A.** Martha Hunt Morgan
    B. Martin Hunt Morgan
    C. Mary H. Morgan
    D. Martine H. Morgan

Directions: For questions 33–35, choose the best answer to each question and mark its letter on the answer sheet.

33. Which one of the following statements about proper telephone usage is NOT always correct? When answering the telephone, you should
    A. know who you are speaking to.
    B. give the caller your undivided attention.
    C. identify yourself to the caller.
    D. obtain the information the caller wishes before you do your other work.

34. Assume that, as a member of a Worker's Safety Committee in your agency, you are responsible for encouraging other employees to follow correct safety practices. While you are working on your regular assignment, you observe an employee violating a safety rule. Of the following, the best action for you to take first is to
    A. speak to the employee about safety practices and order them to stop violating the safety rule.
    B. speak to the employee about safety practices and point out the safety rule they are violating.
    C. bring up the matter in the next committee meeting.
    D. report this violation of the safety rule to the employee's supervisor.

35. Assume that you have been temporarily assigned by your supervisor to do a job that you do not want to do. The best action for you to take is
    A. discuss the job with your supervisor, explaining why you do not want to do it.
    B. discuss the job with your supervisor and tell him or her that you will not do it.
    C. ask a coworker to take your place on this job.
    D. do some other job that you like; your supervisor may give the job you do not like to someone else.

> **Directions:** Answer questions 36–38 solely on the basis of the information contained in the following passage.

The city government is committed to providing a safe and healthy work environment for all city employees. An effective
Line agency safety program reduces accidents
5 by educating employees about the types of careless acts that can cause accidents. Even in an office, accidents can happen. If each employee is aware of possible safety hazards, the number of accidents on the job
10 can be reduced.

Careless use of office equipment can cause accidents and injuries. For example, file cabinet drawers that are filled with papers can be so heavy that the entire cabi-
15 net could tip over from the weight of one open drawer.

The bottom drawers of desks and file cabinets should never be left open, since employees could easily trip over open draw-
20 ers and injure themselves.

When reaching for objects on a high shelf, an employee should use a strong, sturdy object such as a stepstool to stand on. Makeshift platforms made out of
25 books, papers, or boxes can easily collapse. Even chairs can slide out from underfoot, causing serious injury.

Even at an employee's desk, safety hazards can occur. The tangle of wires from
30 phones, computers, surge protectors, and other electrical equipment pose a hazard if not tucked neatly at the rear of the desk and away from a woman's high heels, which could easily catch on them. Com-
35 puter towers need to be out of the walkway so that people can't trip over them. Proper seat height in relation to computers is also important to reduce the number of absences due to back pain and wrist and arm stress.

36. The goal of an effective safety program is to
   A. reduce office accidents.
   B. stop employees from smoking on the job.
   C. encourage employees to continue their education.
   D. eliminate high shelves in offices.

37. Desks and file cabinets can become safety hazards when
   A. their drawers are left open.
   B. they are used as wastebaskets.
   C. they are makeshift.
   D. they are not anchored securely to the floor.

38. What could cause a female employee to trip?
   A. Her chair may be too low.
   B. The computer might fall if it is too close to the edge of the desk.
   C. She could catch her heels on the wires under her desk.
   D. A filing cabinet might be too heavy and collapse.

Directions: For questions 39 and 40, read the question and choose the best answer.

39. Assume that you are assigned to work as a receptionist and your duties are to answer phones, greet visitors, and do other general office work. You are busy with a routine job when several visitors approach your desk. The best action to take is to

A. ask the visitors to have a seat and assist them after your work is completed.

B. tell the visitors that you are busy and they should return at a more convenient time.

C. stop working long enough to assist the visitors.

D. continue working and wait for the visitors to ask you for assistance.

40. Assume that your supervisor has chosen you to take a special course during working hours to learn a new payroll procedure. Although you know that you were chosen because of your good work record, a coworker who feels that they should have been chosen has been telling everyone in your unit that the choice was unfair. Of the following, the best way to handle this situation first is to

A. suggest to the coworker that everything in life is unfair.

B. contact your union representative in case your coworker presents a formal grievance.

C. tell your supervisor about your coworker's complaints and let your supervisor handle the situation.

D. tell the coworker that you were chosen because of your superior work record.

Directions: Answer questions 41–45 solely on the basis of the information contained in the following passage.

The purpose of performance management systems is to facilitate the creation and nurturing of a performance-based
Line culture where the individual employee's
5 performance is aligned with agency and administration objectives, and employees are rewarded for the results they achieve.

Performance management defines the relationship that should exist between state
10 employees and their supervisors. It is an interactive process where upper management communicates the agency's strategic vision and objectives to every manager, supervisor, and employee who then develop
15 program, division, and individual goals designed to achieve the agency's strategic objectives. The agency's strategic objectives should cascade down to the employees in such a way that there is a clear path that
20 connects the individual goals to that agency plan. To be effective, employees must understand how their work contributes to the success of the organization.

Agency management must send a clear
25 and unequivocal message to all employees that performance matters. Each employee at every level of the organization must be held accountable for their participation in this process. Management is also obli-
30 gated to provide sufficient resources for the training and support of all supervisors and managers in the essential components of employee-level performance management. Successful implementation of performance

35 management will enable agencies to create and sustain a performance-based, high-achieving culture.

Performance objectives must be specific, measurable, achievable, and timely and 40 expressed as an outcome or result.

Key components include regular, ongoing coaching, feedback, and communication with employees. Feedback should not be limited to the annual written perfor-45 mance appraisal in which the employee's actual performance is assessed relative to the performance objectives. This annual review is the minimum. Timely, meaningful recognition and reward of the desired per-50 formance should be part of a performance management system. An annual performance-based increase in base salary tied to the performance rating on the appraisal is also an important aspect of the program.

41. What is management obligated to provide supervisors and managers?

A. Performance objectives

B. Annual performance appraisals

C. Resources for training and support

D. Feedback and results

42. What will be the result of the successful implementation of a performance management program?

A. Annual performance reviews

B. Achievable performance objectives

C. A performance-based, high achieving culture

D. Effective feedback

43. *Unequivocal* most nearly means:

A. unchangeable

B. unfeeling

C. unmistakable

D. indecisive

44. In addition to being specific and timely, performance objectives must be

A. measurable and achievable.

B. desired and recognized.

C. communicated and annual.

D. expressed and effective.

45. How often must performance appraisals be conducted?

A. At least every 6 months

B. At least once a year

C. At regular intervals

D. As needed based on performance

Directions: For questions 46–50, read the question, perform the computation, and mark the correct answer on your answer sheet.

46. Assume that your unit ordered 14 staplers at a total cost of $30.20, and each stapler cost the same amount. The cost of one stapler was most nearly
    A. $1.02.
    B. $1.61.
    C. $2.16.
    D. $2.26.

47. Assume that you are responsible for counting and recording licensing fees collected by your department. On a particular day, your department collected in fees 40 checks in the amount of $6 each; 80 checks in the amount of $4 each; 45 $20 bills; 30 $10 bills; 42 $5 bills; and 186 $1 bills. The total amount in fees collected on that day was
    A. $1,406.
    B. $1,706.
    C. $2,156.
    D. $2,356.

48. Assume that you are responsible for your agency's petty cash fund. During the month of February, you pay out seven subway fares at $1.25 each and one taxi fare for $7.30. You pay out nothing else from the fund. At the end of February, you count the money left in the fund and find three $1 bills, four quarters, five dimes, and four nickels. The amount of money you had available in the petty cash fund at the beginning of February was
    A. $4.70.
    B. $11.35.
    C. $16.05.
    D. $20.75.

SHOW YOUR WORK HERE

49. Assume that you are assigned to sell tickets at a city-owned ice skating rink. An adult ticket costs $3.75, and a children's ticket costs $2. At the end of the day, you find that you have sold 36 adult tickets and 80 children's tickets. The total amount of money you collected for that day was

A. $285.50.

B. $295.00.

C. $298.75.

D. $301.00.

50. If each office worker files 487 index cards in one hour, how many cards can 26 office workers file in one hour?

A. 10,662

B. 12,175

C. 12,662

D. 14,266

SHOW YOUR WORK HERE

ANSWER KEY AND EXPLANATIONS

Municipal Office Aide

1. A	11. A	21. A	31. B	41. C
2. D	12. D	22. B	32. A	42. C
3. B	13. B	23. A	33. D	43. C
4. D	14. B	24. C	34. B	44. A
5. C	15. D	25. A	35. A	45. B
6. C	16. C	26. D	36. A	46. C
7. B	17. C	27. A	37. A	47. C
8. B	18. B	28. D	38. C	48. D
9. C	19. B	29. B	39. C	49. B
10. B	20. B	30. B	40. C	50. C

1. **The correct answer is A.** The first step is to discuss the problem with your coworker. Remember that calm, polite discussion is almost always the correct answer when given as a choice.

2. **The correct answer is D.** Obviously, the best thing to do is to be honest with your coworker and to deliver the letter.

3. **The correct answer is B.** The best solution is to work on the areas that your supervisor has told you need improvement so that you can do a better job. If you're committing numerous careless errors, you need to be more careful when doing your work.

4. **The correct answer is D.** The subject of the sentence, the manual, is singular, so the verb must be singular as well. The correct spelling is *describes*.

5. **The correct answer is C.** *Paper* is a singular noun taking the singular verb *wasn't*. The construction *weren't no* constitutes an unacceptable double negative.

6. **The correct answer is C.** *Their* is the possessive. *They're* is the contraction for they are. *There* refers to a place. Choice D is a misspelling.

7. **The correct answer is B.** The correct way to express time is 8:30 a.m.

8. **The correct answer is B.** *The alphabet*—singular—*is*. The phrase *or A to Z sequence* is extra information about the alphabet, so it is enclosed by commas. *Too* means "also" or "excessive" and is the incorrect spelling of *to*.

9. **The correct answer is C.** The numbers in the second set are different: 4144682253 and 4146842253.

10. **The correct answer is B.** The numbers in the first and second sets are different: 5158635578 and 5158365788; 2119786384 and 2119687384.

11. **The correct answer is A.** None of the sets are alike: 1344678986 and 1344768986; 4778633843 and 4778638343; 3398765578 and 3397665578.

12. **The correct answer is D.** All three sets are alike.

13. **The correct answer is B.** The numbers in the second and third sets are different: 0086349252 and 0086347252; 4478875534 and 4478775534.

14. **The correct answer is B.** The second and third sets are different: Birmingham, AL 37184 and Birmingham, AL 37884; Grass Plains, WI 13786 and Grass Plains, WI 13736.

15. **The correct answer is D.** All three sets are the same.

16. **The correct answer is C.** The names in the first set are different: Abigail Marnsey and Abigail Marsney.

17. **The correct answer is C.** See the first sentence of the fourth paragraph.

18. **The correct answer is B.** *E.g.,* means "for example." See the second sentence under Inappropriate Personal Use that states, "For example, greeting cards, video, sound, or other large file attachments... ."

19. **The correct answer is B.** In choices C and D, the numbers are too high for the fluid process. Five copies would be most efficiently reproduced by the photocopy process without preparing a master.

20. **The correct answer is B.** Age is not mentioned in the list. See the second sentence of the last paragraph.

21. **The correct answer is A.** To *retain* is to hold or to keep.

22. **The correct answer is B.** A *routine* is a course of action that is followed regularly.

23. **The correct answer is A.** To *delete* is to strike out or to remove.

24. **The correct answer is C.** The second set is incorrectly coded: MVDBHT–234902 (should be 1).

25. **The correct answer is A.** No sets are correctly coded: BVPTRD–936184 (should be 7); GDPHMB–807029 (should be 46); GMRHMV–827032 (should be 23).

26. **The correct answer is D.** All three sets are correctly coded.

27. **The correct answer is A.** No sets are correctly coded: SGBSDM–489542 (should be 5); MGHPTM–290612 (should be 8); MPBMHT–269301 (should be 2).

28. **The correct answer is D.** All three sets are correctly coded.

29. **The correct answer is B.** The correct alphabetization is: Black, Howard; Black, Howard J.; Black, J. Howard; Black, John H.

30. **The correct answer is B.** The correct alphabetization is: Kingston, Theadore Barth; Kingston, Theodora Garth; Kingston, Thomas; Kingston, Thomas T.

31. **The correct answer is B.** The correct alphabetization is: Huerta, Paul M.; Huerta, Paulette L.; Huerta, Paulette Mary; Huerta, Peter A.

32. **The correct answer is A.** The correct alphabetization is: Morgan, Martha Hunt; Morgan, Martin Hunt; Morgan, Martine H.; Morgan, Mary H.

33. **The correct answer is D.** You must always identify yourself, find out to whom you are speaking, and be courteous to the caller, but sometimes a return call could give information at a later hour or date.

34. **The correct answer is B.** The first thing to do is speak to the employee who may not even be aware of the rule.

35. **The correct answer is A.** Be "up front" with your supervisor. Refusing to do a distasteful task or trying to hand it off to someone else is not proper business procedure.

36. **The correct answer is A.** See the second sentence of the first paragraph.

37. **The correct answer is A.** See the third paragraph.

38. The correct answer is C. See the second sentence in the last paragraph.

39. The correct answer is C. A *receptionist* receives visitors, so the best action is to stop working long enough to assist the visitors.

40. The correct answer is C. No matter how you approach the coworker, you are likely to create ill feeling. Let your supervisor handle this tricky office morale problem.

41. The correct answer is C. See sentence 3 in paragraph 3.

42. The correct answer is C. See the last sentence in paragraph 3.

43. The correct answer is C. *Unequivocal* means "unmistakable."

44. The correct answer is A. See paragraph 4.

45. The correct answer is B. See the last paragraph, where it says that "Feedback should not be limited to the annual written performance appraisal . . . This annual review is the minimum."

46. The correct answer is C. $30.20 ÷ 14 = $2.157; round up to $2.16.

47. The correct answer is C.
40 checks • $6 = $240;
80 checks • $4 = $320;
45 bills • $20 = $900;
30 bills • $10 = $300;
42 bills • $5 = $210;
186 bills • $1 = $186;

$240 + $320 + $900 + $300 + $210 + $186 = $2,156.

48. The correct answer is D.
7 subway fares • $1.25 = $8.75;
1 taxi fare • $7.30 = $7.30;
$8.75 + $7.30 = $16.05, the total amount spent during the month.

3 dollar bills = $3;
4 quarters = $1;
5 dimes = $0.50;
4 nickels = $0.20;
$3 + $1 + $0.50 + $0.20 = $4.70, the total amount left at the end of the month.

$16.05 + $4.70 = $20.75, the total amount at the beginning of the month.

49. The correct answer is B.
36 adults • $3.75 = $135;
80 children • $2 = $160;
$135 + $160 = $295.

50. The correct answer is C. 487 cards • 26 workers = 12,662.

SELF-EVALUATION

On your answer sheet, mark the numbers of the questions that you answered incorrectly and check them against the following charts. If you missed several of any question type, you need more practice with that kind of question. Return to the appropriate chapter and review the rules and practice exercises before moving on to the next sample exam.

SELF-EVALUATION CHART

Question Type	Question Numbers	Chapter(s) to Review
Judgment	1–3, 33–35, 39–40	11
English Grammar and Usage; Spelling	4–8	4 and 5
Clerical Speed and Accuracy	9–16	13
Reading Comprehension	17–20, 36–38, 41–45	10
Synonyms	21–23	6
Coding	24–28	13
Alphabetizing and Filing	29–32	12
Decimals	46–49	15
Work Problems	50	18

ANSWER SHEET PRACTICE TEST 5

Senior Office Typist

1. Ⓐ Ⓑ Ⓒ Ⓓ
2. Ⓐ Ⓑ Ⓒ Ⓓ
3. Ⓐ Ⓑ Ⓒ Ⓓ
4. Ⓐ Ⓑ Ⓒ Ⓓ
5. Ⓐ Ⓑ Ⓒ Ⓓ
6. Ⓐ Ⓑ Ⓒ Ⓓ
7. Ⓐ Ⓑ Ⓒ Ⓓ
8. Ⓐ Ⓑ Ⓒ Ⓓ
9. Ⓐ Ⓑ Ⓒ Ⓓ
10. Ⓐ Ⓑ Ⓒ Ⓓ
11. Ⓐ Ⓑ Ⓒ Ⓓ
12. Ⓐ Ⓑ Ⓒ Ⓓ
13. Ⓐ Ⓑ Ⓒ Ⓓ
14. Ⓐ Ⓑ Ⓒ Ⓓ
15. Ⓐ Ⓑ Ⓒ Ⓓ
16. Ⓐ Ⓑ Ⓒ Ⓓ
17. Ⓐ Ⓑ Ⓒ Ⓓ
18. Ⓐ Ⓑ Ⓒ Ⓓ
19. Ⓐ Ⓑ Ⓒ Ⓓ
20. Ⓐ Ⓑ Ⓒ Ⓓ
21. Ⓐ Ⓑ Ⓒ Ⓓ
22. Ⓐ Ⓑ Ⓒ Ⓓ
23. Ⓐ Ⓑ Ⓒ Ⓓ
24. Ⓐ Ⓑ Ⓒ Ⓓ
25. Ⓐ Ⓑ Ⓒ Ⓓ

26. Ⓐ Ⓑ Ⓒ Ⓓ
27. Ⓐ Ⓑ Ⓒ Ⓓ
28. Ⓐ Ⓑ Ⓒ Ⓓ
29. Ⓐ Ⓑ Ⓒ Ⓓ
30. Ⓐ Ⓑ Ⓒ Ⓓ
31. Ⓐ Ⓑ Ⓒ Ⓓ
32. Ⓐ Ⓑ Ⓒ Ⓓ
33. Ⓐ Ⓑ Ⓒ Ⓓ
34. Ⓐ Ⓑ Ⓒ Ⓓ
35. Ⓐ Ⓑ Ⓒ Ⓓ
36. Ⓐ Ⓑ Ⓒ Ⓓ
37. Ⓐ Ⓑ Ⓒ Ⓓ
38. Ⓐ Ⓑ Ⓒ Ⓓ
39. Ⓐ Ⓑ Ⓒ Ⓓ
40. Ⓐ Ⓑ Ⓒ Ⓓ
41. Ⓐ Ⓑ Ⓒ Ⓓ
42. Ⓐ Ⓑ Ⓒ Ⓓ
43. Ⓐ Ⓑ Ⓒ Ⓓ
44. Ⓐ Ⓑ Ⓒ Ⓓ
45. Ⓐ Ⓑ Ⓒ Ⓓ
46. Ⓐ Ⓑ Ⓒ Ⓓ
47. Ⓐ Ⓑ Ⓒ Ⓓ
48. Ⓐ Ⓑ Ⓒ Ⓓ
49. Ⓐ Ⓑ Ⓒ Ⓓ
50. Ⓐ Ⓑ Ⓒ Ⓓ

51. Ⓐ Ⓑ Ⓒ Ⓓ
52. Ⓐ Ⓑ Ⓒ Ⓓ
53. Ⓐ Ⓑ Ⓒ Ⓓ
54. Ⓐ Ⓑ Ⓒ Ⓓ
55. Ⓐ Ⓑ Ⓒ Ⓓ
56. Ⓐ Ⓑ Ⓒ Ⓓ
57. Ⓐ Ⓑ Ⓒ Ⓓ
58. Ⓐ Ⓑ Ⓒ Ⓓ
59. Ⓐ Ⓑ Ⓒ Ⓓ
60. Ⓐ Ⓑ Ⓒ Ⓓ
61. Ⓐ Ⓑ Ⓒ Ⓓ
62. Ⓐ Ⓑ Ⓒ Ⓓ
63. Ⓐ Ⓑ Ⓒ Ⓓ
64. Ⓐ Ⓑ Ⓒ Ⓓ
65. Ⓐ Ⓑ Ⓒ Ⓓ
66. Ⓐ Ⓑ Ⓒ Ⓓ
67. Ⓐ Ⓑ Ⓒ Ⓓ
68. Ⓐ Ⓑ Ⓒ Ⓓ
69. Ⓐ Ⓑ Ⓒ Ⓓ
70. Ⓐ Ⓑ Ⓒ Ⓓ
71. Ⓐ Ⓑ Ⓒ Ⓓ
72. Ⓐ Ⓑ Ⓒ Ⓓ
73. Ⓐ Ⓑ Ⓒ Ⓓ
74. Ⓐ Ⓑ Ⓒ Ⓓ
75. Ⓐ Ⓑ Ⓒ Ⓓ

76. Ⓐ Ⓑ Ⓒ Ⓓ
77. Ⓐ Ⓑ Ⓒ Ⓓ
78. Ⓐ Ⓑ Ⓒ Ⓓ
79. Ⓐ Ⓑ Ⓒ Ⓓ
80. Ⓐ Ⓑ Ⓒ Ⓓ
81. Ⓐ Ⓑ Ⓒ Ⓓ
82. Ⓐ Ⓑ Ⓒ Ⓓ
83. Ⓐ Ⓑ Ⓒ Ⓓ
84. Ⓐ Ⓑ Ⓒ Ⓓ
85. Ⓐ Ⓑ Ⓒ Ⓓ
86. Ⓐ Ⓑ Ⓒ Ⓓ
87. Ⓐ Ⓑ Ⓒ Ⓓ
88. Ⓐ Ⓑ Ⓒ Ⓓ
89. Ⓐ Ⓑ Ⓒ Ⓓ
90. Ⓐ Ⓑ Ⓒ Ⓓ
91. Ⓐ Ⓑ Ⓒ Ⓓ
92. Ⓐ Ⓑ Ⓒ Ⓓ
93. Ⓐ Ⓑ Ⓒ Ⓓ
94. Ⓐ Ⓑ Ⓒ Ⓓ
95. Ⓐ Ⓑ Ⓒ Ⓓ

answer sheet

Practice Test 5

SENIOR OFFICE TYPIST

95 Questions • 180 Minutes

Directions: For questions 1–8, choose the word that is correctly spelled.

---

1. A. apellate
   B. appelate
   C. appeallate
   D. appellate

2. A. presumption
   B. presoumption
   C. presumsion
   D. presumptsion

3. A. litigiant
   B. litigent
   C. litigant
   D. litigint

4. A. committment
   B. commitment
   C. comittment
   D. comitment

5. A. affidavid
   B. afidavis
   C. affidavit
   D. afidavit

6. A. arraign
   B. arrain
   C. arreign
   D. areign

7. A. cumalative
   B. cummuletive
   C. cummalative
   D. cumulative

8. A. sevarance
   B. severance
   C. severence
   D. severants

Directions: Questions 9 and 10 consist of a CAPITALIZED word that is to be filed correctly among the alphabetized words listed. Choose the word that should come after the capitalized word.

---

9. ERRORS

   A. eras

   B. erasers

   C. errands

   D. eruptions

10. SLANG

   A. slabs

   B. slander

   C. slates

   D. slays

Directions: Questions 11–18 consist of three sentences with one underlined word. One of the underlined words might be spelled incorrectly. Mark the letter of the sentence that contains the incorrectly spelled word. If no sentence contains a misspelled word, choose choice **D**.

---

11. **A.** Punishment must be a planned part of a comprehensive program of treating delinquency.

   B. It is easier to spot inexperienced check forjers than other criminals.

   C. Even young vandals and hooligans can be reformed if given adequate attention.

   D. No error.

12. **A.** The court officer does not have the authority to make exceptions.

   B. Usually the violations are the result of illegal and dangerous driving behavior.

   C. The safety division is required to investigate if the dispatcher files a complaint.

   D. No error.

13. **A.** Violent video games may have a distinct influence on impressionable teens, especially males.

   B. Some of the people behind bars are innocent people who have been put there by mistake.

   C. Educational achievment is closely associated with delinquency.

   D. No error.

14. **A.** Disciplinary action is most effective when it is taken promptly.

   B. Release on "personal recognizance" refers to release without bail.

   C. Parole violators forfeit their freedom.

   D. No error.

15. **A.** Some responsibilities take precedence over preservation of evidence.

   B. Objects should not be touched unless there is some compelling reason.

   C. A juvenile, or youth, detention center houses youth awaiting court hearings or placement in long-term facilities.

   D. No error.

16. **A.** Evidence is inmaterial if it does not prove the truth of a fact at issue.

   B. Without qualms, the offender will lie and manipulate others.

   C. If spectators become disorderly, the court officer may threaten to cite them for contempt of court.

   D. No error.

17. **A.** Under certain conditions, circum-stantial evidence may be <u>admissible</u>.

    B. Just because evidence is circumstantial does not mean that it is <u>irrelevant</u>.

    C. An <u>aggressive</u> offender may appear to be very hostile.

    D. No error.

18. **A.** A victim of <u>assault</u> may want to take revenge.

    B. The result of the trial was put in doubt when the <u>prosecuter</u> produced a surprise witness.

    C. The court officer must maintain order and <u>decorum</u> in the courtroom.

    D. No error.

Directions: Consider each group of names as a unit. Determine where the name printed in boldface would be if the names in the group were correctly alphabetized. If the name in boldface is first, mark **A**; if second, mark **B**; if third, mark **C**; and if fourth, mark **D**.

---

19. Ms. Grace Egan
Greg Eckles
Gail A. Green
G.G. Green

20. Wendy Barron Hardware Limited
45th Street Hardware
2 x 4 Lumber, Inc.
Cathy's Discount Auto Dealership

Directions: For questions 21–27, choose the sentence that is grammatically incorrect.

---

21. **A.** One of us had to reply before tomorrow.

    B. All employees who had served from 40 to 51 years were retired.

    C. The personnel office takes care of employment, dismissals, and etc.

    D. We often come across people with whom we disagree.

22. **A.** The jurors have been instructed to deliver a sealed verdict.

    B. The court may direct the convict to be imprisoned in a county penitentiary instead of a state prison.

    C. Conveying self-confidence is dis-playing assurance.

    D. He devotes as much, if not more, time to his work than the rest of the employees.

23. **A.** In comparison with that laptop, this one is more preferable.

    B. The jurors may go to dinner only with the permission of the judge.

    C. There was neither any intention to commit a crime nor any injury incurred.

    D. It is the sociological view that all weight should be given to the history and development of the individual.

24. **A.** The supervisor, not the employee, makes the suggestions for improvement.

    B. Violations of traffic laws and illegal and dangerous driving behavior con-stitutes bad driving.

    C. Cynics take the position that the criminal is rarely or never reformed.

    D. The ultimate solution to the crime problem may be better schools and better job prospects.

25. **A.** No crime can occur unless there is a written law forbidding the act or omission in question.

    B. If one wants to prevent crime, we must deal with the possible criminals before they reach the prison.

    C. One could reasonably say that the same type of correctional institution is not desirable for the custody of all prisoners.

    D. When you have completed the report, you may give it to me or directly to the judge.

26. **A.** The structure of an organization should be considered in determining the organization's goals.

    B. Complaints are welcomed because they frequently bring into the open conditions and faults in service that should be corrected.

    C. The defendant had a very unique alibi, so the judge dismissed the case.

    D. Court officers must direct witnesses to seats when the latter present themselves in court to testify.

27. **A.** The clerk promptly notified the judge of the fire for which he was highly praised.

    B. There is justice among thieves; the three thieves divided the goods equally among themselves.

    C. If he had been notified promptly, he might have been here on time.

    D. Though doubt may exist about the mailability of some matter, the sender is fully liable for law violation if such matter should be non-mailable.

Directions: For questions 28–32, choose the sentence that is grammatically correct.

---

28. **A.** In high-visibility crimes, it is apparent to all concerned that they are criminal acts at the time when they are committed.

    B. Statistics tell us that more people are killed by guns than by any kind of weapon.

    C. Reliable persons guarantee the facts with regards to the truth of these statements.

    D. Messengers sort and carry mail, documents, or other materials between offices or buildings.

29. **A.** She suspects that the service is so satisfactory as it should be.

    B. The court officer goes to the exhibit table and discovered that Exhibit B is an entirely different document.

    C. The jurors and alternates comprise a truly diverse group.

    D. Our aim should be not merely to reform lawbreakers but striking at the roots of crime.

30. **A.** Close examination of traffic accident statistics reveal that traffic accidents are frequently the result of violations of traffic laws.

B. If you had planned on employing fewer people than this to do the work, this situation would not have arose.

C. As far as good looks and polite manners are concerned, they are both alike.

D. If a murder has been committed with a bow and arrow, it is irrelevant to show that the defendant was well acquainted with firearms.

31. **A.** An individual engages in criminal behavior if the number of criminal patterns that he or she has acquired exceeds the number of non-criminal patterns.

B. Every person must be informed of the reason for their arrest unless arrested in the actual commission of a crime.

C. The one of the following motorists to which it would be most desirable to issue a summons is the one which was late for an important business appointment.

D. The officer should glance around quickly but with care to determine whether his entering the area will damage any evidence.

32. **A.** State troopers typically work on a rotating shift basis, must be available for duty 24 hours a day, they work on holidays in snow and rain.

B. If the budget allows, we are likely to reemploy anyone whose training fits them to do the work.

C. The investigative team went quietly about its work, sifting through the dirt and rubble looking for evidence.

D. Traffic control and enforcement are the mains concerns of state troopers and have limited general police authority.

Directions: Questions 33 and 34 consist of four names. For each question, select the name that should be third if the four names were arranged in alphabetical order in accordance with the rules for alphabetical filing.

---

33. **A.** Mr. Lionel G. Kehr

B. Ms. Judy B. Klein

C. Mr. Margaret Kael

D. Mrs. Trudy Kaminski

34. **A.** Sammy S. Yankovic

B. 12th Pier Shipping, LTD.

C. VP Joanne Chiba

D. Third Column Architecture Co.

Directions: For questions 35–48, compare the name/address/number listings in all three columns. Then choose your answer as follows:

A if the listings in ALL THREE columns are exactly ALIKE.

B if only the listings in the FIRST and THIRD columns are exactly ALIKE.

C if only the listings in the FIRST and SECOND columns are exactly ALIKE.

D if the listings in ALL THREE columns are DIFFERENT.

35. John H. Smith
    238 N. Monroe Street
    Phila., PA 19147
    176-54-326
    5578-98765-33

    John H. Smith
    238 N. Monroe Street
    Phila, PA 19147
    176-54-326
    5578-98765-33

    John H. Smith
    238 N. Monroe Street
    Phila., PA 19147
    176-54-326
    5578-98765-33

36. Evan A. McKinley
    2872 Broadway
    East Amherst, NY 14051
    212-883-5184
    9803-115-6848

    Evan A. McKinley
    2872 Broadway
    East Amherst, NY 14051
    212-883-5184
    9083-115-6848

    Evan A. McKinley
    2872 Broadway
    East Amherst, NV 14051
    212-883-5184
    9803-115-6848

37. Luigi Antonio Cruz Jr.
    2695 East 3435 South
    Salt Lake City, UT 84109
    801-485-1563, x.233
    013-5589734-9

    Luigi Antonio Cruz Jr.
    2695 East 3435 South
    Salt Lake City, UT 84109
    801-485-1563, x.233
    013-5589734-9

    Luigi Antonio Cruz Jr.
    2695 East 3435 South
    Salt Lake City, UT 84109
    801-485-1563, x.233
    013-5589734-9

38. Educational Records Inst.
    P.O. Box 44268a
    Atlanta, Georgia 30337
    18624-40-9128
    63qs5-95YT3-001

    Educational Records Inst.
    P.O. Box 44268a
    Atlanta, Georgia 30337
    18624-40-9128
    63qs5-95YT3-001

    Educational Records Inst.
    P.O. Box 44286a
    Atlanta, Georgia 30337
    18624-40-9128
    63qs5-95YT3-001

39. Sr. Consultant, Labor Rel.
    Benner Mgmt. Group
    86408 W. 3rd Ave.
    Trowbridge, MA 02178
    617-980-1136

    Sr. Consultant, Labor Rel.
    Banner Mgmt. Group
    86408 W. 3rd Ave.
    Trowbridge, MA 02178
    617-980-1136

    Sr. Consultant, Labor Rel.
    Benner Mgmt. Group
    84608 W. 3rd Ave.
    Trowbridge, MA 02178
    617-980-1136

40. Marina Angelika Salvis
    P.O.B. 11283 Gracie Sta.
    Newtown, PA 18940-0998
    215-382-0628
    4168-GNP-78852

    Marina Angelika Salvis
    P.O.B. 11283 Gracie Sta.
    Newtown, PA 18940-0998
    215-382-0628
    4168-GNP-78852

    Marina Angelika Salvis
    P.O.B. 11283 Gracie Sta.
    Newtown, PA 18940-0998
    215-382-0628
    4168-GNP-78852

41. Durham Reichard III
8298 Antigua Terrace
Gaithersburg, MD 20879
301-176-9887-8
0-671-843576-X

    Durham Reichard III
8298 Antigua Terrace
Gaithersburg, MD 20879
301-176-9887-8
0-671-843576-X

    Durham Reichard III
8298 Antigua Terrace
Gaithersberg, MD 20879
301-176-9887-8
0-671-843576-X

42. L. Chamberlain Smythe
Mardikian & Moore, Inc.
Cor. Mott Street at Pell
San Francisco, CA
58312-398401-25

    L. Chamberlain Smythe
Mardikian and Moore, Inc.
Cor. Mott Street at Pell
San Francisco, CA
58312-398401-25

    L. Chamberlain Smythe
Markdikian & Moore, Inc.
Cor. Mott Street at Pell
San Francisco, CA
58312-398401-25

43. Ramona Fleischer-Chris
60646 West Touhy Avenue
Sebastopol, CA 95472
707-998-0104
0-06-408632-0

    Ramona Fleisher-Chris
60646 West Touhy Avenue
Sebastopol, CA 95472
707-998-0104
0-06-408632-0

    Ramona Fleischer-Chris
60646 West Touhey Avenue
Sepabstopol, CA 95472
707-998-0104
0-06-408632-0

44. George Sebastian Barnes
Noble/Encore/Dalton
43216 M Street, NE
Washington, DC 20036
202-222-1272

    George Sebastian Barnes
Noble/Encore/Dalton
43216 M. Street, NE
Washington, DC 20036
202-222-1272

    George Sebastian Barnes
Noble/Encore/Dalton
43216 M Street, NE
Washington, DC 20036
202-222-1272

45. Baldwin Algonquin III
2503 Bartholemew Way
Lemberger, VA 28094-9182
9-1-303-558-8536
683-64-0828

    Baldwin Algonquin III
2503 Bartholemew Way
Lemberger, VA 28094-9182
9-1-303-558-8536
683-64-0828

    Baldwin Algonquin III
2503 Bartholomew Way
Lemberger, VA 28094-9182
9-1-303-558-8536
683-64-0828

46. Huang Ho Cheung
612 Gallopade Gallery, E.
Seattle, WA 98101-2614
001-206-283-7722
5416R-1952TZ-op

    Huang Ho Cheung
612 Gallopade Gallery, E.
Seattle, WA 98101-2614
001-206-283-7722
5416R-1952TZ-op

    Huang Ho Cheung
612 Gallopade Gallery, E.
Seattle, WA 98101-2614
001-206-283-7722
5416R-1952TZ-op

47. Hilliard H. Hyacinth
86529 Dunwoodie Drive
Kanakao, HI 91132
808-880-8080
6-78912-e3e42

    Hilliard H. Hyacinth
86529 Dunwoodie Drive
Kanakao, HI 91132
808-880-8080
6-78912-3e3e42

    Hilliard H. Hyacinth
85629 Dunwoodie Drive
Kanakao, HI 91132
808-880-8080
6-78912-e3e42

48. Anoko Kawamoto
8932 Shimabui Hwy.
O'Reilly Bay, LA 56212
713-864-7253-4984
5634-Ootv5a-16867

    Anoko Kawamoto
8932 Shimabui Hwy.
O'Reillys Bay, LA 56212
713-864-7253-4984
5634-Ootv5a-16867

    Anoko Kawamoto
8932 Shimabui Hwy.
O'Reilly Bay, LA 56212
713-864-7253-4984
5634-Ootv5a-16867

Directions: Questions 49 and 50 provide the name and identification number of an employee. Choose the one answer that has exactly the same identification number and name as those given in the question.

49. H-35446 Ginger Tores

    A. H35446 Ginger Tores

    B. H-35446 Ginger Torres

    C. H-35446 Ginger Tores

    D. H-35446 Ginger Torez

50. F-66786 Philip Potter

    A. F-66786 Phillip Potter

    B. F-67866 Philip Potter

    C. F-66786 Philip Potter

    D. F-66876 Phillip Potter

Directions: Use the information presented in the following tables to answer questions 51–65. You are NOT permitted to use a calculator to arrive at totals.

DAILY LOG OF CASES

Monday

Judge	Date Filed	Sum at Issue	Disposition	Award
Baron	6/5/11	$9,500	Adjourned	X
Lee	4/2/12	$20,000	Dismissed	X
Conlon	12/8/10	$12,000	Settled	X
Ramos	3/31/12	$5,500	Settled	X
Lee	10/8/11	$10,000	Dismissed	X
Jones	1/5/12	$14,000	Found for plaintiff	$15,000
Baron	5/1/13	$7,600	Adjourned	X

Tuesday

Judge	Date Filed	Sum at Issue	Disposition	Award
Ramos	2/2/12	$3,000	Found for plaintiff	$3,375
Amati	8/6/12	$8,000	Dismissed	X
Moro	4/8/11	$11,500	Found for plaintiff	$9,000
Jones	11/17/10	$12,000	Adjourned	X
Conlon	12/4/10	$4,500	Adjourned	X
Amati	6/12/11	$2,000	Settled	$15,000

Wednesday

Judge	Date Filed	Sum at Issue	Disposition	Award
Conlon	1/7/13	$10,000	Dismissed	X
Baron	5/3/12	$5,000	Adjourned	X
Ramos	6/22/11	$7,500	Found for plaintiff	$6,000
Moro	2/15/13	$22,000	Settled	X
Lee	9/7/12	$8,000	Settled	X
Conlon	11/30/10	$16,000	Found for plaintiff	$17,250
Amati	7/10/12	$10,000	Found for plaintiff	$10,850

Thursday

Judge	Date Filed	Sum at Issue	Disposition	Award
Jones	5/18/12	$7,500	Found for plaintiff	$6,000
Amati	3/6/12	$9,250	Settled	X
Conlon	3/31/12	$6,000	Adjourned	X
Moro	8/28/11	$12,000	Adjourned	X
Conlon	10/30/10	$4,600	Found for plaintiff	$5,000

Friday

Judge	Date Filed	Sum at Issue	Disposition	Award
Lee	4/12/12	$6,000	Adjourned	X
Baron	1/28/13	$9,500	Dismissed	X
Ramos	7/17/12	$28,000	Found for plaintiff	$20,000
Amati	12/2/11	$15,000	Settled	X
Lee	2/21/12	$8,000	Found for plaintiff	$8,625
Moro	5/10/11	$22,000	Settled	X
Baron	8/25/11	$11,000	Dismissed	X
Jones	11/4/10	$5,500	Settled	X

DAILY BREAKDOWN OF CASES

	Mon.	Tue.	Wed.	Thurs.	Fri.	Total
Case Status						
Dismissed	2	1	1		2	6
Adjourned	2	2	1	2	1	8
Settled	2	1	2	1	3	9
Found for Plaintiff	1	2	3	2	2	10
Total Cases	7	6	7	5	8	33
Cases by Year Using Original Numbers						
2010	1	2	1	1	1	6
2011	2	2	1	1	3	9
2012	3	2	3	3	3	14
2013	1		2		1	4
Total Cases	7	6	7	5	8	33

SUMMARY OF CASES BY JUDGE/DISPOSITION

Judge	Dismissed	Adjourned	Settled	Found for Plaintiff	Total
Amati	1		3	1	5
Baron	2	3			5
Conlon	1	2	1	2	6
Jones		1	1	2	4
Lee	2	1	1	1	5
Moro		1	2	1	4
Ramos			1	3	4
Total	6	8	9	10	33

51. The judge scheduled to hear the greatest number of cases in the week shown was

  A. Amati.

  B. Lee.

  C. Conlon.

  D. Ramos.

52. The judge who determined no cash awards in the week shown was

  A. Moro.

  B. Jones.

  C. Baron.

  D. Lee.

53. How many judges were assigned to hear more than one case in one day?

  A. 1

  B. 2

  C. 3

  D. 4

54. In how many cases was the sum finally awarded lower than the sum at issue?

  A. 2

  B. 3

  C. 4

  D. 5

55. How many of the cases filed in 2010 were dismissed?

  A. 0

  B. 1

  C. 2

  D. 3

56. Of the cases adjourned, the greatest number were filed in

  A. 2010.

  B. 2011.

  C. 2012.

  D. 2013.

SHOW YOUR WORK HERE

57. Which two judges were scheduled to sit on only three days?
    A. Jones and Baron
    B. Baron and Lee
    C. Lee and Moro
    D. Ramos and Jones

58. In which month were the greatest number of cases filed?
    A. February
    B. May
    C. August
    D. November

59. The total amount of money awarded on Wednesday was
    A. $33,500.
    B. $34,100.
    C. $35,300.
    D. $45,000.

60. The total amount of money awarded by Jones was
    A. $39,000.
    B. $21,500.
    C. $21,000.
    D. $17,500.

61. The amount at issue in the cases that were adjourned on Thursday was
    A. $12,100.
    B. $18,000.
    C. $21,350.
    D. $29,250.

SHOW YOUR WORK HERE

62. When the amount of an award is greater than the sum at issue, the higher award represents an additional sum meant to cover plaintiff's costs in the suit. The total amount awarded this week to cover costs was

- **A.** $4,800.
- **B.** $9,000.
- **C.** $3,500.
- **D.** $17,500.

63. If all the plaintiffs who filed cases in 2013 were awarded exactly the sums for which they sued, they would have received a total of

- **A.** $41,500.
- **B.** $45,100.
- **C.** $48,600.
- **D.** $49,100.

64. The total amount awarded to plaintiffs who filed their cases in 2010 was

- **A.** $1,650.
- **B.** $20,600.
- **C.** $22,250.
- **D.** $22,650.

65. Comparing cases filed in 2011 with cases filed in 2012,

- **A.** four more of the 2011 cases were settled than 2012 cases.
- **B.** two fewer 2012 cases were settled than 2011 cases.
- **C.** an equal number of cases was settled from the two years.
- **D.** three more of the 2011 cases were settled than 2012 cases.

SHOW YOUR WORK HERE

Directions: Questions 66–95 are based on the following passages. Each passage contains several numbered blanks. Read the passage once quickly to get the overall idea. Below each passage are listed sets of words numbered to match the blanks. Read the passage through a second time more slowly, and choose the word from each set that makes the most sense both in the sentence and in the total paragraph.

A large proportion of people __66__ bars are __67__ convicted criminals, __68__ people who have been arrested and are being __69__ until __70__ trials in __71__. Experts have often pointed out that this __72__ system does not operate fairly. For instance, a person who can afford to pay bail usually will not get locked up. The theory of the bail system is that the person will make sure to show up in court when he or she is supposed to; __73__, bail will be forfeited—the person will __74__ the __75__ that was put up. Sometimes a person __76__ can show that he or she is a stable __77__ with a job and a family will be released on "personal recognizance" (without bail). The result is that the well-to-do, the __78__, and family men can often __79__ the detention system. The people who do wind up in detention tend to __80__ the poor, the unemployed, the single, and the young.

66. A. under
    B. at
    C. tending
    D. behind

67. A. always
    B. not
    C. hardened
    D. very

68. A. but
    B. and
    C. also
    D. although

69. A. hanged
    B. freed
    C. held
    D. judged

70. A. your
    B. his
    C. daily
    D. their

71. A. jail
    B. court
    C. fire
    D. judgment

72. A. school
    B. court
    C. detention
    D. election

73. A. otherwise
    B. therefore
    C. because
    D. then

74. A. save
    B. spend
    C. lose
    D. count

75. A. wall
    B. money
    C. front
    D. pretense

76. **A.** whom

B. which

C. what

D. who

77. **A.** citizen

B. horse

C. cleaner

D. clown

78. **A.** handsome

B. athletic

C. employed

D. alcoholic

79. **A.** survive

B. avoid

C. provide

D. institute

80. **A.** become

B. help

C. be

D. harm

___81___ acts are classified according to ___82___ standards. One is whether the ___83___ is major or minor. A major offense, such as murder, would be ___84___ a felony, _ ___85___ , a minor offense, such as reckless driving, would be considered a misdemeanor. ___86___ standard of classification is the specific kind of crime committed. Examples are burglary and robbery, which are ___87___ often used incorrectly by individuals who are ___88___ aware of the actual ___89___ as defined by law. A person who breaks ___90___ a building to commit a ___91___ or other major crime is ___92___ of burglary, while robbery is the felonious taking of an individual's ___93___ from his person or ___94___ his immediate ___95___ by the use of violence or threat.

81. **A.** People's

B. Criminal

C. Felonious

D. Numerous

82. **A.** decent

B. published

C. community

D. several

83. **A.** crime

B. act

C. offender

D. standard

84. **A.** labeled

B. convicted

C. executed

D. tried

85. **A.** moreover

B. because

C. whereas

D. hence

86. **A.** Gold

B. Juried

C. Another

D. My

87. **A.** crimes

B. terms

C. verdicts

D. sentences

88. **A.** sometimes

B. very

C. not

D. angrily

89. A. difference
    B. definitions
    C. crimes
    D. victims

90. A. down
    B. into
    C. apart
    D. from

91. A. felony
    B. burglary
    C. robbery
    D. theft

92. A. accused
    B. convicted
    C. freed
    D. guilty

93. A. life
    B. liberty
    C. property
    D. weapon

94. A. throughout
    B. in
    C. by
    D. for

95. A. lifetime
    B. home
    C. presence
    D. concern

ANSWER KEY AND EXPLANATIONS

1. D	20. D	39. D	58. B	77. A
2. A	21. C	40. A	59. B	78. C
3. C	22. D	41. C	60. C	79. B
4. B	23. A	42. D	61. B	80. C
5. C	24. B	43. D	62. D	81. B
6. A	25. B	44. B	63. D	82. D
7. D	26. C	45. C	64. C	83. A
8. B	27. A	46. A	65. C	84. A
9. D	28. D	47. D	66. D	85. C
10. C	29. C	48. B	67. B	86. C
11. B	30. D	49. C	68. A	87. B
12. D	31. A	50. C	69. C	88. C
13. C	32. C	51. C	70. D	89. A
14. D	33. A	52. C	71. B	90. B
15. C	34. B	53. D	72. C	91. D
16. A	35. B	54. C	73. A	92. D
17. D	36. D	55. A	74. C	93. C
18. B	37. A	56. C	75. B	94. B
19. D	38. C	57. B	76. D	95. C

1. **The correct answer is D.** The correct spelling is *appellate*.

2. **The correct answer is A.** The correct spelling is *presumption*.

3. **The correct answer is C.** The correct spelling is *litigant*.

4. **The correct answer is B.** The correct spelling is *commitment*.

5. **The correct answer is C.** The correct spelling is *affidavit*.

6. **The correct answer is A.** The correct spelling is *arraign*.

7. **The correct answer is D.** The correct spelling is *cumulative*.

8. **The correct answer is B.** The correct spelling is *severance*.

9. **The correct answer is D.** In alphabetical order, *errors* comes after *errands* and before *eruptions*.

10. **The correct answer is C.** In alphabetical order, *slang* comes after *slander* and before *slates*.

11. **The correct answer is B.** The correct spelling is *forgers*.

12. **The correct answer is D.** None of the words are misspelled.

13. **The correct answer is C.** The correct spelling is *achievement*.

14. **The correct answer is D.** None of the words are misspelled.

15. **The correct answer is C.** The correct spelling is *detention*.

16. **The correct answer is A.** The correct spelling is *immaterial*.

17. **The correct answer is D.** None of the words are misspelled.

18. **The correct answer is B.** The correct spelling is *prosecutor*.

19. **The correct answer is D.** Names are alphabetized with importance placed on the last name first, the first name or initial second, and the middle name or initial last. Furthermore, first initials come before spelled out first names and titles such as *Ms.* are disregarded when alphabetizing. Therefore, correct alphabetical order is: Greg Eckles, Ms. Grace Egan, G.G. Green, **Gail A. Green**.

20. **The correct answer is D.** Business names that begin with numerals should be alphabetized as if the numerals are spelled out. Furthermore, the names of organizations, institutions, and buildings are filed according to the order in which each word in the name appears, except where these names include the full names of individuals. In such cases, the last name of the person is filed first. The correct order is: Wendy Barron Hardware Limited, Cathy's Discount Auto Dealership, 45th Street Hardware, **2 x 4 Lumber, Inc.**

21. **The correct answer is C.** There should be no *and* before the "etc." at the end of a series of words.

22. **The correct answer is D.** This is an incomplete comparison. It should read, "He devotes as much as, if not more, time to his work than the rest of the employees."

23. **The correct answer is A.** *More preferable* is a redundancy; *preferable* alone is quite adequate.

24. **The correct answer is B.** The compound subject *violations . . .and. . .behavior* requires the plural form of the verb *constitute*.

25. **The correct answer is B.** This sentence shifts point of view midstream. It could read either "If one wants to prevent crime, one must deal. . .," or, "If we want to prevent crime, we must deal. . ."

26. **The correct answer is C.** *Unique* means that there is only one; therefore, the word can take no qualifier.

27. **The correct answer is A.** This is an ambiguous statement. Was the judge praised for the fire? Was the clerk praised for the fire? It would be better to say, "The clerk was highly praised for promptly notifying the judge of the fire."

28. **The correct answer is D.** Sentence A reads as if all concerned are criminal acts. Since guns are a kind of weapon, sentence B would have to read ". . .than any other kind of weapon." In sentence C, *regards* is the wrong word; the word required is *regard*.

29. **The correct answer is C.** In sentence A, the idiomatic form is *as satisfactory*. Sentence B confuses two verb tenses in the same sentence; it would be correct to say that the court officer *went. . .and discovered*. . . Sentence D requires a parallel construction, either *reforming and striking* or *to reform and to strike*.

30. **The correct answer is D.** In sentence A, *examination*, being singular, requires the singular verb *reveals*. The correct form of sentence B is ". . .would not have arisen." As for sentence C, the word *alike* obviously includes both, so the word both is redundant.

31. **The correct answer is A.** In sentence B, *Every person* is singular and therefore must be informed of the reason for his or her arrest. In sentence C, a motorist is a person, not a thing, so use *to whom* and *who* rather than *to which* and *which*. Sentence D requires the parallelism of quickly but carefully.

32. **The correct answer is C.** Sentence A has several problems. First, it's a run-on sentence. A punctuation mark or conjunction is required between *day* and *they*. The sentence also reads as though the troopers work only on holidays if it snows or rains. The sentence would be clearer if it read: "They work on holidays and in bad weather." In sentence B, *anyone* is singular, so the referent pronoun must also be singular. Sentence D has a problem with clarity. As written, it reads that traffic control and enforcement have limited general police authority.

33. **The correct answer is A.** Names are alphabetized with importance placed on the last name first, the first name or initial second, and the middle name or initial last. Titles such as *Mr.*, *Ms.*, and *Mrs.* are disregarded. Therefore, correct alphabetical order is: Mr. Margaret Kael; Mrs. Trudy Kaminski; Mr. Lionel G. Kehr; Ms. Judy B. Klein. Choice A is the correct answer because Mr. Lionel G. Kehr is third in the order.

34. **The correct answer is B.** Names are alphabetized with importance placed on the last name first, the first name or initial second, and the middle name or initial last. Titles such as *VP* are disregarded. Business names that begin with numerals should be alphabetized as if the numerals are spelled out. Therefore, correct alphabetical order is: VP Joanne Chiba; Third Column Architecture Co.; 12th Pier Shipping, LTD.; Sammy S. Yankovic. Choice B is the correct answer because 12th Pier Shipping, LTD. is third in the order.

35. **The correct answer is B.** There is a difference in the second column: Phila., PA 19147 and Phila, PA 19147.

36. **The correct answer is D.** All three columns are different: East Amherst, NY 14051 and East Amherst, NV 14051 (third column); 9803-115-6848 and 9083-115-6848 (second column).

37. **The correct answer is A.** All three columns are alike.

38. **The correct answer is C.** There is a difference in the third column: P.O. Box 44268a and P.O. Box 44286a.

39. **The correct answer is D.** All three columns are different: Benner Mgmt. Group and Banner Mgmt. Group (second column); 86408 W. 3rd Ave. and 84608 W. 3rd Ave. (third column).

40. **The correct answer is A.** All three columns are alike.

41. **The correct answer is C.** The third column is different: Gaithersburg, MD 20879 and Gaithersberg, MD 20879.

42. **The correct answer is D.** All three columns are different: Mardikian & Moore, Inc., Mardikian and Moore, Inc., and Markdikian & Moore, Inc.

43. **The correct answer is D.** All three columns are different: Ramona Fleischer-Chris and Ramona Fleisher-Chris (second column); 60646 West Touhy Avenue and 60646 West Touhey Avenue (third column).

44. **The correct answer is B.** The second column is different: 43216 M Street, NE and 43216 M. Street, NE.

45. **The correct answer is C.** The third column is different: 2503 Bartholemew Way and 2503 Bartholomew Way.

46. **The correct answer is A.** All three columns are alike.

47. **The correct answer is D.** All three columns are different: 86529 Dunwoodie Drive and 85629 Dunwoodie Drive (third column); 6-78912-e3e42 and 6-78912-3e3e42 (second column).

48. **The correct answer is B.** The second column is different: O'Reilly Bay, LA 56212 and O'Reillys Bay, LA 56212.

49. **The correct answer is C.** Only choice C is written correctly. In choice A, the hyphen in the identification number is missing. Choice B adds an extra r to the employee's last name. Choice D replaces the s in the employee's last name with a z.

50. **The correct answer is C.** In choices A and D, there is an extra *l* in *Phillip*. In choice B, the 6 and 7 are transposed in the number. In choice D, the 8 and 7 are transposed.

51. **The correct answer is C.** Conlon was scheduled to hear 6 cases: 1 on Monday, 1 on Tuesday, 2 on Wednesday, and 2 on Thursday. Amati, Baron, and Lee were scheduled for 5 cases apiece. Jones, Moro, and Ramos were only scheduled for 4.

52. **The correct answer is C.** Of the cases Baron was scheduled to hear, 3 were adjourned (2 on Monday and 1 on Wednesday) and 2 were dismissed (on Friday), so he didn't give any cash awards. Jones gave cash awards in 2 cases, and Moro and Lee gave cash awards in 1 case each.

53. **The correct answer is D.** Lee and Baron were both scheduled for 2 trials on Monday and Friday, Amati was scheduled for 2 on Tuesday, and Conlon was scheduled for 2 on Wednesday and Thursday, for a total of 4 judges.

54. **The correct answer is C.** On Tuesday, Moro awarded $9,000 in a suit for

$11,500; on Wednesday, Ramos awarded $6,000 in a suit for $7,500; on Thursday, Jones awarded $6,000 in a suit for $7,500; and on Friday, Ramos awarded $20,000 in a suit for $28,000, for a total of 4 cases.

55. **The correct answer is A.** Of the 6 cases filed in 2010, 2 were settled (1 on Monday and 1 on Friday), 2 were adjourned (both on Tuesday), and 2 were adjudicated (1 on Wednesday and 1 on Thursday). None of the cases were dismissed.

56. **The correct answer is C.** Three of the 2012 cases were adjourned: 1 on Wednesday, 1 on Thursday, and 1 on Friday. Only one 2013 case was adjourned, and 2 each of 2010 and 2011 cases were adjourned.

57. **The correct answer is B.** Lee and Baron each sat on Monday, Wednesday, and Friday. Jones sat on Monday, Tuesday, Thursday, and Friday. Moro sat on Tuesday, Wednesday, Thursday, and Friday. Ramos sat on Monday, Tuesday, Wednesday, and Friday.

58. **The correct answer is B.** Four cases were filed in May (see the tables for Monday, Wednesday, Thursday, and Friday). Three cases were filed in each of February, August, and November.

59. **The correct answer is B.** $6,000 + $17,250 + $10,850 = $34,100.

60. **The correct answer is C.** $15,000 (on Monday) + $6,000 (on Thursday) = $21,000.

61. **The correct answer is B.** $6,000 (Conlon's first case) + $12,000 (Moro's case) = $18,000.

62. **The correct answer is D.**
$15,000 − $14,000 = $1,000 (Jones on Monday);

$3,375 − $3,000 = $375 (Ramos on Tuesday);

$15,000 - $2,000 = $13,000 (Amati on Wednesday);

$17,250 - $16,000 = $1,250 (Conlon on Wednesday);

$10,850 - $10,000 = $850 (Amati on Wednesday);

$5,000 - $4,600 = $400 (Conlon on Thursday);

$8,625 - $8,000 = $625 (Lee on Friday);

$1,000 + $375 + $13,000 + $1,250 + $850 + $400 + $625 = $17,500.

63. **The correct answer is D.** $7,600 (filed on 5/1/13 and heard on Monday) + $10,000 (filed on 1/7/13 and heard on Wednesday) + $22,000 (filed on 2/15/13 and heard on Wednesday) + $9,500 (filed on 1/28/13 and heard on Friday) = $49,100.

64. **The correct answer is C.** On Wednesday, Conlon awarded $17,250 in a 11/30/10 case; on Thursday, Conlon awarded $5,000 in a 10/30/10 case; $17,250 + $5,000 = $22,250.

65. **The correct answer is C.** An equal number of cases was settled from the two years. Three 2011 cases were settled—one on Tuesday and two on Friday; three 2012 cases were settled—one on Monday, one on Wednesday, and one on Thursday.

66. **The correct answer is D.** People are generally said to be *behind* bars.

67. **The correct answer is B.** The second part of the sentence should lead you to choose the contrasting word *not*.

68. **The correct answer is A.** Again, a contrasting word is needed so the word *but* fits best.

69. **The correct answer is C.** The word that makes the most sense in the context of the sentence is *held*.

70. **The correct answer is D.** Since *people* is plural, you must choose the plural possessive, in this case, *their*.

71. **The correct answer is B.** *Trials* are generally held in *court*.

72. **The correct answer is C.** The paragraph is discussing jailing of people awaiting trial, a form of *detention*.

73. **The correct answer is A.** Reading the two parts of the sentence shows that you need a contrasting word. In this case, *otherwise*.

74. **The correct answer is C.** To *forfeit* bail, as stated earlier in the sentence, means that you *lose* your money.

75. **The correct answer is B.** Since bail is a set amount of cash, *money* is the best choice here.

76. **The correct answer is D.** Since the pronoun refers to a person, *who* is the best answer.

77. **The correct answer is A.** The only choice that makes sense is *citizen*.

78. **The correct answer is C.** As stated earlier, people who are employed can often avoid the *detention* system.

79. **The correct answer is B.** Since these people are released on personal recognizance, they *avoid* the detention system.

80. **The correct answer is C.** *Be* makes the most sense in the context of the sentence.

81. **The correct answer is B.** A quick reading of the paragraph reveals that it is discussing *criminal* acts.

82. **The correct answer is D.** Again, reading over the paragraph reveals that it is discussing more than one, or *several*, standards.

83. **The correct answer is A.** Since the previous sentence was discussing criminal acts, the word *crime* is the best choice here.

84. **The correct answer is A.** *Labeled* fits best in the context of the sentence.

85. **The correct answer is C.** Major and minor offenses are being contrasted here, so choose the contrasting word. In this case, *whereas* is the best choice.

86. **The correct answer is C.** This sentence discusses a second standard, so the best choice is *another*.

87. **The correct answer is B.** This sentence is talking about definitions, so *terms* is the best choice.

88. **The correct answer is C.** Since the terms are used incorrectly, the people who use them are *not* aware of their legal definitions.

89. **The correct answer is A.** This sentence is clearly discussing the *difference* between the two terms.

90. **The correct answer is B.** Typically, a person breaks *into* a building.

91. **The correct answer is D.** Since this part of the sentence is defining robbery, it doesn't make sense to reuse the term *felony*, so choice A can be eliminated. In addition, you already know that a *burglary* (choice B) isn't the same thing as a *robbery* (choice C), making these choices incorrect. Therefore, the best choice is *theft* (choice D).

92. **The correct answer is D.** When a person commits the crime of burglary, they are *guilty* of burglary.

93. **The correct answer is C.** Robbery generally means taking someone's *property*.

94. **The correct answer is B.** The word *in* fits the context of the sentence best.

95. **The correct answer is C.** The only choice that makes sense in the context of the sentence is *presence*.

SELF-EVALUATION

On your answer sheet, mark the numbers of the questions that you answered incorrectly and check them against the following charts. If you missed several of any question type, you need more practice with that kind of question. Return to the appropriate chapter and review the rules and practice exercises before moving on to the next sample exam.

SELF-EVALUATION CHART

Question Type	Question Numbers	Chapter to Review
Spelling	1–8, 11–18	5
English Grammar and Usage	21–32	4
Clerical Speed and Accuracy	35–50	13
Tabular Completions	51–65	17
Effective Expression	66–95	9
Alphabetizing and Filing	9–10, 19–20, 33–34	12

PART VI
APPENDIXES

Occupations Available in the Federal Government

FEDERAL JOB TYPES

The employment opportunities within the federal government are diverse and far-ranging. You don't need to work in Washington, D.C. or even in the United States to become a federal worker. You also don't need to pursue a standard 9 to 5 desk job.

All federal civil service occupations fall under one of two broad categories: "professional" or "trade, craft, or labor." Professional occupations are defined as "positions whose primary duty requires knowledge or experience of an administrative, clerical, scientific, artistic, or technical nature and is not related to trade, craft, or manual labor work," according to *usajobs.gov*. Most professional jobs are paid according to the General Schedule (GS) pay grade system.

As the name suggests, trade, craft or labor occupations are occupations that involve "the performance of physical work and require knowledge or experience of a trade, craft, or manual labor nature." If you work in one of these roles, you'll most likely be paid according to the Federal Wage System (FWS).

Within each system, similar occupations are grouped together into families, or "series." To see which federal jobs might be right for you or something you want to work toward, review the complete, current list of occupation series below. (Text is excerpted, with some modification, from *usajobs.gov*.)

PROFESSIONAL OCCUPATIONS

0000 – Miscellaneous Occupations
These positions include those whose duties are to administer, supervise, or perform work that cannot be included in other occupational groups, either because the duties are unique or because they are complex and come in part under various groups.

0100 – Social Science, Psychology, and Welfare
This category includes those positions whose duties are to advise on, administer, supervise, or perform research or other professional and scientific work, subordinate technical work, or related clerical work in one or more of the social sciences; in psychology; in social work; in recreational activities; or in the administration of public welfare and insurance programs.

0200 – Human Resources Management

These positions include those whose duties are to advise on, administer, supervise, or perform work involved in the different phases of human resources management.

0300 – General Administrative, Clerical, and Office Services

This category includes those positions whose duties are to administer, supervise, or perform work involved in management analysis; stenography, typing, correspondence, and secretarial work; mail and file work; the operation of office equipment; the operation of communications equipment, use of codes and ciphers, and procurement of the most effective and efficient communications services; the operation of microform equipment, peripheral equipment, mail processing equipment, duplicating equipment, and copier/duplicating equipment; and other work of a general clerical and administrative nature.

0400 – Natural Resources Management and Biological Sciences

These positions include those whose duties are to advise on, administer, supervise, or perform research or other professional and scientific work or subordinate technical work in any of the fields of science concerned with living organisms, their distribution, characteristics, life processes, and adaptations and relations to the environment; the soil (its properties and distribution) and the living organisms growing in or on the soil; and the management, conservation, or utilization thereof for particular purposes or uses.

0500 – Accounting and Budget

This category includes those positions whose duties are to advise on, administer, supervise, or perform professional, technical, or related clerical work of an accounting, budget administration, related financial management, or similar nature.

0600 – Medical, Hospital, Dental, and Public Health

These positions include those whose duties are to advise on, administer, supervise, or perform research or other professional and scientific work, subordinate technical work, or related clerical work in the several branches of medicine, surgery, and dentistry or in related patient-care services such as dietetics, nursing, occupational therapy, physical therapy, pharmacy, and others.

0700 – Veterinary Medical Science

This category includes positions whose duties are to advise on, administer, manage, supervise, or perform professional or technical support work in the various branches of veterinary medical science.

0800 – Engineering and Architecture

These positions include those whose duties are to advise on, administer, supervise, or perform professional, scientific, or technical work concerned with engineering or architectural projects, facilities, structures, systems, processes, equipment, devices, material, or methods. Positions in this group require knowledge of the science or art, or both, by which materials, natural resources, and powers are made useful.

0900 – Legal and Kindred

This category includes positions whose duties are to advise on, administer, supervise, or perform work of a legal or similar nature. (Also see 1200 – Copyright, Patent, and Trademark.)

1000 – Information and Arts

These positions include those that involve professional, artistic, technical, or clerical work in one of the following areas:

- the communication of information and ideas through verbal, visual, or pictorial means

- the collection, custody, presentation, display, and interpretation of art works, cultural objects, and other artifacts

- a branch of fine or applied arts such as industrial design, interior design, or musical composition

Positions in this group require writing, editing, and language ability; artistic skill and ability; knowledge of foreign languages; the ability to evaluate and interpret informational and cultural materials; or the practical application of technical or esthetic principles combined with manual skill and dexterity or related clerical skills.

1100 – Business and Industry

These positions include those whose duties are to advise on, administer, supervise, or perform work pertaining to and requiring a knowledge of business and trade practices, characteristics and use of equipment, products, or property, or industrial production methods and processes, including the conduct of investigations and studies; the collection, analysis, and dissemination of information; the establishment and maintenance of contacts with industry and commerce; the provision of advisory services; the examination and appraisement of merchandise or property; and the administration of regulatory provisions and controls.

1200 – Copyright, Patent, and Trademark

This category includes positions whose duties are to advise on, administer, supervise, or perform professional scientific, technical, and legal work involved in the cataloging and registration of copyrights, in the classification and issuance of patents, in the registration of trademarks, in the prosecution of applications for patents before the Patent Office, and in the giving of advice to government officials on patent matters.

1300 – Physical Sciences

These positions include those whose duties are to advise on, administer, supervise, or perform research or other professional and scientific work, or subordinate technical work, in any of the fields of science concerned with matter, energy, physical space, time, nature of physical measurement, and fundamental structural particles; and the nature of the physical environment.

1400 – Library and Archives

These positions are for those whose duties are to advise on, administer, supervise, or perform professional and scientific work or subordinate technical work in the various phases of library and archival science.

1500 – Mathematical Sciences

This category includes positions whose duties are to advise on, administer, supervise, or perform research or other professional and scientific work or related clerical work in basic mathematical principles, methods, procedures, or relationships, including the development and application of mathematical methods for the investigation and solution of problems; the development and application of statistical theory in the selection, collection, classification, adjustment, analysis, and interpretation of data; the development and application of mathematical, statistical, and financial principles to programs or problems involving life and property risks; and any other professional and scientific or related clerical work requiring primarily and mainly the understanding and use of mathematical theories, methods, and operations.

1600 – Equipment, Facilities, and Services

These positions include those whose duties are to advise on, manage, or provide instructions and information concerning the operation, maintenance, and use of equipment, shops, buildings, laundries, printing plants, power plants, cemeteries, or other government facilities, or other work involving services provided predominantly by persons in trades, crafts, or manual labor operations.

1700 – Education

This category includes positions whose duties are to involve administering, managing, supervising, performing, or supporting education or training work when the paramount requirement of the position is knowledge of, or skill in, education, training, or instruction processes.

1800 – Inspection, Investigation, Enforcement, and Compliance

These positions include those whose duties are to advise on, administer, supervise, or perform inspection, investigation, enforcement, or compliance work primarily concerned with alleged or suspected offenses against the laws of the United States, or such work primarily concerned with determining compliance with laws and regulations.

1900 – Quality Assurance, Inspection, and Grading

This category includes positions whose duties are to advise on, supervise, or perform administrative or technical work primarily concerned with the quality assurance or inspection of material, facilities, and processes; or with the grading of commodities under official standards.

2000 – Supply

The positions in this category involve work concerned with furnishing all types of supplies, equipment, material, property (except real estate), and certain services to components of the federal government, industrial, or other concerns under contract to the government, or receiving supplies from the federal government. Included are positions concerned with one or more aspects of supply activities from initial planning, including requirements analysis and determination, through acquisition, cataloging, storage, distribution, and utilization to ultimate issue for consumption or disposal.

2100 – Transportation

This category includes positions whose duties are to advise on, administer, supervise, or perform clerical, administrative, or technical work involved in the provision of transportation service to the government, the regulation of transportation utilities by the government, or the management of government-funded transportation programs, including transportation research and development projects.

2200 – Information Technology

The administrative positions in this category involve managing, supervising, leading, administering, developing, delivering, and supporting information technology (IT) systems and services. This series covers only those positions for which the principal requirement is knowledge of IT principles, concepts, and methods (e.g., data storage, software applications, networking). Information technology refers to systems and services used in the automated acquisition, storage, manipulation, management, movement, control, display, switching, interchange, transmission, assurance, or reception of information. Information technology includes computers, network components, peripheral equipment, software, firmware, services, and related resources.

TRADE, CRAFT, OR LABOR OCCUPATIONS

2500 – Wire Communications Equipment Installation and Maintenance

The occupations here are involved in the construction, installation, maintenance, repair, and testing of all types of wire communications systems and associated equipment that are predominantly electrical-mechanical.

2600 – Electronic Equipment Installation and Maintenance

These occupations involve the installation, repair, overhaul, fabrication, tuning, alignment, modification, calibration, and testing of electronic equipment and related devices such as radio, radar, loran, sonar, television, and other communications equipment; industrial controls; fire control, flight/landing control, bombing-navigation, and other integrated systems; and electronic computer systems and equipment.

2800 – Electrical Installation and Maintenance

Occupations in this category are involved in the fabrication, installation, alteration, maintenance, repair, and testing of electrical systems, instruments, apparatus, and equipment.

3100 – Fabric and Leather Work

This category includes occupations that involve the fabrication, modification, and repair of clothing and equipment made of: (1) woven textile fabrics of animal, vegetable, or synthetic origin; (2) plastic film and filaments; (3) natural and simulated leather; (4) natural and synthetic fabrics; and (5) paper.

3300 – Instrument Work

These occupations involve fabricating, assembling, calibrating, testing, installing, repairing, modifying, and maintaining instruments and instrumentation systems for measuring, regulating, and computing physical quantities such as mass, moment, force, acceleration, displacement, stress, strain, vibration or oscillation frequency, phase and amplitude, linear or angular velocity, space-time position and attitude, pressure, temperature, density, viscosity, humidity, thermal or electrical conductivity, voltage, current, power, power factor, impedance, and radiation.

3400 – Machine Tool Work

Occupations in this category involve setting up and operating machine tools and using hand tools to make or repair (shape, fit, finish, assemble) metal parts, tools, gauges, models, patterns, mechanisms, and machines; and machining explosives and synthetic materials.

3500 – General Services and Support Work

These occupations are not specifically covered by another work family and require little or no specialized training or work experience. These occupations usually involve work such as moving and handling materials (e.g., loading, unloading, digging, hauling, hoisting, carrying, wrapping, mixing, pouring, spreading); washing and cleaning laboratory apparatus, cars, and trucks, etc.; cleaning and maintaining living quarters, hospital rooms and wards, office buildings, grounds, and other areas; and doing other general maintenance work by hand or using common hand tools and power equipment. Responsibilities may involve heavy or light physical work and various skill levels.

3600 – Structural and Finishing Work

Occupations in this category are not specifically covered by another work family and involve doing structural and finishing work in construction, maintenance, and repair of surfaces and structures (e.g., laying brick, block, and stone; setting tile; finishing cement and concrete; plastering; installing, maintaining, and repairing asphalt, tar, and gravel; roofing; insulating and glazing).

3700 – Metal Processing

These occupations involve processing or treating metals to alter their properties or produce desirable qualities such as hardness or workability, using processes such as welding, plating, melting, alloying, casting, annealing, heat treating, and refining.

3800 – Metal Work

The occupations in this category involves shaping and forming metal and making and repairing metal parts or equipment and includes such work as the fabrication and assembly of sheet metal parts and equipment; forging and press operations; structural iron working, boiler making, ship fitting, and other plate metal work; rolling, cutting, stamping, riveting, etc. It does not include machine tool work.

3900 – Motion Picture, Radio, Television, and Sound Equipment Operation

These occupations involve setting up, testing, operating, and making minor repairs to equipment such as microphones, sound and radio controls, sound recording equipment, lighting and sound effects devices, television cameras, magnetic video tape recorders, motion picture projectors, and broadcast transmitters used in the production of motion pictures and radio and television programs. It also includes occupations that involve related work such as operating public address system equipment.

4000 – Lens and Crystal Work

Occupations in this category involve making precision optical elements, crystal blanks or wafers, or other items of glass, crystalline substances, synthetics, polished metals, or similar materials, using such methods as cutting, etching, grinding, and polishing.

4100 – Painting and Paperhanging

The occupations listed here are those that involve hand or spray painting and decorating interiors and exteriors of buildings, structures, aircraft, vessels, mobile equipment, fixtures, furnishings, machinery, and other surfaces; finishing hardwoods, furniture, and cabinetry; painting signs; covering interiors of rooms with strips of wallpaper or fabric, and so on.

4200 – Plumbing and Pipe-fitting

Occupations in this category involve the installation, maintenance, and repair of water, air, steam, gas, sewer, and other pipelines and systems as well as related fixtures, apparatus, and accessories.

4300 – Pliable Materials Work

These occupations involve shaping, forming, and repairing items and parts from nonmetallic moldable materials such as plastic, rubber, clay, wax, plaster, glass, sand, or other similar materials.

4400 – Printing Family

Occupations in this category involve letterpress (relief), offset-lithographic, gravure (intaglio), or screen printing. These occupations include layout, hand composition, photoengraving, plate making, printing, and finishing operations.

4600 – Wood Work

Occupations here are involved in the construction, alteration, repair, and maintenance of wooden buildings and other structures as well as the fabrication and repair of wood products such as furniture, foundry patterns, and form blocks, using power and hand tools.

4700 – General Maintenance and Operations Work

Occupations in this category consist of various combinations of work that are involved in constructing, maintaining, and repairing buildings, roads, grounds, and related facilities; manufacturing, modifying, and repairing items or apparatus made from a variety of materials or types of components; or repairing and operating equipment or utilities. These jobs require the application of a variety of trade practices associated with occupations in more than one job family (unless otherwise indicated) and the performance of the highest level of work in at least two of the trades involved.

4800 – General Equipment Maintenance

In this category, occupations involve the maintenance or repair of equipment, machines, or instruments that are not coded to other job families because the equipment is not characteristically related to one of the established subject matter areas, such as electronics, electrical, industrial, transportation, instruments, engines, aircraft, ordnance, and so on, or because the nature of the work calls for limited knowledge/skill in a variety of crafts or trades as they relate to the repair of such equipment, but not a predominate knowledge of any one trade or craft.

5000 – Plant and Animal Work

These occupations involve general or specialized farming operations; gardening, including the general care of grounds, roadways, nurseries, greenhouses, and so on; trimming and felling trees; and propagating, caring for, handling, and controlling animals and insects, including pest species.

5200 – Miscellaneous Occupations

Occupations in this category are not covered by the definition of any other job family or are of such a general or miscellaneous character as to preclude placing them within another job family.

5300 – Industrial Equipment Maintenance

These occupations involve the general maintenance, installation, and repair of portable and stationary industrial machinery, tools, and equipment such as sewing machines, machine tools, woodworking and metalworking machines, printing equipment, processing equipment, driving machinery, power generating equipment, air conditioning equipment, heating and boiler plant equipment, and other types of machines and equipment used in the production of goods and services.

5400 – Industrial Equipment Operation

The occupations in this category are involved in the operation of portable and stationary industrial equipment, tools, and machines to generate and distribute utilities such as electricity, steam, and gas for heat or power; treat and distribute water; collect, treat, and dispose of waste; open and close bridges, locks, and dams; lift and move workers, materials, and equipment; manufacture and process materials and products, and so on.

5700 – Transportation/Mobile Equipment Operation

These occupations involve the operation and operational maintenance of self-propelled transportation and other mobile equipment (except aircraft) used to move materials or passengers, including motor vehicles, engineering and construction equipment, tractors, and so on, some of which may be equipped with power takeoff and controls to operate special purpose equipment; ocean-going and inland waterway vessels, harbor craft, and floating plants; and trains, locomotives, and train cars.

5800 – Transportation/Mobile Equipment Maintenance

Occupations in this category involve repairing, adjusting, and maintaining self-propelled transportation and other mobile equipment (except aircraft), including any special purpose features with which they may be equipped.

6500 – Ammunition, Explosives, and Toxic Materials Work

The occupations in this category involve the manufacturing, assembling, disassembling, renovating, loading, deactivating, modifying, destroying, testing, handling, placing, and discharging of ammunition, propellants, chemicals and toxic materials, and other conventional and special munitions and explosives.

6600 – Armament Work

These occupations are involved in the installation, repair, rebuilding, adjustment, modification, and testing of small arms and artillery weapons and allied accessories. Artillery includes, but is not limited to, field artillery, antitank artillery, anti-aircraft weapons, aircraft and shipboard weapons, recoilless rifles, rocket launchers, mortars, cannons, and allied accessories. Small arms includes, but is not limited to, rifles, carbines, pistols, revolvers, helmets, body armor, shoulder-type rocket launchers, machine guns, and automatic rifles.

7000 – Packing and Processing

These occupations involve determining the measures required to protect items against damage during movement or storage; selecting proper method of packing, including type and size of container; cleaning, drying, and applying preservatives to materials, parts, or mechanical equipment; and packing equipment, parts, and materials.

7300 – Laundry, Dry Cleaning, and Pressing

Occupations in this category involve receiving, sorting, washing, drying, dry cleaning, dyeing, pressing, and preparing for delivery clothes, linens, and other articles requiring laundering, dry cleaning, or pressing.

7400 – Food Preparation and Serving

These occupations are involved in the preparation and serving of food.

7600 – Personal Services

In this category, the occupations are concerned with providing grooming, beauty, or other personal services to individuals, patrons, guests, passengers, entertainers, etc., or attending to their personal effects.

8200 – Fluid Systems Maintenance

Occupations in this category involve the repair, modification, assembly, and testing of fluid systems and fluid system components of aircraft, aircraft engines, missiles, and mobile and support equipment.

8600 – Engine Overhaul

These occupations are concerned primarily with the manufacture, repair, modification, and major overhaul of engines (except where covered by another group), including the disassembly, reassembly, and test phases of engine overhaul programs.

8800 – Aircraft Overhaul

In this category, the occupations are concerned primarily with the overhaul of aircraft, including the disassembly, reassembly, and test phases of aircraft overhaul programs.

9000 – Film Processing

These occupations involve processing film—for example, operating motion picture developers and printers; cleaning, repairing, matching, cutting, splicing, and assembling films; and mixing developing solutions. The work does not include processing work that requires specialized subject-matter knowledge or artistic ability.

State and Municipal Government Jobs

The list below shows representative jobs in state and local government entities. The list is typical of all states and the largest municipalities. The number of jobs in a municipality depends on the size of the city, township, or village. The larger the governmental unit, the more jobs there are. At the local municipal level, the school district is often the largest employer.

The responsibilities of state and local governments are typically divided among a number of departments, agencies, offices, commissions, boards, and councils at the administrative and legislative levels. The titles depend on the state or locality. Jobs range from administrative assistants and clerks to lawyers and paralegals to facilities managers and food service workers. States and local governments also have judiciaries and employ lawyers, bailiffs and corrections officers, court reporters, and administrators. State and municipal office buildings and courthouses require maintenance personnel and security guards.

Some states also have strong county governmental structures. (In Louisiana, they are called parishes.) These may include county prosecutor/district attorney offices, county welfare departments, municipal water districts that connect several cities or townships, county public works departments that take care of county roads, and transportation districts that coordinate countywide networks of buses, subways, trolleys, and trains. All these services need to be staffed.

To find out about state or local government jobs in your area, go online to your state government website. Some states list local government job postings as well as state openings. If you can't find local job announcements on the state site, check the website for the municipality you're interested in working for.

Not all jobs on the state and municipal levels require civil service exams. Some jobs are listed as non-civil service while others—such as administrative and clerical positions—may be either, depending on the department or agency the job is with.

ADMINISTRATIVE, ACCOUNTING, AND FISCAL CONTROL

Government officials need updated financial information to make decisions. Accountants and auditors prepare, analyze, and verify financial reports that inform those decisions. In addition, auditors, economists, and statisticians work for other areas of government that require their expertise. Lawyers also provide services to many departments within state and local governments as well as staff the Attorney General's office at the state level and the district attorney/prosecutor level at municipal and county levels.

Accident record reviewer

Accountant

Actuary

Appeals examiner

Auditor/examiner

Audit account clerk

Budget analyst

Business analyst

Economist

Human resources assistant, supervisor

Insurance investigator

Legal assistant/paralegal

Life and health insurance policy examiner

Management analyst

Medical malpractice claims examiner, supervisor

Municipal court administrator

Pensions benefit specialist

Purchasing agent

Real estate appraiser, technician, specialist

Retirement administrator

Retirement benefits specialist, supervisor, technician

Staff attorney

Statistician

Unemployment compensation tax agent

Workers' compensation analyst

CLERICAL

Clerks perform a variety of administrative and clerical duties necessary to run state and local governments. Often, applicants must pass a written clerical and verbal abilities test.

Cashier

Clerk bookkeeper

Clerical and secretarial

Clerk transcriber

Clerk typist

Computer operator: keyboarding clerk, purchasing assistant, account clerk

Payroll clerk

Records specialist, supervisor

Secretarial supervisor

Stenographer

Stock clerk

EDUCATION

In addition to the traditional pre-kindergarten to 12th-grade educational systems, states and local municipalities offer other types of educational services. Correctional institutions on the state and county level may offer high school and vocational courses.

Adult basic and literacy education teacher
Adult basic education teacher
Alcohol education teacher
Business occupations teacher
Career and technical education teacher
Corrections activities specialist
Corrections education teacher
Corrections school principal
Curriculum specialist
Early childhood education teacher
Education administrator
Education aide
Education certification evaluator
Educational assessment specialist
Educator, K–12
Environmental education specialist
Food and nutrition services advisor
Guidance counselor
Nursing educator
Professional librarian
Special education teacher
Vocational teacher

ENGINEERING AND ENVIRONMENTAL CONTROL

Although many engineers work in design and development positions, others work in testing, production, operations, and maintenance.

Air monitoring equipment specialist
Air quality engineer and engineering specialist
Aquatic resources program specialist
Architect
Bridge and structural designer
Chemist
Civil engineer, manager: hydraulic, bridge, transportation
District utility manager
Drafter, drafter/designer
Ecological program specialist
Electrical engineer
Environmental engineer, interpretive technician

Environmental project construction inspector, supervisor

Environmental protection compliance specialist

Forester, program specialist, technician

Geologic scientist, specialist

Highway drafter, designer

Materials technicians

Mechanical engineer

Mineral resources program specialist

Mining engineer, specialist, permit and compliance specialist

Natural resources specialist

Nuclear safety specialist

Park manager, ranger

Plant pathologist

Radiation health physicist

Roadway programs specialist, manager, coordinator

Surveyor, technician

Traffic control specialist, technician

Transportation construction inspector, supervisor, manager

Wildlife biologist

INFORMATION TECHNOLOGY

A great variety of opportunities exist in the area of information technology. Jobs range from data-entry operators to computer specialists in applied programming. Much of the work involves database entry and management.

Applications developer and administrator

Data administrator

Data analyst

Database analyst and administrator

Information technology generalists and administrators

Information technology technicians

Computer service technician

Network specialists and administrators

Telecommunications specialists

LAW ENFORCEMENT, INVESTIGATION, AND SAFETY

There are more than 17,000 state and local law enforcement agencies divided among local police forces such as municipal, county, tribal, and regional forces; state police and highway patrol; special jurisdiction police such as housing authority police and school security; and deputy sheriffs who police local jails and serve court summonses and warrants. Other jobs in enforcement include corrections officers who oversee prisons.

Investigative positions include investigators who examine claims for benefits or compensation to ensure that they are valid and conform to regulations, gather evidence of fraud and other wrongdoing that is then used in legal actions, and discover violations of rules and regulations.

While villages and small towns and cities may rely heavily on volunteer firefighters, they may also have some full-time firefighters. Larger cities have paid fire companies. Some include EMTs. In addition to putting out fires, fire departments are responsible for fire prevention and education.

Agricultural commodity inspector
Agricultural products inspector, technician
Campus police officer
Capitol police officer
Case monitor, juvenile justice
Code enforcement officer
Commissioned boiler inspector, supervisor,
Community corrections center director
Corrections officer
Court clerk
Court liaison program specialist
Domestic animal health inspector
Driver license center manager, inspector
Emergency management watch officer, specialist
Forensic scientist
Institutional parole assistant
Institutional safety manager
Laboratory system quality specialist
Milk sanitarian
Mine electrical inspector
Mine inspector
Mine safety emergency response and training specialist
Mortuary inspector
Operations center monitor
Parole agent, supervisor, counselor
Plant industry field technician, inspector
Public utility enforcement officer
Railroad safety inspector
Regional traffic management center operator and supervisor
Regulatory enforcement inspector, supervisor
Securities investigator
Security officer
Seed analyst
Special investigator
Building inspector, supervisor, plans examiner
Elevator inspector, supervisor
Workers' compensation health and safety training specialist

MEDICAL AND HEALTH SERVICES

With the continuing growth of medical knowledge and the increasing demands of an aging population, state and local governments increasingly need physicians, medical researchers, nurses, physician's assistants, physical therapists, occupational therapists, and similar healthcare workers.

Certified registered nurse practitioner

Clinic nurse

Clinical dietitian

Community health nurse

Dental hygienist, dentist

Disability physician specialist

Drug program specialist

Epidemiologist, epidemiology program specialist, research associate

Health facility quality examiner, supervisor

Health systems specialist

Laboratory technologists

Licensed occupational therapist, assistant

Licensed practical nurse

Medical assistance program technician

Medical facility and records examiner, supervisor

Medical records assistant, supervisor

Medical technologist

Nurse manager, nursing director

Nursing practice adviser

Nursing services consultant

Occupational therapist

Pharmacist, assistant

Physical therapist, registered assistant

Public health nutrition consultant, physician

Registered nurse

Registry technician, specialist

Speech, language, and hearing specialist

Veterinary laboratory diagnostician

Veterinary medical field officer

SOCIAL AND EMPLOYMENT SERVICES

People who work in the social welfare field are community troubleshooters. Through direct counseling, referral to other services, or policymaking and advocacy, they help individuals, families, and groups cope with their problems. Often, the problems are related to unemployment. State employment offices, known as American Job Centers, are a major source of help for the unemployed.

Aging care manager, case aide, program assessor

Childcare caseworker, supervisor

County care management manager, supervisor, caseworker, program specialist

Drug and alcohol case management specialist, prevention program specialist, program analyst, treatment specialist

Employment counselor

Meal transporter and van driver

Mental health/mental disabilities staff specialist, county social work training specialist, community services area manager, unit manager

Senior Center manager, program specialists, aides

Social worker, supervisor, manager

Therapeutic activities aide

Unemployment claims examiner, supervisor, intake interviewer

Veterans' employment representative

Vocational rehabilitation counselor

Youth development counselor, aide, supervisor

TRADES AND MAINTENANCE

Increasingly, formal training acquired in high school, vocational or technical school, community college, or in the armed services is an asset for those entering the trades. Some trades also provide apprenticeship programs, but the number of apprentices accepted in any location is usually small. Many maintenance positions require no formal education, qualification, or experience. Some jobs, such as those that involve lifting heavy objects, may require a physical exam.

Automotive and diesel mechanic, supervisor, equipment foreman

Boiler plant operator

Building construction inspector

Carpenter

Construction inspector supervisor and manager

Corrections industry foreman and supervisor

Custodial supervisor and manager

Electrical construction inspector

Electrician

Food service personnel

Forest and park maintenance supervisor

Highway drilling operator

Housekeeper

Maintenance repairer, foreman, supervisor

Mason

Painter

Parks maintenance

Plasterer

Plumber

Semi-skilled laborer

Steamfitter

Wastewater treatment plant operator

Water treatment plant operator

Hiring Veterans

Feds Hire Vets (**fedshirevets.gov**) is the "single site for Federal employment information for Veterans, transitioning military service members, their families, and Federal hiring officials." Feds Hire Vets is the Office of Personnel Management's government-wide Veterans Employment website, a joint effort of the Departments of Defense, Labor, Veterans Affairs, Homeland Security, and other federal agencies. The website is part of the federal government's strategy for recruiting and employing veterans.

On the Feds Hire Vets website, you can find a dashboard for job seekers and hiring officials; a directory of federal agencies with contact names, numbers, and email addresses; and numerous success stories to provide an overview of how other veterans and their family members have gotten jobs in the federal government. The "About Us" page offers a list of FAQs about government policies for hiring veterans. In addition, the site offers lists of tips for job hunters and scheduled webinars on topics of interest to those wishing to work for the federal government.

Like other federal job seekers, the primary tool for veterans looking for jobs is USAJOBS (**usajobs.gov**), the employment site of the Office of Personnel Management. This site lists all the federal job openings available anywhere in the nation as well as around the world. The site offers tutorials, FAQs, and a "Resume Builder." You can set up an account, work on your resume and store it for later submission, and apply for jobs through USAJOBS.

VETERANS' PREFERENCE POINTS

Giving veterans preference in hiring has been a federal government policy since the Civil War. A law enacted in 1944 and amended several times since sets up a hiring preference system for disabled veterans and those who served on active duty during certain military actions or time periods. Members of all five branches of the armed forces are eligible: Army, Navy, Air Force, Marine Corps, and Coast Guard. The law entitles them "to preference over others in hiring from competitive lists of [those] eligible and also in retention during reductions in force." The law also applies to family members under certain circumstances. Not all jobs in the federal government are open to the use of preference points, but many are.

Appendix C

If you qualify, you can add either 5 or 10 points to your civil service exam score or rating, giving your job application an automatic boost. (You need to have passed your civil service exam before adding points, however.) The rules for veterans' preference can be complicated, but there are two basic criteria:

- You must have served in active duty and been released with an honorable or general discharge. (For non-disabled veterans, "active duty" does not include National Guard or Reserve training service. For disabled veterans, it does.)

- Military retirees with a rank of major, lieutenant commander, or higher are not eligible for veterans' preference unless they are disabled veterans. (This rule does not apply to some Reservists.)

5-Point Preference

In addition to meeting the criteria above, to gain 5 points, you must have served during any of these periods:

- For more than 180 consecutive days, other than for training, any part of which occurred during the period beginning September 11, 2001, and ending on August 31, 2010, the last day of Operation Iraqi Freedom, *or*

- During the Gulf War, between August 2, 1990 and January 2, 1992, *or*

- For more than 180 consecutive days, other than for training, any part of which occurred after January 31, 1955 and before October 15, 1976, *or*

- Between April 28, 1952 and July 1, 1955, *or*

- In a war, campaign or expedition for which a campaign medal or badge has been authorized.

10-Point Preference

To be eligible for 10 points, you must qualify as one of the following:

- A veteran with a service-connected disability

- A veteran receiving compensation, disability benefits, or a pension from the military

- A veteran who has received a Purple Heart (this qualifies you as a disabled veteran)

- The unmarried spouse of a veteran who is deceased (certain restrictions apply)

- The spouse of a veteran who cannot work because of a service-related disability

- The parent of a veteran who died during service

- The parent of a permanently and totally disabled veteran

For additional information on preference points, click on the "Veterans" menu option on the **opm.gov** main site and then select "Veterans Services," which has links to a number of information sources including the Vet Guide.

STATE RECOGNITION OF VETERANS' PREFERENCE POINTS

State governments also have programs providing preference points to veterans who have served in the armed forces honorably, whether sustaining a service-connected disability or not. The state programs generally follow the federal government's criteria and points system, but some states also grant preference points for service in their state's National Guard. Spouses, including partners in civil unions, may also be included in some state programs.

Hiring People with Disabilities

The federal government actively recruits and hires people with disabilities. President Barack Obama signed an Executive Order in 2010 directing the federal government to "become a model for the employment of individuals with disabilities." Under the Executive Order, departments and agencies are to increase their recruitment, hiring, and retention of people with disabilities. The reasons for these activities are twofold: it's the right thing to do, and it enlarges the candidate pool of highly qualified people.

There are two routes to employment for those with disabilities. One is noncompetitively through Schedule A Authority, and the other is through the traditional or competitive process.

To be eligible to be considered for employment under Schedule A, a person must have a severe physical disability, a psychiatric disability, or an intellectual disability. To prove eligibility, a candidate must be qualified for the job (i.e., have the competencies and relevant experience); show proof of disability, which is a Schedule A letter of disability; and possibly (but not necessarily) provide a certification of job readiness, meaning that he or she is able to perform the duties of the job under consideration.

A doctor, licensed medical professional, or licensed vocational rehabilitation specialist may write the letter documenting a candidate's disability. The hiring agency will also accept a letter from any federal, state, or local agency that issues or provides disability benefits. Some agencies may accept the certification of job readiness as part of the proof of disability letter or they may require a separate letter. You may find that an agency will accept your resume as enough proof of your ability to perform the duties of the job you're interested in.

The Office of Personnel Management (OPM) is very clear that being eligible for a Schedule A appointment does not guarantee a person a job, but it does help in the hiring process. Once hired, a person who received a Schedule A appointment undergoes a probationary period, which may last up to two years. The amount of time depends on the job. While on probation, the employee is expected to perform the job at the same level of competency as other employees.

The U.S. Equal Employment Opportunity Commission's initiative to tackle the declining number of employees with targeted disabilities in the federal workforce is known as LEAD (Leadership for the Employment of Americans with Disabilities). On the LEAD website, **eeoc.gov/eeoc/initiatives/lead/index.cfm**, you can download *The ABCs of Schedule A*, which is a handy reference guide for applying for federal jobs under Schedule A.

GETTING HELP IN THE FEDERAL HIRING PROCESS

One of the first things that the OPM website advises potential candidates to do is to contact their Selective Placement Program Coordinator (SSPC) for help and advice. SPCCs help agencies recruit, hire, and accommodate people with disabilities, and help assist potential candidates in navigating the hiring process.

Most federal agencies have established the SPPC position. Each agency with SPPCs maintains regional field offices with coordinators who are there to assist hiring managers and candidates. SPPCs can help individuals learn about job opportunities and the types of jobs that become available in their agencies. SSPCs can also advise on reasonable accommodations for jobs. Among their duties for hiring managers, SPPCs identify the essential duties of a job and any physical barriers to successful employment of a person with a disability for that job. They suggest possible modifications to the physical environment and reasonable accommodations.

You can find a directory of regional field offices with the names and contact information of the local coordinators on the SPPC website at **www.opm.gov/policy-data-oversight/disability-employment/ selective-placement-program-coordinator-directory/**. You can search by state to find all SSPCs in the state or by department if you are interested in a job in a particular department, such as Agriculture or Homeland Security. Many agencies also have a Disability Program Manager.

Veterans with service-connected disabilities are eligible for special consideration in the hiring process. These individuals may have 10 preference points added to their passing exam score or rating. Family members of veterans with service-connected disabilities may also, under certain circumstances, receive 10 preference points toward their passing exam score or rating. For more information, visit **fedshirevets.gov**.

PROVIDING ACCOMMODATIONS

Federal agencies are required under the Rehabilitation Act of 1973 to provide reasonable adjustments to the work environment for employees and candidates for jobs who have disabilities. A reasonable accommodation as defined by the OPM is "any change in the work environment or the way things are usually done that enables an individual with a disability to enjoy Equal Employment Opportunity." A reasonable accommodation would be a sign language interpreter or a workstation that is accessible for an employee in a wheelchair.

The Americans with Disabilities Act of 1990 (ADA), as amended, extended reasonable accommodations to all Americans in work situations, among other rights. State and local governments also cannot discriminate in hiring practices against those with disabilities and must provide reasonable accommodations as defined by law.

The Law

The ADA extends to applicants and employees of most private employers, state and local governments, educational institutions, employment agencies, and labor organizations. Titles I and V of the ADA protect qualified individuals with disabilities from discrimination in hiring, promotion, termination, pay, fringe benefits, job training, classification, referral, and other aspects of employment.

Disability discrimination includes refraining from making reasonable accommodation to the known physical or mental limitations of an otherwise qualified applicant or employee who has a disability. However, the word reasonable qualifies this situation. The employer does not have to comply if the accommodation would cause undue hardship to the employer. The requirement to provide reasonable accommodation is a key component of ADA.

State and Municipal Hiring Practices

In looking for information on state hiring practices, you may find a disclaimer on a state employment site that the state is an equal opportunity employer. A state may also have an affirmative action policy that directs its hiring managers in state departments and agencies to make all efforts to hire people with disabilities. Even if you can't find such a statement or policy, ADA requires nondiscrimination in the hiring of people with disabilities. The same is true for county, city, town, village, and special district employers.

NOTES

NOTES